MONASTICISM AND MANUSCRIPT CULTURE IN MEDIEVAL EUROPE

MONASTICISM AND MANUSCRIPT CULTURE IN MEDIEVAL EUROPE

STUDIES IN CLUNIAC HISTORY, C. 900–1200

SCOTT G. BRUCE

CORNELL UNIVERSITY PRESS
Ithaca and London

Copyright © 2025 Scott Bruce

Except:
Chapter 1 copyright © 2020 Oxford University Press
Chapter 2 copyright © 2020 Cambridge University Press
Chapter 8 copyright © 2023 Brepols Publishers n.v., Turnhout, Belgium
Chapter 13 copyright © 2019 Brepols Publishers n.v., Turnhout, Belgium

All rights reserved. Except for brief quotations in a review, this book, or parts thereof, must not be reproduced in any form without permission in writing from the publisher. For information, address Cornell University Press, Sage House, 512 East State Street, Ithaca, New York 14850. Visit our website at cornellpress.cornell.edu.

First published 2025 by Cornell University Press

Librarians: A CIP catalog record for this book is available from the Library of Congress.

ISBN 9781501784651 (hardcover)
ISBN 9781501784668 (paperback)
ISBN 9781501784996 (pdf)
ISBN 9781501784675 (epub)

GPSR EU contact: Sam Thornton, Mare Nostrum Group B.V., Mauritskade 21D, 1091 GC, Amsterdam, NL, gpsr@mare-nostrum.co.uk.

For Drew Jones

Die Sterne in dem Sommertuch
die brech ich auf
ich finde nichts
und wieder nichts
und dann ein Wort
in einer fremden Sprache.

—Elisabeth Borchers

Contents

Abbreviations   ix

Introduction: A Centuries-Old Murmuring   1

1. The Benedictines   11
2. Sources for the History of Monasticism in the Central Middle Ages (c. 800–1100)   27
3. An Abbot Between Two Cultures: Maiolus of Cluny Considers the Muslims of La Garde-Freinet   44
4. Clandestine Codices in the Captivity Narratives of Abbot Maiolus of Cluny   59
5. Local Sanctity and Civic Typology in Early Medieval Pavia: The Example of the Cult of Abbot Maiolus of Cluny   72
6. The Social Life of an Eleventh-Century Shrine in the *Miraculorum sancti Maioli libri duo* (*BHL* 5186), with W. Tanner Smoot   88
7. Lurking with Spiritual Intent: On the Origin and Functions of the Monastic Roundsman (*Circator*)   109
8. Monastic Sign Language in the Cluniac Customaries   124
9. The Relics of Cluny   142

10. Cluny and the Crusades   162

11. *Nunc homo, cras humus*: A Twelfth-Century Cluniac Poem on the Certainty of Death   180

12. Abbot Peter the Venerable's Two Missions to England (1130 and 1155/1156)   196

13. Curiosity Killed the Monk: The History of an Early Medieval Vice   217

14. The Dark Age of Herodotus: Shards of a Fugitive History in Early Medieval Europe   236

Epilogue: A Treasure of Secrets   262

Acknowledgments 277
Bibliography 279
Index 317

Abbreviations

AASS	*Acta sanctorum quotquot toto orbe coluntur*, ed. J. Bolland et al. (Paris, 1643–1940).
BB	*Recueil des chartes de l'abbaye de Cluny*, ed. A. Bernard and A. Bruel, 6 vols. (Paris, 1876–1903).
BC	*Bibliotheca Cluniacensis*, ed. M. Marrier and A. Duchesne (Paris, 1618; repr., Brussels and Paris, 1914).
BHL	*Bibliotheca Hagiographica Latina: Antiquae et Mediae Aetatis*, 2 vols. (Brussels, 1898–1901) with supplemental volumes published in 1911 and 1986 (cited by *BHL* number).
BM	Bibliothèque municipale.
BnF	Bibliothèque nationale de France, Paris.
Bernard	Bernard of Cluny, *Ordo Cluniacensis sive Consuetudines*, in *Vetus Disciplina Monastica*, ed. M. Herrgott (Paris, 1726), pp. 136–364 (cited by book, chapter, and page number).
CCCM	Corpus christianorum: Continuatio mediaevalis.
CCM	Corpus consuetudinum monasticarum.
CCMA	*A Companion to the Abbey of Cluny in the Middle Ages*, ed. S. G. Bruce and S. Vanderputten (Leiden, 2021).
CCSL	Corpus christianorum: Series latina.
CHMM	*The Cambridge History of Medieval Monasticism in the Latin West*, ed. A. Beach and I. Cochelin, 2 vols. (Cambridge, 2020).
CLA	*Codices latini antiquiories: A Palaeographical Guide to Latin Manuscripts Prior to the Ninth Century*, ed. E. A. Lowe, 11 vols. and supplement (Oxford, 1934–1971) (cited by volume, page, and number).
CSEL	Corpus scriptorum ecclesiasticorum latinorum.
MGH	Monumenta Germaniae historica.
MM	*Miracula sancti Maioli libri duo* (*BHL* 5186), in *BC*, cols. 1787–1814 (cited by book and chapter number).
PL	*Patrologia cursus completus: Series latina*, ed. J.-P. Migne, 221 vols. (Paris, 1844–1888) (cited by volume and column number).

RB	*Regula Benedicti*, ed. and trans. A. de Vogüé, in *La règle de saint Benoît*, SC 81–86, 7 vols. (the last of which is not included in the SC series) (Paris, 1971–1972).
RM	*Regula magistri*, ed. and trans. A. de Vogüé, in *La règle de Maître*, SC 105–107, 3 vols. (Paris, 1964–1965).
SBO	*Sancti Bernardi Opera*, ed. J. Leclercq, H. M. Rochais, and C. H. Talbot, 9 vols. (Rome, 1957–1977) (cited by volume and page number).
SC	Sources chrétiennes.
Statuta	Peter the Venerable, *Statuta*, ed. G. Constable, in *Consuetudines Benedictinae variae (saec. XI-saec. XIV)*, CCM 6 (Siegburg, 1975), pp. 19–106 (cited by chapter and page number).
Ulrich	Ulrich of Zell, *Consuetudines Cluniacensis*, PL 149, cols. 643–779 (cited by book, chapter, and column number).

MONASTICISM AND MANUSCRIPT CULTURE IN MEDIEVAL EUROPE

Introduction
A Centuries-Old Murmuring

> The library... was then a place of long, centuries-old murmuring, an imperceptible dialogue between one parchment and another, a living thing, a receptacle of powers not to be ruled by a human mind, a treasure of secrets emanated by many minds, surviving the death of those who had produced them or had been their conveyors.
>
> —Umberto Eco, *The Name of the Rose*[1]

The chapters gathered in this book investigate questions about religious practice at the abbey of Cluny between the tenth and twelfth centuries by examining medieval monks in their roles as the makers and readers of manuscripts. Medieval books preserved for posterity information inherited from the ancient world, biblical history from creation to the present, Christian traditions handed down from patristic authorities, and pastoral texts rehearsed in parish churches and missionary fields across Western Europe. Throughout the Middle Ages, monks turned to their manuscripts for answers to inquiries about a vast array of topics. Those living in cloistered communities with well-stocked libraries were fortunate to have written resources close at hand, whereas others relied on networks of patronage and friendship to secure copies of the books they needed. Their encounters with texts were often generative. Monastic authors frequently responded to what they had read by writing. In doing so, they built on the foundations of their literary inheritance with textual monuments of their own, which revealed not only the contemporary concerns that compelled them to write but also the lineaments of the library holdings at their fingertips.

---

1. U. Eco, *The Name of the Rose*, trans. Richard Dixon (New York, 2014), p. 306.

Communities of Benedictine monks offer the most abundant evidence for reading habits and literary production in medieval Europe. In the post-Carolingian world, the abbey of Cluny stands out as especially rich in its written remains.[2] Between its foundation in 910 and its apogee in the early twelfth century, this monastic community amassed an enormous library of texts by pagan and Christian authors, while also producing saints' lives, miracle collections, letters, polemical treatises, historical narratives, customary laws, and devotional poetry as well as thousands upon thousands of charters. The investigation of these source materials by modern scholars has been selective. For much of the twentieth century, the study of Cluniac monasticism was dominated by institutional and legislative histories with an emphasis on the growth of a "Cluniac order" through the affiliation of new communities and the imposition of monastic customs.[3] Over time, however, Cluny's reputation as a monolithic entity with an uncompromising identity and an inescapable reach has retreated before the advance of new research by scholars who have examined how cloistered communities resisted Cluniac encroachment or adopted its customs selectively and pragmatically without giving up their independence.[4] Even so, historical approaches to Cluny remain stubbornly teleological with the abbey's fortunes following a predictable rise-and-fall narrative determined largely by the extent of its legislative influence.[5]

This book offers a different view of Cluniac monasticism, one informed primarily by cultural history with close attention given to manuscript evidence. Instead of emphasizing the exceptionalism of the great Burgundian abbey and the ways in which it imposed its distinctive brand of religious practice on other communities, the chapters in this book underscore the interconnectedness of Cluniac devotional practices and written culture with contemporary Benedictine houses,

---

2. For an introduction to the abbey of Cluny and its place in the history of western monasticism, see *CCMA*, esp. pp. 11–102 ("Part 1: A Brief History of Cluny and Cluniac Monasticism").

3. For a useful survey of Cluniac historiography until the early 1980s, see B. Rosenwein, *Rhinoceros Bound: Cluny in the Tenth Century* (Philadelphia, 1982), pp. 3–29.

4. See, for example, J. Diehl and S. Vanderputten, "Cluniac Customs Beyond Cluny: Patterns of Use in the Southern Low Countries," *Journal of Religious History* 41 (2017): 22–41; and S. Vanderputten, "'I Would Be Rather Pleased if the World Were to be Rid of Monks': Resistance to Cluniac Integration in Late Eleventh- and Early Twelfth-Century France," *Journal of Medieval History* 47 (2021): 22–41.

5. See J. Wollasch, *Cluny, Licht der Welt: Aufstieg und Niedergang der klösterlichen Gemeinschaft* (Düsseldorf and Zürich, 1996); and more generally J. G. Clark, *The Benedictines in the Middle Ages* (Woodbridge, 2011); and G. Melville, *The World of Medieval Monasticism: Its History and Forms of Life*, trans. J. D. Mixton (Collegeville, MN, 2016).

even those, like the Cistercians, commonly seen as being at odds with the brethren of Cluny. The first two chapters signal this approach by highlighting common features of the medieval Benedictine tradition to which Cluny belonged (§§ 1-2). The chapters that follow trace the contours of Cluny's interdependence with contemporary cloistered communities in its most well-documented devotional practices, from the veneration of relics to participation in the crusades, and in almost every genre of monastic literary culture produced at the abbey between the tenth and twelfth centuries. Four of these chapters focus on the career and cult of Maiolus, who was abbot of Cluny from 954 to 994 (§§ 3-6), and four more chapters examine aspects of Cluniac discipline and devotion in the eleventh and twelfth centuries (§§ 7-10). The final four chapters investigate texts and problems that fall squarely within the abbacy of Peter the Venerable (1122-1156), but they range widely in time and space in their search for answers (§§ 11-14). Throughout this book, I argue that we gain a better understanding of Cluniac monasticism by examining the abbey's textual histories within the context of influential European-wide currents than we do by considering them in isolation from its many interlocutors. As these chapters show, Cluny was a center of cultural production at once receptive and influential, embedded in a dynamic field of monastic institutions, some friendly, some competitive, but all participating in a vibrant cross-pollination of written texts studied by monks in the safety of their cloister and carried by them throughout Europe from Spain to England to Italy and across the Mediterranean Sea to the Holy Land and beyond.

A synthetic history of Cluny's textual culture and literary production in the three centuries after its foundation remains unwritten.[6] Although no record exists of the initial endowment of books made to the community under its first abbot, Berno (r. 910-27), the abbey's nascent library was soon bolstered by the arrival of his future successor Odo (r. 927-942), who allegedly brought one hundred manuscripts with him to Cluny after he retired from life as a secular canon at Tours.[7] Some of Cluny's oldest surviving manuscripts have been identified on paleographical grounds as products of the scriptorium at Tours and likely traveled with Odo to Burgundy. These include a Carolingian copy

---

6. E. M. Wischermann, *Grundlagen einer cluniacensischen Bibliotheksgeschichte* (Munich, 1988) is a rare exception. For an exemplary study of Cluny's later medieval archive, see S. Barret, *La mémoire et l'écrit: L'abbaye de Cluny et ses archives (Xe-XVIIIe siècle)* (Munster, 2004).

7. John of Salerno, *Vita Odonis* 1.23: "At ille sumptis secum centum voluminibus librorum, mox ad idem demigravit monasterium." *PL* 133, col. 54.

of the fourth-century Latin adaption of Flavius Josephus's account of the First Roman-Jewish War attributed to Pseudo-Hegesippus (Paris, BnF, Nouvelle acquisition latine 1490), as well as a badly damaged early ninth-century compilation of orations by Cicero copied from an ancient exemplar (London, British Library, Additional 47678 + Geneva, Bibliothèque Publique et Universitaire, Latin 169).[8] Odo was a prolific author, whose direct citations and indirect echoes of earlier writers provide a valuable index of other works that may have made up his private library. As Isabelle Rosé reminds us, "la culture d'Odon est, en definitive, éminemment carolingienne," not only because of his familiarity with authors who wrote in the eighth and ninth centuries, like Bede, John Scotus, and Paschasius Radbertus, but also because he shared the preference of Carolingian theologians for writings by Augustine, especially *On the City of God*, and by Gregory the Great, including the *Morals on the Book of Job*, the *Pastoral Rule*, and the *Dialogues*.[9] Odo's prose writings betray his familiarity with many works that plausibly found a place in his library, including hagiographical traditions related to the cult of Martin of Tours, Latin translations of Greek patristics, ascetic literature from late antiquity, and eucharistic theology composed in the Carolingian period.[10] His sprawling poem on salvation history, the *Occupatio*, resonates with phrases borrowed from poets of Roman antiquity like Virgil, Horace, Juvenal, and Persius, as well as Christian composers of biblical epic, like Caelius Sedulius, Avitus of Vienne, and Arator.[11] Odo may have possessed complete copies of these works, but it is also likely that he had access to thematic florilegia that collected some of the texts in question, like the exemplar of an early eleventh-century compendium of hagiographical texts and excerpts from Gregory the Great and Bede made at Saint Martial in Limoges (Paris, BnF, Latin 5601).[12]

---

8. E. K. Rand, *A Survey of the Manuscripts of Tours*, 2 vols. (Cambridge, MA, 1929), vol. 1, pp. 104–105 (Cicero) and 142 (Hegesippus). Further on the Cicero manuscript, which is a crucial witness to the orations that it preserves, see B. M. Olsen, *L'étude des auteurs classiques latins aux XIe et XIIe siècles*, 5 vols. (Paris, 1982-2020), vol. 1, pp. 207–208; and *Texts and Transmission: A Survey of the Latin Classics*, ed. L. D. Reynolds (Oxford, 1983), pp. 61–62.

9. I. Rosé, *Construire une société seigneuriale: Itinéraire et ecclésiologie de l'abbé Odon de Cluny (fin du IXe-milieu du Xe siècle)* (Turnhout, 2008), p. 95.

10. L. Kolmer, *Odo, der erste Cluniacenser Magister* (Deggendorf, 1913), pp. 9–21; and Rosé, *Construire une société seigneuriale*, pp. 186–209.

11. See the full discussion in *The Occupatio of Odo of Cluny: Edition, Translation, and Commentary*, ed. and trans. C. A. Jones, 2 vols. (Turnhout, 2025).

12. For the possible connection between Odo and this manuscript, see B. Judic, "Lire Grégoire le Grand à Saint-Martial de Limoges," *Studia Patristica* 36 (2001): 126–33.

Evidence for the industry of Cluny's scriptorium first appeared in the later tenth century during the abbacy of Maiolus (r. 954–994). For more than a decade, Maiolus had served his predecessor Aymard (r. 942–954) as the custodian (*armarius*) of Cluny's book collection (*bibliotheca*), so he was intimate with its contents and its shortcomings.[13] More than a dozen manuscripts survive from his four-decade tenure as abbot.[14] Maiolus clearly privileged the production of books devoted to texts by Latin theologians of late antiquity like Augustine (six manuscripts), Jerome (five manuscripts), and Ambrose (three manuscripts) as well as works by Hilary of Poitiers, Cassiodorus, Gennadius of Marseille, and Gregory the Great (one manuscript each). Carolingian thinkers received some attention as well, including Hrabanus Maurus (three manuscripts) and Remigius of Auxerre (one manuscript). This heavy emphasis on biblical exegesis and gospel homilies by patristic authorities met the need for explanations of scripture to be read aloud during the Night Office and in the refectory, as mandated by the *Rule of Benedict* (*RB* 9). Maiolus also commissioned at least one work of history (Gregory of Tours's *History of the Franks*), a treatise on grammar (Priscian), a sample of eastern patristics in Latin translation (Didymus the Blind's discourse on the Holy Spirit), and a collection of capitulary legislation forged in the ninth century (Pseudo-Isidore). Two tenth-century manuscripts boasted colophons that identified Maiolus directly in the production of the book and its subsequent donation to the abbey: Ambrose of Milan's commentary on the Gospel of Luke (Paris, BnF, Nouvelle acquisition latine 1438) and Hrabanus Maurus's ninth-century commentary on the book of Jeremiah (London, British Library, Additional 22820).[15]

Manuscript production did not abate during the abbacy of Odilo (994–1049), who commissioned lavishly decorated books like the Bible that bears his name in dedicatory verses appropriated from a poem written to Charlemagne by Alcuin (Paris, BnF, Latin 15176) and a florilegium of excerpts from Augustine's commentaries on the letters of Paul made for Emperor Henry II (Bamberg, Staatsbibliothek, Msc. Bibl.

---

13. Syrus, *Vita sancti Maioli* 1.13, ed. D. Iogna-Prat, in *Agni Immaculati: Recherches sur les sources hagiographiques relatives à saint Maieul de Cluny (954–994)* (Paris, 1988), p. 200.

14. For a list of tenth-century manuscripts from Cluny, see M.-C. Garand, "Copistes de Cluny au temps de saint Maieul (948–994)," *Bibliothèque de l'Ecole des Chartes* 136 (1978): 5–36, at p. 8. Wischermann assigned the production of thirteen of these manuscripts firmly to the time of Maiolus's abbacy (*Grundlagen einer cluniacensischen Bibliotheksgeschichte*, p. 40).

15. See L. Delisle, *Inventaire des manuscrits de la bibliothèque nationale: Fonds du Cluni* (Paris, 1884), pp. 44–45 (no. 19); and R. Kottje, *Verzeichnis der Handschriften mit den Werken des Hrabanus Maurus* (Hanover, 2012), p. 87 (no. 487), respectively.

126). These luxury manuscripts were produced for elite consumption. In contrast, the eleventh-century customary known as the *Liber tramitis* preserved evidence of a tradition of book-borrowing at the great Burgundian abbey that provides a rich sample of the kinds of manuscripts available to the brethren for private reading in the 1040s. According to this custom, each monk was expected to read one book per year, which was distributed on the first Monday of Lent.[16] On that day, the community gathered in the chapter room, where they returned the books in their possession from the previous year and selected a new manuscript from those laid out on a large carpet. The *Liber tramitis* incorporated the custodian's record of the names of sixty-four individuals who took part in this tradition and the titles of the manuscripts that they had borrowed for the year.[17]

In his unsurpassed study of this record, André Wilmart identified the five kinds of writings on which the brethren of Cluny ruminated in their private hours: the Bible, patristic theology, ascetic literature and hagiography, history, and especially biblical exegesis.[18] According to the *Liber tramitis*, four readers borrowed manuscripts of individual works of scripture, including the Book of Kings, the letters of Paul, and two psalters. Fourteen others chose specimens of patristic theology represented primarily by the writings of Augustine, including his magisterial *On the City of God* but also works by Isidore of Seville, Julian of Toledo, and Alcuin. Eleven monks selected samples of ascetic literature and saints' lives that evoked the penitential hardships of the eastern desert, like the *Collations* of John Cassian, the *Sayings* of Basil of Caesarea, a sermon attributed to Ephrem the Syrian called *On the Compunction of the Heart*, and the *Life of Mary of Egypt*. Six of the brethren studied histories of antiquity and the early church by Josephus, Eusebius of Caesarea, Paul Orosius, Aethicus Ister, Bede, and perhaps surprisingly, the Roman historian Livy. Almost half of the borrowers, however, chose works of biblical exegesis composed by patristic authorities like Origen, Ambrose, Jerome, John Chrysostom, Augustine, Cassiodorus, Gregory the Great, and Bede, as well as Carolingian thinkers like Hrabanus Maurus, Remigius, and Haimo of Auxerre. When pauses in the relentless

---

16. Further on this custom, see K. Christ, "In Caput Quadragesimae," *Zentralblatt für Bibliothekswesen* 60 (1943): 33–59.

17. *Liber tramitis aevi Odilonis abbatis* 2.190, ed. P. Dinter, CCM 10 (Siegburg, 1980), pp. 261–64. The precise year in question is unknown.

18. A. Wilmart, "Le couvent et la bibliothèque de Cluny vers le milieu du XIe siècle," *Revue Mabillon* 11 (1921): 89–124.

cycle of liturgical rituals permitted opportunities for private reading, the brethren of Cluny filled this time primarily by ruminating on the Bible mediated by patristic authorities and by immersing themselves in theological arguments formulated at the end of antiquity.

The full panoply of Cluny's manuscript holdings was, in fact, even more extensive than any of these tenth- and eleventh-century examples attests. A catalog of the community's library composed during the abbacy of Hugh III (1158–1161) described the contents of a staggering 570 volumes, many of which contained multiple texts by different authors.[19] The relatively small number of eleventh- and twelfth-century authors in this catalog—a mere 15 out of 206—and the absence of significant works of theology and philosophy by contemporary luminaries like Abelard, Peter of Poitiers, John of Salisbury, Anselm of Canterbury, and Hugh of Saint Victor led Veronika von Büren to argue convincingly that the core of this inventory was the product of the eleventh century, which the brethren later updated as needed.[20] The catalog is now lost, but descriptions of it left by Maurist visitors to the abbey in the seventeenth century allow us to reconstruct its unusual appearance. The text was originally written on parchment sheets affixed to four large panels of wood mounted on a wall. At the end of the catalog at the bottom of the fourth panel was an illustration of a monk offering a book to an abbot named Hugh. Like so many artifacts of medieval Cluny, this catalog did not survive the ravages of the French Revolution. Fortunately, early modern transcriptions of its inventory of books reveal the contents of the abbey's library at its height in the twelfth century.

By the death of Abbot Peter the Venerable in 1156, Cluny's book collection rivaled those of the great monastic houses of the Carolingian age. The discursive character of its book catalog provides us with the opportunity not only to survey the hundreds of manuscripts owned by the community but also to leaf through their rich and varied contents. The author of the catalog organized the books under headings according to topic and author, but the relationship between manuscripts in each section tended to be associative rather than strict. Works of scripture assumed pride of place at the beginning of the catalog, both whole

---

19. Delisle, *Inventaire des manuscrits*, pp. 337–73 (appendix A).

20. See V. von Büren, "Le grand catalogue de la bibliothèque de Cluny," in *Le gouvernement d'Hugues de Semur à Cluny* (Cluny, 1988), pp. 245–63; and V. von Büren, "Le catalogue de la bibliothèque de Cluny du XIe siècle reconstitué," *Scriptorium* 46 (1992): 256–67.

bibles (*bibliothecae*) and volumes containing separate biblical units, like the major and minor prophets, or collections of patristic sermons keyed to the liturgical calendar (nos. 1–16). Next followed works of history ranging from the imperial records of Roman antiquity to the triumphal accounts of the rise of the early church to the conversion of barbarian peoples to the Christian faith (nos. 17–33). Patristic literature dominated the first half of the catalog with a section devoted to writings by Gregory the Great (nos. 34–64), the works of early church fathers listed collectively under a heading for Gregory Nazianzen and Cyprian of Carthage (nos. 65–89), Ambrose of Milan (nos. 90–105), John Chrysostom (nos. 106–22), Augustine (nos. 123–87), Jerome (nos. 188–219), Origen of Alexandria (nos. 220–52), and Bede followed by sundry Carolingian exegetes (nos. 253–99). Two early abbots of Cluny (Odo and Odilo) took their place in this lineage (nos. 300–307) before the theme of the catalog shifted to hagiography with an emphasis on the cult of Saint Martin of Tours (nos. 308–37). Hrabanus Maurus marked the return of Carolingian authorities in a section that soon lost thematic coherence (nos. 338–91) until a cluster of writings by Isidore of Seville restored a semblance of order (nos. 392–417). There followed collections of canon law and the acts of church councils (nos. 433–50). The catalog concluded with miscellaneous titles, including ancient medicine, philosophy, and literature (nos. 451–523), and a robust section devoted to poetry, both classical and Christian (nos. 524–70).

The destruction of the abbey of Cluny in the aftermath of the French Revolution scattered and destroyed most of these manuscripts, but the few survivors still have stories to tell. The oldest extant manuscript from Cluny's library was a copy of Paul Orosius's *Seven Books of History Against the Pagans* (Paris, BnF, Latin 9665), which was made in the decades around 800 at the abbey of Luxueil.[21] Originally composed in the second decade of the fifth century, Orosius's history was a grim chronicle of the misfortunes that had befallen Rome before the time of Christ written in response to pagans who had blamed the empire's neglect of the gods for the sack of Rome in 410.[22] This Carolingian copy may have arrived at Cluny in the early tenth century as one of the

---

21. B. Bischoff, "Manuscripts in the Age of Charlemagne," in B. Bischoff, *Manuscripts and Libraries in the Age of Charlemagne*, ed. and trans. M. M. Gorman (Cambridge, 1994), pp. 20–55, at p. 34, n. 67; and L. B. Mortensen, "The Diffusion of Roman Histories in the Middle Ages: A List of Orosius, Eutropius, Paulus Diaconus and Landulfus Sagax Manuscripts," *Filologia mediolatina* 6–7 (1999–2000): 101–200, at p. 143 (no. 157).

22. On Orosius, see Peter Van Nuffelen, *Orosius and the Rhetoric of History* (Oxford, 2012).

hundred books that Odo brought with him when he entered the community. The second abbot of Cluny certainly knew his Orosius, for echoes from the *Seven Books of History* recurred both in his *Collations* as well as his *Occupatio*.[23] Over the generations, other monks of Cluny clearly read this manuscript as well. In the 1040s, an individual named Bernard chose Orosius's history for private study during the annual book-borrowing custom practiced on the first Monday of Lent.[24] A century later, it appeared in the first column on the "wall catalog" of Cluny's great library among other accounts of the ancient past.[25] Peter the Venerable consulted it in the early years of his abbacy. There he learned the story of the vengeance of King Cyrus against the river Gyndes for drowning his favorite horse, which he repeated in the late 1130s in his treatise against the Petrobrusian heretics.[26] The antiquity of this venerable Orosius manuscript—it was more than three hundred years old by the twelfth century—may have inspired Peter to commission a second copy of it for the abbey's library. Both manuscripts survived until the seventeenth century, when a Cluniac librarian made a new inventory of Cluny's books. His list included two copies of Orosius: the Carolingian exemplar "written in scribal hands of great antiquity and outstanding in their proficiency" (*optimae et antiquae manus*), which survives to the present day, and the twelfth-century copy made at the request of Peter, now lost.[27]

Cluny's venerable Orosius manuscript tells a different story than the luxury volumes of monastic production that have attracted the lion's share of attention in modern scholarship, like the heavily illustrated copy of Ildefonsus's seventh-century treatise on the virginity of Mary made in the late eleventh century for an elite patron in Spain (Parma, Biblioteca Palatina, Ms. Parm. 1650) or the lavishly illuminated commemoration of Cluny's history, music, and liturgical rituals produced in the first decades of the thirteenth century at the request of Abbot William II (1207-1215) at a moment of institutional change (Paris,

---

23. *The Occupatio of Odo of Cluny*, ed. and trans. Jones.
24. *Liber tramitis* 2.190: "frater Bernardus Orosium," ed. Dinter, p. 264, with Wilmart, "Le couvent et la bibliothèque de Cluny," p. 114.
25. Delisle, *Inventaire des manuscrits*, p. 338: "Volumen in quo continetur historia Pauli Orosii" (no. 20), with von Büren, "Le grand catalogue," p. 255: "Le manuscrit contenant Orose (no. 20) . . . est écrit dans le style de Luxeuil et il est sans doute parvenu avec Odon à Cluny."
26. Peter the Venerable, *Contra Petrobrusianos* 121, ed. J. Fearns, CCCM 10 (Turnhout, 1968), pp. 71-72.
27. Delisle, *Inventaire des manuscrits*, p. 384 (nos. D and E).

BnF, Latin 17716).[28] Yet, middling and modest manuscripts made contributions no less important to our understanding of the abbey's history than these deluxe volumes produced for elite consumption. The chapters collected here find their origin in medieval books of this kind and the texts they preserve, like the inelegant late eleventh-century collection of *vitae* and miracles related to the cult of Abbot Maiolus owned by the abbey of Saint Martial of Limoges (Paris, BnF, Latin 5611), or the scrappy twelfth-century pamphlet preserving accounts of relic translations from the Holy Land to Cluny in the aftermath of the First Crusade (Paris, BnF, Latin 12603), or the contemporary workaday chapter book for nuns that featured an unusual line drawing of a monk ascending a ladder as a preface to the *Rule of Benedict* (Admont, Benediktinerstift, Codex 567). Together they offer a new contribution to the history of religious culture at the abbey of Cluny in the Middle Ages informed by the texts preserved in manuscripts that the brethren read and reread for centuries in the solemn stillness of their church or the quiet corners of their cloister.

---

28. On the so-called Parma Ildefonsus, see the classic work by M. Shapiro, *The Parma Ildefonsus: A Romanesque Illuminated Manuscript from Cluny and Related Works* (New York, 1964). For a study of Paris, BnF, Latin 17716, with reference to earlier bibliography, see S. Boynton, "Music and the Cluniac Vision of History in Paris, Bibliothèque nationale de France, MS lat. 17716," in *Chant, Liturgy, and the Inheritance of Rome: Essays in Honour of Joseph Dyer*, ed. D. J. DiCenso and R. Maloy (London, 2017), pp. 407–30.

CHAPTER 1

The Benedictines

Since the seventeenth century, historians have used the term *Benedictine* to describe communities of cloistered men and women, who lived between the sixth century and the present. The name derives from the indebtedness of most monks, both male and female, to the religious principles outlined in the *Rule of Benedict* (*Regula Benedicti*).[1] A sixth-century handbook for the organization and orchestration of cenobitic communities written in Latin by an Italian abbot, the *Rule* became the most authoritative word on monastic practice in Europe after it was endorsed by Carolingian rulers in the early ninth century. Benedict's handbook for monks is without question one of the most influential and enduring monastic texts written in the Middle Ages, but the term *Benedictine* is not medieval in origin, and thus it requires some qualification by scholars who use it. In this chapter, I examine the early history of the *Rule* and its reputed author

---

Originally published as "The Benedictines," in *The Oxford Handbook of Christian Monasticism*, ed. B. Kaczynski (New York, 2020), pp. 218-31. Reproduced with permission of The Licensor through PLSclear. Copyright © 2020 Oxford University Press.

1. The standard Latin edition and French translation remains *La règle de saint Benoît*, ed. and trans. A. de Vogüé and J. Neufville, SC 181-86, 7 vols. (the last of which is not included in the SC series) (Paris, 1971-1972). English translations include *The Rule of Benedict*, trans. C. White (New York, 2008); and *The Rule of Saint Benedict*, trans. B. Venarde (Cambridge, MA, 2011).

Benedict of Nursia (c. 480–c. 550) to pinpoint where and when the text achieved the designation of *regula sancta* in the Middle Ages. I also consider how modern scholarship has called into question many of the received traditions about the author of the *Rule*, the date of its composition, and the authenticity of the earliest texts that mention it, particularly works long attributed to Pope Gregory the Great (c. 540–604).

I then turn to the word *Benedictine* and its history. The application of this term to medieval cloistered communities is useful insofar as it distinguishes monks inspired by the principles espoused in the *Rule of Benedict* from other religious vocations in the Christian tradition (mendicants, canons, hermits), but it regrettably obscures the rich diversity and historical development of monastic practice in the Middle Ages, because it implies that all Benedictine communities shared the same relationship with the *Rule* and the same reverence for its author. In fact, abbeys and nunneries across medieval Europe frequently braided selections of the *Rule* with prescriptions culled from other rules, and they habitually amplified and nuanced its tenets with discrete revisions, silent omissions, and sprawling commentaries. These accommodations were due, in no small part, both to the laconic character of the *Rule* and to changes in Christian devotional practices that had no precedent in Benedict's time. In short, despite the widespread adoption of principles inspired by the *Rule*, several examples will show that each community's relationship with this influential text was different.

Lastly, I call attention to three neglected areas of research in the premodern Benedictine tradition. First, I identify the later Middle Ages (c. 1200–1500) as a period of monastic activity that has received little notice from historians.[2] There are several reasons for this. The rise of the new mendicant and military orders claims the lion's share of scholarly attention in this period. The Cistercians are also a popular subject of historical inquiry, but scholars almost always treat them as distinct from the Benedictine tradition rather than as an integral part of it.[3] Moreover, despite evidence to the contrary, a tenacious

---

2. Welcome exceptions include J. G. Clark, *A Monastic Renaissance at St. Albans: Thomas Walsingham and His Circle, c. 1350–1440* (Oxford, 2004); M. Heale, *Monasticism in Late Medieval England, c. 1300–1535* (Manchester, 2009); and S. Falk, *The Light Ages: The Surprising Story of Medieval Science* (New York, 2020), all of which focus on later medieval England.

3. Cistercian exceptionalism is on full display in Boydell Press's book series Monastic Orders, which has published both J. G. Clark, *The Benedictines in the Middle Ages* (Woodbridge, 2011) and J. Burton and J. Kerr, *The Cistercians in the Middle Ages* (Woodbridge, 2011). Likewise,

narrative arc in scholarly literature depicts a decline of traditional monasticism in the later Middle Ages. This has made it challenging for historians to frame questions about the influence of cloistered monks in the thirteenth century and beyond. Second, I argue for a more systematic inclusion of female religious in the history of the Benedictines. Some of the very earliest evidence for the use of the *Rule of Benedict* in the seventh century appears in rules of conduct written specifically for women. The choices made by the authors who redacted the *Rule* for their female charges reveal a great deal about the differences that they perceived and constructed between the monastic project as pursued by men and women. Third, I cast light on monastic poetry as an overlooked source for the history of Benedictine culture and spirituality in the Middle Ages. Modern research has underscored the centrality of Latin verse in the program of monastic education that was familiar from the Carolingian period well into the twelfth century and beyond. Despite its evident importance in the social, religious, and political lives of monks, medieval monastic poetry remains an uncharted landscape that only a few intrepid explorers have begun to investigate.

The *Rule of Benedict* and Its Author

The *Rule of Benedict* is a normative guide for cloistered monks written in the early sixth century. It is a concise work comprising a prologue, seventy-two short chapters, and an epilogue, which combine theoretical reflections on the goals of the monastic vocation with practical insight about the day-to-day workings of a small religious house, based on the firsthand experience of its author. The *Rule* presumes a group of like-minded laypeople, who renounced their families, social status, and personal wealth to live in prayerful simplicity with the goal of meriting their own salvation before God. According to the *Rule*, monks achieved this aim by cultivating the virtues of obedience, humility, and silence while taking part in manual labor, sacred reading, and rendering praise to God in liturgical offices distributed throughout the day and night. During these offices (vigils, lauds, prime, terce, sext, none, vespers, and

---

the *Oxford Handbook of Christian Monasticism* places the present chapter on the Benedictines side-by-side with a separate chapter devoted to "The Cistercians." For the latter, see A. E. Lester, "The Cistercians," in *The Oxford Handbook of Christian Monasticism*, ed. B. Kaczynski (New York, 2020), pp. 232–47.

compline), monks gathered as a community to recite psalms and hear readings from scripture and from patristic authorities, working their way through the 150 psalms of the Psalter in a week's time. They conducted this way of life under the watchful eyes of their abbot, who acted as the spiritual adviser, teacher, and administrator of the entire community.[4] The *Rule* drew its inspiration from the collective wisdom of the desert fathers, mediated through the writings of Basil and John Cassian, and borrowed freely from handbooks written for other monastic communities, most notably the near-contemporary *Rule of the Master*.[5] The *Rule of Benedict*, however, stood out from other rules of the time because of its author's sense of moderation; his consideration of contingencies, such as climate; and his compassionate view of human weakness.

Medieval readers never questioned the authorship of the *Rule*. They attributed the work to Benedict of Nursia, an otherwise obscure Italian abbot who flourished in the early sixth century, and who left no other writings that bear his name. In the twentieth century, however, some scholars called into question received traditions about the *Rule* and its author. This discussion began with the relationship between the *Rule of Benedict* and the *Rule of the Master*, which share the same prologue and several early chapters on the spiritual program of the abbey. Monastic historians had always presumed that the *Rule of the Master* was "an interpolated and somewhat eccentric enlargement" of the *Rule of Benedict* until 1940, when Augustin Genestout argued just the opposite: that the author of the *Rule of Benedict* had read the *Rule of the Master* and judiciously pruned its contents for use in his own rule.[6] Since the 1980s, other scholars have challenged traditional assumptions about the *Rule of Benedict* and the earliest witnesses to the life of Benedict of Nursia. Against much opposition, Francis Clark has argued at length that the *Dialogues* of Gregory the Great were the work of a seventh-century forger and therefore do not provide evidence of the pope's esteem for Abbot Benedict and his rule for monks.[7] Moreover, Adalbert de Vogüé has

---

4. A. de Vogüé, *Community and Abbot in the Rule of Benedict* (Kalamazoo, MI, 1979).

5. *Regula magistri*, ed. A. de Vogüé, in *La règle de Maître*, 3 vols., SC 105-107 (Paris, 1964-1965).

6. On the history of the controversy, see A. Genestout, "La Règle du Maître et la Règle de S. Benoît," *Revue d'Ascétique et de Mystique* 21 (1940): 51-112; D. Knowles, *Great Historical Enterprises: Problems in Monastic History* (London, 1963), pp. 139-95; and B. Jaspert, *Die Regula Benedicti-Regula Magistri Kontroverse*, 2nd ed. (Hildesheim, 1977). For the quotation, see A. Sillem, "St. Benedict (c. 480-c. 550)," in *Benedict's Disciples*, ed. D. H. Farmer (Leominster, 1980), pp. 21-40, at p. 29.

7. F. Clark, *The Pseudo-Gregorian Dialogues*, 2 vols. (Leiden, 1987); and F. Clark, *The 'Gregorian' Dialogues and the Origins of Benedictine Monasticism* (Leiden, 2003). For a summary of the

shown that the attribution to Gregory of the *Commentary on 1 Kings* that bears his name, which includes an early citation from the *Rule of Benedict*, is not secure. In all likelihood, the author was Peter of Cava-Venosa, a twelfth-century abbot who braided his own commentary with some of Gregory's lost writings.[8] If we jettison Gregory's *Dialogues* and *Commentary on 1 Kings* as the earliest independent testimonies for the *Rule of Benedict* and the historical Benedict, then the first evidence for its use only appears in seventh-century Francia. We know that some cloistered communities there, both male and female, adopted a rule of this name, either on its own or (more commonly) excerpted and grafted onto other monastic legislation, like Caesarius of Arles's *Rule for Virgins* and the *Rule of Columbanus*.[9]

Despite the controversies surrounding its early history, it is clear that the *Rule of Benedict* became popular during the Carolingian period, in no small part because of imperial sponsorship.[10] At the Aachen assemblies of 816–817, Emperor Louis the Pious's adviser Abbot Benedict of Aniane promoted the adoption of one rule and one custom *(una regula, una consuetudo)* in all Frankish abbeys. The one rule was the *Rule of Benedict*; the one custom was Benedict of Aniane's supplementary regulations to it.[11] Although this legislation was not entirely successful, owing to the tenacity of local monastic traditions, from this point onward, the *Rule* overshadowed all other ancient rules as the most authoritative guide to governing a cloistered community. Its authority was not challenged until the emergence of the new monastic orders of the twelfth and thirteenth centuries.

---

rebuttals to Clark's thesis, see S. Boesch Gajano, "Gregorio Magno agiografo," in *Hagiographies: Histoire internationale de la littérature hagiographique latine et vernaculaire en Occident des origines à 1550*, ed. G. Philippart, M. Goullet, and F. Peloux, 9 vols. to date (1992–2024), vol. 7, pp. 11–94, at pp. 26–27.

8. A. de Vogüé, "L'auteur du *Commentaire des Rois* attribué à Saint Grégoire: Un moine de Cava?" *Revue bénédictine* 106 (1996): 319–31; and F. Clark, "Authorship of the Commentary *In 1 Regum*: Implications of A. de Vogüé's Discovery," *Revue bénédictine* 108 (1998): 61–79.

9. M. Dunn, *The Emergence of Monasticism: From the Desert Fathers to the Early Middle Ages* (Oxford, 2000), pp. 158–90. See also n. 37, below.

10. M. de Jong, "Carolingian Monasticism: The Power of Prayer," in *The New Cambridge Medieval History*, vol. 2, *c. 700–c. 900*, ed. R. McKitterick (Cambridge, 1995), pp. 622–53. See also A. Diem and P. Rousseau, "Monastic Rules (Fourth to Ninth Century)," and R. Kramer, "Monasticism, Reform, and Authority in the Carolingian Era," in *CHMM*, vol. 1, pp. 162–94 and 432–49, respectively.

11. J. Semmler, "Benedictus II: Una regula, una consuetudo," in *Benedictine Culture, 750–1050*, ed. W. Lourdaux and D. Verhelst (Louvain, 1983), pp. 1–49.

The *Benedictine Centuries*

Given the prominence of Benedict and his rule in the lives of early medieval monks, scholars have occasionally referred to the span of European history between 600 and 1100 as the *Benedictine centuries*.[12] Indeed, in almost every aspect of cultural production in this period—manuscript production and scribal innovation, artistic creations across diverse media from book illumination to monumental sculpture, literary industry in a wide array of genres, the development of Christian music and liturgical chant, the writing of history, medicine, and even scientific inquiry—we find the guiding hands and acquisitive intellect of cloistered monks. The phrase *Benedictine centuries* remains troubling as a generic appellation, however, because it implies a uniformity of religious practice in early medieval abbeys that did not exist, and it thereby veils the rich diversity of local traditions observed, cherished, and protected in cloistered communities across Western Europe. An anonymous late twelfth-century continuator of Folcuin's *Deeds of the Abbots of Lobbes* stated plainly that the brethren at the abbey of Lobbes in the 1120s did not follow the *Rule of Benedict* to the letter and, for that matter, neither did any other cloistered community![13] We cannot dismiss this kind of testimony lightly. No one can deny that the so-called *Benedictine centuries* witnessed the rise of Benedict of Nursia as a significant saint in the Christian tradition and the ascent of the *Rule* as the most authoritative guide to the monastic life in this period. We must nonetheless agree with John Howe's assessment that "if Benedictinism is literal adherence to the Rule, then the so-called 'Benedictine Centuries' saw precious little of it."[14]

The *Rule of Benedict* was a useful and inspiring document of practice for medieval monks, but it was clearly not sufficient on its own. Indeed,

---

12. See, for example, J. H. Newman, "The Mission of St. Benedict," in J. H. Newman, *Historical Sketches*, 3 vols. (London, 1906), vol. 2, pp. 365–87, at p. 371: "[Benedict] is the representative of Latin monasticism for the long extent of six centuries, while monachism was one; and even when at length varieties arose, and distinct titles were given to them, the change grew out of him; — not the act of strangers who were his rivals, but of his own children, who did but make a new beginning in all devotion and loyalty to him."

13. *Gesta abbatum Lobbiensium* 18, ed. W. Arndt, MGH Scriptores 21 (Hanover, 1869), p. 320; with S. Vanderputten, "A Time of Great Confusion: Second-Generation Cluniac Reformers and Resistance to Monastic Centralization in the County of Flanders (c. 1125–1145)," *Revue d'histoire ecclésiastique* 102 (2007): 47–75.

14. J. Howe, *Church Reform and Social Change in Eleventh-Century Italy: Dominic of Sora and His Patrons* (Philadelphia, 1997), p. 92.

its combination of theoretical principles, pragmatic advice, and fair-minded consideration of the frailty of individuals was a strength that contributed to its enduring appeal. In its long history, however, we find few cloistered communities that adopted the *Rule* to the exclusion of supplementary customs, that is, local and idiosyncratic responses to practical and devotional issues that find no expression in this authoritative source. From the eighth century onward, monks expounded on those portions of the *Rule of Benedict* that defied an easy interpretation, while at the same time collecting and writing down their community's traditions in documents known as customaries.[15] The implication of their industry is clear: the precepts of the *Rule of Benedict* were not self-explanatory to medieval readers, and they did not carry the same value in every cloistered community. The passage of centuries and the emergence of a new readership of the *Rule* in northern Europe only contributed to the problems attendant on the recovery of its author's original meaning.

The phrase *Benedictine Centuries* also masks the significant developments in monastic practices between 800 and 1100 that had little or no precedent in the *Rule of Benedict*. First and foremost, the size of monastic communities increased dramatically in the Carolingian period, in no small part because of the patronage of royal sponsors such as Charlemagne and Louis the Pious, who directed monks to pray for their well-being.[16] Secular rulers took an active interest in regulating and standardizing religious practice in their kingdom to ensure the efficacy of those prayers. From the eighth century onward, the goal of the monastic vocation broadened to include not only the salvation of the individual monk but also the spiritual health of the entire Christian community, especially the royal family. This new role increased the prestige of the monastic vocation and swelled the demand for new recruits, especially those who were untainted by contact with the secular world. Carolingian families responded to this need by offering their children as oblates (offerings) to cloistered communities, where they would spend their entire lives as religious specialists in the prayerful

---

15. *From Dead of Night to End of Day: The Medieval Customs of Cluny / Du coeur de la nuit à la fin du jour: Les coutumes clunisiennes au moyen âge*, ed. S. Boynton and I. Cochelin, Disciplina Monastica 3 (Turnhout, 2005); and *Consuetudines et Regulae: Sources for Monastic Life in the Middle Ages and the Early Modern Period*, ed. C. M. Malone and C. Maines, Disciplina Monastica 10 (Turnhout, 2014).

16. de Jong, "Carolingian Monasticism."

intervention that had become so important in Carolingian society.[17] Although the *Rule of Benedict* devoted a chapter to the entry of children into the abbey (*RB* 58), a sixth-century abbot such as Benedict could scarcely imagine that monasteries would become bustling communities like the one imagined in the ninth-century Plan of Saint Gall. The Plan numbered hundreds of monks and a comparable number of secular artisans, servants, and helpers, who took care of the mundane needs of the brethren whose time was increasingly consumed by the demands of corporate prayer at the expense of manual labor.[18] Moreover, this period also saw the rise of new expressions of Christian devotion that the *Rule of Benedict* could not have anticipated, including the clericalization of monks and the development of the cult of the dead, which placed a significant importance on the near-constant celebration of funerary masses in abbeys across Western Europe.[19]

The brethren of the great Burgundian abbey of Cluny, founded in 910 by Duke William of Aquitaine, epitomized how monastic communities could esteem the *Rule of Benedict* yet also augment its precepts in creative ways to accommodate both the devotional developments and the practical realities of their time. The Cluniacs cultivated the discipline of silence in their abbeys, as the *Rule* recommended, but they also developed a silent language of hand signs that had no precedent in early medieval monasticism to safeguard their tongues from sinful words when they interacted with one another in the kitchens, the refectory, or the oratory.[20] Influenced by the emphasis on liturgical intervention that characterized the Carolingian reforms of monasticism, the brethren of Cluny earned renown for their commitment to an exhausting regime of liturgical prayer that far exceeded the recitation of 150 psalms a week usual in late antique abbeys.[21] They did so,

---

17. M. de Jong, *In Samuel's Image: Child Oblation in the Early Medieval West* (Leiden, 1996).

18. R. Sullivan, "What Was Carolingian Monasticism? The Plan of St. Gall and the History of Monasticism," in *After Rome's Fall: Narrators and Sources of Early Medieval History*, ed. A. C. Murray (Toronto, 1998), pp. 251–87; and G. Constable, "Carolingian Monasticism as Seen in the Plan of St. Gall," in *Le monde carolingien: Bilan, perspectives, champs de recherches*, ed. W. Fałkowski and Y. Sassier (Turnhout, 2010), pp. 199–217.

19. D. Iogna-Prat, "The Dead in the Celestial Bookkeeping of the Cluniac Monks Around the Year 1000," in *Debating the Middle Ages: Issues and Readings*, ed. L. Little and B. H. Rosenwein (Oxford, 1998), pp. 340–62.

20. S. G. Bruce, *Silence and Sign Language in Medieval Monasticism: The Cluniac Tradition, c. 900–1200* (Cambridge, 2007).

21. K. Hallinger, "Überlieferung und Steigerung im Mönchtum des 8. bis 12. Jahrhunderts," in *Eulogia: Miscellanea Liturgica in onore di P. Burckhard Neunheuser O.S.B.* (Rome, 1979), pp. 125–87.

however, at the expense of manual labor, which was undertaken mostly by servants, even though the *Rule* stated that "it is when they live by the work of their hands, like our fathers and apostles, that they are truly monks."[22] In the eleventh century, the Cluniacs composed massive books of customary legislation to augment the guidelines of the *Rule*, both as a way of imposing order on received traditions and as a template for other monasteries that desired to emulate their particular way of life.[23] Cluny's fame did not protect its brethren from criticism, however. In the twelfth century, Cistercian monks condemned the practices of the Cluniacs because their customs had strayed too far from the literal meaning of the sacred authority enshrined in the *Rule*. As Idung of Prüfening wrote in his *Dialogus duorum monachorum*: "The customs of Cluny are a deviation from the law given to us by God, that is, from the *Rule*. And thereby they bring dishonor on the giver of the law, that is, on God, and on the expounder of that law, that is, on Saint Benedict."[24]

Given the prevalence of the term *Benedictine* in academic discourse, it may come as a surprise that premodern monks never used this word to refer to themselves. Although some in the later Middle Ages referred to themselves as monks of the Order of Saint Benedict (*ordo sancti Benedicti*), much of the ambiguity surrounding the term *Benedictine* when applied to medieval cloistered communities arises from the fact that it is an anachronism, first coined in the seventeenth century.[25] It emerged as a category of historical analysis only in the late nineteenth century, through its use by pioneering historians of Benedictine monasticism, such as Cardinal John Henry Newman and Cuthbert Butler. The currency of the term increased because of its adoption in the title of one of the foremost venues for the publication of research on monastic history and literature, the *Revue bénédictine*, founded in 1884 at the Abbaye de Maredsous in Belgium. The term thus owes its popularity to the success of the so-called Benedictine revival of the

---

22. *RB* 48.8: "Quia tunc uere monachi sunt si labore manuum suarum uiuunt, sicut et Patres nostri et apostoli."

23. I. Cochelin, "Customaries as Inspirational Sources," in *Consuetudines and Regulae*, ed. Malone and Maines, pp. 27-72.

24. Idung, *Dialogus duorum monachorum*, 1.27: "Tui oris confessio et tuae sententiae concessio convincit Cluniacensem consuetudinem legis a deo nobis datae, id est Regulae, esse prevaricatricem et per hoc datoris legis, id est dei, et latoris legis, id est sancti Benedicti, esse inhonoratricem." ed. R. B. C. Huygens, in *Le moine Idung et ses deux ouvrages: "Argumentum super quatuor questionibus" et "Dialogus duorum monachorum"* (Spoleto, 1980), p. 102.

25. J. Leclercq, *Aux sources de la spiritualité occientale* (Paris, 1964), p. 30.

1800s, which witnessed the recovery of the black monks from the dark days of the French Revolution and the reorganization of Benedictine houses under an international governing body known as the Benedictine Confederation of the Order of Saint Benedict, established in 1893 by Pope Leo XIII.[26]

How, then, did cloistered men and women of the Middle Ages refer to themselves if they did not use the term *Benedictine*? The most common name for monks in medieval Latin sources was *monachus*. The word first appears in fourth-century papyrus documents from Egypt, and its meaning was widely discussed throughout the Middle Ages.[27] According to Giles Constable: "Most writers agreed that the first part (*mona-*) meant 'one' in the sense of alone, single, or, more rarely, united, but they were less certain about the second part (*-chus*), which they thought might come from *cor* or *oculus*, because monks were supposed to have one heart, like the apostles in Acts 4.32, and a single eye, as in the Gospels, which saw no evil and was directed toward heaven."[28] In addition to *monachus*, monks were also commonly referred to as *fratres* (brethren). Comparable names applied to cloistered women (*sorores*, in particular), but they were most often called *sanctimoniales*, from the noun *sanctimonium* (piety), or simply *moniales*.

Medieval Benedictines were also called black monks (*monachi nigri*) because of the dark color of their woolen robes. The term was primarily descriptive, but in the twelfth century, the color of monastic clothing became a source of contention between traditional brethren such as the Cluniacs and reform-minded monks such as the Cistercians, who considered the liturgical opulence and material extravagance of large abbeys like Cluny to be at odds with Benedict's precepts.[29] Agitating for a return to the literal observance of the *Rule of Benedict*, which did not specify the color of monastic clothing (*RB* 55), the early Cistercians wore robes of undyed wool, which contemporaries described as white or gray in color. The plain habits of the white monks broadcast both their disdain for the world and their loyalty to a literal reading of the *Rule*. For their part, the black monks dismissed this convention as a

---

26. D. Rees, "The Benedictine Revival in the Nineteenth Century," in *Benedict's Disciples*, ed. Farmer, pp. 282–307.
27. E. A. Judge, "The Earliest Use of *Monachos* for 'Monk': (P. Coll. Youtie 77) and the Origins of Monasticism," *Jahrbuch für Antike und Christentum* 20 (1977): 72–89.
28. Constable, "Carolingian Monasticism as Seen in the Plan of St. Gall," p. 8.
29. For what follows, see G. Constable, *The Reformation of the Twelfth Century* (Cambridge, 1996), pp. 188–89.

superficial conceit. In his commentary on the *Rule*, the early twelfth-century theologian and exegete Rupert of Deutz wryly speculated that "perhaps if we had used white clothes, they would now use black."[30]

New Avenues of Inquiry

Historians have marked the end of the *Benedictine centuries* in the decades around 1100 and have viewed the rise of new religious orders (such as the canons regular, the military orders, and the mendicants) as responses to the ascetic laxity and material prosperity of traditional monasticism, which contemporary critics (like the Cistercians) claimed had strayed from the ideals of the *Rule of Benedict*. In an important revisionist article published in 1986, John Van Engen scrutinized the notion of a "crisis of cenobitism" in this period by evaluating the health of traditional monastic communities in the late eleventh and early twelfth centuries based on some important metrics. He concluded that "in four crucial areas—recruitment, revenue, quality of personnel, and leadership in the Church—the evidence indicates rather that Benedictine houses held their own or even increased in prosperity during the years 1050-1150."[31] Nevertheless, the lingering influence of the idea that Benedictine monasticism suffered a decline in the twelfth century has had a lasting impact on modern scholarship. As a result, inquiry into the religious and political activities of cloistered monks in the period between the thirteenth century and the Reformation has fallen far behind modern advances in research that characterize the study of monasticism in the early Middle Ages and the Enlightenment.[32]

The later Middle Ages are fertile ground for inquiries into the intellectual influence, political power, and devotional and administrative practices of traditional monastic communities in Western Europe. Like bees who leave the safety of their hive but do not forget their common purpose, Benedictine monks were active in the vibrant and often turbulent intellectual culture beyond their cloister walls. In the thirteenth century, they flocked to the universities in significant numbers.

---

30. Rupert of Deutz, *In regulam sancti Benedicti*, 3.13: "Fortisan si nos albidis vestibus usi fuisemus [sic], ipsi nunc nigris uterentur." *PL* 170, col. 521.

31. J. Van Engen, "The 'Crisis of Cenobitism' Reconsidered: Benedictine Monasticism in the Years 1050-1150," *Speculum* 61 (1986): 269-304, at pp. 275-76.

32. Dunn, *The Emergence of Monasticism*; D. Beales, *Prosperity and Plunder: European Catholic Monasteries in the Age of Revolution, 1650-1815* (Cambridge, 2003); and U. Lehner, *Enlightened Monks: The German Benedictines, 1740-1803* (Oxford, 2011).

22   CHAPTER 1

Between 1229 and 1500, scholars have identified by name more than 650 monks who were students or teachers of theology or canon law at the University of Paris alone.[33] Many Benedictine monks returned to their cloisters with new literary tastes and clandestine interests, including the practice of natural magic.[34] The tissue of evidence for the lives of most of these individuals is thin, but some of them rose to positions of authority in monastic and ecclesiastical hierarchies.

None rivaled the heights reached by Abbot Mathieu of Vendôme.[35] Despite the fact that he did not receive a university education and rose through the ranks as a simple monk, in 1258, Mathieu was elected abbot of the royal monastery of Saint-Denis in Paris, one of the richest and most influential religious communities in Western Europe. As abbot, Mathieu defended the interests of his community in disputes with other religious institutions and lay lords, even with the government of King Louis IX. At the same time, he promoted the cult of Saint-Denis through the translation of relics and the founding of new feast days formalized and encouraged through the creation of opulent service books. The abbot's responsible stewardship of Saint-Denis earned him respect and authority at the highest levels of secular society. Toward the end of Louis IX's reign, Mathieu sat as a judge at the Parlement of Paris, the highest court of appeal in the French kingdom. Even more significantly, when the great king embarked on his second and final expedition to the East in 1270, he named the abbot of Saint-Denis as one of the two coregents of his realm (the other was the lay aristocrat, Simon of Clermont, Lord of Nesle). When Louis died in Tunis later that year, Mathieu's final service to his king was to act as the executor of his last will and testament.

Another lacuna in the history of Benedictine monasticism is the application of the *Rule of Benedict* in communities of religious women. Mostly ignored in monastic historiography until the 1970s, when the feminist movement drew scholars to the topic of female spirituality, the devotional practices of medieval Christian women and their active role in the production of manuscripts have become subjects of intense

---

33. T. Sullivan, *Benedictine Monks at the University of Paris, A.D. 1229-1500: A Biographical Register* (Leiden, 1995).

34. Clark, *A Monastic Renaissance at St. Albans*; and S. Page, *Magic in the Cloister: Pious Motives, Illicit Interests, and Occult Approaches to the Medieval Universe* (University Park, PA, 2013).

35. W. C. Jordan, *A Tale of Two Monasteries: Westminster and Saint-Denis in the Thirteenth Century* (Princeton, 2009), pp. 25-35, 66-73, and 130-34.

and fruitful discussion for the past three decades.[36] Even so, despite this surge of interest in a wide array of topics relating to premodern female monasticism, the meaning of the *Rule of Benedict* for cloistered women remains an open question. The lack of attention to this problem is even more puzzling when one considers that some of the earliest evidence for the adoption of the *Rule* in northern Europe appears in the context of female houses. This evidence includes the rule for women compiled by Bishop Donatus of Besançon as well as the anonymous *Regula cuiusdam ad virgines*, both composed in the mid-seventh century.[37] These two early witnesses to the use of the *Rule of Benedict* raise the same question: to what degree can we consider the *Rule* to have been appropriate, in theoretical and practical terms, for women as well as for men?[38]

The issue of the applicability and adaptation of the *Rule of Benedict* for women persisted long after its adoption in the ninth century as the legal foundation for all cloistered communities.[39] At the turn of the twelfth century, there was acute concern about whether religious women could live according to the *Rule*. In a well-known letter to her spiritual adviser Abelard, Abbess Heloise of the Paraclete (near Paris) requested that he compose a new set of monastic precepts suitable for

---

36. See, for example, J. A. McNamara, *Sisters in Arms: Catholic Nuns Through Two Millennia* (Cambridge, MA, 1996); A. Beach, *Women as Scribes: Book Production and Monastic Reform in Twelfth-Century Bavaria* (Cambridge, 2004); A. E. Lester, *Creating Cistercian Nuns: The Women's Religious Movement and Its Reform in Thirteenth-Century Champagne* (Ithaca, 2011); *The Oxford Handbook of Women and Gender in Medieval Europe*, ed. J. M. Bennett and R. M. Karras (Oxford, 2013); F. Lifshitz, *Religious Women in Early Carolingian Francia: A Study of Manuscript Transmission and Monastic Culture* (New York, 2014); and K. Bugyis, *The Care of Nuns: The Ministries of Benedictine Women in England during the Central Middle Ages* (New York, 2019).

37. *Regula Donati*, ed. V. Zimmerl-Panagl and M. Zelzer, in *Monastica 1: Donati Regula, Pseudo-Columbani Regula monialium (frg.)*, CSEL 98 (Berlin, 2015), pp. 139-88; and *Regula cuiusdam ad virgines*, ed. and trans. A. Diem, in *The Pursuit of Salvation: Community, Space, and Discipline in Early Medieval Monasticism*, Disciplina Monastica 13 (Turnhout, 2021), pp. 60-151.

38. A. Diem, "Rewriting Benedict: The *regula cuiusdam ad virgines* and Intertextuality as a Tool to Construct a Monastic Identity," *Journal of Medieval Latin* 17 (2007): 313-28; and A. Diem, "New Ideas Expressed in Old Words: The *Regula Donati* on Female Monastic Life and Monastic Spirituality," *Viator* 43 (2012): 1-38.

39. L. de Seilhac, "L'utilisation de le Règle de saint Benoît dans les monastères féminins," in *San Benedetto nel suo tempo: Atti del 7. Congresso internazionale di studi sull'alto Medioevo (Norcia, Subiaco, Cassino, Montecassino, 29 Settembre-Ottobre 1980)*, 2 vols. (Spoleto, 1982), vol. 2, pp. 527-49; K. Bodarwé, "Eine Männerregel für Frauen: Die Adaption der Benediktsregel im 9. und 10. Jahrhundert," in *Female "Vita Religiosa" Between Late Antiquity and the High Middle Ages: Structures, Developments and Spatial Contexts*, ed. G. Melville and A. Müller (Munster, 2011), pp. 235-72; and S. Vanderputten, *Dark Age Nunneries: The Ambiguous Identity of Female Monasticism, 800-1050* (Ithaca, 2018).

the women of her community. She stated that the *Rule* was "clearly written for men alone [and as such] it can only be fully obeyed by men."[40] Heloise drew attention to those precepts of Benedict that were inappropriate for women, including the frequent mention of clothing worn exclusively by men, the practice of wearing tight-fitting tunics and woolen garments that were impractical during a woman's menstrual cycle, and the liturgical and social responsibilities of the abbot, which an abbess could not hope to emulate. There was no unanimity among medieval legislators about how to deal with these problems. Some addressed the issue with a minimum of intervention, like the author of an early thirteenth-century Old French translation of the *Rule of Benedict* written for an unidentified female Cistercian community near Dijon, who simply changed the gender of the male pronouns to female and otherwise left the substance of the text unaltered.[41]

A final avenue of inquiry that remains little explored in the history of Benedictine monasticism is poetry. From late antiquity until the end of the Middle Ages, black monks composed thousands of lines of Latin verse on moral and devotional themes and recast hundreds of saints' lives in heroic meter.[42] Only in the past two decades have monastic historians advanced with tentative steps into this promising field of inquiry. A pathbreaking contribution is Anna Taylor's *Epic Lives and Monasticism in the Middle Ages, 800–1050*, which examines the social, political, and didactic value of saints' lives written in epic verse in post-Carolingian abbeys.[43] Taylor's book has revealed an intensely literary world in which the consumption and composition of poetry in the monastic classroom played a formative role in the cultivation of friendships, the currying of favor with powerful patrons, and the devotional reading practices of the brethren.

---

40. Heloise, *Ep.* 6.4: "Quam sicut uiris solummodo constat scripta esse, ita et ab ipsis tantum impleri posse tam subiectis pariter quam prelatis," ed. and trans. D. Luscombe, in *The Letter Collection of Peter Abelard and Heloise* (Oxford, 2013), pp. 218–59, at pp. 220–21; with R. Mohr, "Der Gedankenaustausch zwischen Heloisa und Abaelard über eine Modifizierung der Regula Benedicti für Frauen," *Regulae Benedicti Studia* 5 (1976/1977): 307–33.

41. "Ancienne traduction française des *Ecclesiastica officia, Instituta generalis Capituli, Usus conversorum* et *Regula sancti Benedicti*," publié d'après le manuscrit 352 de la bibliothèque publique de Dijon," ed. P. Guignard, in *Les monuments primitifs de la règle Cistercienne* (Dijon, 1878), pp. 407–42 (appendix I).

42. F. Dolbeau, "Un domaine négligé de la littérature médiolatine: Les textes hagiographiques en vers," *Cahiers de Civilisation Médiévale* 45 (2002): 129–39; and A. Taylor, "Hagiography and Early Medieval History," *Religion Compass* 7 (2013): 1–14.

43. A. Taylor, *Epic Lives and Monasticism in the Middle Ages, 800–1050* (Cambridge, MA, 2013).

Despite the central importance of Latin verse in Benedictine cloisters, the history of monastic poetry in the Middle Ages has not yet been written. Fortunately, an increasing number of case studies of individual poems written between the tenth and twelfth centuries have highlighted the virtuosity of monastic poets and the importance of their literary works for our understanding of how medieval monks thought about themselves, their bodies, their place in a world dominated by powerful laymen, and their hope of a life to come.[44] To take one example, Odo of Cluny's 5,755-line *Occupatio*, an early tenth-century spiritual meditation that provided its monastic audience with an object of moral and intellectual rumination, has been examined by Christopher A. Jones as an expression of the anxieties attendant with the danger of homosexual longing in the cloister.[45] Seldom integrated into the wider context of Cluniac spirituality, in no small part because it is so prolix and challenging to read, the *Occupatio* emerges in Jones's study as a formative statement of tenth-century ideals and concerns about monastic sexual conduct that no historian of medieval Christianity can afford to ignore.

Likewise, the rehabilitation of verse saints' lives is underway, as scholars realize that the recasting of prose texts in Latin meter provided cloistered poets with the opportunity to confront and resolve issues of contemporary concern. Reginald of Canterbury's late eleventh-century poetic rendering of Jerome's fourth-century *Life of Malchus* is a good example of the promise that these poems hold as topics of historical research.[46] In Jerome's story, Malchus was a monk who endured captivity among Saracens in the desert, where he had to overcome his temptation for the female captive that his new master bestowed on him as a wife. The primary message of the *Life of Malchus* was explicitly an exhortation to chastity. Centuries later, when Reginald retold the story in a sprawling work of 3,344 rhymed hexameter lines organized into six books, he expanded on themes that had no precedent in the original but that had a strong currency in the age of the Gregorian reform. These themes included not only the importance of celibacy

---

44. See, for example, *The Relatio metrica de duobus ducibus: A Twelfth-Century Cluniac Poem on Prayer for the Dead*, ed. and trans. C. A. Jones and S. G. Bruce (Turnhout, 2016); and chapter 11, below.

45. C. A. Jones, "Monastic Identity and Sodomitic Danger in the *Occupatio* by Odo of Cluny," *Speculum* 82 (2007): 1–53.

46. Reginald of Canterbury, *Vita Malchi*, ed. L. Lind, in *The Vita Sancti Malchi of Reginald of Canterbury: A Critical Edition* (Urbana, IL, 1942).

for monks but also the value of domestic and agricultural labor, which Reginald couched in Virgilian allusions borrowed from the *Georgics*.[47]

The men and women who found inspiration for their cloistered vocation in the precepts outlined in the sixth-century *Rule of Benedict* were the most numerous and influential monks in the premodern Christian tradition. Despite the antiquity of their calling and the vitality of their devotional practices, the Benedictines remain difficult to define beyond their mutual esteem for Benedict as a legislator inspired by God and their common use of his rule, which they believed to have been established by the Holy Spirit. Modern scholarship has recognized that this shared observance did not constitute a European-wide monastic order, as it would develop in later centuries. Rather, the Benedictines were like the stars in the night sky: seemingly numberless; variable in their luminosity; on the move yet constant in their collective ambition; singular yet often allied with their neighbors and far-flung friends. Beyond esteem for the *Rule of Benedict* and reverence for its holy author, it is the diversity of monastic customs as responses to local conditions and broader changes in Christian devotion that best characterizes Benedictine communities in the millennium after Benedict composed his rule. Future inquiry into the history of Benedictine monasticism should concentrate on the evidence for local and regional adaptations of the *Rule*. These adaptations were expressions of the creativity and resourcefulness of monastic legislators in the face of innumerable practical and devotional contingencies that had no precedent in Benedict's handbook for monks.

---

47. S. Parsons and D. Townsend, "Gender," in *The Oxford Handbook of Medieval Latin Literature*, ed. R. J. Hexter and D. Townsend (Oxford, 2012), pp. 423–46, at pp. 436–37.

CHAPTER 2

Sources for the History of Monasticism in the Central Middle Ages (c. 800–1100)

Imagining the contents of monastic libraries in the central Middle Ages (c. 800–1100) also encompasses a contemplation of their loss. The violence of plunderers, the rapaciousness of early modern bookhunters, and the destruction wrought by fire, moisture, and vermin have taken such a toll on these once formidable collections that only a small fraction of the manuscripts painstakingly produced by monk-scribes have survived the last millennium to hint at the lost horizons of this vibrant textual culture.[1] It has been estimated, in fact, that only a small fraction (less than 10 percent) of the books produced in the early Middle Ages have survived.[2] To take one egregious example of this destruction, in the tenth century, the brethren of the abbey of Novalesa in Piedmont fled before the advance of Muslim

---

Originally published as "Sources for the History of Monasticism in the Central Middle Ages (c. 800–1100)," in *The Cambridge History of Medieval Monasticism in the Latin West*, ed. A. Beach and I. Cochelin, 2 vols. (Cambridge, 2020), vol. 1, pp. 382–98. Reproduced with permission of The Licensor through PLSclear. Copyright © 2020 Cambridge University Press.

1. On monastic libraries, see E. Schlotheuber and J. McQuillen, "Books and Libraries within Monasteries," in *CHMM*, vol. 2, pp. 975–97.

2. See E. Buringh, *Medieval Manuscript Production in the Latin West: Explorations with a Global Database* (Leiden, 2011).

raiders, leaving behind not only their home but also the six thousand books in their library.³

Fortunately, many of the administrative documents, volumes of legislation, and compilations of devotional literature composed in medieval abbeys *have* endured to inform us about the lived experience and religious ideals of cloistered monasticism in post-Carolingian Europe. I make no claim to treat every source relevant to this topic. The chapter begins by cleaving closely to three genres of medieval texts that are arguably the most important for our understanding of monasticism in this period: charters (*libri privilegiorum, preceptorum sive cartarum*), rules and customaries (*regulae et consuetudines*), and saints' lives (*passiones et vitae sanctorum*). Taken together, these sources provide unparalleled insight into the ways in which monks interacted with the world outside of their abbeys, comported themselves in their cloisters, and imagined and promoted their ideals of sanctity. The richness of these texts as sources for monastic history is commensurate with the challenges involved in parsing the information that they contain, especially because medieval authors had their own interests and agendas in mind when composing, deploying, and preserving these documents. For this reason, in this chapter, I also highlight some of the difficulties presented by these sources in our reconstruction of the medieval past and some of the ways in which material culture has enhanced our understanding of monastic history in this period. The exclusion from this discussion of service books, sermons, patristic commentaries, exegetical material, histories, and other texts copied and read by monks is a practical necessity that does not in any way suggest their lack of importance for the study of medieval monasticism. The same is true for artistic production.⁴

Charters

Monastic charters preserve in writing the grants, donations, and sales of property to and by a religious house as well as the transfer of privileges to a cloistered community by kings, bishops, and popes.⁵ Individual monastic charters are unassuming documents that preserve in

---

3. *Chronicon novaliciense* 4.26 [*sic* for 4.25]: "Et inter cetera delati sunt libri sex mille," ed. G. Pertz, MGH Scriptores 7 (Hanover, 1846), p. 108.

4. See A. Cohen, "Monastic Art and Architecture, c. 700–1000: Material and Immaterial Worlds," in *CHMM*, vol. 1, pp. 519–41.

5. For general orientation, see R. Clemens and T. Graham, *Introduction to Manuscript Studies* (Ithaca, 2007), pp. 222–39 (chapter 14: "Charters and Cartularies").

formulaic language a moment in time when an abbey entered into or renewed a relationship with a lay man or woman and their family that was important enough to record for future reference. Despite their laconic nature, charters are expressive of a host of historical information that rarely surfaces in religious texts. The pathbreaking modern study, which used the evidence of monastic charters (those of Cluny) to reconstruct the changing social and political structures of an entire region, was Georges Duby, *La société aux XIe et XIIe siècles dans la region mâconnaise*, published in 1953.[6]

The contents of charters allow us to map the landholdings of religious communities and thereby plot their influence in secular society; to chart their relationships with elite and lesser families, who relied on the monks for redemptive prayers, often over many generations; and to make informed inferences about the role of gift-giving in central medieval culture. Their witness lists are invaluable sources for the names of the officeholders in these abbeys and their relationship to local aristocratic families, as well as for the agency of lay women in these transactions, whether as consenting partners of their spouses or as independent actors (most often in the case of widows). Even the literary confections of these documents promise to tell us something about the ways that monks wished to preserve and remember the social relationships that underlie each of these transactions.

No single source survives from the central Middle Ages in the same abundance as monastic charters because of the efforts taken by monks to safeguard in their archives the valuable information that they contained. The raw numbers are staggering. The brethren of Fulda produced about two thousand charters in this period.[7] The monks of Cluny composed even more—almost three thousand charters that can be dated before 1049—in no small part because of the enthusiasm of abbots like Maiolus (954–994) and Odilo (994–1049) in promoting the efficacy of Cluniac prayers in releasing the souls of the Christian faithful from the torments of purgatory.[8] Lastly, more than eight hundred individual charters written at the monastery of Saint

---

6. G. Duby, *La société aux XIe et XIIe siècles dans la région mâconnaise* (Paris, 1953).
7. J. Raaijmakers, *The Making of the Monastic Community of Fulda, c. 744–c. 900* (Cambridge, 2012), pp. 198–213.
8. B. H. Rosenwein, *To Be the Neighbor of Saint Peter: The Social Meaning of Cluny's Property, 909–1049* (Ithaca, 1989); and M. Innes, "On the Material Culture of Legal Documents: Charters and Their Preservation in the Cluny Archive, Ninth to Eleventh Centuries," in *Documentary Culture and the Laity in the Early Middle Ages*, ed. W. Brown et al. (Cambridge, 2013), pp. 283–320.

Gall before the year 920 survive in their original form.[9] This collection is especially precious because most of the early medieval charters known to us today are later copies preserved in massive compendia known as cartularies.

In the past three decades, monastic cartularies have become the object of intense study in their own right.[10] In the nineteenth and twentieth centuries, scholars tended to treat cartularies as static repositories of original charters and paid no attention to their structure and purpose. In fact, however, as Patrick Geary has taught us, "each cartulary is the result of a process of neglect, selection, transformation, and suppression."[11] The monks who compiled cartularies made selective and creative use of the documents they had at hand. Institutional crises often prompted the creation of a customary and inflected its contents. The cartulary compiled by the brethren of Saint Calais in 863 to dispute the claims of the bishop of Le Mans is one such example.[12] Some cartularies comprised earlier charters copied verbatim; others contained summaries of relevant information culled from them; and yet others preserved forged charters created with the intention of forwarding the interests of the monastic community. Every cartulary is thus expressive of the choices that monks made in the preservation and manipulation of the documents relevant to the history of their abbeys.

Charters can also provide evidence about early medieval culture that has nothing to do with their original purpose. For example, charters from the abbey of Cluny allow us to glimpse administrative interactions between the monks and local Jews in the tenth and eleventh centuries, a commerce attested in no other source from Cluny in this period and completely at odds with Abbot Peter the Venerable's stinging invective

---

9. R. McKitterick, *The Carolingians and the Written Word* (Cambridge, 1989), pp. 77–134; and M. Innes, "Archives, Documents and Landowners in Carolingian Francia," in *Documentary Culture and the Laity*, ed. Brown et al., pp. 152–88.

10. Exemplary in this regard is P. Geary, *Phantoms of Remembrance: Memory and Oblivion at the End of the First Millennium* (Princeton, 1996), esp. pp. 81–114. See also G. Declercq, "Originals and Cartularies: The Organization of Archival Memory (Ninth-Eleventh Centuries)," in *Charters and the Use of the Written Word in Medieval Society*, ed. K. Heidecker (Turnhout, 2000), pp. 147–70; and C. Bouchard, "Monastic Cartularies: Organizing Eternity," in *Charters, Cartularies, and Archives: The Preservation and Transmission of Documents in the Medieval West: Proceedings of a Colloquium of the Commission Internationale de Diplomatique (Princeton and New York, 16–18 September 1999)*, ed. A. Kosto and A. Winroth (Toronto, 2002), pp. 22–32.

11. Geary, *Phantoms of Remembrance*, p. 83.

12. See W. Goffart, *The Le Mans Forgeries: A Chapter in the History of Church Property in the Ninth Century* (Cambridge, 1966).

against the Jews written in the 1140s on the eve of the Second Crusade.[13] Moreover, as the work of Georges Duby and Barbara Rosenwein has shown, these sources are crucial for our understanding of aristocratic society.[14] Indeed, we know more about influential landowning families in the central Middle Ages from monastic charters than we do from any other source that survives from this period. For example, on the basis of hundreds of charters preserved by the monks of Gorze and Saint Maximin in the ninth and tenth centuries, John Nightingale has argued that "relations with monasteries had a crucial role in the elite's inheritance strategies, strengthening the position of direct heirs at the expense of competing interests of the wider kin."[15] This important insight relies heavily on the recordkeeping habits of cloistered communities.

Like many sources for monastic history in this period, research on charters and cartularies progresses apace with the availability of source materials.[16] New editions of significant texts continue to appear in print, sometimes with facsimile reproductions of the charters, although not with the regularity that one would like.[17] Fortunately, in the past decade, online resources for the study of charters have opened up this field of research to a new generation of scholars by making the source materials much more easily accessible. To take one example, in the case of the abbey of Cluny, scholars can use the *Cartae Cluniacenses Electronicae* (CCE) maintained by the Westfälische Wilhelms-Universität in Munster to search the contents of the *Recueil des chartes de l'abbaye de Cluny* edited by Auguste Bernard and Alexandre Bruel and originally published in six volumes between 1876 and 1903.[18] The CCE is especially welcome because the editors of the *Recueil* died before they could complete the

---

13. For a convenient summary of the evidence, see D. Iogna-Prat, *Order and Exclusion: Cluny and Christendom Face Heresy, Judaism, and Islam (1000–1150)*, trans. G. R. Edwards (Ithaca, 2003), p. 278.

14. See Duby, *La société aux XIe et XIIe siècles*; and Rosenwein, *To Be the Neighbor of Saint Peter*.

15. J. Nightingale, *Monasteries and Patrons in the Gorze Reform: Lotharingia, c. 850–1000* (Oxford, 2001), p. 8.

16. For a sample of new directions of research, see the essays collected in *Problems and Possibilities of Early Medieval Charters*, ed. J. Jarrett and A. McKinley (Turnhout, 2013). For charters from early medieval England in particular, see S. Keynes, "Anglo-Saxon Charters: Lost and Found," in *Myth, Rulership, Church, and Charters: Essays in Honour of Nicholas Brooks*, ed. J. Barrow and A. Vareham (Aldershot, 2008), pp. 45–66.

17. See, for example, *Les plus anciens documents originaux de l'abbaye de Cluny*, ed. H. Atsma and J. Vezin, 3 vols. (Paris, 1997–2002); and the following editions by C. Bouchard: *The Cartulary of Flavigny, 717–1113* (Cambridge, MA, 1991); and *The Cartulary of Montier-en-Der, 666–1129* (Toronto, 2004).

18. *Cartae Cluniacenses Electronicae*, hosted by the Institut für Frühmittelalterforschung at the Universität Münster.

indices to their edition and the absence of any instruments of reference makes their important edition of the Cluniac charters difficult to use. Unfortunately, despite the central importance of monastic charters for medieval scholarship, many individual charters and voluminous cartularies remain unpublished.

Rules and Customaries

In the early ninth century, the *Rule of Benedict* (*Regula Benedicti*) emerged as the most authoritative handbook for cloistered life in Western Europe. Written in the sixth century by an otherwise obscure Italian abbot known as Benedict of Nursia (c. 480–c. 550), the rule was a concise work comprising a prologue, seventy-two short chapters, and an epilogue that promoted a set of religious principles for monks informed by the firsthand experience of its author. After two centuries of relative obscurity, the *Rule of Benedict* became popular in the Carolingian period in no small part because of imperial sponsorship by Charlemagne and his son Louis the Pious (r. 814–40), both of whom believed that the efficacy of monastic prayers were instrumental for the military success and spiritual well-being of their kingdom.[19] To this end, they sought to impose uniformity of practice and worship on the cloistered communities in the Frankish heartlands. At the Aachen assemblies of 816/817, Abbot Benedict of Aniane (d. 821) promoted the adoption of one rule and one custom (*una regula, una consuetudo*) in all of the abbeys of the realm. The one rule was the *Rule of Benedict*, and the one custom was Benedict's own supplementary regulations to it.[20] Although the promotion of the rule by the Carolingians elevated this sixth-century text to the status of *regula sancta* in the monasteries of Western Europe, there was considerable resistance to the adoption of a single set of ancillary legislation, as individual abbeys clung tenaciously to their age-old customs.

The *Rule of Benedict* carried an unprecedented authority in the post-Carolingian period, but the interpretation of its text posed numerous

---

19. On the centrality of monasticism to the political ambitions of the Carolingians, see M. de Jong, "Carolingian Monasticism: The Power of Prayer," in *The New Cambridge Medieval History*, vol. 2, c. 700–c. 900, ed. R. McKitterick (Cambridge, 1995), pp. 622–53. See also A. Diem and P. Rousseau, "Monastic Rules (Fourth to Ninth Century)," and R. Kramer, "Monasticism, Reform, and Authority in the Carolingian Era," in *CHMM*, vol. 1, pp. 162–94 and 432–49, respectively.

20. J. Semmler, "Benedictus II: Una regula, una consuetudo," in *Benedictine Culture, 750–1050*, ed. W. Lourdaux and D. Verhelst (Leuven, 1983), pp. 1–49.

problems for monastic legislators. To begin with, by the turn of the first millennium, the rule was already hundreds of years old and some of its late antique Italian terminology regarding articles of clothing and units of measurement were alien to the vocabularies of monks who lived north of the Alps. When Paul the Deacon (d. c. 799) sent Charlemagne a manuscript of the rule copied from the exemplar believed to have been written by Benedict himself, he felt the need to include a letter explaining words and phrases that would have been unclear to the great king and his religious advisers.[21] Moreover, although the laconic character of the *Rule of Benedict* was part of the appeal of this text, it also left readers with an impressionistic understanding of its principles. For example, the author of the rule placed a strong emphasis on the cultivation of silence among monks, but later readers were left to puzzle out the distinction between the word "silence" (*silentium*) and the several cases in which the rule refers to "the utmost silence" or "total silence" (*summum silentium* or *omne silentium*).[22] In the middle of the ninth century, Hildemar of Corbie (fl. c. 845) attempted to reconcile these distinctions in his *Expositio regulae sancti Benedicti*.[23]

To make matters worse, the centuries separating the composition of the *Rule of Benedict* and its widespread adoption in northern Europe also witnessed the development of aspects of Christian devotional practice that had no precedent in Benedict's lifetime, such as the cult of the dead. By the eleventh century, most monks were also ordained priests, who occupied much of their day with funerary masses intoned for the souls of the faithful departed to free them from the fires of purgatory.[24] This emphasis on near-constant liturgical activity came at the expense of manual labor, which was increasingly performed by servants, despite the recommendation of the rule that true monks, like the apostles, should live by the work of their hands.[25]

---

21. Paul the Deacon, *Epistula ad regem Karolum de monasterio sancti Benedicti*, in *The Rule of Benedict*, ed. and trans. B. Venarde (Cambridge, MA, 2011), pp. 230–43.

22. *RB* 38.5 (*summum fiat silentium*), 48.5 (*cum omni silentio*), and 52.2 (*cum summo silentio*).

23. *Expositio regulae sancti Benedicti* 38, ed. R. Mittermüller, in *Vita et Regula SS. P. Benedicti una cum Expositio Regulae a Hildemaro tradita* (Regensburg, 1880), p. 424.

24. See G. Blennemann, "Ascetic Prayer for the Dead in the Early Medieval West," in *CHMM*, vol. 1, pp. 278–96. See also D. Iogna-Prat, "The Dead in the Celestial Bookkeeping of the Cluniac Monks Around the Year 1000," in *Debating the Middle Ages: Issues and Readings*, ed. L. Little and B. H. Rosenwein (Oxford, 1998), pp. 340–62; and more generally G. Constable, "The Commemoration of the Dead in the Early Middle Ages," in *Early Medieval Rome and the Christian West: Essays in Honour of Donald A. Bullough*, ed. J. M. H. Smith (Leiden, 2000), pp. 169–95.

25. *RB* 48.

CHAPTER 2

Because the precepts of the *Rule of Benedict* were not always clear and did not always bear directly upon the devotional practices current in cloistered communities around the turn of the first millennium, monastic legislators augmented its tenets with supplementary customs of their own devising. From the eighth century onward, monks began to explain in lengthy commentaries those parts of the rule that resisted a straightforward interpretation, like the *expositio* composed by Smaragdus of Saint Mihiel (d. c. 826).[26]

At the same time, cloistered communities preserved their local customs, first as oral traditions and later in expansive collections of monastic legislation known as customaries.[27] Monastic customaries were often elaborations on the *Rule of Benedict*, but they offered much more in terms of immediate and detailed historical information about the lived practice of medieval monasticism than the laconic precepts provided by Benedict's little handbook.[28] These compilations treated topics as diverse as liturgical ceremonies, the duties of monastic officials, and the instruction of novices. The function of these texts for medieval readers is a subject of some debate, in particular the degree to which a given customary was descriptive or directive in character.[29] There is some indication that large abbeys like Cluny recorded their customs in writing because of disagreements among the brethren about received tradition, as was the case for the late eleventh-century *ordo Cluniacensis* by Bernard.[30] Ample evidence also suggests, however, that monks composed customaries to serve as

---

26. Smaragdus, *Expositio in regulam sancti Benedicti*, ed. A. Spannagel and P. Engelbert, in *Smaragdi abbatis expositio in regulam s. Benedicti*, CCM 8 (Siegburg, 1974); English translation: *Smaragdus of Saint-Mihiel, Commentary on the Rule of Benedict*, trans. D. Berry (Kalamazoo, 2007). See also M. Ponesse, "Smaragdus of St. Mihiel and the Carolingian Monastic Reform," *Revue bénédictine* 116 (2006): 367–92.

27. K. Hallinger, "*Consuetudo*: Begriff, Formen, Forschungsgeschichte, Inhalt," in *Untersuchungen zu Kloster und Stift* (Göttingen, 1980), pp. 140–66; *From Dead of Night to End of Day: The Medieval Customs of Cluny / Du coeur de la nuit à la fin du jour: Les coutumes clunisiennes au moyen âge*, ed. S. Boynton and I. Cochelin, Disciplina Monastica 3 (Turnhout, 2005); *Regulae—Consuetudines—Statuta: Studi sulle fonti normative degli ordini religiosi nei secoli centrali del Medioevo*, ed. C. Andenna and G. Melville (Munster, 2005); and *Consuetudines et Regulae: Sources for Monastic Life in the Middle Ages and the Early Modern Period*, ed. C. M. Malone and C. Maines, Disciplina Monastica 10 (Turnhout, 2014).

28. L. Donnat, "Les coutumiers du Moyen Âge et la règle de saint Benoît," *Regulae Benedicti Studia* 16 (1989): 37–54.

29. See, for example, Hallinger, "*Consuetudo*"; L. Donnat, "Les coutumiers monastiques: Une nouvelle entreprise et un territoire nouveau," *Revue Mabillon*, n.s. 3 (1992): 5–21, esp. pp. 14–16; and A. Davril, "Coutumiers directifs et coutumiers descriptifs: D'Ulrich à Bernard de Cluny," in *From Dead of Night to End of Day*, ed. Boynton and Cochelin, pp. 23–28.

30. Bernard of Cluny, *Ordo Cluniacensis sive Consuetudines*, in *Vetus Disciplina Monastica*, ed. M. Herrgott (Paris, 1726), pp. 136–364.

models of religious practice for distant communities.[31] In both cases, customaries were primarily commemorative and indicative in character and tended to reflect actual customs rather than the normative ideals of monastic legislators. It is clear, however, that customaries did not carry the universal authority of the *Rule of Benedict* and thus were not, in the words of Gert Melville, "understood by the entire monastic congregation to be generally binding."[32]

Irrespective of their original purpose, monastic customaries provide us with invaluable information about lived experience in cloistered communities and are unrivaled in their scope and detail by other sources from this period.[33] Since the 1990s, historians have mined them for evidence and insight on a wide range of topics, including the role played by oblates in the liturgy; the principles of monastic silence and the use of sign language in the abbey; regulations for the care of sick monks and the protocols governing their interaction with healthy brethren in the abbey; and the rites performed in preparation for the imminent death of individuals, including the duties of relevant officials, final communion for the dying monk, and the preparation of his body for burial.[34] Moreover, the customaries allow us to reconstruct in detail aspects of monastic practice otherwise rendered invisible because of a paucity of relevant source material. For instance, liturgists and architectural historians have turned to descriptions of rituals and buildings in these texts for insight into the content and orchestration of corporate worship and its physical setting in the absence of liturgical manuscripts and monastic structures from this period.[35] These studies,

---

31. I. Cochelin, "Customaries as Inspirational Sources," in *Regulae et Consuetudines*, ed. Malone and Maines, pp. 27–72, with references to earlier literature.

32. G. Melville, "Action, Text, and Validity: On Re-Examining Cluny's Consuetudines and Statutes," in *From Dead of Night to End of Day*, ed. Boynton and Cochelin, pp. 67–83, at p. 77.

33. See I. Cochelin, "Discipline and the Problem of Cluny's Customaries," in *CCMA*, pp. 204–22.

34. See, respectively, S. Boynton, "The Liturgical Role of Children in Monastic Customaries from the Central Middle Ages," *Studia Liturgica* 28 (1998): 194–209; S. G. Bruce, *Silence and Sign Language in Medieval Monasticism: The Cluniac Tradition, c. 900–1200* (Cambridge, 2007); R. Cristiani, "Integration and Marginalization: Dealing with the Sick in Eleventh-Century Cluny," in *From Dead of Night to End of Day*, ed. Boynton and Cochelin, pp. 287–95; and F. Paxton, *The Death Ritual at Cluny in the Central Middle Ages / Le rituel de la mort à Cluny au Moyen Âge central*, Disciplina Monastica 9 (Turnhout, 2013).

35. S. Boynton, "The Customaries of Bernard and Ulrich as Liturgical Sources,"; K. Krüger, "Monastic Customs and Liturgy in the Light of the Architectural Evidence: A Case Study on Processions (Eleventh-Twelfth Centuries),"; and C. M. Malone, "Interprétation des pratiques liturgiques à Saint-Bénigne de Dijon d'après ses coutumiers d'inspiration clunisienne," in *From Dead of Night to End of Day*, ed. Boynton and Cochelin, pp. 109–30, 191–220, and 221–50, respectively.

aided immeasurably by the availability of new critical editions of some of the most important texts, have moved the customaries of the central Middle Ages into the mainstream of contemporary monastic scholarship. The series *Corpus consuetudinum monasticarum* (1963–present), in particular, has been instrumental in publishing critical editions of monastic legislation from the Middle Ages.[36]

Saints' Lives

Stories about the virtues and the miracles of Christian saints were the most popular narrative texts produced and consumed by monks in the central Middle Ages.[37] Saints' lives provided models of virtuous behavior for pious readers and presented their holy subjects as active intercessors between heaven and earth. Christian hagiography is a literary form with a long history; the earliest accounts of martyrdom date back to the second century.[38] It is also a derivative genre; most saints' lives drew their authority from the repetition of themes and conventions borrowed from late antique traditions of sacred Christian biography.[39] In Latin literature, Evagrius's translation of Athanasius's *Life of Anthony* and Sulpicius Severus's *Life of Martin of Tours*, both written in the late fourth century, exerted a profound influence on the structure and content of most of the saints' lives composed over the next millennium, including those written about women.[40]

---

36. See William of Hirsau, *Constitutiones Hirsaugienses*, ed. C. Elvert and P. Engelbert, CCM 15.1-2, 2 vols. (Siegburg, 2010).

37. There is no general guide in English for the study of western medieval hagiography. See instead J. Dubois and J.-L. Lemaitre, *Sources et methods de l'hagiographie médiévale* (Paris, 1993); and R. Aigrain, *L'hagiographie: Ses sources, ses methods, son histoire*, 2nd ed. (Brussels, 2000). On the etymology and development of the word "hagiography," see G. Philippart, "Hagiographes et hagiographie, hagiologes et hagiologie: Des mots et des concepts," *Hagiographica* 1 (1994): 1–16.

38. See A.-M. Helvétius, "Re-Reading Monastic Traditions: Monks and Nuns, East and West, from the Origins to c. 750," in *CHMM*, vol. 1, pp. 40–72. See also S. A. Harvey, "Martyr Passions and Hagiography," in *The Oxford Handbook of Early Christian Studies*, ed. S. A. Harvey and D. G. Hunter (Oxford, 2008), pp. 603–27; *Greek and Latin Narratives About the Ancient Martyrs*, ed. and trans. E. Rebillard (Oxford, 2017); and M. Lapidge, *The Roman Martyrs: Introduction, Translations, and Commentary* (Oxford, 2018).

39. R. Bartlett, *Why Can the Dead Do Such Great Things? Saints and Worshippers from the Martyrs to the Reformation* (Princeton, 2013), esp. pp. 504–86 on "The Literature of Sanctity." For examples in translation, see *Soldiers of Christ: Saints and Saints' Lives from Late Antiquity and the Early Middle Ages*, ed. T. F. X. Noble and T. Head (University Park, PA, 1995).

40. J. M. H. Smith, "The Problem of Female Sanctity in Carolingian Europe, c. 780–920," *Past & Present* 146 (1995): 3–37. See also *Sainted Women of the Dark Ages*, ed. J. A. McNamara and

Library catalogs from the central Middle Ages articulate both the ubiquity of hagiography in the lives of medieval monks and the variety of venues in which the brethren ruminated on these stories. Saints' lives played a central role in the liturgy as the primary reading on the feast day of a given saint, but time restrictions prevented the monks from reading more than a few chapters at a time, especially during the night office, the round of prayers celebrated in the middle of the night.[41] Likewise, the refectory often resounded with stories about the saints. Since late antiquity, monks and nuns habitually read hagiographical works aloud to one another while they were eating, so that the words might nourish their souls at the same time that the food nourished their bodies.[42] In the early twelfth century, Abbot Peter the Venerable of Cluny took for granted that his brethren knew the saints' lives written by and about Pope Gregory the Great because "they are recited and heard and read and understood daily and almost without interruption by innumerable and even unlearned and simple brothers."[43] Lastly, times set aside for private reading allowed individual monks to read saints' lives at their leisure in a quiet corner of the cloister or the seclusion of their cell. In the 1040s, for example, we find brethren of Cluny borrowing copies of hagiographical literature for this very purpose.[44]

Although most authors of medieval hagiography patterned their work on these authoritative models of the lives of Antony and Martin, some departed from received tradition and tailored their stories to address contemporary concerns, often invoking the voices of their

---

J. Halborg (Durham, NC, 1992); and R. Alciati, "The Invention of Western Monastic Literature: Texts and Communities," in *CHMM*, vol. 1, pp. 144–61.

41. On this point, see T. Snijders, "Celebrating with Dignity: The Purpose of Benedictine Matins Readings," in *Understanding Monastic Practices of Oral Communication (Western Europe, Tenth-Thirteenth Centuries)*, ed. S. Vanderputten (Turnhout, 2011), pp. 115–36.

42. See, for example, *RB* 38 on the duties of the weekly reader.

43. Peter the Venerable, *Contra Petrobrusianos* 256: "Quid autem beatus et magnus papa Gregorius de hoc uel scripserit uel dixerit, uel ipse in suo monasterio Rome fecerit, quoniam et Vita eius et Omelie et Dialogus eius ab innumerabilibus minusque etiam eruditis ac simplicibus fratribus cotidie ac pene sine intermissione et recitantur et audiuntur, et leguntur et intelliguntur, non nobis uidetur necessarium per singula enarrare," ed. J. Fearns, CCCM 10 (Turnhout, 1968), p. 151; trans. G. Constable, in *Three Treatises from Bec on the Nature of Monastic Life*, ed. G. Constable (Toronto, 2008), p. 11, n. 28.

44. *Liber tramitis aevi Odilonis abbatis* 2.190: "Humbertus *Uita sancti Siluestri* . . . Rodbertus *Uitam sancti Theuterii* . . . Iohannes *Uita Mariae Egyptiacae* . . . Ebrardus *Uitam Iohannis Heleymonis*," ed. P. Dinter, CCM 10 (Siegburg, 1980), pp. 262–63. On the custom of book borrowing by individual monks at eleventh-century Cluny, see A. Wilmart, "Le couvent et la bibliothèque de Cluny vers le milieu du XIe siècle," *Revue Mabillon* 11 (1921): 89–124; and K. Christ, "In Caput Quadragesimae," *Zentralblatt für Bibliothekswesen* 60 (1943): 33–59.

holy subjects to lend their authority to current issues. Since the 1960s, historians have become much more adept both at recognizing the conventions of this genre and at parsing the information particular to the historical milieu in which the work was written.[45] This sensitivity to the limits and possibilities of saints' lives as sources for medieval history has generated a vast industry of scholarship. Many studies have been especially attentive to the importance of examining the variations introduced during the rewriting of hagiography, in no small part because the repetition of age-old literary models exerted such a dominant influence in this conservative genre.[46]

Hagiography remains central to our understanding of ideals of sanctity and the promotion of Christian virtue in the central Middle Ages, but this genre can also provide answers to questions about the ways in which monks made use of these texts beyond their obvious devotional purpose. Historians are beginning to appreciate that early medieval readers were not limited in the ways in which they understood the contents of saints' lives as sources for information about the world around them. For example, in the middle of the ninth century, we find Ratramnus of Corbie consulting the *Life of Christopher* in his abbey library to determine whether the dog-headed men (*cynocephali*) who allegedly dwelt in the far north of Europe had humans souls and were therefore open to the possibility of salvation through their conversion to Christianity.[47] Hagiography was an important resource in

---

45. See, for example, F. Lotter, "Methodisches zur Gewinnung historischer Erkenntnisse aus hagiographischen Quellen," *Historische Zeitschrift* 229 (1979): 298–356; P. Fouracre, "Merovingian History and Merovingian Hagiography," *Past & Present* 127 (1990): 3–38, repr. in P. Fouracre, *Frankish History: Studies in the Construction of Power* (Burlington, 2013), no. II; P. Geary, "Saints, Scholars, and Society: The Elusive Goal," in *Saints: Studies in Hagiography*, ed. S. Sticca (Binghamton, 1996), pp. 13–20, repr. in P. Geary, *Living with the Dead in the Middle Ages* (Ithaca, 1994), pp. 9–29; and J. Kreiner, *The Social Life of Hagiography in the Merovingian Kingdom* (Cambridge, 2014). For a useful overview, see J. Palmer, *Early Medieval Hagiography* (Kalamazoo, MI, 2018).

46. See M. Goullet, *Ecriture et réécriture hagiographiques: Essai sur les réécriture de Vies de saints dans l'Occident latin medieval (VIIIe-XIIIe s.)* (Turnhout, 2005); as well as the volumes edited by M. Goullet, M. Heinzelmann, and C. Veyrard-Cosme: *La réécriture hagiographique dans l'Occident médiéval: Transformations formelles et idéologiques* (Ostfildern, 2003); *Miracles, vies et réécriture dans l'Occident médiéval: Actes de l'Atelier 'La réécriture des Miracles' (IHAP, juin 2004) et SHG X–XII: Dossiers des saints de Metz et Laon et de saint Saturnin de Toulouse* (Ostfildern, 2006); and *L'hagiographie mérovingienne à travers ses réécritures* (Ostfildern, 2010).

47. For what follows, see S. G. Bruce, "Hagiography as Monstrous Ethnography: A Note on Ratramnus of Corbie's Letter Concerning the Conversion of the Cynocephali," in *Insignis Sophiae Arcator: Essays in Honour of Michael Herren on his 65th Birthday*, ed. Gernot Wieland, Carin Ruff, and Ross C. Arthur (Turnhout, 2006), pp. 45–56.

this case because some versions of the *Life of Christopher* depict him as a dog-headed man. In Ratramnus's opinion, his successful conversion to Christianity opened up the possibility that others like him could be saved, despite their monstrous appearance. Moreover, scholars have become acutely aware that monks may have had a more nuanced understanding of saints' lives than the modern word "hagiography" implies. In fact, the arbitrary distinctions between "historical" sources and "hagiographical" sources that have preoccupied historians of the Middle Ages for more than a century are anachronisms that have limited our comprehension of "hagiography" as an important source for monastic "history."[48]

Perhaps the most important development in the study of monastic hagiography in the central Middle Ages is the new attention being paid to saints' lives written in poetic meter.[49] Long dismissed as derivative of its original source material and therefore not useful as sources for historical research, verse hagiography has remained a largely uncharted frontier in medieval monastic scholarship. Poetic composition and consumption clearly played a formative role, however, in the education of the brethren and had a strong currency in the world outside of the classroom. As Anna Taylor has argued, between the ninth and eleventh centuries, monks composed thousands of metered lines of hagiography to promote the saintly patrons of their abbeys, to educate young monks in classical literature and devotional themes, to spar with other poets for the valued patronage of important lords and prelates, to refute the claims and resist the encroachment of other monastic communities, and to provide spiritual *ruminatio* for their brethren.[50] Verse hagiography was not strictly the domain of male authors. In the tenth century, Hrotswitha of Gandersheim made poetic adaptations of many legends of the saints for an audience of female readers.[51] The recent discovery of

---

48. The *locus classicus* remains F. Lifshitz, "Beyond Positivism and Genre: 'Hagiographical' Texts as Historical Narrative," *Viator* 25 (1994): 95-114. See also I. N. Wood, "The Use and Abuse of Latin Hagiography in the Early Medieval West," in *East and West, Modes of Communication: Proceedings of the First Plenary Conference at Merida*, ed. E. Chrysos and I. N. Wood (Leiden, 1999), pp. 93-109; and A. Taylor, "Hagiography and Early Medieval History," *Religion Compass* 7 (2013): 1-14.

49. J.-Y. Tilliette, "Les modèles de sainteté du IXe au XIe siècle d'après le témoignage des récits hagiographiques en vers métriques," in *Santi e demoni nell'alto medioevo occidentale (secoli V-XI)* (Spoleto, 1988), pp. 381-406; and F. Dolbeau, "Un domaine négligé de la littérature médiolatine: Les textes hagiographiques en vers," *Cahiers de Civilisation Médiévale* 45 (2002): 129-39.

50. A. Taylor, *Epic Lives and Monasticism in the Middle Ages, 800-1050* (Cambridge, 2013).

51. Hrosvit, *Opera Omnia*, ed. W. Berschin (Munich and Leipzig, 2001).

the value of verse hagiography as an historical source is without doubt the most important advance in scholarship on the literary culture of medieval abbeys in the past two decades, but, with dozens and dozens of these poems still unedited and unstudied, research in this new field of inquiry has only just begun.

Monastic Materials

The tissue of evidence for the history of Christian monasticism in Carolingian and post-Carolingian Europe is particularly thick, but even in their abundance, the surviving texts do not tell the full story of the cloistered life in this period. Since the 1990s, scholars have turned with greater frequency than ever before to nontextual sources to illuminate aspects of medieval monastic history. Manuscripts play an important role as historical sources not only for the texts that they contain but also for what their production and movement reveal about material resources and networks of knowledge exchange in cloistered communities.[52] Books had a symbolic potency that made them attractive as diplomatic gifts at the highest level of early medieval society, often to the benefit of monastic communities.[53] In the early ninth century, Louis the Pious received from Emperor Michael II a modest manuscript written in Greek uncials containing the theological works and letters of Dionysius the Areopagite. Unable to read the book, Louis deposited it at the abbey of Saint-Denis, where the remains of Dionysius lay buried.[54] This Greek manuscript soon served as the basis for two Latin translations of the *corpus Dionysiacum* made by monks of Saint Denis, which played an important role as conduits of Greek learning to western monasteries.[55] As Carmela Franklin has shown, early medieval manuscripts, even the smallest fragments of them, had

---

52. See *The European Book in the Twelfth Century*, ed. E. Kwakkel and R. Thomson (Cambridge, 2018); and S. Meeder, *The Irish Scholarly Presence at St. Gall: Networks of Knowledge in the Early Middle Ages* (London, 2018). For the Carolingian period, see McKitterick, *The Carolingians and the Written Word*, pp. 135–210.

53. J. Lowden, "The Luxury Book as Diplomatic Gift," in *Byzantine Diplomacy*, ed. J. Shepard and S. Franklin (Aldershot, 1992), pp. 249–60.

54. Paris, BnF, Grec 437. See A. Taylor, "Books, Bodies, and Bones: Hilduin of St-Denis and the Relics of St. Dionysius," in *The Ends of the Body: Identity and Community in Medieval Culture*, ed. S. C. Akbari and J. Ross (Toronto, 2013), pp. 25–60.

55. See *Hilduin of Saint-Denis: The Passio S. Dionysii in Prose and Verse*, ed. and trans. M. Lapidge (Leiden, 2017), pp. 61–62 (on the dates) and 70–71 (on the identity and method of the translators). On Euriugena's translation and its reception, see T. Budde, "The *Versio Dionysii* of John Scottus Eriugena: A Study of the Manuscript Tradition and Influence of Eriugena's

afterlives that bear witness to the use and reuse of monastic books well beyond the Middle Ages.[56]

Like manuscripts, the relics of the saints and the ornate containers that housed them (reliquaries and portable altars) have been the subjects of intense study in modern scholarship. As Julia Smith has argued, the collection of sacred remains provides insight into the daily practices of monastic devotion that are not always evident in the surviving texts.[57] These materials traveled great distances from points of origin in the Holy Land or sacred cities like Rome to the monasteries of northern Europe, allowing us to track the networks of communication and commerce that facilitated their movement and to reconstruct the systems of elite patronage required for the acquisition of prestige relics, like fragments of the True Cross.[58] Reliquaries have invited scrutiny as objects that mediated the devotional experience of relics for the viewer and thereby construct and control the religious experience of their contents.[59]

Despite their popularity, medieval criticism of devotional practices involving relics and reliquaries betrays a lack of unanimity about the purpose of holy remains. For example, mystery shrouds the origins of an exquisite ninth-century gold talisman in the shape of a cross that allegedly contained hair of the Virgin Mary, but medieval tradition holds that it was discovered around the neck of Charlemagne (*crucem auream, quae in collo eius pependit*) when Emperor Otto III opened his tomb in Aachen in the year 1000.[60] The emperor's habit of wearing a personal reliquary would have been completely at odds, however, with the opinion of his most learned monastic counselor, Alcuin (d. 804),

---

Translation of the *Corpus Areopagiticum* from the Ninth through the Twelfth Century" (PhD diss., University of Toronto, 2011).

56. C. V. Franklin, *Material Restoration: A Fragment from Eleventh-Century Echernach in a Nineteenth-Century Parisian Codex* (Turnhout, 2010).

57. J. H. M. Smith, "Portable Christianity: Relics in the Medieval West (c. 700–1200)," *Proceedings of the British Academy* 181 (2012): 143-67, at p. 145.

58. On the early medieval relic trade and the literature it inspired, see M. Heinzelmann, *Translationsberichte und andere Quellen des Reliquienkultes*, Typologie des sources du moyen age occidental 33 (Turnhout, 1979); P. Geary, *Furta Sacra: Thefts of Relics in the Central Middle Ages*, 2nd ed. (Princeton, NJ, 1990); and J. M. H. Smith, "Old Saints, New Cults: Roman Relics in Carolingian Francia," in *Early Medieval Rome and the Christian West*, ed. Smith, pp. 317-39.

59. C. Hahn, *Strange Beauty: Issues in the Making and Meaning of Reliquaries, 400–circa 1204* (College Park, PA, 2012).

60. Thietmar, *Chronicon* 4.47, ed. R. Holzmann, MGH Scriptores Rerum Germanicarum n.s. 9 (Berlin, 1935), p. 285. On Charlemagne's relic collection and its influence, see Hahn, *Strange Beauty*, pp. 179-83.

who derided carrying relics or Gospel texts in this way as a "superstition befitting the Pharisees" (*pharisaica superstitio*).[61]

No source for monastic history in the central Middle Ages is as evocative as the Plan of Saint Gall, a schematic blueprint for an ideal abbey preserved in an early ninth-century manuscript.[62] Although the Plan does not represent any particular monastery, the spatial organization of its church and monastic precincts relative to nearby workshops and gardens has called attention to the fact that the experience of the cloistered life extended well beyond the *claustum* in this period.[63] Beginning with Kenneth Conant's excavation of the abbey of Cluny between 1927 and 1950, monastic archaeology matured rapidly over the course of the twentieth century.[64] New excavations have privileged a holistic approach to the environment in which the brethren lived, taking the focus away from the primary buildings of the monastic community (the church, the cloister, and so on) and drawing attention to lesser studied structures, like latrines, as well as overlooked aspects of an abbey's infrastructure, such as its waterways and fishponds.[65] Garbage pits and refuse piles can also tell us as much about the monastic life as the remains of buildings. The animal bones excavated at the Cluniac dependency of La Charité-sur-Loire, for example, reveal details about the diet of the brethren that are absent in written sources.[66] These discoveries have, in turn, informed new research in medieval environmental history,

---

61. G. Snoek, *Medieval Piety from Relics to the Eucharist: A Process of Mutual Interaction* (Leiden, 1995), pp. 354–55, with reference to other Carolingian authors who voiced the same concern.

62. Saint Gallen, Stiftsbibliothek, Codex Sangallensis 1092. The classic study remains W. Horn and E. Born, *The Plan of St. Gall*, 3 vols. (Berkeley, 1979). See also G. Constable, "Carolingian Monasticism as Seen in the Plan of St. Gall," in *Le monde carolingien: Bilan, perspectives, champs de recherches*, ed. W. Falkowski and Y. Sassier (Turnhout, 2009), pp. 199–217; and M. Lauwers, "Constructing Monastic Space in the Early and Central Medieval West (Fifth to Twelfth Century)," in *CHMM*, vol. 1, pp. 317–39, esp. p. 329 (figure 16.4).

63. See I. Cochelin, "Monastic Daily Life (c. 750–1100): A Tight Community Shielded by an Outer Court," in *CHMM*, vol. 1, pp. 542–60.

64. K. Conant, *Cluny: Les églises et la maison du chef d'ordre* (Mâcon, 1968). See also S. Bully, E. Destefanis, and E. Marron, "The Archaeology of the Earliest Monasteries in Italy and France (Second Half of the Fourth Century to the Eighth Century)," in *CHMM*, vol. 1, pp. 232–57. State-of-the-question surveys on monastic archaeology include S. Bonde and C. Maines, "The Archaeology of Monasticism: A Summary of Recent Work in France, 1970–1987," *Speculum* 63 (1988): 794–825; and *Monastic Archaeology*, ed. G. Keevill, M. Aston, and T. Hall (Oxford, 2001).

65. See H. Röckelein, "Monastic Landscapes," in *CHMM*, vol. 2, pp. 816–30.

66. F. Audoin-Rouzeau, *Ossements animaux de moyen âge au monastère de La Charité-sur-Loire* (Paris, 1986).

in which monks play a decisive role in the management and exploitation of natural resources.[67]

The central Middle Ages (c. 800–1100) are a period rich in textual and material sources for the history of monasticism in Western Europe. In the centuries following the collapse of Charlemagne's sprawling empire, many cloistered communities turned to writing to preserve and promote their relationships with the lay patrons whose donations sustained them, with like-minded religious institutions that inspired them, and with the holy men and women whose intercession protected them. Cartularies, customaries, and works of hagiography all cast light on the ways in which monks made use of the written word to articulate and confect their sense of purpose as communities of intercessory prayer, as emulators of an angelic way of life, and as protégés of the saints. Despite the dispersal and destruction of almost every monastic library from this period, the centuries-old murmuring of texts composed in abbeys around the turn of the first millennium urges us to question old presumptions and ask new questions about the significance of the cloistered life in medieval Europe.

---

67. The classic study remains R. C. Hoffmann, "Economic Development and Aquatic Ecosystems in Medieval Europe," *The American Historical Review* 101 (1996): 631–69. See also C. Berman, "Later Monastic Economies," in *CHMM*, vol. 2, pp. 831–47.

Chapter 3

An Abbot Between Two Cultures

Maiolus of Cluny Considers the Muslims of La Garde-Freinet

Most studies of religious encounters between adherents of Islam and Christianity in the premodern era have focused on the period between the formulation of Abbot Peter the Venerable of Cluny's enterprise to translate the Qur'an into Latin in the 1140s and the military successes of Sultan Mehmed II that propelled the Turks across the Bosporus in the middle of the fifteenth century.[1] In specialized studies, however, scholars have also begun to chart the lesser-known waters of early medieval contact between the religious cultures of Christian Europe and the Muslim Mediterranean from the rise of Islam in the early seventh century to the capture of Jerusalem in 1099

Originally published as "An Abbot Between Two Cultures: Maiolus of Cluny Considers the Muslims of La Garde-Freinet," *Early Medieval Europe* 15 (2007): 426–40. Reprinted with permission.

1. Important works on this topic include R. W. Southern, *Western Views of Islam in the Middle Ages* (Cambridge, MA, 1962); B. Z. Kedar, *Crusade and Mission: European Approaches Toward the Muslims* (Princeton, 1984); N. Daniel, *Islam and the West: The Making of an Image*, rev. ed. (Oxford, 1993); and T. E. Burman, *Reading the Qur'an in Latin Christendom, 1140–1560* (Philadelphia, 2007). On Peter the Venerable's view of the Muslims in particular, see D. Iogna-Prat, *Order and Exclusion: Cluny and Christendom Face Heresy, Judaism, and Islam (1000–1150)*, trans. G. R. Edwards (Ithaca, 2002), pp. 323–57; and S. G. Bruce, *Cluny and the Muslims of La Garde-Freinet: Hagiography and the Problem of Islam in Medieval Europe* (Ithaca, 2015).

by participants in the First Crusade.² Despite a burgeoning interest in evidence for cross-cultural commerce between Christians and Muslims in the Middle Ages, no study of this topic has given full attention to an unprecedented tenth-century episode involving a fateful encounter between a Cluniac abbot and a band of Muslim warriors. In July 972, raiders from the Muslim enclave of La Garde-Freinet (near modern Saint-Tropez, in Provence) abducted Abbot Maiolus of Cluny and his entourage as they camped at the top of the Great Saint Bernard Pass (Mons Jovis) in the western Alps while en route from Rome to Burgundy. The abbot managed to secure a ransom for their release and returned to Cluny unharmed, but the story did not end there. Upon Maiolus's death in 994, Christian communities hailed him as a saint who held the power to intercede with God on their behalf.³ Between the years 1000 and 1150, no fewer than five Cluniac authors related the tale of the abbot's kidnapping as they told and retold the history of his deeds and virtues.⁴ As knowledge of Muslim beliefs filtered slowly into

---

2. See, for example, M. T. d'Alverny, "La connaissance de l'Islam en Occident du IXe au milieu du XIIe siecle," in *L'Occidente e l'Islam nell'alto medioevo, Spoleto 2-8 aprile 1964*, 2 vols. (Spoleto, 1965), vol. 1, pp. 577-602, repr. in M. T. d'Alverny, *La connaissance de l'Islam dans l'Occident médiéval* (Aldershot, 1994), no. V; E. Rotter, *Abendland und Sarazenen: Das okzidentale Araberbild und seine Entstehung im Frühmittelalter* (Berlin, 1983); and K. S. Beckett, *Anglo-Saxon Perceptions of the Islamic World* (Cambridge, 2003). For the case of Spain, where Christian authors had ready access to information about Islamic beliefs than northern Europeans, see K. B. Wolf, "The Earliest Spanish Christian Views of Islam," *Church History* 55 (1986): 281-93; and K. B. Wolf, "Christian Views of Islam in Early Medieval Spain," in *Medieval Christian Perceptions of Islam: A Book of Essays*, ed. J. V. Tolan (New York, 1996), pp. 85-108.

3. On popular saint-making in the early Middle Ages, see A. Vauchez, *Sainthood in the Later Middle Ages*, trans. J. Birrell (Cambridge, 1997), pp. 13-21.

4. These texts include (1) Anonymous, *Vita breuior sancti Maioli* (BHL 5180), BC, cols. 1763-82. A monk of Pavia composed this text shortly after Maiolus's death (c. 1000). See D. Iogna-Prat, *Agni Immaculati: Recherches sur les sources hagiographiques relatives à saint Maieul de Cluny (954-994)* (Paris, 1988), pp. 27-29; and chapter 5, below. (2) Syrus, *Vita sancti Maioli* (BHL 5177/79), ed. Iogna-Prat, *Agni lmmaculati*, pp. 163-285. Syrus was a Cluniac monk writing around 1010 in response to Pavia's claim on Maiolus. (3) Odilo, *Vita sancti Maioli* (BHL 5182/84), in BC, cols. 279-90, repr. In PL 142, cols. 943-62. This *vita* was the work of Maiolus's successor as abbot of Cluny. It was written in 1031 or 1033. (4) Rodulphus Glaber, *Historiarum Libri Quinque* 1.4.9, ed. and trans. J. France, in *Rodulfus Glaber: The Five Books of Histories and The Life of Abbot William* (Oxford, 1989), pp. 22-24. Glaber was a monastic chronicler who resided at Cluny in the early 1030s and composed the *Histories* in the 1040s (see n. 25, below). (5) Nalgod, *Vita sancti Maioli* (BHL 5181): "Vita ex prolixoribus coaevorum actis a Nalgodo monacho post sesqui secum contracta," AASS Maii 2, pp. 657-67: "ex codice cluniacensi." This early twelfth-century *vita* was a reworking of Syrus's *Vita sancti Maioli* (no. 2, above). For more on the *dossier hagiographique* of Maiolus, see D. logna-Prat, "Panorama de l'hagiographie abbatiale clunisienne (v. 940-v. 1140)," in *Manuscrits hagiographiques et travail des hagiographes*, ed. M. Heinzelmann (Sigmaringen, 1992), pp. 77-118, at pp. 87-89; repr. in D. logna-Prat, *Études clunisiennes* (Paris, 2002), pp. 35-73, at pp. 44-46.

CHAPTER 3

northern Europe after the turn of the first millennium, the story of the abduction, particularly the verbal exchanges between Maiolus and his captors, changed significantly in the telling in ways that reflected the transformation of western attitudes toward Islam from ambivalence to curiosity to grave concern.[5]

In this chapter, I focus on the earliest textual evidence for the harrowing events of July 972: a hastily written note that Maiolus sent to the monks of Cluny to inform them of his plight and to request payment for his release and the release of his fellow captives. The significance of this document is twofold. First, it is the only contemporary record of the kidnapping incident. Resonant with Old Testament imagery drawn from the Second Book of Samuel and the Psalter, this text provides the most immediate and concrete information about Maiolus's perception of his abductors. As such, it is a neglected witness to an encounter between a Christian intellectual and Muslims in northern Europe near the close of the first millennium.[6] Second, although the ransom letter is brief, it contributes substantially to our understanding of the mental world of Maiolus. Unlike other abbots of Cluny, Maiolus did not produce a corpus of sermons, treatises, or letters that provides insight into his thoughts and ideals. The document's biblical resonances capture an exegetical moment that illuminates the deftness of his application of scripture to comprehend and cope with the fearful circumstances that confronted him. I analyze the text of the abbot's ransom letter to identify and contextualize the Old Testament passages that Maiolus used to characterize his dire situation. I trace the history of these passages in the Christian exegetical tradition, giving special attention to the writings of the apostle Paul, to capture their received interpretation at tenth-century Cluny. Most important, I attempt to determine whether the biblical components of the ransom letter betray any hint of the abbot's awareness of the religion of his captors.

In the waning days of July 972, Maiolus of Cluny and his entourage set out from Rome to return to their home in Burgundy. A persuasive diplomat, tireless powerbroker for kings and popes, and enthusiastic reformer of religious life, Maiolus traveled continuously during his

---

5. Bruce, *Cluny and the Muslims of La Garde-Freinet*, pp. 41–62.
6. Although several scholars have drawn attention to the abduction of Maiolus, none of them has scrutinized the text of his ransom letter. See Southern, *Western Views of Islam*, p. 28, n. 25; and Kedar, *Crusade and Mission*, pp. 42–43.

forty-year tenure as abbot of Cluny (954–994).[7] On this occasion, the path before him was familiar. Hospices and abbeys punctuated the road running north from Rome through Siena, Lucca, and Pavia, to the southern foothills of the Alps.[8] In Pavia, Maiolus and his party were joined by a host of pilgrims, who believed that his holy presence would assure them a safe crossing over the perilous path before them, an alpine route that later became known as the Great Saint Bernard Pass. In the summer months, this mountain pass was a primary artery for pilgrim and merchant traffic moving between the Italian peninsula and northern Europe. Devout men and women from as far away as England braved its precipitous heights to visit the shrines of the Roman martyrs. So, too, did enterprising merchants, who traded the hardships of the road for the promise of profits to be made from luxury goods like silk, spices and exotic animals, in the courts and regional markets of the north.[9]

The perils of crossing the Great Saint Bernard Pass were considerable. Early medieval prayers for people about to embark on long voyages beseeched God to protect them specifically from the dangers of wild animals, hostile weather, and brigands.[10] Attacks by wolves and the threat of avalanches and snowstorms were always feared in the Alps, but in the early tenth century a new danger emerged. Throughout this

---

7. On Maiolus's travels in Italy, see L. Bourdon, "Les voyages de Saint Mayeul en Italie: Itineraires et chronologie," *Melanges d'archéologie et d'histoire* 43 (1926): 63–89. More generally on the abbot and his influence, which extended to the highest secular and ecclesiastical circles, see Iogna-Prat, *Agni Immaculati; Saint Mayeul et son temps: Actes du congrès international de Valensole, 12–14 Mai 1994* (Dignes-les-Bains, 1997); and *San Maiolo e le Influenze Cluniacensi nell'Italia del Nord: Atti del Convegno Internationale nel Millenario di San Maiolo (994–1994) Pavia-Novara, 23–24 settembre 1994*, ed. E. Cau and A. Settia (Como, 1998).

8. This route and its hostels are detailed minutely in a catalog of way-stations recorded in 990 by Archbishop Sigeric of Canterbury upon his return from Rome to England. See V. Ortenberg, "Archbishop Sigeric's Journey to Rome in 990," *Anglo-Saxon England* 19 (1990): 197–246, esp. the map on p. 230. For more on these and other hospices for medieval travelers through the Alps, see J. E. Tyler, *The Alpine Passes: The Middle Ages (962–1250)* (Oxford, 1930), pp. 21–38; and, more generally on this topic, see O. R. Constable, *Housing the Stranger in the Mediterranean World: Lodging, Travel and Trade in Late Antiquity and the Middle Ages* (New York, 2003).

9. A list of tolls for transalpine trade goods drawn up in 960 by Bishop Giso of Aosta included tariffs for weapons, armor, salt, metals, and animals such as horses, hawks, and apes. See Tyler, *Alpine Passes*, pp. 151–52. For the broader context of transalpine commerce in the early medieval period, see M. McCormick, *Origins of the European Economy: Communications and Commerce* (Cambridge, 2001).

10. A. Franz, *Die kirchlichen Benediktionen im Mittelalter*, 2 vols. (Graz, 1960), vol. 2, pp. 261–71. For more on long-distance travel around the year 1000 and the hazards associated with it, see H. Fichtenau, "Reisen und Reisende," in H. Fichtenau, *Beiträge zur Mediävistik: Ausgewählte Aufsätze*, 3 vols. (Stuttgart, 1975–86), vol. 3, pp. 1–79.

period, Muslim pirates held sway over the southern coast of Provence. Largely unhindered by local Christian lords, who lacked the organization and resources necessary to curb their initial onslaught, these raiders seized a Christian citadel called *Fraxinetum* (modern La Garde-Freinet, near Saint-Tropez) and used it as a base to pillage monasteries and towns throughout the region.[11] They also made predatory forays into the Alpine Passes to harry and waylay pilgrim and merchant traffic. At first, their methods were crude and brutal. In the early 920s, they reportedly murdered Anglo-Saxon pilgrims by triggering avalanches and then looted their corpses.[12] When they realized, however, that they could exact a heavy and renewable toll in ransoms, these raiders changed their method from murder to kidnapping.[13]

The Muslims who inhabited La Garde-Freinet in the tenth century were not recognized as a polity or outpost of any Islamic central government in the Iberian Peninsula or in the East. They are best understood as an autonomous, entrepreneurial community that flourished for decades as mercenaries, taking part in the small-scale conflicts of local Christian lords while also profiting from piracy and brigandage in the lawless countryside of Provence and in the coastal waters of the Mediterranean Sea.[14] They produced no documents of their own, so little is known of the origin, size, and composition of the community,

---

11. Liudprand of Cremona, *Antapodosis* 1.2–4, ed. P. Chiesa, in *Liudprandi Cremonensis Opera Omnia*, CCCM 156 (Turnhout, 1998), pp. 6–7. For what follows, see B. Luppi, *I saraceni in Provenza, in Liguria e nelle Alpi occidentali* (Bordighera, 1952); J.-T. Reinaud, *Muslim Colonies in France, Northern Italy and Switzerland*, trans. H. Kahn Sherwani (Lahore, 1955); J.-P. Poly, *La Provence et la société féodale (879–1166): Contribution à l'étude des structures dites féodales dans le Midi* (Paris, 1976), pp. 3–29; P. Sénac, *Musulmans et sarrasins dans le sud de la Gaule: VIIIe au XIe siècle* (Paris, 1980); and P. Sénac, *Provence et piraterie sarrasine* (Paris, 1982).

12. Flodoard, *Annales*, anno 921: "Anglorum Romam proficiscentium plurimi inter angustias Alpium lapidibus a Sarracenis sunt obruti," and anno 923: "Multitudo Anglorum limina sancti Petri orationis gratia petentium inter Alpes a Sarracenis trucidatur," ed. P. Lauer, in *Les Annales de Flodoard* (Paris, 1905), pp. 5 and 19.

13. Flodoard, *Annales*, anno 951: "Sarraceni meatum Alpium obsidentes, a viatoribus Romam petentibus tributum accipiunt, et sic eos transire permittunt," ed. Lauer, p. 132. For similar activities in Italy, see Liudprand, *Antapodosis* 2.44: "Nemo etiam ab occasu sive ab arcturo orationis gratia ad beatissimorum apostolorum limina Romam transire poterat, qui ab his aut non caperetur aut non modico dato precio dimittererur," ed. Chiesa, p. 53. Sources from late medieval Spain provide much more explicit evidence for the price of ransoms and the resources available for captives and their families to raise funds for the release of individuals from Muslim captivity. See J. Rodriguez, "Financing a Captive's Ransom in Late Medieval Aragon," *Medieval Encounters* 9 (2003): 164–81.

14. On conditions in Provence in this period and the rationales of contemporaries for the ills besetting the countryside, see S. Weinberger, "Paiens et mauvais chrétiens: L'explication du mal dans la Provence des Xe et XIe siècles," *Annales du Midi* 98 (1986): 317–26.

except what can be gleaned from contemporary Christian sources.¹⁵ Liudprand of Cremona believed that they hailed originally from Spain, but such a group could have been composed of dissolute or opportunistic individuals from Muslim lands around the Mediterranean rim.¹⁶ The aborted effort of Count Hugh of Arles to destroy their stronghold in 942 with a coordinated assault by land forces and a blockade of Byzantine ships wielding Greek fire implies that the community was substantial, perhaps numbering several hundred fighting men at any given time.¹⁷ The longevity of La Garde-Freinet—some eight decades had elapsed between its putative founding in the 890s and its destruction in 972—suggests that the community may have had periodic support from outside Provence (plausibly from Spain) and that its numbers were bolstered further by the presence of women and children, like those attested at a contemporary Muslim enclave near Mount Garigliano in Italy.¹⁸ Little else is known for certain about the character and composition of the community.

On the night of July 21/22, 972, raiders from La Garde-Freinet abducted Abbot Maiolus, his entourage, and the pilgrim host accompanying them as they crossed the Great Saint Bernard Pass.¹⁹ From captivity, the abbot sent a desperate letter to his brethren in Burgundy, as recorded first by the abbot's earliest Cluniac biographer, Syrus, and

---

15. La Garde-Freinet received mention in several Arabic geographies from the tenth to the thirteenth centuries, but these texts do not provide any details about the tenth-century Muslim community. See P.-A. Février et al., *La Provence des origines à l'an mil: Histoire et archéologie* (Paris, 1989), pp. 487–91.

16. Liudprand, *Antapodosis* 1.3: "ex Hispania egressi," ed. Chiesa, p. 6. Luidprand made an explicit distinction between this group from Spain and the African Muslims active in central and southern Italy, whom he considered to be much more savage. See Luidprand, *Antapodosis* 2.44, ed. Chiesa, p. 53. John of Gorze's embassy to the court of Caliph 'Abd al-Rahman III in Cordoba in 953–956 may have been a diplomatic response by Emperor Otto I to the Muslim raids in Provence, thus implying a Spanish origin for the raiders. See John of Saint Arnulf, *Vita Iohannis abbatis Gorziensis* 115–29, ed. and trans. P. C. Jacobsen, in *Die Geschichte vom Leben des Johannes, Abt des Klosters Gorze*, MGH Scriptores rerum Germanicarum 81 (Wiesbaden, 2016), pp. 414–53. If this was indeed the goal of John's embassy, it was unsuccessful, for more than a decade later, in a letter dated to 968, Otto expressed his desire to destroy the Muslim enclave at La Garde-Freinet once and for all: Widukind, *Res Gestae Saxonicae* 3.70: "per Fraxinecum ad destruendos Sarracenos, Deo cornice, iter arripiemus," ed. P. Hirsch, in *Die Sachsengeschichte des Widukind von Korvei*, MGH Scriptores rerum Germanicarum 60 (Hanover, 1935), p. 147.

17. Liudprand, *Antapodosis* 5.9, ed. Chiesa, p. 128. On the failure of this offensive, see A. R. Lewis, *Naval Power and Trade in the Mediterranean, A.D. 500–1100* (Princeton, 1951), p. 150.

18. Liudprand, *Antapodosis* 2.44, ed. Chiesa, p. 53.

19. On the date of this encounter, see P. A. Amargier, "La capture de saint Maieul de Cluny et l'expulsion des Sarrasins de Provence," *Revue bénédictine* 73 (1963): 316–23.

again several decades later by a monastic chronicler closely associated with Cluny, Rodulphus Glaber. In response, the monks of Cluny quickly ransacked the ornaments of their church and gathered a considerable sum—one thousand pounds of silver, according to Glaber—to secure the release of their spiritual father.[20] Their efforts were successful. Maiolus and his entourage went free, but the audacity of their abductors outraged Christian leaders and galvanized the will of local lords. Within a year of the incident, Count William of Aries and his allies marshaled an army and laid waste to Fraxinetum, effectively erasing the Muslim presence from Provence and the Alpine Passes.[21]

Maiolus's original ransom letter is lost, but recollections of it have been preserved in two early eleventh-century accounts of the kidnapping episode written at Cluny. The earliest of these appeared in a hagiographical portrait of the abbot composed between the years 1000 and 1010 by a Cluniac monk named Syrus (*BHL* 5177/79).[22] In this version of the story, Syrus described how Maiolus wrote the ransom letter with his own hand and had it delivered to his brethren by means of another captured monk, who was released by their abductors to secure the payment.[23] In a very few words, the abbot evoked a situation fraught with life-threatening peril: "Maiolus, a captive, wretched and in chains, sends greetings to his lords and brothers, the monks of Cluny. The hordes of Belial have surrounded me; the snares of death have seized me. Please send a ransom payment for me and those held captive with me."[24]

The text of the ransom letter also appeared around 1040 with slight, but significant, variations in Glaber's *Five Books of Histories*, which was

---

20. Rodulphus Glaber, *Historiarum Libri Quinque* 1.4.9: "Insuper pecunie pondus atque numerum ei determinantes indixerunt. Fuit enim mille librarum argenti, ut uidelicet singulis libra una in partem proueniret," ed. France, p. 18. The ransoming of captives was an expression of Christian charity with roots in late antiquity. On the development of this tradition, see W. Klingshirn, "Charity and Power: Caesarius of Aries and the Ransoming of Captives in Sub-Roman Gaul," *Journal of Roman Studies* 75 (1985): 183-203.

21. Rodulphus Glaber, *Historiarum Libri Quinque* 1.4.9, ed. France, p. 22. The expulsion of the Muslims from La Garde-Freinet loomed large in Cluniac hagiography (see n. 4, above), but left no impression in contemporary charters and other documents of practice from Provence. See M. Zerner, "La capture de Maïeul et la guerre de libération de Provence: Le départ des sarrasins à travers les cartulaires provençaux," in *Saint Mayeul et son temps*, pp. 199-210.

22. Syrus, *Vita sancti Maioli* 3.1-9, ed. Iogna-Prat, pp. 247-60.

23. Syrus, *Vita sancti Maioli* 3.5, ed. Iogna-Prat, p. 253.

24. Syrus, *Vita sancti Maioli* 3.5: "Dominis et fratribus cluniensibus, Maiolus miser captus et catenatus. Torrentes Belial circumdederunt me, preoccupauerunt me laquei mortis. Redemptionis pretium, si placet, mittite pro me et his qui una mecum capti tenentur," ed. Iogna-Prat, p. 253.

dedicated to Odilo, Maiolus's successor as abbot of Cluny: "Maiolus, wretched and captive, sends greetings to his lords and brothers, the monks of Cluny. The hordes of Belial have surrounded me; the snares of death have seized me. In view of this, by all means please send a ransom for those held captive with me."[25]

The minor differences in the wording of the ransom letter in these two accounts are more stylistic than substantive, but they indicate quite clearly that Glaber did not copy the contents of this document directly from Syrus's text. Glaber's version did not include Syrus's reference to Maiolus as *catenatus* ("in chains"). Moreover, the final plea for the ransom in Glaber's account added a note of urgency with the words *nunc vero* ("in view of this, by all means") before the request for payment, which Glaber called simply a *redemptio* in contrast to Syrus's descriptive phrase *pretium redemptionis*. The fact that Syrus wrote about Maiolus's travails several decades before Glaber and may have even had the opportunity to hear the story from the saintly abbot before his death in 994 places his account closer to contemporary witnesses to the kidnapping, but does not prove conclusively that the text of the ransom letter presented by him is a more accurate reproduction of Maiolus's original letter than the version preserved in Glaber's *Five Books of Histories*. Either author could have been working from memory or both were in a position to consult the original ransom letter in the abbey archives, if the brethren of Cluny in fact chose to preserve it.

These textual variations are of little importance, however, for the purpose of this chapter, because the heart of the letter, in which Maiolus characterized the nature of his captivity— "The hordes of Belial have surrounded me; the snares of death have seized me" (*Torrentes Belial circumdederunt me, praeoccupauerunt me laquei mortis*)—is identical in both accounts. The abbot of Cluny drew the central images of his ransom letter directly from his memory of an Old Testament hymn of praise preserved in the Second Book of Samuel and repeated with minor variations in the Book of Psalms: "I will call upon the Lord, who is worthy of praise, and I will be saved from my enemies, for the miseries of death

---

25. Rodulphus Glaber, *Historiarum Libri Quinque* 1.4.9: "Dominis et fratribus Cluniensibus, frater Maiolus miser et captus. Torrentes Belial circumdederunt me, praeoccupauerunt me laquei mortis. Nunc uero si placet et his qui mecum capti tenentur redemptionem mittite," ed. France, pp. 20–22. Glaber was a monk—although not a very good one by his own reckoning—who spent a considerable amount of time at Cluny while composing his work. See J. France, "Rodulfus Glaber and the Cluniacs," *Journal of Ecclesiastical History* 39 (1988): 497–508.

surround me. The hordes of Belial frighten me. The cords of Hell have entangled me. The snares of death have hindered me."[26]

In this ancient poem, a king of Israel gives thanks to God for help in defeating his enemies. The hymn begins with a confession of faith in God's protective power: "I love you, O my Lord, my strength. The Lord is my foundation and my refuge and my deliverer."[27] There follows the series of short metaphorical descriptions of the king's tribulations (quoted above), from which Maiolus borrowed images of entrapment and captivity to communicate the difficulty of his situation to his Cluniac brethren. The hymn concluded with an account of the Lord's intervention in battle, leading to the defeat of the ancient king's enemies and his ascendancy as a ruler of an empire at peace.

Given the richness of the liturgical psalmody at tenth-century Cluny and the impact of its language on the monastic imagination, it is not at all surprising that Maiolus chose to express the gravity of his plight by echoing the adversities that faced an Old Testament king of Israel, who relied on his faith in the Lord for deliverance and victory.[28] It is the abbot's use of the word Belial, however, that complicates our understanding of his perception of his captors. Unlike the phrase "the snares of death have seized me," which could apply generically to any dangerous situation, Belial was a proper name that was resonant with ancient and infamous associations. The discovery of the meaning of this name in a tenth-century monastic context is imperative for our understanding of the abbot's response to his captivity and his perception of his captors.

Maiolus's application of the term Belial to his Muslim captors is unprecedented in the Christian tradition of writing about Islam in the early Middle Ages. Northern Europeans were much more likely to

---

26. 2 Sam. 22:4-6: "Laudabilem invocabo Dominum et ab inimicis meis salvus ero quia circumdederunt me contritiones mortis torrentes Belial terruerunt me funes inferi circumdederunt me praeverunt me laquei mortis." Compare Ps. 17:4-6: "Laudans invocabo Dominum et ab inimicis meis salvus ero circumdederunt me dolores mortis et torrentes iniquitatis conturbaverunt me dolores inferni circumdederunt me praeoccupaverunt me laquei mortis."

27. Ps. 17:2-3: "Diligam te Domine fortitude mea Dominus firmamentum meum et refugium meum et liberator meus."

28. The tenth-century Cluniacs emulated the liturgical customs instituted in the early ninth century by Abbot Benedict of Aniane, who ordered the singing of 138 psalms on feast days. This was a substantial increase from the thirty-seven psalms prescribed in the sixth-century *Rule of Benedict*, which served as the template for monastic life throughout the Middle Ages. See K. Hallinger, "Überlieferung und Steigerung im Mönchtum des 8. bis 12. Jahrhunderts," in *Eulogia: Miscellanea liturgica in onore di P. Burckhard Neunheuser O.S.B.* (Rome, 1979), pp. 125-87, at pp. 145-46.

identify the followers of Mohammed with the Ishmaelites or Hagarenes of the Old Testament, who were also known collectively as Saracens.[29] According to early medieval exegesis of the Book of Genesis, the peoples who dwelt in the desert lands of the Arabian Peninsula were the descendants of Ishmael, the ill-favored son of Abraham by his slave woman Hagar. Destined by a prophecy of God to a legacy of conflict— "his hand against every man and every man's hand against him" (Gen. 16:12)—the sons of Ishmael elided easily in the western imagination with adherents to Islam whose war machine conquered the Byzantine settlements of North Africa and the Visigothic kingdom of Spain in the seventh and early eighth centuries. In late antiquity, Jerome and his contemporaries applied the term Saracen (*Saraceni*) to pre-Islamic pagan Arabs, but early medieval exegetes understood it to be the name taken by the Muslims to claim their descent from Abraham's wife, Sarah, and thereby to conceal their ignoble ancestry.[30] Before the eleventh century, this collective of names (Ishmaelite, Hagarene, Saracen) carried a specific religious association. In early medieval thought, people known by these names were commonly believed to be pagans who worshipped idols of Apollo, Venus, and Mohammed, as well as other gods of classical antiquity. Popular epic poems, like the *Song of Roland*, preserved this false perception in the European imagination even centuries after more accurate information about Islamic beliefs became available in the West.[31]

---

29. On the meaning of these terms, their application by late ancient and early medieval Christian authors, and their religious associations, see Rotter, *Abendland und Sarazenen*, pp. 77-130; Beckett, *Anglo-Saxon Perceptions of the Islamic World*, pp. 18-19 and 69-139; and J. V. Tolan, *Saracens: Islam in the Medieval European Imagination* (New York, 2002), pp. 105-34.

30. See, for example, Jerome, *Vita Malchi*, ed. and trans. C. Gray, in *Jerome, Vita Malchi: Text, Translation, and Commentary* (Oxford, 2015), pp. 167-69. For a useful catalog of sources that refer to pre-Islamic Saracens and their interaction with late Roman Christians, see P. Mayerson, "Saracens and Romans: Micro-Macro Relationships," *Bulletin of the American Schools of Oriental Research* 274 (1989): 71-79.

31. See, for example, *La Chanson de Roland*, lines 7-8: "Li reis Marsilie la tient, ki Deu nen aimet. / Mahumet sert e Apollin recleimet," ed. L. Cortés, in *La Chanson de Roland* (Paris, 1994), p. 160. The fullest discussion of the depiction of Muslims in the *Song of Roland* remains K. Heisig, "Die Geschichtsmetaphysik des Rolandsliedes und ihre Vorgeschichte," *Zeitschrift für romanische Philologie* 60 (1935): 1-87. For more on the representation of Saracens in medieval epic poetry, see W. W. Comfort, "The Literary Role of the Saracens in the French Epic," *Proceedings of the Modern Language Association* 55 (1940): 628-59; and C. M. Jones, "The Conventional Saracen of the Songs of Geste," *Speculum* 17 (1942): 201-25.

In contrast, the term Belial was an ancient Hebrew noun that had no relation to the Old Testament racial taxonomies favored by Christian exegetes in their descriptions of Muslim peoples. There is no consensus of scholarly opinion with regard to its etymology, but the word is generally understood to mean "worthlessness" or "wickedness."[32] Old Testament authors used it most commonly in apposition to describe individuals who had committed crimes against the Israelite religion or sought to disrupt the social order. In the Book of Deuteronomy, people who incited the worship of false gods were called "sons of Belial" (*filii Belial*) and put to the sword, along with their supporters and their cattle.[33] Two men who bore false witness against Naboth in the First Book of Kings were likewise called "sons of Belial."[34] This term was especially prevalent in the Books of Samuel, where "sons of Belial" designated individuals who were inhospitable to guests and "man of Belial" (*vir Belial*) signaled one who had offered insult to his sovereign.[35] By the Hellenistic period, however, the word took on a more specific association. In apocalyptic Jewish literature, Belial (sometimes written as Beliar) became the name of the adversarial entity who opposed the will of God, that is, the Devil. He was a creature of darkness, who with the aid of attendant spirits dominated the will of evil men and held the present age under his control. Although Belial was depicted as a powerful force in the immediate present, his future downfall was foretold as a war in which God and his angels would defeat him and his minions by imprisoning them in chains or hurling them into an everlasting fire.

It was this apocalyptic understanding of Belial as an opponent of God and an adversary of humankind that informed the only reference to his name in New Testament literature.[36] In the Second Letter to the Corinthians, the apostle Paul deployed the word in a pronouncement on the proper relationship between Christians and pagans. Using a

---

32. For what follows, see H. W. Huppenbauer, "Belial in den Qumrantexten," *Theologische Zeitschrift* 15 (1959): 81–89; J. B. Russell, *The Devil: Perceptions of Evil from Antiquity to Primitive Christianity* (Ithaca, 1977), pp. 174–220, esp. p. 188, n. 17; and *Dictionary of Deities and Demons in the Bible*, ed. K. van der Toorn et al. (Leiden, 1995), cols. 320–27, *s.v.* Belial, with references to earlier literature.

33. Deut. 13:12–18.
34. 1 Kings 21:8–14.
35. 1 Sam. 25:17; and Sam. 16:7 and 20:1.
36. Russell, *The Devil*, pp. 221–49.

series of rhetorical juxtapositions, he emphasized the conceptual and spiritual gulf that divided the faithful from the unfaithful:

> Do not lead the yoke with unbelievers. Indeed, what partnership has justice with iniquity or what fellowship has light with darkness? What accord has Christ with Belial or what does a believer have in common with an unbeliever?[37]

In Paul's mind, Belial was no less than the Devil himself, the opposite of Christ, and a spirit synonymous with iniquity, darkness, and false belief. The name Belial was not mentioned by any other New Testament author, so Paul's use of the word was particularly important for its transmission into the vocabularies of early Christian communities. Moreover, his investment of Belial with such dark meanings shaped the reception and understanding of the name in the early Middle Ages.

The contrast of Belial with Christ in Paul's Second Letter to the Corinthians drew the attention of several early medieval exegetes, whose topical concerns influenced the polemical application of the word in their writings. Most of them treated the name as a collective metaphor for religious rivals that threatened or opposed Christian society. In the mid-seventh century, Pope Martin I (649–655) applied the term to those spreading false doctrines. Just as there is no accord between Christ and Belial, he wrote, so too is there no accord between the consensus of the orthodox and heretical thinkers.[38] Echoing Paul's letter, he warned his readers to guard their hearts by avoiding all social commerce with those who denied the true faith. A few decades later, in an allegorical commentary on the Books of Samuel, Bede applied the name Belial even more broadly to include not only errant Christians but Jews as well. "The sons of Belial," he maintained, "are the sons of the Jewish priesthood, the blind sons of light, and those without a yoke, that is, those who are ignorant of the teaching of Christ. They do not follow the commandments of divine law, but rather the decrees of

---

37. 2 Cor. 6:14–15: "Nolite iugum ducere cum infidelibus quae enim participatio iustitiae cum iniquitate aut quae societas luci ad tenebras quae autem conventio Christi ad Belial aut quae pars fideli cum infidele."

38. Pope Martin I, *Ep.* 13 *(ad ecclesiam Thessalonicensium de Pauli damnatione eiusque haeresi fugienda)*: "Nec conventio Christi ad Belial, nec pars fideli cum infidelibus, neque consensus orthodoxorum cum haereticis." *PL* 87, col. 197.

their own traditions."³⁹ This association of Belial was repeated in the early ninth century in a letter of complaint about the mounting influence of Jews in the Frankish kingdoms, addressed to Emperor Louis the Pious by Archbishop Agobard of Lyons. The archbishop employed Paul's juxtaposition of Christ and Belial to argue that it was inappropriate and reprehensible for devout Christians like the emperor to share company and commerce with unbelievers. As a solution to this dangerous situation, Agobard advised a strict segregation of Jewish people living in Christian society.⁴⁰

Metaphorical applications of Belial to the religious adversaries of Christianity were much more numerous than the direct identification of the name with the person of the Devil in early medieval thought. This latter use is most apparent in the writings of a Carolingian monk of Fulda named Haimo, who studied under Alcuin at Tours and later became a monk of Hirschfeld (around 839) and bishop of Halberstadt (841).⁴¹ In his commentary on Paul's Second Letter to the Corinthians, Haimo emphasized the relationship between Belial and the Devil:

> *What accord has Christ with Belial?* Belial means 'without the yoke,' signifying the Devil, who threw off from his neck the yoke of almighty God. For it is said in the Book of Samuel: They are said to be men of Belial, that is, men without the yoke of God. What accord or what fellowship does Christ have with the Devil? None whatsoever.⁴²

---

39. Bede, *In Samuelem prophetam allegorica expositio* 5: "*Porro filii Heli, Filii Belial, etc.* Filii sacerdotii Judaici, filii caeci luminis, sive absque jugo (utrumque enim Belial sive Beliar sonat) exstitere, quotquot Christi doctrinam nesciebant; non divinae legis jussa, sed suarum statuta traditionum sequentes." *PL* 91, col. 512.

40. Agobard of Lyons, *De iudaicis superstitionibus et erroribus (ad Ludouicum)* 2: "*Que conuentio Christi ad Belial?* In quo aduertendum est, quia, sicut infideles sponte sequestrantur ab ecclesi astica communione, ut in nullis uelint mysteriis participare fidelibus, ita et fideles deuote separare se debent et conuictu et societate infidelium," ed. L. Van Acker, in *Agobardi Lugdunensis Opera Omnia*, CCCM 52 (Turnhout, 1981), p. 208. On the context of Agobard's conflict with the Jews of Lyons, see B.-S. Albert, "*Adversus Iudaeos* in the Carolingian Empire," in *Contra Iudaeos: Ancient and Medieval Polemics Between Christians and Jews*, ed. O. Limor and G. Stroumsa (Tubingen, 1996), pp. 119–42; and J. Heil, "Agobard, Amolo, das Kirchengut und die Juden von Lyon," *Francia* 25 (1998): 39–76.

41. On Haimo's life and work, see *Lexikon des Mittelalters*, ed. Robert Autry et al., 9 vols (Munich and Zurich, 1980–98), vol. 4, col. 1864, *s.v.* Haimo 2: Haimo von Halberstadt. For more on the monastic community at Fulda in the Carolingian period, see J. Raaijmakers, *The Making of the Monastic Community of Fulda, c. 744–c. 900* (Cambridge, 2012).

42. Haimo, *Expositio in epistolam II ad Corinthios* 6: "Quae autem conventio Christi ad Belial? Belial inpretatur (sic) absque jugo, significans diabolo qui jugum omnipotentis Dei de collo suo excussit. Dicitur et in libro Samuelis: Qui dixerunt viri Belial, id est absque jugo Dei. Quae conventio, sive quae societas Christi ad diabolum? Nulla." *PL* 117, col. 639.

Haimo also expressed this diabolical affinity in a homily delivered on the second Sunday before Lent. In this work, he presented his audience with an inventory of the names by which the Devil was known in the New Testament and commented on their meaning. He placed Belial at the top of the list, perhaps because of its perceived antiquity, and identified the name as a Hebrew word meaning "without a yoke."[43] This association of Belial with the Devil was the exception rather than the rule for Christian exegetes in the early Middle Ages as most commentators applied the term generally to religious communities that were hostile and threatening to the Christian faith.

This reconstruction of the exegetical history of the name Belial allows us to consider Maiolus's letter with new insight. The abbot's deployment of this ancient and infamous word in his characterization of the Muslims of La Garde-Freinet suggests that he recognized his captors as adherents to a rival system of belief that was opposed to Christianity. The polemical resonances of the term strongly imply that Maiolus understood his captors in the same terms as his contemporaries understood heretics and Jews, that is, as credible adversaries of the Christian faith. Maiolus's perceptions were particularly important because as one of the foremost religious leaders of his age he was uniquely situated to inform and influence the viewpoints of powerful individuals, lay and religious alike. Later accounts of the abduction written in the eleventh and early twelfth centuries expanded on the premise that religious tension freighted the encounter between Maiolus and his captors. In their accounts of the virtuous deeds of the saintly abbot, Cluniac authors populated his experience in captivity with Muslim warriors who recognized his holiness and either converted to Christianity or died for their obstinacy.[44] Although these pious fictions say more about their authors' anxieties concerning Islam than they do about the historical events of July 972, the use of the term Belial in Maiolus's ransom letter suggests that these later tales were elaborations on a received historical tradition rather than complete fabrications.

While it is impossible to ascertain the exact nature of Maiolus's understanding of Islam as a system of belief, it is now plausible to assert that some recognition of his captors' religion informed the text of the

---

43. Haimo, *Homilia* 22 *(Dominica in sexagesima):* "Ab isto qui hoc evangelium scripsit, diabolus qui latro sive criminator vel deorsum fluens, Hebraice Belial, quod incerpretatur absque jugo, dicitur." *PL* 118, cols. 167-68.

44. Bruce, *Cluny and the Muslims of La Garde-Freinet*, pp. 41-62.

ransom letter that he sent to his brethren in Burgundy. Read in this light, it would not be anachronistic to interpret Maiolus's application of the word *Belial* to the Muslims of La Garde-Freinet as a self-conscious act of ordering and exclusion that foreshadowed and perhaps even influenced Peter the Venerable's characterization of Islam in the twelfth century, as a "diabolical heresy."[45] On the perilous heights of the Great Saint Bernard Pass, Maiolus of Cluny evoked an ancient appeal to God to characterize his captors as enemies of Christianity. While awaiting the arrival of the ransom that would free him and his associates from captivity, he may have been strengthened by the promise of deliverance at the conclusion of the psalm that had come so readily to his mind: "You exalted me above my adversaries. You delivered me from men of violence. For this I extol you, O Lord, among the nations, and sing praises to your name."[46]

---

45. See the works cited in n. 1, above.

46. Ps. 17:48–50: "Deus qui dat vindictas mihi et subdidit populos sub me liberator meus de gentibus iracundos et ab insurgentibus in me exaltabis me a viro iniquo eripies me propterea confitebor tibi in nationibus Domine et psalmum dicam nomini tuo."

CHAPTER 4

Clandestine Codices in the Captivity Narratives of Abbot Maiolus of Cluny

The violent death of the Anglo-Saxon archbishop and missionary Boniface in the summer of 754 is perhaps the most famous account of traveling manuscripts from the early Middle Ages. According to the *vitae* written to promote his sanctity, Boniface and his entourage were slain by local brigands while preaching among the pagans of Friesland in the far north of Europe.[1] When they ransacked the goods of their victims, the bandits were disappointed to find "manuscripts instead of gold vessels, pages of sacred texts instead of silver plate," and they set about "littering the fields with the books they found, throwing some of them into reedy marshes, hiding others in widely different places."[2] Arriving at the scene of the slaughter,

---

Originally published as "Clandestine Codices in the Captivity Narratives of Abbot Maiolus of Cluny," in *Teaching and Learning in Medieval Europe: Essays in Honour of Gernot R. Wieland*, ed. G. Dinkova-Bruun and T. Major, Publications of the Journal of Medieval Latin 11 (Turnhout, 2017), pp. 149-61. Reprinted with permission.

1. The earliest account, composed around 760, is Willibald, *Vita Bonifatii* 8, ed. W. Levison, in *Vitae sancti Bonifatii archiepiscopi Moguntini*, MGH Scriptores rerum Germanicarum 57 (Hanover and Leipzig, 1905), pp. 49-51; and S. Godlove, "The First Life of Boniface: Willibald's *Vita Bonifatii*," in *A Companion to Boniface*, ed. M. Aaij and S. Godlove (Leiden, 2020), pp. 152-73.

2. Willibald, *Vita Bonifatii* 8: "Et confractis librorum repositoriis, etiam pro auro voluminia et pro argento divinae scienciae cartas reppererunt. Sicque pretioso auri argenteae pretio privati, codices quos invenerunt alios per campi planitiem disparserunt, alios siquidem paludum

associates of Boniface who came to retrieve his body allegedly found several of his precious manuscripts intact: the sixth-century Victor Codex containing the Gospel harmony of Tatian alongside books of the New Testament; the Cadmug Gospel, an elegant eighth-century Gospel *Taschenbuch*; and the Ragyndrudis Codex, a compilation of anti-Arian texts and other theological writings compiled in the decades around 700.[3] By the tenth century, the Ragyndrudis Codex had taken on a more important role in the narrative of Boniface's death, for a tradition had developed that the damage to the manuscript had been caused when the saint held it over his head to ward off the killing blow of a brigand's weapon; with the passage of time, this codex became a contact relic.[4]

Narratives about the transport of personal manuscripts and their use to travelers are vanishingly rare in sources from the early Middle Ages, but a cluster of hagiographical texts written at the abbey of Cluny in the eleventh and twelfth centuries provides us with the opportunity to consider the role of books for itinerant prelates, especially when they found themselves in perilous situations. Maiolus of Cluny (abbot from 954–994) was traveling with personal manuscripts of biblical and patristic texts in the summer of 972 when Muslim adventurers kidnapped him and his entourage as they crossed the Great Saint Bernard Pass through the Alps en route from Rome to their abbey in Burgundy.[5] These brigands hailed from Fraxinetum (modern La Garde-Freinet, near Saint-Tropez), a Muslim enclave in Provence, from which they made seasonal forays into the mountains to harry and waylay

---

arundineto inferentes, alios etiam in diversis quibusque locis abscondentes proiecerunt," ed. Levison, p. 51; trans. T. Head and T. F. X. Noble in *Soldiers of Christ: Saints and Saints' Lives from Late Antiquity and the Early Middle Ages* (University Park, PA, 1995), p. 136.

3. L. E. von Padberg, "Bonifatius und die Bücher," in *Der Ragyndrudis-Codex des Hl. Bonifatius*, ed. L. E. von Padberg and H.-W. Stork (Paderborn, 1994), pp. 7–75.

4. For a summary of this development, which derived from an early tenth-century *Vita Bonifatii* attributed to Bishop Radbod of Utrecht, see M. Aaij, "Boniface's Booklife: How the Ragyndrudis Codex Came to be a *Vita Bonifatii*," *The Heroic Age* 10 (May 2007).

5. The flurry of scholarly industry that greeted the millennial anniversary of Maiolus' death in 1994 has since died down. Key starting points for the study of the fourth abbot of Cluny and his cult are D. Iogna-Prat, *Agni Immaculati: Recherches sur les sources hagiographiques relatives à saint Maieul de Cluny (954–994)* (Paris, 1988); *Saint Maïeul, Cluny et la Provence: Expansion d'une abbaye à l'aube du moyen âge*, ed. D. Iogna-Prat and B. Rosenwein (Mane, 1994); *Saint Mayeul et son temps: Actes du congrès international de Valensole, 12–14 mai 1994* (Dignes-les-Bains, 1997); and *San Maiolo e le Influenze Cluniacensi nell'Italia del Nord: Atti del Convegno Internazionale nel Millenario di San Maiolo (994–1994), Pavia-Novara, 23–24 settembre 1994*, ed. E. Cau and A. Settia (Como, 1998). On the abbot's frequent journeys over the Alpine Passes into Italy, see L. Bourdon, "Les voyages de Saint Mayeul en Italie: Itinéraires et chronologie," *Mélanges d'archéologie et d'histoire* 43 (1926): 63–89.

pilgrim and merchant traffic that crossed the Alpine Passes in the summer months.[6] Over the course of the eleventh and twelfth centuries, the brethren of Cluny told and retold the story of Maiolus's abduction in works of history and hagiography that celebrated the virtuous life of their holy father.[7] Two of the Cluniac authors who recounted the abbot's abduction called attention to the role played by books during his captivity. According to his hagiographers, the abbot's manuscripts functioned both as a provocation to religious debate with his Muslim captors and also as a solace for the hardships that the abbot endured among them.

These accounts deserve our attention, in no small part because Maiolus was unusually laconic for an abbot of Cluny. Even though he fostered the industry of his monastic scriptorium, such that Cluny emerged in the late tenth century as one of the foremost centers for manuscript production in northern Europe, the abbot left behind no treatises or sermons or works of hagiography, not even a single line of poetry that would provide insight into the texts that he read.[8] Although we know that Maiolus was active as a reformer of religious houses as far afield from Cluny as Paris, Rome, and Pavia, where he served as an influential power broker in the court of Emperors Otto II and Otto III, the paucity

---

6. On the Muslim presence in Provence and the Alpine Passes in this period, see B. Luppi, *I saraceni in Provenza, in Liguria e nelle Alpi occidentali* (Bordighera, 1952); J. T. Reinaud, *Muslim Colonies in France, Northern Italy and Switzerland*, trans. H. Sherwani (Lahore, 1955); J.-P. Poly, *La Provence et la société féodale (879–1166): Contribution à l'étude des structures dites féodales dans le Midi* (Paris, 1976), pp. 3-29; P. Sénac, *Musulmans et sarrasins dans le sud de la Gaule: VIIIe au XIe siècle* (Paris, 1980); and P. Sénac, *Provence et piraterie sarrasine* (Paris, 1982). On the date of their encounter with Maiolus, see P.-A. Amargier, "La capture de saint Maieul de Cluny et l'expulsion des Sarrasins de Provence," *Revue bénédictine* 73 (1963): 316-23.

7. These narratives are a rich source of information concerning Cluniac perceptions of Islam in this period, a topic explored more fully in S. G. Bruce, *Cluny and the Muslims of La Garde-Freinet: Hagiography and the Construction of Islam in Medieval Europe* (Ithaca, 2015).

8. For evidence of increased scribal activity at Cluny in the late tenth century, see M.-C. Garand, "Copistes de Cluny au temps de saint Maieul (948–994)," *Bibliothèque de l'Ecole des Chartes* 136 (1978): 5-36; and F. Crivello, "Les débuts de l'activité artistique dans le *scriptorium* de Cluny: Fondements et œuvres," in *Cluny: Les moines et la société au premier âge féodal*, ed. D. Iogna-Prat et al. (Rennes, 2013), pp. 197-208. This is not to suggest that Maiolus wrote nothing at all. We know, for instance, that he corresponded with Gerbert of Aurillac, later Pope Sylvester III (999-1002), a renowned scholar and, like Maiolus, a frequent presence at the Ottonian court. In 986, Gerbert entreated the abbot of Cluny to investigate the contested abbacy of Oylbold of Fleury, who took office with the support of laymen against the wishes of his brethren. Unfortunately, only Gerbert's side of the correspondence has survived. See Gerbert of Aurillac, *Correspondance: Lettres 1 à 220*, ed. and trans. P. Riché and J.-P. Callu (Paris, 2008), pp. 170-71 (no. 69) and 204-207 (no. 87); with P. Riché, "Gerbert d'Aurillac et Saint Mayeul," in *Saint Mayeul et son temps*, pp. 191-97.

of texts attributed to him has made it difficult for historians to measure the arc and aggregate of his abbatial career.[9] I begin this chapter with a survey of surviving manuscripts that may have been in the personal possession of Maiolus. Remarkably, no fewer than three late tenth-century books provide some indication that they once belonged to the abbot of Cluny. After considering these volumes, I turn my analysis to the role of clandestine books in the accounts of the abbot's abduction preserved in Rodulphus Glaber's *Five Books of Histories*, written in the 1040s, and Nalgod of Cluny's *Life of Maiolus*, composed at the request of Peter the Venerable, who was abbot of Cluny from 1122 to 1156. In their narratives, both Rodulphus and Nalgod took it for granted that their monastic audiences would find it plausible, indeed probable, that Maiolus carried manuscripts with him while he traveled and that he would turn to them for support and comfort during the trials of his captivity.

Maiolus's Manuscripts

Although we have little direct information about the intellectual currents that shaped and informed Maiolus of Cluny's ideas, three pieces of manuscript evidence provide some tantalizing clues about the kinds of texts that he may have read. During a five-day visit to Cluny in May 1682, Jean Mabillon pored over the one hundred or so medieval manuscripts that still remained in the abbey library. In his *Burgundian Journey*, the Maurist scholar singled out two tenth-century volumes for comment because of their clear connection to Abbot Maiolus.[10] Fortunately, both of these manuscripts survived the dissolution of the great Burgundian abbey at the time of the French Revolution. The first was the abbot's personal copy of Ambrose of Milan's commentary on the Gospel of Luke, which is now preserved in the Bibliothèque nationale de France (Paris, BnF, Nouvelle acquisition latine 1438).[11] At the end of this manuscript, a scribe has written: "This book was offered at the altar

---

9. On Maiolus's activity in the Ottonian court at Pavia and the representation of that city and its inhabitants as the recipients of his favor in the earliest hagiographical account of the abbot's life (*BHL* 5180), see Bruce, *Cluny and the Muslims of La Garde-Freinet*, pp. 32–33 and 42–49.

10. Jean Mabillon's *Itinerarium Burgundicum* was published posthumously in *Ouvrages posthumes de Jean Mabillon et de Thierri Ruinart*, ed. V. Thuillier, 2 vols. (Paris, 1724), vol. 2, pp. 1–33, at p. 22.

11. For a description of this book, see L. Delisle, *Inventaire des manuscrits de la bibliothèque nationale: Fonds du Cluni* (Paris, 1884), pp. 44–45 (no. 19). For the Latin text, see Ambrose, *Expositio evangelii secundum Lucam*, ed. M. Adriaen, CCSL 14 (Turnhout, 1957).

of Saint Peter at the abbey of Cluny by a vow of the lord and most reverent abbot Maiolus" followed by a malediction formula to ward against the theft of the manuscript.[12] The second volume associated directly with Maiolus was a manuscript of Hrabanus Maurus's ninth-century commentary on the book of Jeremiah (*Expositiones in Hieremiam*; now London, British Library, Additional 22820).[13] A colophon on the final leaf of this sumptuous manuscript reads: "This book was written by the order of the lord abbot Maiolus by Herimann, a priest, albeit unworthy and the least of all monks, and it was offered to Saint Peter at the abbey of Cluny by the vow of the beloved father."[14] Although it is rare to have such a clear indication that particular books were linked so closely to an early abbot of Cluny, the lack of contemporary marginalia in these manuscripts and the absence of any writings by Maiolus means that we cannot map with confidence how he may have read or understood these works of late antique and Carolingian biblical exegesis.

Parts of a composite manuscript now housed in the Vatican Library (Vatican City, Biblioteca Apostolica Vaticana, Reg. Lat. 1709) may have once belonged to Maiolus as well.[15] This collection of ancient and early medieval poetry includes sections composed in the ninth, tenth, and eleventh centuries that preserve works of pagan authors like Priscian and Ovid alongside those of Christian poets like Venantius Fortunatus and Sedulius.[16] The portion of the manuscript devoted to Ovid's *Fasti* (fols. 36-99) bears the title "Ovidius Maiolii" (fol. 36). This title has led

---

12. Paris, BnF, Nouvelle acquisition latine 1438, p. 308: "Liber oblatus ad altare sancti Petri Cluniensis coenobii ex voto domni atque reuerentissimi Maioli abbatis. Si quis illum a iam dicto loco abstaxerit, seu furtim abtulerit, sit anathema maranatha, et dicat omnis populus: Fiat. Fiat. Fiat. Amen. Amen. Amen." On monastic curse formulas, see L. Little, *Benedictine Maledictions: Liturgical Cursing in Romanesque France* (Ithaca, 1993).

13. *Catalogue of Additions to the Manuscripts in the British Museum in the Years 1854-1860: Additional MSS. 19,720-24,026* (London, 1875), p. 739 (no. 22,820); and R. Kottje, *Verzeichnis der Handschriften mit den Werken des Hrabanus Maurus* (Hanover, 2012), p. 87 (no. 487), with references to earlier literature.

14. London, British Library, Additional 22820, fol. 327v: "Hic liber descriptus est jussu domini Maioli abbatis ab Herimanno sacerdote, licet indigno, et monachorum omnium ultimo et praelibati patris uoto oblatus S. Petro Cluniacensi coenobio."

15. For a description of this manuscript and its contents, see *Les manuscrits classiques latins de la bibliothèque Vaticane II.1: Fonds Patetta et fonds de la Reine*, ed. E. Pellegrin et al. (Paris, 1978), pp. 383-86.

16. As Anna Taylor has shown, this marriage of Roman and Christian poets in a single manuscript was not at all unusual in a tenth-century monastic context, in which proficiency in the composition of Latin poetry was central to the intellectual formation of early medieval monks. See A. L. Taylor, *Epic Lives and Monasticism in the Middle Ages, 800-1050* (Cambridge, MA, 2013).

some scholars to speculate that this portion of the book or its exemplar was once in the possession of the abbot of Cluny.[17] Paleographical affinities suggest strongly that parts of this manuscript originated at the abbey of Fleury-sur-Loire, which was reformed by Maiolus's predecessor Abbot Odo of Cluny (927-942), and had close ties with the great Burgundian abbey throughout the tenth century. This lends weight to the claim that parts of the manuscript may have once belonged to Maiolus, but the lack of any other corroborating evidence prevents us from using Maiolus's "Ovid" as a source for the literary predilections of the abbot of Cluny. Ultimately, it is the silence of Maiolus that conspires most successfully against the reconstruction of the books that he may have actually read.[18]

Clandestine Codices

The kidnapping of Maiolus of Cluny loomed large in the imagination of Cluniac monks throughout the eleventh and twelfth centuries. Accounts of this harrowing episode appeared no fewer than four times between the years 1000 and 1150 in several works of hagiography dedicated to extolling the virtues of the holy abbot of Cluny: (a) an anonymous *Life of Maiolus*, composed by a monk of Pavia in the late 990s to commemorate the rededication of a church in his honor;[19] (b) a second *Life of Maiolus* written around 1010 by a Cluniac monk named Syrus at the request of Abbot Odilo to counter the Pavians's claim to a special relationship with Maiolus and to secure control of the cult at Cluny;[20] (c) a condensed account of the life of Maiolus composed by Abbot Odilo around 1033 for the liturgical use of the brethren of Romainmôtier;[21] and lastly (d) a thorough rewriting of this tradition by Nalgod of Cluny

---

17. *Les manuscrits classiques latins de la bibliothèque Vaticane II.1*, ed. Pellegrin, p. 385: "Le titre du f. 36: OVIDIUS MAIOLII signifierait que cette partie a appartenu à S. Maieul abbé de Cluny (d. 984) [sic for 994]?"

18. The only surviving document plausibly composed by Maiolus himself was a brief ransom note dictated while he was in captivity in the summer of 972. See chapter 3, above.

19. *Vita breuior sancti Maioli* (*BHL* 5180), in *BC*, cols. 1763-82. D. Iogna-Prat, *Agni Immaculati*, pp. 27-29 has persuasively argued that *BHL* 5180 is the earliest account of Maiolus's life and not a redaction of the early eleventh-century *Vita sancti Maioli* by Syrus of Cluny (cited in the next note), as the Bollandists presumed.

20. Syrus, *Vita sancti Maioli* (*BHL* 5177/79), ed. Iogna-Prat, in *Agni Immaculati*, pp. 163-285. For more on this competition between Pavia and Cluny, see chapter 5, below.

21. Odilo, *Vita sancti Maioli* (*BHL* 5182/84), in *BC*, cols. 279-90, repr. in *PL* 142, cols. 959-62.

at the request of Abbot Peter the Venerable (1122-1156).²² Another version of the abduction story appeared in a chronicle written by Rodulphus Glaber, a monk who had spent significant time at Cluny in the 1030s and dedicated his *Five Books of Histories* to Abbot Odilo, perhaps to reconcile himself with his old master after his dismissal from the abbey.²³ Each of these narratives differed in terms of their presentation of the virtues of the saint, the motives and behavior of his Muslim captors, and the circumstances surrounding the abbot's release.²⁴ This should not surprise us. As many studies have shown, medieval hagiographers often tailored their work to address contemporary concerns in the authoritative voices of their holy subjects.²⁵

Two tales of the kidnapping of Maiolus mentioned specific books that the abbot carried hidden on his person. Was it common for prelates to travel with personal manuscripts in the tenth century? Undoubtedly so, but historians must rely on incidental allusions in narrative genres from the period for evidence of this practice and the sources are not as forthcoming as one might like. For his part, Maiolus seems to have traveled with a small library of books. Nalgod's account of his kidnapping remarks that the abbot was surprised to find a small codex hidden beneath his cloak (*sub amictu suo repositum*) after all of his other manuscripts had been lost.²⁶ But such explicit references are rare. Hagiographical texts are much more likely to remark on the movement of large collections of books from one monastic community to another than the habitual transport of personally owned manuscripts by individuals. For example, in his early tenth-century *Life of Odo*, John of Salerno reported that, upon his retirement from life as a secular

---

22. Nalgod, *Vita sancti Maioli* (BHL 5181): *Vita ex prolixoribus coaevorum actis a Nalgodo monacho post sesqui secum contracta*, AASS Maii 2, pp. 657-67.

23. Rodulphus Glaber, *Historiarum Libri Quinque*, ed. and trans. J. France, in *Rodulfus Glaber: The Five Books of Histories and the Life of St. William* (Oxford, 1989), pp. 1-253. For more on Glaber's fraught relationship with Odilo of Cluny, see J. France, "Rodulfus Glaber and the Cluniacs," *Journal of Ecclesiastical History* 39 (1988): 497-508.

24. Bruce, *Cluny and the Muslims of La Garde-Freinet*, pp. 41-62.

25. The rewriting of saints' lives and *miracula* in the early Middle Ages and the opportunities presented to historians by these interventions have attracted considerable attention since the early 2000s. See, for example, the volumes edited by M. Goullet and M. Heinzelmann: *La réécriture hagiographique dans l'Occident médiéval: Transformations formelles et idéologiques* (Ostfildern, 2003); *Miracles, vies et réécriture dans l'Occident médiéval: Actes de l'Atelier 'La réécriture des Miracles' (IHAP, juin 2004) et SHG X-XII: Dossiers des saints de Metz et Laon et de saint Saturnin de Toulouse* (Ostfildern, 2006); and *L'hagiographie mérovingienne à travers ses réécritures* (Ostfildern, 2010).

26. Nalgod, *Vita Maioli* 23: "Cumque ablatis sibi aliis libris suis," AASS Maii 2, p. 662.

canon at Tours, Odo brought one hundred manuscripts with him to the fledging monastery of Cluny.[27] More than century later, a chronicler named Hariulf went one step further by listing the titles of the thirty-six manuscripts that Gerwin of Saint-Vanne brought with him to Normandy in 1045 when he became the abbot of the Norman monastery of Saint-Riquier.[28] In both cases, the movement of the personal libraries of Odo and Gerwin bolstered their integrity and authority as well-read and thus well-qualified monastic leaders.

Codicem, bibliotecam uidelicet

The earliest account of the abduction of Maiolus to feature a clandestine manuscript was Glaber's *Five Books of Histories*, written before its author's death in 1046. Although narrower in scope than his ambitions imply, Glaber claimed that he wrote this chronicle "to tell of what happened in the four parts of the globe" to a contemporary audience bereft of historical writing comparable with Bede and Paul the Deacon.[29] His account of Maiolus's kidnapping appeared in the first book of the *Histories*, in which he related many stories about the early history of Cluny and its abbots.[30] What makes Glaber's *Histories* so distinctive in the literary tradition of Maiolus's abduction, however, is an aside about the beliefs of the abbot's captors. The context for this digression is provided by two short episodes about Maiolus's experience in captivity, both of which Glaber employed to illuminate the sanctity of the holy man. The chronicler's comment is prompted by the discursive activity of the characters that populate his text, the details of which have no parallel in earlier accounts of the kidnapping but may harken back to oral tradition at Cluny. In the first episode, the Muslims offered Maiolus meat and hard bread to eat in captivity, but the abbot declined, saying: "If I should be hungry, then it is the Lord who will provide. I will not eat this, for it is not what I am

---

27. John of Salerno, *Vita Odonis* 1.23: "At ille sumptis secum centum voluminibus librorum, mox ad idem demigravit monasterium." *PL* 133, col. 54

28. Hariulfus, *Chronicon* 4.32, ed. F. Lot, in *Hariulf, Chronique de l'Abbaye de Saint-Riquier (Ve siecle-1104)* (Paris, 1894), pp. 262-64. I am grateful to Steven Vanderputten for sharing this reference with me.

29. Glaber, *Historiarum Libri Quinque* 1.1: "quoniam de quatuor mundani orbis partium euentibus relaturi sumus," ed. France, p. 2.

30. For what follows, see Glaber, *Historiarum Libri Quinque* 1.9, ed. France, pp. 18-23.

used to."[31] Moved by compassion (*pietate ductus*), one of the Muslims responded by rolling up his sleeves, washing his shield, and baking upon it a fresh loaf of bread, which he offered to Maiolus with great reverence, because he recognized the abbot as a man of God. Not all of the Muslims interacted so sympathetically with their captive, however. While carving a piece of wood with a knife, another warrior placed his foot on the bible manuscript (*codicem, bibliotecam uidelicet*) that Maiolus always carried on his person.[32] The abbot reacted to this sacrilege with horror and "certain of the less ferocious" Muslims (*aliqui minus feroces ex ipsis*) recognized that this action was an affront to God and reprimanded their companion. Moved by divine judgment, these warriors later attacked their friend and cut off the foot with which he had offended the Lord.[33] After the discovery and misuse of this manuscript, the key moment in Glaber's narrative arrives when some of the Muslims allegedly recognized the prophets in the abbot's *bibliotheca* as their own. This scene provided the chronicler with an opportunity to digress at length on the error of Muslim belief with respect to Christian prophecy.[34]

Glaber's use of the word *bibliotheca* to describe Maiolus's manuscript raises questions about what kind of codex the abbot may have been carrying on his person when he was captured. In the early Middle Ages, the term *bibliotheca* usually denoted the Bible and this was almost certainly the case here, as Glaber's digression on the Muslim view of the Hebrew prophets suggests.[35] This book may well be the very same codex listed in a library catalog compiled at Cluny in the eleventh century, which included among its bible manuscripts an entry for a

---

31. Glaber, *Historiarum Libri Quinque* 1.9: "Nam cum ei hora prandii obtulissent cibos quibus uescebantur, carnes uidelicet panemque admodum asperum, et dicerent: 'Comede,' respondit: 'Ego enim si esuriero, Domini est me pascere. Ex his tamen non comedam, quia non mihi olim in usu fuerunt'." ed. France, p. 20
32. On the use of the word *bibliotheca* to describe this manuscript, see n. 35, below.
33. Glaber, *Historiarum Libri Quinque* 1.9, ed. France, p. 20.
34. Glaber, *Historiarum Libri Quinque* 1.9, ed. France, pp. 20-22.
35. M. Duchet-Suchaux and Y. Lefèvre, "Les noms de la Bible," in *Bible de Tous les Temps 4: Le Moyen Age et la Bible* (Paris, 1984), pp. 13-23. The term could also denote other comprehensive collections of authoritative materials, like the "library of histories" (*bibliotheca historiarum*), an extensive liturgical compendium, commissioned from Hrabanus Maurus by Emperor Lothar I in the early 850s. See M. de Jong, "The Empire as *Ecclesia:* Hrabanus Maurus and Biblical *Historia* for Rulers," in *The Uses of the Past in the Early Middle Ages*, ed. Y. Hen and M. Innes (Cambridge, 2000), pp. 191-226, at pp. 191-94.

bibliotheca that once belonged to Maiolus.[36] But what manner of bible was it? Single-volume bibles (often called pandects) were exceedingly rare in the early Middle Ages.[37] Most of the surviving examples were hefty large-format manuscripts intended for public reading in the church, like the sumptuous codex that Oswald of Worchester donated to Ramsey Abbey in the late tenth century.[38] Easily portable bibles of the kind that individuals might carry while traveling did not appear until the late twelfth century and became common only in the thirteenth.[39] Either Maiolus was carrying a very early example of a private portable bible, the likes of which have not survived from the tenth century, or his personal *biblioteca* did not contain the sum of Christian scriptures. Given Glaber's mention of the Hebrew prophets, the abbot of Cluny was probably carrying a codex containing a selection of books from the Old Testament. Monastic communities purposefully created manuscripts dedicated to the books of the prophets for liturgical readings between Passion Sunday and Holy Week and for the months of November and December, when they read Ezechiel, Daniel, the minor prophets, and Isaiah in preparation for Christmas Week.[40]

---

36. See Delisle, *Inventaire des manuscrits*, p. 337 (no. 3): "Volumen secunde bibliothece, que fuit beati Mayoli." For the argument that the core of this catalog belonged to the abbacy of Hugh the Great (1049–1109) rather than that of Hugh III (1158–1161), see V. von Büren, "Le grand catalogue de la Bibliothèque de Cluny," in *Le gouvernement d'Hugues de Semur à Cluny: Actes du Colloque scientifique international* (*Cluny, septembre 1988*) (Mâcon, 1990), pp. 245–63.

37. For an introduction to early medieval bibles, see M. P. Brown, "Spreading the Word," in *In the Beginning: Bibles Before the Year 1000*, ed. M. P. Brown (Philadelphia, 2006), pp. 45–75. For examples of single-volume bibles from this period, see C. de Hamel, *The Book: A History of the Bible* (New York, 2001), pp. 36–37, 50–52, and 72–77.

38. Byrhtferth, *Vita Oswaldi* 5.11: "Inter cetera magnifica munera que ibidem dependit, dedit gloriosum pandecten, id est, bibliothecam egregiam." ed. M. Lapidge, in *Byrhtferth of Ramsey: The Lives of St. Oswald and St. Ecgwine* (Oxford, 2009), p. 172. This manuscript has not survived, but compare London, British Library, Royal I.E.VII–VIII, the sole surviving pandect from Anglo-Saxon England, created at Christ Church, Canterbury, in the decades around 1000: *Catalogue of Western Manuscripts in the Old Royal and King's Collections*, ed. G. F. Warner and J. P. Gilson, 4 vols. (London, 1921), vol. 1, pp. 20–21; and H. Gneuss and M. Lapidge, *Anglo-Saxon Manuscripts: A Bibliographical Handlist of Manuscripts and Manuscript Fragments Written or Owned in England up to 1100* (Toronto, 2014), p. 370 (no. 449). I am grateful to Tessa Webber for the reference to Byrhtferth.

39. The modest Waltham Abbey Bible (created around 1200) is one of the earliest examples of a portable bible of this kind. See *The Libraries of the Augustinian Canons*, ed. A. G. Webber and A. G. Watson, Corpus of British Medieval Library Catalogues 6 (London, 1998), p. 428. For further examples from the thirteenth century, see de Hamel, *The Book*, pp. 114–39.

40. For a list of eleventh-century examples from Montecassino, see R. Gyug, "Early Medieval Bibles, Biblical Books, and the Monastic Liturgy in the Beneventan Region," in *The Practice of the Bible in the Middle Ages: Production, Reception, and Performance in Western Christianity*, ed. S. Boynton and D. J. Reilly (New York, 2011), pp. 34–60, at p. 45.

In fact, several examples of volumes containing the major and minor prophets appear in Cluny's eleventh-century library catalog.[41] It seems likely, then, that Maiolus's *biblioteca* was a portable manuscript of the books of the Old Testament prophets rather than a complete bible.

Cogitis me

By the turn of the twelfth century, stories about Maiolus of Cluny were in wide circulation. In addition to a robust hagiographic tradition, reports of the abbot's miracles enjoyed a strong currency in monastic circles, so much so that in the 1140s Abbot Peter the Venerable of Cluny could make the claim that more legends were told about the virtues of Maiolus throughout all of Europe than any other saint in Christendom besides the Virgin Mary.[42] Peter may have had in mind the dozens of miracles attested at the abbot's tomb in Souvigny, which the brethren of that community recorded throughout the eleventh century before the translation of his holy remains back to Cluny in the 1090s.[43] He was also undoubtedly familiar with a popular *exemplum* allegedly narrated by Maiolus on the benefits of prayer for the dead. Written in the orbit of Cluny in the mid-twelfth century, this story circulated widely in prose and verse retellings in Benedictine and Cistercian houses alike.[44] Peter the Venerable augmented this robust tradition further when he commissioned a monk named Nalgod to compose new accounts of the lives of Cluny's two most illustrious tenth-century abbots, Odo and Maiolus.[45] His concerns were both aesthetic and pragmatic. Nalgod was instructed to improve the literary quality of older hagiographic

---

41. Delisle, *Inventaire des manuscrits*, p. 338 (nos. 7, 10, and 11).

42. Peter the Venerable, *De miraculis* 2.32: "Hac miraculorum gratia in tantum iam per centum sexaginta et duos annos, hoc est a tempore mortis sue claruit, ut post sanctum Dei genitricem, nullum sanctorum in tota Europa nostra in huiusmodi operibus parem habeat," ed. D. Bouthillier, CCCM 83 (Turnhout, 1988), p. 162.

43. *Miraculorum sancti Maioli abbatis libri duo* (BHL 5186), in *BC*, cols. 1787-1814. For more on this miracle collection, see chapter 6, below.

44. For a study of this story cycle, see *The Relatio metrica de duobus ducibus: A Twelfth-Century Cluniac Poem on Prayer for the Dead*, ed. and trans. C. A. Jones and S. G. Bruce (Turnhout, 2016); C. A. Jones, "Relatio prosaica de duobus ducibus/Relatio metrica de duobus ducibus," in *La Trasmissione dei testi latini del medioevo/Medieval Latin Texts and their Transmission* 8, ed. L. Castaldi (Florence, 2023), pp. 145-64; as well as J. Delmulle, "Notes on the Text of the Twelfth-Century Cluniac *Relatio metrica de duobus ducibus*" and G. Hays, "Additional Notes on the *Relatio metrica de duobus ducibus*," *Journal of Medieval Latin* 34 (2024): 71-100 and 101-110, respectively.

45. For a brief account of Nalgod's career, see *Histoire Litteraire de la France*, 47 vols. (Paris, 1733-2021), vol. 11, pp. 167-68, *s.v.* "Nalgode, religieux de l'abbaye de Cluni."

stories about these saintly abbots, but he also attempted to liberate these tales from historical details that no longer aligned with twelfth-century realities, especially with regard to the presentation of Cluny's foundation and Odo's succession as abbot.[46]

Nalgod's retelling of the abduction episode borrowed many of its narrative features from other early eleventh-century *vitae* of Maiolus: the capture of the abbot and his entourage high in the mountain passes, the miraculous healing of the wound that Maiolus received on his hand when he protected a monk from a sword stroke, the power of prayer to unlock the heavy chains that bound the captives, the raising of the ransom at Cluny, and the extirpation of the Muslim community at the hands of a Christian host.[47] But the monk also embroidered his account with new details that were unprecedented in the story's century-old history. Among these was a miracle that began with the unexpected discovery of yet another book. As we have seen, Cluniac tradition held that Maiolus usually traveled with books in his possession. According to Nalgod, while the abbot was in captivity, he marveled to find hidden in the folds of his cloak a short treatise on the Assumption of the Virgin attributed to Jerome, for he presumed that it had been lost, like all of his other books, when the Muslims captured him.[48] This book was in fact not the work of Jerome at all, but in all likelihood the apocryphal treatise known as *Cogitis me*, composed by the ninth-century Carolingian theologian Paschasius Radbertus.[49] Irrespective of its authorship, the discovery of the manuscript brought the abbot great joy. He quickly calculated the number of days until the Feast of the Assumption (August 15) and prayed to Mary that he would be set free by then to celebrate this feast in the company of Christians. Sure enough, when Maiolus woke up the next morning, his chains had fallen away and all subsequent attempts by his captors to bind him again

---

46. This tendency was much more evident in Nalgod's rewriting of John of Salerno's *vita Odonis* than it was in his *vita Maioli*. See D. Iogna-Prat, "La geste des origines dans l'historiographie clunisienne des XIe et XIIe siècles," *Revue bénédictine* 102 (1992): 135–91, at pp. 183–87; repr. in D. Iogna-Prat, *Études clunisiennes* (Paris, 2002), pp. 161–200, at pp. 194–98.

47. Nalgod, *Vita Maioli* 22–25, *AASS* Maii 2, pp. 662–63.

48. Nalgod, *Vita Maioli* 23: "Cumque ablatis sibi aliis libris suis, libellum beati Hieronymi de Assumptione perpetuae Virginis, quem in sinu suo familiari reverentia circumferre solebat, sub amictu suo repositum invenisset," *AASS* Maii 2, p. 662.

49. For the Latin text, see *Pascasius Radbertus, De partu Virginis/De assumptione sanctae Mariae Virginis*, ed. E. A. Matter and A. Ripberger, CCCM 56C (Turnhout, 1985), pp. 97–162. There is helpful commentary on this work in E. A. Matter, *The Voice of My Beloved: The Song of Songs in Western Medieval Christianity* (Philadelphia, 1990), pp. 152–53.

failed when he made the sign of the cross. In the next chapter, Nalgod related that the abbot's prayer had been answered, for a delegation of monks from Cluny soon arrived with the ransom and allowed him to return home before the Feast of the Assumption. If this episode has any historical veracity, then it implies that Maiolus was in captivity for less than three weeks, because he was captured on July 23/24 and freed in time to return to Cluny by August 15.

While the dearth of source material written by Maiolus makes it almost impossible to reconstruct the texts that informed and inspired his forty-year tenure as abbot of Cluny, these accounts of his captivity among the Muslims of La Garde-Freinet in the summer of 972 have preserved a tradition that books were important to Maiolus, for he habitually had them in his possession during his frequent travels abroad. Although the authors of these tales marshaled this information primarily to promote the sanctity of their abbot, their stories must carry at least a kernel of plausibility to meet the expectations of their medieval audiences. Both of these anecdotes—the provocation of the Muslims who discovered their captive's *biblioteca* in Glaber's *Five Books of Histories* and the solace obtained by the abbot upon the miraculous discovery of a treatise about the Virgin deemed lost in Nalgod's *Life of Maiolus*—carry the potent reminder that, in the hands of itinerant prelates, the meaning and value of manuscripts extended far beyond the intellectual pursuits of the cloister to provide hope and comfort even on the darkest days of travel through the bleakest wilderness.

CHAPTER 5

Local Sanctity and Civic Typology in Early Medieval Pavia

The Example of the Cult of Abbot Maiolus of Cluny

Abbot Maiolus of Cluny was a tireless advocate of religious life in tenth-century Europe.[1] He traveled extensively during his forty-year tenure as abbot of Cluny (954–994), both as a reformer of monastic communities and as a broker of peace at the highest level of secular and religious affairs. Maiolus spent considerable time in northern Italy at the city of Pavia, a seat of Ottonian power, where he restored the abbeys of Saint Maria, Saint Salvatore and Saint Pietro in Ciel d'Oro, and negotiated a reconciliation between the estranged German empress Adelaide and her son Otto II.[2] Shortly after the abbot's

---

Originally published as "Local Sanctity and Civic Typology in Early Medieval Pavia: The Example of the Cult of Maiolus of Cluny," in *Cities, Texts and Social Networks, 400–1500: Experiences and Perceptions of Medieval Urban Space*, ed. C. Goodson, A. E. Lester, and C. Symes (Aldershot, 2010), pp. 177–91. Reproduced by permission of Taylor & Francis Group.

1. Maiolus of Cluny has received considerable scholarly attention in the last two decades, in no small part due to the millennial anniversary of his death in 1994. See D. Iogna-Prat, *Agni Immaculati: Recherches sur les sources hagiographiques relatives à saint Maieul de Cluny (954–994)* (Paris, 1988); *Saint Maïeul, Cluny et la Provence: Expansion d'une abbaye à l'aube du moyen âge*, ed. D. Iogna-Prat et al. (Mane, 1994); and *Saint Mayeul et son temps: Actes du congrès international de Valensole, 12–14 mai 1994* (Dignes-les-Bains, 1997).

2. On early medieval Pavia, in general, see D. A. Bullough, "Urban Change in Early Medieval Italy: The Example of Pavia," *Papers of the British School at Rome* 34 (1966): 82–130; and A. Settia, "Economia e società nella Pavia ottoniana," *Archivio storico Lombardo* 122 (1996): 11–28. On the activity of Maiolus in Pavia in particular, see *San Maiolo e le influenze Cluniacensi*

death in 994, a monk of Pavia was the first to hail Maiolus as a saint by composing a *vita* to commemorate his holy life.³ This work of hagiography was an important vehicle of self-promotion for the inhabitants of Pavia in that it portrayed their city as the setting for Maiolus's miracles and exhibited its citizens as the special recipients of the saint's favor. The anonymous author of the earliest *Life of Maiolus* emphasized the relationship between the people of Pavia and the Cluniac holy man by explicitly comparing their city to the ancient port-towns of Sidon and Tyre, whose inhabitants Christ had singled out for their penitent character. He also made direct references in the *vita* both to local venues where miracles took place and to local individuals healed by the abbot's prayers.

This study argues that the self-conscious localization of the manifest *virtus* of Abbot Maiolus in the urban landscape of Pavia constructed and confirmed a privileged relationship between the Cluniac saint and the city's inhabitants.⁴ After taking account of the abbot's activities in Italy and his involvement with the Ottonian court, I examine in this chapter how the author of the earliest *Life of Maiolus* employed a typology of biblical cities to make the case that Pavia and its inhabitants enjoyed the special protection of the abbot of Cluny. In doing so, the author deliberately elided the tenth-century experiences of the citizens of Pavia with those of their counterparts in Sidon and Tyre, thus fostering the perception that the manifest holiness of Christ's earthly ministry was also active in and around their city through the activity of one of his saints, Maiolus of Cluny. This claim on the abbot's sanctity did not escape the attention of monks in Burgundy. Within a decade of the composition of the earliest *Life of Maiolus*, the Cluniacs commissioned

---

nell'*Italia del Nord: Atti del Convegno Internationale nel Millenario di San Maiolo (994–1994) Pavia-Novara, 23-24 settembre 1994*, ed. E. Cau and A. Settia (Como, 1998). There is no comprehensive study of the relationship between the Ottonians and the abbey of Cluny, but for general orientation, see S. Barret, "Cluny et les Ottoniens," in *Ottone III e Romualdo di Ravenna: Impero, monasteri e santi asceti*, Atti del XXIV convegno del Centro Studi Avellaniti, Fonte Avellana, 2002 (Verona, 2003), pp. 179–213.

3. *Vita breuior sancti Maioli* (BHL 5180), in *BC*, cols. 1763-82. The significance of this *vita* as the earliest account of Maiolus's life, rather than a redaction of the early eleventh-century *vita* by Syrus of Cluny (*BHL* 5177/79), as the Bollandists presumed, has been persuasively demonstrated by Iogna-Prat (*Agni Immaculati*, pp. 20–29). For the sake of simplicity, I am assuming that the work had a single author, but it may have been the collective endeavor of several members of a monastic community.

4. For another study of the function of early medieval hagiography as an expression of a local, civic identity, although without reference to biblical typologies, see K. Krönert, "Le role de l'hagiographie dans la mise en place d'une identité locale aux Xe-XIe siècles: L'exemple de Trèves," in *Constructions de l'espace au Moyen Âge: Practique et representations* (Paris, 2007), pp. 379-89.

74   CHAPTER 5

a new account of his life that excised many of the urban details specific to Pavia and thereby revoked the Pavians' claim on the sanctity of their spiritual father. I conclude this chapter with a consideration of the significance of this initiative for the rise of Cluniac abbatial hagiography in the eleventh century.

A Tenth-Century Abbot at Work

Maiolus of Cluny remains very much in the shadow of his abbatial successors, Odilo (994–1049) and Hugh the Great (1049–1109), in part because the tenures of these long-lived and influential abbots coincided with a period of unprecedented growth at the great Burgundian monastery.[5] Over the course of the eleventh century, monastic vocations at Cluny tripled from approximately one hundred individuals to more than three hundred, an increase that strained from the resources of the community and challenged the integrity of personal discipline among the brethren.[6] Moreover, the physical fabric of the abbey complex expanded apace with this dramatic rise in vocations. In autumn 1095, a month before preaching the First Crusade at Clermont, Pope Urban II consecrated the high altar of Cluny's new basilica (known to historians as Cluny III), which upon its completion became the largest church in western Christendom.[7] When Hugh the Great died in 1109, few alive could remember a time when he was not the abbot of Cluny and no monastic community in Europe could rival the Cluniacs in terms of their religious and political influence and the awe-inspiring opulence of their primary place of worship.

The eleventh-century achievements for which the Cluniacs are best remembered were constructed on a foundation laid in the tenth century.[8] Much of Cluny's success as a religious community belongs

---

5. Most general studies of Cluny's history emphasize the eleventh century as a period of expansion. See N. Hunt, *Cluny Under Saint Hugh, 1049–1109* (Notre Dame, IN, 1967); and J. Wollasch, *Cluny, Licht der Welt: Aufstieg und Niedergang der klösterlichen Gemeinschaft* (Düsseldorf and Zürich, 1996).

6. For a summary of the evidence, see Hunt, *Cluny Under Saint Hugh*, pp. 82–83. On the strategies employed by the Cluniacs and others to prevent lapses in discipline in large monastic communities, see chapter 7, below.

7. On Cluny III, see N. Stratford, "The Documentary Evidence for the Building of Cluny III," in N. Stratford, *Studies in Burgundian Romanesque Sculpture*, 2 vols. (London, 1998), vol. 1, pp. 41–59.

8. On Cluny's place in tenth-century monasticism, see B. H. Rosenwein, *Rhinoceros Bound: Cluny in the Tenth Century* (Philadelphia, 1982); and G. Constable, "Cluny in the Monastic World of the Tenth Century," in *Il secolo di ferro: Mito e realtà del secolo X (Spoleto,*

to the active promotion by Maiolus and his successors of the efficacy of Cluniac prayer in releasing the souls of the sinful dead from torment. According to Dominique Iogna-Prat, donations of revenue-producing land to Cluny in exchange for monastic prayers on behalf of Christian souls increased exponentially in the second half of the tenth century. Contracts expressing the terms of these agreements survive in modest numbers from Cluny's early years—29 from the abbacy of Berno (910-927); 126 from the abbacy of Odo (927-942); and 194 from the abbacy of Aymard (942-954)—before rising to unprecedented heights under Maiolus (1,096 charters dating from 954-994), when the reputation of the Cluniacs as intercessors for the dead reached its peak.[9] The creation of a special day of prayerful intercession for all Christian souls (November 2) by Maiolus's successor Odilo should be understood as a response to the popularity of prayer for the dead at Cluny that had gained its momentum during the abbacy of Maiolus.[10] Moreover, it was under Maiolus that the Cluniac scriptorium first emerged as an important venue of manuscript production in tenth-century Europe.[11] Following their abbot's direction, scribes also composed the earliest collection of the liturgical customs of Cluny, an important step toward the massive efforts to

---

19-25 aprile 1990) (Spoleto, 1991), pp. 391-437, repr. in G. Constable, *The Abbey of Cluny: A Collection of Essays to Mark the Eleven-Hundredth Anniversary of Its Foundation* (Berlin, 2010), pp. 43-79.

9. D. Iogna-Prat, *Order and Exclusion: Cluny and Christendom Face Heresy, Judaism, and Islam (1000-1150)*, trans. G. R. Edwards (Ithaca, 2002), p. 224.

10. The Cluniac sources for this tradition include: Jotsaldus, *Vita Odilonis* 2.15, ed. J. Staub, in *Iotsald von Saint-Claude, Vita des Abtes Odilo von Cluny*, MGH Scriptores rerum Germanicarum 68 (Hanover, 1999), pp. 218-20; and Rodulphus Glaber, *Historiarum libri quinque* 5.1.13, ed. J. France, in *Rodulphus Glaber: The Five Books of Histories and the Life of St. William* (Oxford, 1989), pp. 234-37. For more on prayer for the dead at Cluny in this period, see D. Iogna-Prat, "The Dead in the Celestial Bookkeeping of the Cluniac Monks Around the Year 1000," in *Debating the Middle Ages*, ed. L. Little and B. H. Rosenwein (Oxford, 1998), pp. 340-62; and U. Longo, "Riti e agiografia: L'istituzione della *commemoratio omnium fidelium defunctorum* nelle *Vitae* di Odilone di Cluny," *Bullettino dell'Istituto storico italiano per il Medio Evo e Archivio Muratoriano* 103 (2002): 163-200.

11. For evidence of scribal industry at Cluny in the late tenth century, see M.-C. Garand, "Copistes de Cluny au temps de saint Maieul (948-994)," *Bibliothèque de l'Ecole des Chartes* 136 (1978): 5-36; and F. Crivello, "Les débuts de l'activité artistique dans le *scriptorium* de Cluny: Fondements et œuvres," in *Cluny: Les moines et la société au premier âge féodal*, ed. D. Iogna-Prat et al. (Rennes, 2013), pp. 197-208. More generally on the Cluniac scriptorium, see J.-P. Aniel, "Le scriptorium de Cluny au Xe et XIe siècle," in *Le gouvernement d'Hugues de Semur à Cluny* (Mâcon, 1990), pp. 265-81; and S. Barret, "Cluny et son scriptorium (Xe-XIe siècles)," in *Cluny ou la puissance des moines: Histoire de l'abbaye et de son ordre, 910-1790* (Dijon, 2001), pp. 48-53.

codify the abbey's received traditions and legal records that occurred in the late eleventh century.¹²

During his forty-year tenure as abbot, Maiolus traveled repeatedly over the Alps to Pavia in pursuit of his religious ideals and in defense of Cluniac interests.¹³ The perils of long-distance travel in the tenth century were considerable. In July 972, Muslim brigands from the citadel of *Fraxinetum* (modern La Garde-Freinet, near Saint-Tropez in Provence) abducted the abbot and his entourage as they crossed the Great Saint Bernard Pass en route from Italy to Burgundy.¹⁴ These adventurers supplemented their income as mercenaries and pirates by kidnapping and ransoming merchants and pilgrims who crossed the Alps in great numbers during the summer months. A ransom note from Maiolus sent the monks of Cluny scrambling to raise the funds to free him. This affront to such a well-respected individual kindled the ire of local lords. Shortly after the abbot's release, an army led by Count William of Arles destroyed the Muslim enclave at *Fraxinetum* and effectively eliminated the threat they posed to Provence and the Alpine Passes.

Maiolus's saintly reputation attracted the attention of Emperor Otto I and his wife Adelaide of Italy, who enlisted his expertise to reform several monastic communities in their Italian territories, including Saint Apollinare in Classe near Ravenna.¹⁵ The abbot of Cluny soon became Otto and Adelaide's religious adviser and confidant—"the ear and repository of imperial secrets"—and spent considerable time at the imperial palace in Pavia.¹⁶ His relationship with the royal couple was

---

12. *Consuetudines Cluniacensium antiquiores cum redactionibus derivatis*, ed. Kassius Hallinger, CCM 7.2 (Siegburg, 1983). The late eleventh-century customaries of Bernard and Ulrich have received considerable attention since the early 2000s, but both works still await modern critical editions. See Bernard of Cluny, *Ordo Cluniacensis sive Consuetudines*, ed. M. Herrgott, in *Vetus Disciplina Monastica* (Paris, 1726), pp. 136–364; and Ulrich of Zell, *Consuetudines Cluniacensis*, PL 149, cols. 643–779. For a collection of studies that highlights the value of the Cluniac customaries as historical sources, see *From Dead of Night to End of Day: The Medieval Customs of Cluny / De coeur de la nuit à la fin du jour: Les coutumes clunisiennes au moyen âge*, ed. S. Boynton and I. Cochelin, Disciplina Monastica 3 (Leiden, 2005).

13. L. Bourdon, "Les voyages de Saint Mayeul en Italie: Itinéraires et chronologie," *Mélanges d'archéologie et d'histoire* 43 (1926): 63–89.

14. For what follows, see P. A. Amargier, "La capture de saint Maieul de Cluny et l'expulsion des Sarrasins de Provence," *Revue bénédictine* 73 (1963): 316–23; and chapter 3, above.

15. Syrus, *Vita sancti Maioli* 2.20, ed. Iogna-Prat, *Agni Immaculati*, p. 239. On the reform of Saint Apollinare in Classe, which occurred toward the end of 971, see Syrus, *Vita sancti Maioli* 2.23, ed. Iogna-Prat, *Agni Immaculati*, pp. 243–44.

16. Syrus, *Vita sancti Maioli* 2.22: "Hunc imperator habebat auricularium, hunc a secretis fidum internuntium," ed. Iogna-Prat, *Agni Immaculati*, pp. 242–43. The translation is from L. M. Smith, *The Early History of the Monastery of Cluny* (Oxford, 1920), p. 105.

such that anyone who had obtained an audience with the emperor first sought out the abbot to act as an intermediary on their behalf.[17] Shortly after Otto's death in 973, Adelaide and her son Otto II nominated Maiolus as pope, but he demurred, explaining that he could not abandon the souls in his care at Cluny and predicting that the citizens of Rome would chafe under the rule of a bishop from Gaul.[18] When relations between Adelaide and Otto II soured in 978 after the latter's marriage to the Byzantine princess Theophanu, it was the abbot of Cluny who brokered the peace between them.[19] This close relationship with the Ottonian dynasty made Maiolus one of the most powerful and influential prelates in all of tenth-century Europe.

Because of his ever-increasing eminence and his frequent sojourns in Pavia, Maiolus became the spiritual father of several local monastic communities at the behest of a wide range of sponsors.[20] In the summer of 967, a judge of the imperial court named Gaidulf sold a small chapel in Pavia to Adalgis, a local priest, who immediately donated the property to Cluny. The chapel, rededicated to Saints Mary and Michael, became a Cluniac dependency under the direction of Maiolus.[21] A few years later, in 972, Empress Adelaide bequeathed the abbey of Saint Salvatore near Pavia to the abbot of Cluny, who agreed to enforce the precepts of the *Rule of Benedict* among the monks who lived there.[22] Finally, in 987, Pope John XV invited Maiolus to undertake the reform of Saint Pietro in Ciel d'Oro in Pavia, a task that he embraced with enthusiasm.[23] Ties of spiritual affiliation bound the abbot of Cluny to many of Pavia's religious communities. By the end of his life, Maiolus was undoubtedly the most prominent figure in the religious landscape of the imperial capital and a firm fixture in the imagination of its citizens.

---

17. Syrus, *Vita sancti Maioli* 2.22: "Si quis apud imperatorem aliquod haberet negotium, mediatorem beatum quaerebat Maiolum," ed. Iogna-Prat, *Agni Immaculati*, p. 243.

18. Syrus, *Vita sancti Maioli* 3.10, ed. Iogna-Prat, *Agni Immaculati*, pp. 260-63.

19. Syrus, *Vita sancti Maioli* 3.11, ed. Iogna-Prat, *Agni Immaculati*, pp. 263-66. See also *Annales Magdeburgensis* (anno 978), ed. Georg Pertz, MGH Scriptores 16 (Hanover, 1859), p. 154.

20. For what follows, see J. Leclercq, "S. Maiolo fondatore e reformatore di monasteri a Pavia," in *Atti del 4° congresso internazionale di studi sull'alto medioevo, Pavia-Scaldasole-Monza-Bobbio, 10-14 settembre 1967* (Spoleto, 1969), pp. 155-73, at pp. 155-57; and Rosenwein, *Rhinoceros Bound*, pp. 51-55.

21. For the documents relevant to this donation and the dispute that resulted from it due to the disaffection of Gaidulf's heirs, see BB, vol. 2, pp. 308-19 (nos. 1228 and 1229, dated 967).

22. A. Colombo, "I diplomati ottoniani e adelaidini e la fondazione del monastero di S. Salvatore di Pavia," *Biblioteca della Società storica subalpine* 130 (1932): 1-39.

23. *Vita breuior sancti Maioli* 18, in BC, col. 1775.

Hagiography and Civic Typology

Given the strong associations between Maiolus of Cluny and the city of Pavia, it is not surprising that a local monastic community took the initiative to publicize the benefits of this relationship in a work of hagiography. As André Vauchez reminds us, the papacy did not begin to reserve the right to recognize holy people through the process of canonization until the late eleventh century.[24] With few exceptions, the decades around 1000 witnessed the creation of local saints by bishops, secular prelates, and abbots, without any intervention on the part of the popes. In the case of Maiolus, the occasion for the composition of his earliest *vita* was in probably the rededication of a Pavian church in honor of his memory. In the late 990s, with the consent of Abbot Odilo of Cluny, the local monastery of S. Maria became the church of Saint Maiolo.[25] In all likelihood, the earliest *Life of Maiolus* was a literary commemoration of the late abbot's association with Pavia in general and with the monks of the renamed abbey church in particular, a hypothesis supported by the prominence that the author affords to the city in the last chapters of the *vita*.

Although the earliest *Life of Maiolus* follows literary conventions familiar from other works of early medieval hagiography, the content of the text differed considerably from contemporary saints' lives in two ways: first, the author devoted a great deal of attention to Maiolus's harrowing encounter with Muslim adventurers; and second, the *vita* singled out the citizens of Pavia as the special recipients of the saint's attention, as witnessed by the abbot's miraculous interventions among them. The twenty-six chapters of the *Life of Maiolus* fall roughly into five thematic parts. The opening chapters treat the youth and early religious career of Maiolus and recount his first miracle.[26] The second part of the

---

24. A. Vauchez, *Sainthood in the Later Middle Ages*, trans. J. Birrell (Cambridge, 1997), pp. 13–21.

25. Jotsaldus, *Vita Odilonis* 1.14: "Apud Papiam sancti Maioli nobilissimus locus," ed. Staub, in *Iotsald von Saint-Claude*, p. 172. The implication is that Odilo endorsed the renaming of the abbey but did not sanction the Pavian *vita* that was written to celebrate it. For the date of this event, which is contested, see C. Manaresi, "La fondazione del monasterio di S. Maiolo di Pavia," in *Spiritualità Cluniacense, 12-15 ottobre 1958* (Todi, 1960), pp. 274–85; and M. A. Casagrande, "Fondazione e suiluppo del monasterio cluniacense di San Maiolo di Pavia nei primi secoli," in *Atti del 4o congresso internazionale di studi sull'alto medioevo*, pp. 335–51. On Odilo's industry with respect to constructing new churches both at home and abroad, see J. Hourlier, "Saint Odilon bâtisseur," *Revue Mabillon* 51 (1961): 303–24.

26. *Vita breuior sancti Maioli* 1–4, in *BC*, cols. 1763–67.

vita follows his entry into monastic life at Cluny, his election as abbot, and his activities as the head of the community.[27] The author of the *vita* then devotes several chapters to the abduction of Maiolus by Muslim brigands in the summer of 972, making this episode the central feature of the work. This captivity narrative, which is based on eyewitness accounts from monks in the abbot's entourage who were kidnapped with him, is unprecedented in the early medieval hagiographical tradition.[28] There follows an enumeration of the miracles performed by Maiolus, many of which took place in the city of Pavia.[29] Finally, the *vita* concludes with an unusually laconic report of the final days of the abbot.[30] Unlike many contemporary works of hagiography, there is no mention of postmortem manifestations of the saint's miraculous powers, perhaps because the work was undertaken so soon after the abbot's death. The earliest *Life of Maiolus* did not enjoy a wide circulation after its composition. The text, or portions thereof, survive in only four manuscripts and in an early seventeenth-century edition based on two medieval witnesses that are no longer extant. In addition, two medieval breviaries include short excerpts from the work for liturgical use and twelfth-century account of the death of Maiolus paraphrases the preface and first chapter of the text.[31]

By composing a *vita* about the abbot of Cluny, the newly rededicated community of Saint Maiolo in Pavia made public its claim to the special protection of a powerful holy man who had been a frequent resident of their city. To this end, the earliest *Life of Maiolus* had a decidedly local inflection. Several of the miracle stories related in the *vita* took place in the city of Pavia. The author of the work underscored the importance of the city as a venue for the saint's manifest *virtus* in two distinct ways. First, he praised Pavia as the hub of a far-flung network of commerce comparable to the biblical cities of Sidon and Tyre. Like the inhabitants of these eastern Mediterranean entrepôts, the author claimed that the people of Pavia were especially repentant in character and thus receptive to the miraculous intervention of the Cluniac saint, just as those of Sidon and Tyre had been open to the message of Christ and duly rewarded with miracles. Second, among the Pavian miracle stories the

---

27. *Vita breuior sancti Maioli* 5–6, in *BC*, cols. 1767–69.
28. *Vita breuior sancti Maioli* 7–13, in *BC*, cols. 1769–72.
29. *Vita breuior sancti Maioli* 14–26, in *BC*, cols. 1772–81.
30. *Vita breuior sancti Maioli* 26, in *BC*, cols. 1781–82.
31. On the manuscript tradition of *BHL* 5180, see Iogna-Prat, *Agni Immaculati*, pp. 24–27.

vita mentions by name a prominent imperial official who had benefited from the healing power of Maiolus. This anecdote rooted the power of the saint in the living fabric of the city while providing contemporary Pavian readers and listeners with a concrete referent to the lasting impact of the abbot's presence among them.

The earliest *Life of Maiolus* compares the city of Pavia explicitly with Sidon and Tyre, biblical port towns of Phoenician origin, which lay about twenty miles apart on the coastline of what is now modern Lebanon.[32] Both Sidon and Tyre were bustling commercial centers in the ancient world.[33] They were current in the early medieval imagination through accounts of the journeys of the apostle Paul, who tarried in Tyre for a week at the end of his third mission to Greece and Asia Minor (Acts 21:3–7) and later docked in Sidon at the beginning of his fateful voyage to Malta, which ended in shipwreck (Acts 27:3). Although they are often mentioned as a pair, Tyre enjoyed a privileged place over its neighbor and rival because of its most renowned industry, the production of an expensive purple dye cultivated from a marine snail common in eastern Mediterranean waters, the Murex brandaris.[34] This dye was highly prized in the Roman period and well into the Middle Ages both for its extraordinary color and for the tenacity of its hue. The widespread use of "Tyrrean purple" in the royal courts of early medieval Europe and Byzantium sustained an enduring image of Tyre as a city that had grown prosperous through commercial enterprise.[35]

By the year 1000, the comparison of Tyre and Sidon to Pavia was a plausible one. Although the evidence is not abundant, it seems quite clear that the imperial seat of the Ottonians in northern Italy was a thriving commercial center well situated on a lucrative transalpine route

---

32. *Vita breuior sancti Maioli* 17: "Quae multiplicibus populorum referta turbis, nobilium et diuersarum mercium speciebus insignis, quasi quaedam Tyrus et Sydon videtur remansisse, quibus complacet ad sui mercimonii comparationem et venditionem venire," in *BC*, col. 1775.

33. In a lamentation for Tyre, the prophet Ezekiel called the city "merchant of the peoples on many coastlines" (Ezek. 27:3).

34. For what follows, see L. B. Jensen, "Royal Purple of Tyre," *Journal of Near Eastern Studies* 22 (1963): 104–18. Later Roman mythographers credited the discovery of this commodity to Hercules, who noticed that his dog had stained its mouth a deep purple while chewing on these snails. See, for example, Julius Pollux, *Onomasticon* 1.45–49, ed. E. Bethe, in *Pollucis Onomasticon*, 3 vols. (Leipzig 1900–37), vol. 1, pp. 14–15.

35. See the work of A. Muthesius, whose most important articles have been collected in *Studies in Byzantine and Islamic Silk Weaving* (London, 1995); *Studies in Silk in Byzantium* (London, 2004); and *Studies in Byzantine, Islamic and Near Eastern Silk Weaving* (London, 2008).

that connected northern Europe with the riches of the Mediterranean.[36] An early eleventh-century account of the duties of imperial officials at the Ottonian court in Pavia (*Honorantiae Civitatis Papiae*) paints a vivid portrait of an artery of trade stretching from England to Venice, along which moved a slow and steady traffic of animals, slaves, cloth, precious metals, and weapons.[37] In the ninth and tenth centuries, silk and other fine goods made their way up the Po River from Venice to the markets of Pavia. In the 890s, Venetian traders active in the city sought out the saintly nobleman Gerald of Aurillac to sell him their wares, including cloaks and spices, as he camped near Pavia en route from Rome to Burgundy.[38] By the early eleventh century, Pavia and Ferrara, a market town in the Po watershed near Ravenna, enjoyed a monopoly on the sale of silks in Italy.

Long-distance trade made the citizens of Pavia prosperous, a fact that found expression in a rich array of religious and domestic building projects. In 924, the chronicler Flodoard of Reims characterized the city as a place brimming with people and crowded with magnificent structures (*Papiam quoque urbem populosissimam atque opulentissimam*).[39] According to his chronicle, a Magyar raid on Pavia damaged forty-four churches, which suggests a high density of sacred buildings within the city limits.[40] Moreover, charter evidence from the tenth century suggests that Pavia boasted a large number of impressive private residences. Some of these may have been the homes of successful merchants; others were owned by churches in Pavia or the surrounding area and were probably rented to Venetian traders and others like them who spent months at a time in the city while participating in the local economy.[41]

---

36. The fullest account remains A. Schulte, *Geschichte des mittelalterlichen Handels und Verkehrs zwischen Westdeutschland und Italien mit Ausschluss von Venedig*, 2 vols. (Leipzig, 1900), vol. 1, pp. 1–79.

37. Edited by A. Hofmeister as *Instituta regalia et ministeria camerae regum Longobardorum et honorantiae civitatis Papiae*, in MGH Scriptores 30.1 (Hanover, 1934), pp. 1444–60 (hereafter *Honorantiae Civitatis Papiae*). On the routes of trade that linked northern Europe with the Mediterranean Sea in the early Middle Ages, see M. McCormick, *Origins of the European Economy: Communications and Commerce AD 300–900* (Cambridge, 2002).

38. Odo of Cluny, *Vita sancti Geraldi Auriliacensis* 1.27, ed. A.-M. Bultot-Verleysen, in *Odon de Cluny, Vita sancti Geraldi Auriliacensis: Édition critique, traduction française, introduction et commentaires* (Brussels, 2009), p. 174.

39. Flodoard, *Annales* 6 (anno 924), ed. P. Lauer, in *Les Annales de Flodoard* (Paris, 1905), p. 22.

40. Bullough, "Urban Change in Early Medieval Italy," pp. 119–29 (Appendix III: Evidence for Churches in Pavia before the Sack of the City in 924).

41. Bullough, "Urban Change in Early Medieval Italy," pp. 105–108.

The presence of an imperial mint in Pavia by the late tenth century and the protection afforded to a city that was often home to the emperor and his entourage were distinct advantages that undoubtedly helped to create an environment that was conducive to the high volumes of commerce on which the Pavians depended for their wealth.

Even more significant than the commercial parallels between Sidon and Tyre and their medieval counterpart was the implicit comparison of the moral disposition of their respective inhabitants. Both of these ancient port cities enjoyed the special attention of Christ during his earthly ministry because the people who lived there were especially receptive to his message of repentance. It was in the vicinity of Sidon and Tyre that Christ encountered a Canaanite woman whose daughter had been possessed by a demon. Even though she was a Gentile, her acceptance of Christ's message allowed her daughter to be healed (Matt. 15:21-28; also Mark 7:24-30, where the woman is identified as a Greek). Moreover, residents of both cities came to hear the Sermon on the Plain and have their ailments relieved by Christ's healing presence (Luke 6:17-19). Most tellingly, however, Christ singled out the virtues of the people of Sidon and Tyre when upbraiding many of the towns in which he had performed miracles, where the citizens were too hard-hearted to change their ways: "Woe to you, Corazin! Woe to you, Bethsaida! For if the mighty works done in you had been done in Tyre and Sidon, they would have repented long ago in sackcloth and ashes. But I tell you, it shall be more tolerable on the day of judgment for Tyre and Sidon than for you" (Matt. 11:21-22). Implicit in the evocation of these biblical cities, which would have been well known to monastic readers who were familiar with these Gospel stories from their repetition in the liturgy, is the notion that the miracles of the abbot of Cluny took place in Pavia because the inhabitants of the city, like those of Sidon and Tyre, had a disposition of repentance that merited the manifest *virtus* of the saint.

The earliest *Life of Maiolus* supported the claim that the citizens of Pavia deserved the special attention of the saintly abbot by relating two miracles that occurred at local landmarks that would have been familiar to the audience of the *vita*. As a whole, the miracles attributed to Maiolus are quite modest in character, perhaps because the reservoir of available stories of the saint's interventions was not very deep so soon after his death.[42] They include an unanticipated discovery of mush-

---

42. A similar problem troubled Eadmer, the early twelfth-century biographer of Anselm of Canterbury, who contented himself with recording miracles of the most mundane sort

rooms, the rescue of a ship and its crew on the Rhine, the protection of a book from a candle that was left to burn upon it, an unexpected catch of fish, and the pardon of a criminal. The two miracles that the abbot performed in Pavia are similarly mundane. The first occurred in the church of Saint Syrus.[43] On this occasion, while the abbot of Cluny tarried in the city, he and two monks from his entourage made a nocturnal visit to the church for the purpose of prayer. As they approached the building, their lantern was suddenly extinguished, although no wind or jostling had disturbed it. Unmoved by this, the abbot approached the doors of the church in the pitch darkness and spoke a prayer, which caused the candle of the lantern to burst into flame. His companions rejoiced that the words of the abbot had rekindled the lantern and thereby turned their fear of the darkness to rejoicing at the power of God. The second of the Pavian miracles took place near a chapel on the outskirts of the city, where Maiolus retired on occasion to escape the bustle of the capital.[44] The only road from the city center to the chapel was swampy and difficult to traverse. Although the abbot had recommended its repair with woodwork and stone, no action was taken to improve it. Nonetheless, the frequent passage of the holy abbot did what the civic authorities would not, taming the ground beneath his feet to make the pathway accessible to all and causing the hagiographer to exclaim that even "the unperceiving earth heeded the imperial command of father Maiolus."[45] The power of God, through the agency of Maiolus, performed a task of much-needed urban renewal that the imperial administration had been slow to act on.

While these two stories anchored the manifest *virtus* of the saint firmly in the civic fabric of Pavia, a third presented a miracle experienced by a prominent imperial official who would have been well known to the local audience of the *vita*: Hildebrand, a master of the royal mint

---

precisely because grander miracles were in short supply. In the words of Richard W. Southern, "As compared with the ancient saints, it was not much." See Southern, *Saint Anselm: A Portrait in a Landscape* (Cambridge, 1990), p. 426.

43. *Vita breuior sancti Maioli* 17, in *BC*, cols. 1774-75. On the church of Saint Syrus, see also *Honorantiae Civitatis Papiae* 16, ed. Hofmeister, p. 1457. On the cult of Saint Syrus in Pavia, see G. Vocino, "Hagiography as an Instrument for Political Claims in Carolingian Northern Italy: The Saint Syrus Dossier (*BHL* 7976 and 7978)," in *An Age of Saints? Power, Conflict, and Dissent in Early Medieval Christianity*, ed. P. Sarris, M. Dal Santo, and P. Booth (Leiden, 2011), pp. 169-86.

44. *Vita breuior sancti Maioli* 19, in *BC*, col. 1775.

45. *Vita breuior sancti Maioli* 19: "Sic insensibile elementum terrae obseruat adhuc, ut uidimus et audiuimus, praeceptum patris Maioli imperiale," in *BC*, col. 1775.

(*magister monetariorum Papiensis provinciae*).⁴⁶ Bedridden by an illness that caused him excruciating pain, Hildebrand had given up hope until the prayers of the Cluniac abbot led to his complete recovery. Explicit reference to an imperial official of high standing distinguishes this story from innumerable accounts of miraculous healings in contemporary hagiographical texts. By virtue of his office, Hildebrand must have been one of the most powerful individuals in late tenth-century Pavia. He was probably the master of the imperial treasury, who oversaw "nine noble and wealthy masters above all other moneyers" in the supervision of the mint and the regulation of the currency.⁴⁷ Although public recognition of Hildebrand would certainly have lent this miracle story a strong capital among local readers, the fact that he was an imperial official directly in charge of the mint and therefore deeply implicated in the city's commercial success reinforced the analogue of Pavia and the trade centers of Sidon and Tyre. This identification underscored the hagiographer's claim that the residents of Pavia deserved the special attention of the Cluniac abbot because, like the citizens of these biblical port towns, their repentant character made them worthy vessels for the miraculous manifestations of the saint's power. In other words, the earliest *Life of Maiolus* created the perception that Pavia was a plausible venue for the miracles of the Cluniac saint by drawing an explicit comparison between the commercial activity and virtuous character of its inhabitants and those of the ancient entrepôts Sidon and Tyre, among whom Christ had cast out demons and healed the sick.

Cluny's Response

Abbatial hagiography was not a medium of Cluniac self-perception or self-promotion in the tenth century.⁴⁸ The Pavian *Life of Maiolus* (c. 1000) was only the second such work to extol the virtues of an abbot of Cluny. The first was John of Salerno's *Life of Odo*, an account of the holy character of Cluny's second abbot written shortly after his death in 942.⁴⁹ The author of this work was not a monk of the fledging Burgun-

---

46. *Vita breuior sancti Maioli* 20, in *BC*, col. 1776.
47. *Honorantiae Civitatis Papiae* 8: "Ministerium autem monete Papie debet habere novem magistros nobiles et divites super omnes alios monetarios," ed. Hofmeister, p. 1454. For context, see R. Naismith, *Making Money in the Early Middle Ages* (Princeton, 2023), pp. 345–52.
48. S. Vanderputten, "Imagining Early Cluny in Abbatial Biographies," in *CCMA*, pp. 105–24, at pp. 106–109.
49. John of Salerno, *Vita Odonis*, PL 133, cols. 43–86.

dian monastery but an Italian who had first met Odo in Rome and then journeyed with him to Pavia, where John took the monastic vow.[50] John dedicated the *Life of Odo* to his brethren at Salerno, where by the 940s he had become the spiritual father of a religious community with ties to Cluny. For these Italian monks, the abbot of Cluny provided a model of personal virtue worthy of emulation. Moreover, the *Life of Odo* demonstrated the lengths to which the monks of Gaul were prepared to go to uphold the angelic ideal (*coeletis disciplina*) fostered by Odo in fulfillment of the abbey's foundation charter, which encouraged the brethren specifically "to seek and desire with full commitment and inner order the heavenly way of life."[51] Perhaps because John's enterprise was a work of local consumption written at a time when the Cluniacs were not self-conscious about controlling the public image of the sanctity of their abbots, John of Salerno's *Life of Odo* did not invite critical scrutiny from Cluny until the early twelfth century, when Abbot Peter the Venerable commissioned a monk named Nalgod to rewrite the lives of some of his abbatial predecessors.[52]

In contrast, the earliest *Life of Maiolus* quickly drew the attention of the Cluniacs. The reason for this is clear. As discussed previously, the abbacy of Maiolus marked a turning point for the Burgundian monastery in terms of the sheer number of donations that the community received in return for prayers for the dead. Maiolus's successor as abbot was Odilo (994–1049), who spent the early years of his abbacy supporting the image of Cluny as a religious house whose monks were so virtuous in their conduct that their prayers were especially efficacious in securing the release of souls from infernal punishment. It was in the

---

50. On the career of John of Salerno, see I. Rosé, *Construire une société seigneuriale: Itinéraire et ecclésiologie de l'abbé Odon de Cluny (fin du IXe–milieu du Xe siècle)* (Turnhout, 2008). On the ambiguities surrounding his monastic affiliation in Salerno, see the comments of Sitwell in *St. Odo of Cluny*, p. 44, n. 3; and p. 59, n. 1.

51. On the concept of *coelestis disciplina*, see Odo of Cluny, *Sermo* 3 (*De sancto Benedicto abbate*), PL 133, cols. 721-29, at col. 722a. For a similar ideal expressed in Cluny's foundation charter, see *Charta qua Vuillelmus, comes et dux, fundat monasterium cluniacense*, in BB, vol. 1, pp. 125-26 (no. 112): "Ita duntaxat ut ibi venerabile oracionis domicilium votis ac subplicationibus fideliter frequentetur, conversatioque celestis omni desideratio et ardore intimo perquiratur et expetatur, sedule quoque oraciones, postulationes atque obsecrationes Domino dirigantur, tam pro me quam pro omnibus, sicut eorum memoria superius digesta est."

52. In the preface of his work, Nalgod complained explicitly about John of Salerno's redundancy (*PL* 133, col. 85b). On this otherwise obscure author, see *Histoire Littéraire de la France*, 47 vols. (Paris, 1733-2021), vol. 11, pp. 167-68, *s.v.* "Nalgode, religieux de l'abbaye de Cluni." Nalgod's reworking of Cluniac hagiography deserves further study in the context of Peter the Venerable's reforms.

early eleventh century that a legend began to circulate concerning a hermit who had a vision of the souls of the damned escaping the grasp of demons because of the agency of the vigils and almsgiving of the brethren of Cluny. News of this vision allegedly inspired Odilo to establish the Feast of All Souls (November 2).[53] This new feast day, unprecedented in its ecumenical approach to the souls of all Christians, made the prayers of the Cluniacs available to everyone, living and dead; at the same time, it asserted a monopoly on prayerful intercession for all Christendom.

It was in this climate of self-conscious self-promotion that the Cluniacs responded to the Pavian *Life of Maiolus*. There is no way to know exactly how and when they had learned that the monks of Pavia had honored their recently deceased abbot with a *vita*, but by the year 1010 a new *Life of Maiolus* appeared, commissioned by Abbot Odilo and composed by a monk of Cluny named Syrus.[54] Compared with the Pavian *vita*, this Cluniac production was a sprawling work, comprising sixty chapters organized into three books. What is most striking for our purposes, however, is the Cluniac treatment of the Pavian claims on their abbot, which had given the earliest *Life of Maiolus* its local inflection. Syrus included in his work two of the miracles that took place in Pavia: the rekindling of the candle in the church of Saint Syrus and the healing of Hildebrand the master of the mint.[55] The Cluniac author played down the local significance of both miracles, however, by omitting from his work any reference to Pavia as an equivalent of Sidon and Tyre, thereby removing the rationale for the saint's activity among the penitential Pavians that loomed so large in the earliest *Life of Maiolus*. Although these miracles of illumination and healing elided easily with the growing corpus of miracle stories that Syrus include in his account of the abbot's life, the miracle of urban renewal that appeared in the Pavian *vita* did not find its way into the official Cluniac version, most probably because it was so localized that it would have held little relevance to readers who were not familiar with the city of Pavia. In the end, the Cluniacs won out over their northern Italian competitors. Based on the surviving manuscript evidence, Syrus's *Life of Maiolus* enjoyed a much wider readership than the Pavian *vita* and eventually overshadowed it completely.[56]

---

53. See n. 10, above.

54. Syrus, *Vita sancti Maioli* (BHL 5177/79), ed. Iogna-Prat, *Agni Immaculati*, pp. 163–285.

55. Syrus, *Vita sancti Maioli* 3.15 (healing of Hildebrand the *monetarius*) and 3.19 (miracle at the church of Saint Syrus), ed. Iogna-Prat, *Agni Immaculati*, pp. 270–71 and 274–76.

56. On the manuscript tradition of *BHL* 5177/79, see Iogna-Prat, *Agni Immaculati*, pp. 71–98.

The author for the earliest *Life of Maiolus* made the case for Pavia as a fitting venue for the manifest *virtus* of the abbot of Cluny by drawing an explicit comparison between the northern Italian city and the Mediterranean port towns of Sidon and Tyre, whose citizens Christ had praised for their penitential character. The application of this civic typology rested firmly on the fact that Pavia, like its ancient counterparts, was a thriving center of commerce. The *vita* made public the claim that Pavia boasted a special relationship with the Cluniac abbot, which found expression in miracles that took place in and around the city for the benefit of its residents. In a period before the intervention of the papacy in the recognition of saints' cults, the composition of the earliest *Life of Maiolus* was enough to legitimize the claim of the Pavians. This declaration did not go uncontested, however. Within a decade of the composition of the earliest *Life of Maiolus*, Abbot Odilo of Cluny commissioned a new *vita* that challenged the Pavians' claim to be the singular recipients of the saint's favor. This Cluniac *Life of Maiolus* put control of the abbot's legacy firmly in the hands of his Burgundian brethren by subsuming some of the Pavian episodes into the growing corpus of his miracles and by excising others from the tradition completely. Lost from view in the dominant Cluniac tradition was the Pavians' innovative use of civic typology informed by the depiction of Sidon and Tyre in the New Testament to create the perception that their city was a venue worthy of the miraculous powers of the saintly abbot of Cluny.

CHAPTER 6

The Social Life of an Eleventh-Century Shrine in the *Miraculorum sancti Maioli libri duo* (BHL 5186)

Maiolus (c. 909-94) remains the most obscure of the early abbots of the so-called golden age of the monastery of Cluny from its founding in 910 to the death of Abbot Peter the Venerable in 1156. Although Maiolus governed the great Burgundian abbey for four decades—from around 954, when he succeeded the blind and ailing Aymard, to his death in 994, when Odilo succeeded him—little is known directly about his personal principles or his abbatial ambitions. Unlike other abbots of early Cluny, Maiolus left no writings in his own hand or voice; there are no letters, no treatises, no sermons or homilies that could cast light on the kind of person he was or the kind of religious leader he strived to be. His frequent trips to his native Provence and across the Alps to Rome and Pavia, the seat of the Ottonians, suggest his restless energy as a reformer of monastic communities and as a power broker in imperial politics, but we are left to deduce his character and ideals indirectly from the hundreds of charters created during his abbacy, from the industry of Cluny's scriptorium under his leadership, and from the idealized portraits presented in the rich

---

Written with W. Tanner Smoot. Originally published as "The Social Life of an Eleventh-Century Shrine in the *Miracula Maioli* (BHL 5186)," *Journal of Medieval Monastic Studies* 12 (2023): 27-52. © Brepols Publishers n.v., Turnhout, Belgium. Reprinted with permission.

hagiographical tradition written throughout the eleventh and twelfth centuries to commemorate his worldly achievements and otherworldly sanctity.[1] Without the direct evidence of personal testimony, however, the personality of Cluny's fourth abbot remains elusive.

The dearth of information about Maiolus's life did little to dissuade his brethren from writing voluminously about his merits in the two hundred years following his death. Throughout the eleventh and twelfth centuries, monks of Cluny and other abbeys where Maiolus played a leadership role were eager to tell and retell stories about his sanctity.[2] Central to these narratives was the abbot's abduction by the Muslims of La Garde-Freinet in the summer of 972, during which Maiolus and his entourage endured the cruelty of their captors and, in some versions of the story, won them over to the Christian faith.[3] Cluniac monks also identified Maiolus as a powerful proponent of prayerful intercession for the dead.[4] When his abbatial successor Odilo (994–1049) established the Feast of All Souls (November 2) sometime after 1024, he was building on momentum gathered in the later tenth century during the abbacy of Maiolus, when the number of charters that requested prayers for the benefit of the donor's soul (*pro remedio animae*) increased exponentially. This association of Maiolus with the cult of the dead persisted well into the twelfth century, when Cluniacs and Cistercians alike popularized testimony attributed to him about the efficacy of suffrages in a story that circulated in prose and in verse about an army of the dead that came to the aid of a pious duke at war against his malevolent rival. Maiolus was, in fact, such a popular saint in the twelfth century that Abbot Peter the Venerable (1122–1156) made the claim in his treatise *De miraculis* that more legends were told

---

1. On Maiolus's activity in Pavia and his commemoration there, see chapter 5, above. For evidence of increased scribal activity at Cluny in the late tenth century, see M.-C. Garand, "Copistes de Cluny au temps de saint Maieul (948–994)," *Bibliothèque de l'Ecole des Chartes* 136 (1978): 5–36; and F. Crivello, "Les débuts de l'activité artistique dans le *scriptorium* de Cluny: Fondements et œuvres," in *Cluny: Les moines et la société au premier âge féodal*, ed. D. Iogna-Prat et al. (Rennes, 2013), pp. 197–208.

2. D. Iogna-Prat, "Panorama de l'hagiographie abbatiale clunisienne (v. 940–v. 1140)," in *Manuscrits hagiographiques et travail des hagiographes*, ed. M. Heinzelmann (Sigmaringen, 1992), pp. 77–118, at pp. 87–89; repr. in D. Iogna-Prat, *Études clunisiennes* (Paris, 2002), pp. 35–73, at pp. 44–46.

3. S. G. Bruce, *Cluny and the Muslims of La Garde-Freinet: Hagiography and the Problem of Islam in Medieval Europe* (Ithaca, 2015).

4. For what follows, see *The Relatio metrica de duobus ducibus: A Twelfth-Century Cluniac Poem on Prayer for the Dead*, ed. and trans. C. A. Jones and S. G. Bruce (Turnhout, 2016), pp. 3–9.

about the virtues of this holy man than about any other saint in Europe besides the Virgin Mary.[5]

It is thus surprising that the richest collection of medieval stories related to the cult of Maiolus has been completely neglected in modern scholarship: the eleventh-century *Miraculorum sancti Maioli libri duo* (BHL 5186), hereafter *Miracula*.[6] This compilation of fifty-three miracles was the result of the industry of a monk of Souvigny, a Cluniac dependency about ninety miles due west of the great Burgundian abbey.[7] Maiolus had died at this sleepy priory in 994, en route from Cluny to Paris to reform the abbey of Saint Denis. The abbot's tomb soon attracted all manner of pilgrims from across the Auvergne, notably cure-seekers hoping to benefit from Maiolus's heavenly intercession.[8] The crowds of people seeking divine aid at the tomb of Maiolus grew so large that Abbot Odilo of Cluny felt compelled to enlarge Souvigny's church in the early eleventh century.[9] Many of these pilgrims experienced curative miracles at the abbot's tomb. According to the preface of the *Miracula*, the posthumous *virtus* of Maiolus further induced Odilo to order the community at Souvigny to commit the accounts of his predecessor's miraculous intercessions to writing.[10] The fact that the author of the *Miracula* made no mention of Odilo's

---

5. Peter the Venerable, *De miraculis* 2.32: "Hac miraculorum gratia in tantum iam per centum sexaginta et duos annos, hoc est a tempore mortis sue claruit, ut post sanctam Dei genitricem, nullum sanctorum in tota Europa nostra in huiusmodi operibus parem habeat," ed. D. Bouthillier, CCCM 83 (Turnhout, 1988), p. 162.

6. Transcribed from an unknown manuscript under the title "Miraculorum sancti Maioli abbatis Cluniacensis IIII" and attributed to "authore quodam, ut uidetur, Monacho Siluiniacensi," in *BC*, cols. 1787–1814, at col. 1787. See also *AASS* Maii 2, cols. 690–700, a reprint of the *BC* text published in 1680 with helpful commentary on the identity of place names.

7. On the history of the priory of Souvigny and its relationship to Cluny, see G. Constable, "Souvigny and Cluny," in G. Constable, *The Abbey of Cluny: A Collection of Essays to Mark the Eleven-Hundredth Anniversary of Its Foundation* (Berlin, 2010), pp. 213–34

8. Maiolus had already been dubbed *sanctissimus* in a lay grant dating from 978/979, more than a decade before his death. See D. Iogna-Prat, *Order and Exclusion: Cluny and Christendom Face Heresy, Judaism, and Islam (1000–1150)*, trans. G. R. Edwards (Ithaca, 2003), p. 58 and n. 129. On the tombs of Maiolus and Odilo, who was also buried at Souvigny, see M.-É. Gautier, "Les aménagements liturgiques de la prieurale de Souvigny et les tombeaux des saints abbés de Cluny, Mayeul et Odilon," *Bulletin Monumental* 162 (2004): 67–85. More generally on the cult of the saints at Cluny, see chapter 9, below.

9. M.-É. Gautier, "Les sépultures des saints abbés de Cluny, Mayeul et Odilon, à Souvigny: État de la question et réflexions nouvelles (XIe-XIVe siècle)," *Hortus Artium Mediaevalium* 10 (2004): 133–42, at p. 133. See also P. Chevalier, "Le tombeau et les monuments funéraires médiévaux des saints abbés Mayeul et Odilon de Cluny," *Hortus Artium Mediaevalium* 10 (2004): 119–32, at pp. 119–20.

10. *MM*, preface to book 1: "Hos ex parte aliqua pro paterno imperio domni ac reuerentissimi Odilonis abbatis obedimus mandare scriptis."

death in 1049 or his subsequent burial at Souvigny alongside Maiolus strongly suggests that this collection was composed in the first half of the eleventh century.

Surviving in whole or in part in no fewer than five manuscripts from the late eleventh to the early thirteenth centuries, this robust collection of miracles casts light on the social life of the shrine of an influential tenth-century abbot.[11] Scholars have long recognized the value of miracle collections as sources for social history, employing a number of methodologies to explore the lived experiences and perspectives of cure-seekers.[12] The so-called socio-statistical approach, first pioneered by Ronald Finucane and Pierre-André Sigal, involves the identification of social taxonomies to examine historical patterns in *miracula* collections.[13] Such an approach remains a vital first step in the study of any saint's cult, as it grants important insight both into the types of people who visited a given shrine and the ailments from which they sought relief.[14] Statistical analyses alone, however, tend to ignore the social meaning of pilgrims' experiences at saints' shrines, glossing over the importance of human relationships in the cure-seeking process and reducing illness to simplistic categories.[15] Consequently, scholars like Simon Yarrow, Irina Metzler, and Rachel Koopmans have demonstrated the value of a cultural approach in analyzing *miracula*, with

---

11. The *Miracula* have survived in full in three manuscripts: Paris, BnF, Latin 5611, fols. 50r–83r (late eleventh century); Angers, BM 803, fols. 14v–35r (twelfth century); and Angers, BM 820, fols. 39v–80v (twelfth century). Two other manuscripts preserve selections of miracles from this collection: Paris, BnF, Latin 18304, fols. 42v–44v and 57r–72v (twelfth century); and Paris, BnF, Latin 5365, fols. 1r–5r (twelfth/thirteenth century).

12. Several recent studies have worked to reassess the importance of miracle collections as sources for medieval monastic culture, medical practices, pilgrimage patterns, and more. See C. Trenery, *Madness, Medicine and Miracle in Twelfth-Century England* (Abingdon, 2019); *Travel, Pilgrimage and Social Interaction from Antiquity to the Middle Ages*, ed. J. Kuuliala and J. Rantala (Abingdon, 2020); and *A Companion to Medieval Miracle Collections*, ed. S. Katajala-Peltomaa, J. Kuuliala, and I. McCleery (Leiden, 2021), esp. E. Jamroziak, "Miracles in Monastic Culture," pp. 36–53.

13. R. C. Finucane, *Miracles and Pilgrims: Popular Beliefs in Medieval England*, 2nd ed. (New York, 1995); and P.-A. Sigal, *L'homme et le miracle dans la France médiévale: XIe–XIIe siècle* (Paris, 1985).

14. I. McCleery, "Christ More Powerful Than Galen? The Relationship Between Medicine and Miracles," in *Contextualising Miracles in the Christian West, 1100–1500: New Historical Approaches*, ed. M. M. Mesley and L. E. Wilson (Oxford, 2014), pp. 127–54, at p. 140; and R. J. Salter, *Saints, Cure-Seekers and Miraculous Healing in Twelfth-Century England* (York, 2021), p. 22.

15. S. Ritchey, "Health, Healing, and Salvation: Hagiography as a Source for Medieval Healthcare," in *Hagiography and the History of Latin Christendom, 500–1500*, ed. S. K. Herrick (Leiden, 2020), pp. 417–36, at pp. 420–21; and McCleery, "Christ More Powerful Than Galen?," pp. 142–43.

special focus on the language employed and experiences described in miraculous anecdotes.[16] Such an emphasis on textual analysis, combined with an attention to local context, has clarified the ways in which shrines allowed pilgrims to express and potentially resolve social anxieties.[17] Historians like Iona McCleery and Ruth J. Salter have called for the integration of these two approaches, citing the importance of both statistical data and literary analysis for a thorough interpretation of how medieval cure-seekers understood, experienced, and participated in holy healing.[18]

In this chapter, we adopt an integrated approach to reconstruct the social features of the cult of Maiolus of Cluny in Souvigny as well as the shrine's geographic range of influence. We begin this chapter with a statistical analysis of the pilgrims themselves. The accounts preserved in the *Miracula* allow us to build a social profile of the people who visited the shrine, including such details as their names, genders, ages, and backgrounds. In some cases, we can even identify named pilgrims from other contemporary sources. The miracle collection also provides detailed information about the maladies from which these pilgrims sought relief at the abbot's shrine. Moreover, particular attention to the language of illness used within the *Miracula* provides insight into the experience of illness and healing at Souvigny, enhancing our understanding of how contemporaries perceived the curative process. Lastly, these accounts make frequent mention of the place of origin of those who traveled to the tomb, thus providing us with the opportunity to chart the cult's full range of influence in the Auvergne and beyond. Since many of the pilgrims seeking the saint's aid had difficulty traveling because of impairment of mobility or sight, the *Miracula* also offer firsthand information about the social networks that pilgrims mobilized to facilitate their journey to the shrine as well as the inventive means of conveyance that they employed to overcome their physical challenges. Taken together, the evidence of this miracle collection

---

16. S. Yarrow, *Saints and Their Communities: Miracle Stories in Twelfth-Century England* (Oxford, 2006); R. Koopmans, *Wonderful to Relate: Miracle Stories and Miracle Collecting in High Medieval England* (Philadelphia, 2011); I. Metzler, *Disability in Medieval Europe: Thinking About Physical Impairment During the High Middle Ages, c. 1100–1400* (London, 2006); and McCleery, "Christ More Powerful Than Galen," pp. 143–44.

17. Yarrow, *Saints and Their Communities*, p. 20.

18. Salter, *Saints, Cure-Seekers and Miraculous Healing*, pp. 22–24; and McCleery, "Christ More Powerful Than Galen," p. 152.

provides an especially vivid portrait of the social life of a bustling saint's shrine in what is now central France that highlights the risks and rewards of pilgrim travel in the early eleventh century.

Pilgrims at the Tomb of Maiolus

The vast majority of the miracles associated with Maiolus's shrine concerned the healing of individuals suffering from physical maladies. The *Miracula* recorded accounts of fifty-three separate miracles involving many dozens of pilgrims, as supplicants often traveled to the saint's tomb in groups or accompanied by family members. Visitors to the abbot's tomb came from all walks of life, from the ranks of the Capetian kings to the lowliest of local villagers. In most instances, the *Miracula* recorded only the gender of the supplicant who received a miraculous cure through the saint's intervention, but in a few cases, the author of the miracle collection also provided some indication of a pilgrim's age, his or her social rank, and even their name. This information allows us to make some general inferences about the type of people attracted to this early eleventh-century shrine.

The *Miracula* identified fifty-four individual pilgrims according to their gender (table 1). Among them, thirty-five were men (65 percent) and nineteen were women (35 percent). This ratio represents almost exactly what one would expect in terms of the gender balance of medieval cure-seekers based on studies of central and later medieval cult sites, which suggest a ratio of 66 percent men to 33 percent women. This appears to have been the norm both in Capetian France and throughout Western Europe more generally.[19] In contrast, the age and social status of these pilgrims is much more elusive than their

Table 1. Gender distribution of cure-seekers in the *Miracula Maioli*

GENDER	NUMBER	PERCENTAGE
Male	35	65%
Female	19	35%
Total	**54**	**100%**

---

19. Sigal, *L'homme et le miracle*, pp. 300–301; Finucane, *Miracles and Pilgrims*, p. 143; and Salter, *Saints, Cure-Seekers and Miraculous Healing*, pp. 93–96.

CHAPTER 6

Table 2. Age distribution of cure-seekers in the *Miracula Maioli*

AGE	MALE	FEMALE	TOTAL	PERCENTAGE
Youth	5	1	6	11%
Adult/Unspecified	26	18	44	82%
Elder	4	0	4	7%

genders (table 2). The author of the *Miracula* tended not to mention the age of pilgrims, although he often supplied anecdotal information that presumes their adulthood. He did, however, specifically identify six individuals as adolescents or children (11 percent of the total sample), five of whom were men (83 percent) and one of whom was a woman (17 percent).[20] Likewise, the miracle collection specifically mentioned four elderly pilgrims (7 percent of the total sample), all of whom were men.[21]

The *Miracula* were also laconic with respect to the social class of the pilgrims who came to the abbot's tomb in Souvigny. In general, men were more likely to be designated by their social rank than women. The most distinguished of them were King Hugh Capet, Count Bouchard of Vendôme, and his son Bishop Rainald of Paris, who together witnessed the miraculous healing of a blind man when they visited the abbot's tomb around 995.[22] All of the other pilgrims described in social terms in the *Miracula* came from the middle and lower ranks of medieval society. Seven of them were men, three of a religious background and four laymen. Two monks and one of their relatives or associates were singled out as the recipients of miracles, as were a cleric and a stonemason,

---

20. Male adolescents and children: *MM* 1.11 (*puer quidam*), 1.12 (*quidam puer . . . puerilis aetatis non transcendens terminum*), 1.14 (*quidam . . . cuius iuuenile corpus foedauerat grauis contractio manuum ac pedum*), 2.1 (*quidam attingens annos puerilis aetatis*), and 2.10 (*quidam infans . . . qui ab ipso matris utero iam paene septennium annorum transiens*). Female adolescent or child: *MM* 1.22 (*paupercula . . . a parentibus ad sancti Maioli sepulchrum est adducta*).

21. *MM* 1.13 (*quidam ueteranus*), 1.20 (*quidam in iam perfecta aetate corporis*), 1.23 (*ueteranam barbam et cigneum caput detrahebat manibus*), and 2.14 (*quidam in decrepita aetate*).

22. *MM* 2.3. King Hugh Capet's visit to the shrine must have taken place between the abbot's death on May 11, 994, and the king's death on October 24, 996. See J. Hourlier, *Saint Odilon, abbé de Cluny* (Louvain, 1964), p. 54, n. 9. Maiolus had associated with the king throughout his life. In fact, the abbot died at Souvigny en route to the royal monastery of Saint-Denis in Paris, which Hugh had asked him to reform. Likewise, Count Bouchard had previously commissioned Maiolus to reform the monastery of Saint-Maur-des-Fossés. See J. Dubois, "Au temps des premiers Capétiens les moines en pleine expansion affirment leurs libertés," in *Pouvoirs et libertés au temps premiers Capétiens*, ed. É. Magnou-Nortier (Maulevrier, 1992), pp. 197–214, at pp. 198–200; and Constable, "Souvigny and Cluny," pp. 219–20.

who was part of the crew that constructed the shrine.[23] A farmer also received healing at the church near the saint's tomb.[24] Lastly, a pilgrim who came from the town of Petra seeking a remedy for his lameness was described in vague terms as a man "of not ignoble descent."[25] In contrast, the three women singled out by their social rank in the *Miracula* were all laywomen from the lowest classes of society. The author characterized two of the women disparagingly as ignorant rustics and the third was the daughter of a man described as "the poorest of the poor" (*pauperum pauperrimus*).[26]

Providing the names of the beneficiaries of the saint's miracles was a way for the author to lend credence to his accounts of their efficacy. As the custodians of a newly established cult of a recently deceased saint, the monks of Souvigny had a particular interest in substantiating claims of Maiolus's intercessory power. Among the dozens of pilgrims and their associates and relatives mentioned in the *Miracula*, twenty-three of them were explicitly named in the text. Some of them were religious and secular elites well known from other sources, like the Capetian king Hugh Capet and his entourage.[27] Another was a monk of Cluny named Vivianus, who came to the saint's shrine to seek relief from pain caused by an ingrown toenail.[28] This was very likely the same well-attested Vivianus who served as the prior of Cluny under Abbots Maiolus and Odilo between 983 and 1018.[29] Likewise, a cleric named Bernardus who came on horseback from Chartres to petition Maiolus to cure his withered foot and leg may be plausibly identified with any of the several church officials with this common name recorded in the necrology of Saint Mary's cathedral composed during the time of Bishop Fulbert of Chartres (1006–1028), but there is no way to know for certain which one it

---

23. Monks: *MM* 1.7 (*quidam frater*) and 2.5 (*quidam e fratribus Cluniacensis monasterii*); relative: *MM* 1.2 (*quidam uero associatus magni conuentus populo*); cleric: *MM* 2.7 (*clericus*); and stonemason: *MM* 1.3 (*inter ceteros cementariorum artifices extitit quidam*).

24. *MM* 2.11 (*agricola*).

25. *MM* 2.17 (*quidam non de ignobili genere*). The author of the *Miracula* situated *villa Petra* in *pagus Siciacus*, both of which remain unidentified. The Bollandists suggested the county of Saissac, Aude, as a possible location for the *pagus Siciacus*, but its great distance from Souvigny (more than two hundred miles) mitigates against this identification. See *AASS* Maii 2, p. 698, n. *p*.

26. *MM* 1.5 (*mulier... satis rustica et intellectu scientiarum nescia*), 1.18 (*quidam pauperum pauperrimus filiam unicam habebat*), and 1.25 (*quaedam rusticarum mulierum inscia*).

27. See n. 22, above.

28. *MM* 2.5 (*quidam e fratribus Cluniacensis monasterii nomine Uiuianus*).

29. M. Chaume, "Les grands prieurs de Cluny: Compléments et rectifications à la liste de la *Gallia Christiana*," *Revue Mabillon* 28 (1938): 147–52, at p. 148.

might be.³⁰ The rest of the named pilgrims in the *Miracula* resist identification with individuals of the same name known from contemporary sources. Thirteen of them were men, including the stonemason Constantius; a monk of Souvigny named Odo; a farmer called Durannus; and pilgrims named Herbertus, Constantius, Heldinus, Bernardus, Cristianus, Heinricus, Goszaldus, Armannus, Ascellinus, and Iterius. Five of them were women with the names Stephana, Heldeardis, Hildeburgis, Helena, and Ermengardis. Lastly, the *Miracula* also mention in passing the name of an individual whose association with the shrine was a matter of serendipity rather than an act of devotion. When the pilgrim named Armannus received a cure for his lameness, he donated to God and the saint not only the oxen that had brought him to the shrine but also an unfree servant (*servus*) named Guidricus.³¹

The *Miracula* thus provide a wealth of information about the kinds of pilgrims who visited the abbot's shrine in Souvigny in the early eleventh century. Like other pilgrimage destinations in this period, male supplicants outnumbered their female counterparts by a ratio of two to one. Evidence for the social status of these pilgrims is elusive, but it suggests that the saint's reputation as an active intercessor for those in need attracted cure-seekers from across a wide social spectrum, from powerful secular figures like kings and counts to members of the most destitute families. Such appeal and fame allowed the compiler of the *Miracula* to present the saint as a socially inclusive intercessor, who was responsive to the needs of elite patrons and common folk alike. Although a small number of these pilgrims are known from other sources, most of the recipients of the abbot's blessings are otherwise unattested in the documentary record. Moreover, it is clear that the *Miracula* did not provide a complete account of pilgrim activity at the shrine in the early eleventh century. It made no mention, for example, of two of the most famous visitors to the abbot's tomb: Empress Adelaide, who came to Souvigny in the company of Abbot Odilo in 999, and King Robert II the Pious, who paid his respects to the saint in 1131.³² Likewise, it offered no

---

30. *MM* 2.7: "Quidam Carnotensis aecclesiae clericus nomine Bernardus." For church officials named Bernard in the necrology from Saint Mary's cathedral, see *Necrologium ecclesiae beatae Mariae Carnotensis*, in *Un manuscript chartrain du XIe siècle: Fulbert, évêque de Chartres*, ed. R. Merlet and A. Clerval (Chartres, 1893), pp. 155, 166, 169, 172, and 173. But the pilgrim may not have been a canon of Saint Mary's cathedral at all.

31. *MM* 2.17: "Pro qua recompensatione tradidit Deo et sancto Maiolo boues qui remanserant et tradidit quendam sui iuris seruum nomine Guidricum."

32. Adelaide: Odilo, *Epitaphium domine Adelheide Auguste* 16 (XVII), ed. H. Paulhart, in *Die Lebensbeschreibung der Kaiserin Adelheid von Abt Odilo von Cluny* (Graz and Cologne, 1962), p. 41.

indication of the visit that Bishop Fulcran of Lodève made to the shrine before his death in 1006.[33] While it may seem unusual that the author of the *Miracula* did not take the opportunity to promote the saint's shrine by drawing attention to these distinguished pilgrims, their visits may not have merited mention because they did not provide an occasion for a manifestation of the abbot's miraculous intercession.

Maladies and Miracles

The tomb of Maiolus thus attracted pilgrims from all ranks of society in the early eleventh century. Judging by the accounts contained in the *Miracula*, the intercessory power of Maiolus was localized to the abbot's tomb. Out of the fifty-three miracle accounts recorded in the collection, forty-four of them (83 percent) occurred either before the tomb of Maiolus or in and around the monastic church at Souvigny. The nature of these petitions sheds light on the distinctive characteristics of the abbot's shrine.[34] Although pilgrims to Souvigny sought the saint's intervention for relief from a range of physical or material hardships, the author of the *Miracula* depicted the holy man's tomb primarily as a place of healing. Around 81 percent of all the miracles recorded (forty-eight of the fifty-nine cases) involved some kind of curative element (table 3).[35] Most medieval saints' shrines had a therapeutic bent, but the *Miracula* ascribed an exceptionally high number of healings to Maiolus in comparison to other cults from this period.[36] Likewise, the collection featured relatively few accounts of noncurative miracles popular among

---

Robert: Helgaud of Fleury, *Epitoma vitae regis Rotberti Pii*, ed. R.-H. Bautier (Paris, 1965), p. 126.

33. *Vita sancti Fulcrani*, ed. F. Dolbeau, in "Vie inédite de Saint Fulcran, évêque de Lodève," *Analecta Bollandiana* 100 (1982): 515-44, at pp. 535-37.

34. In the past few decades, many studies analyzing local and regional cult activity have greatly enhanced our understanding of the distinctive characteristics of the shrines of specific saints. See D. Gonthier and C. le Bas, "Analyse socio-économique de quelques recueils de miracles dans la Normandie du XIe au XIIIe siècle," *Annales de Normandie* 24 (1974): 3-36; B. Ward, *Miracles and the Medieval Mind* (Philadelphia, 1982); D. Rollason, "The Miracles of St. Benedict: A Window on Early Medieval France," in *Studies in Medieval History Presented to R. H. C. Davis*, ed. H. Mayr-Harting and R. I. Moore (London, 1985), pp. 73-90; H. Mayr-Harting, "Functions of a Twelfth-Century Shrine: The Miracles of St. Frideswide," in *Studies in Medieval History*, ed. Mayr-Harting and Moore, pp. 193-206; C. Vulliez, "Le miracle et son approche dans les recueils de *miracula* Orléanais du IXe au XIIe siècle," in *Miracles, Prodiges et Merveilles au Moyen Age* (Sorbonne, 1995), pp. 89-113; and Yarrow, *Saints and Their Communities*.

35. Although the author(s) of the *Miracula* cataloged their information in fifty-three chapters, several chapters include multiple miraculous events.

36. Sigal, *L'homme et le miracle*, pp. 227-64; Vauchez, *Sainthood in the Later Middle Ages*, pp. 466-77; and Finucane, *Miracles and Pilgrims*, pp. 142-51.

Table 3. Distribution of posthumous miracles in the *Miracula Maioli*

MIRACLE TYPE	NUMBER OF MIRACLES	PERCENTAGE
Healing	48	81.3%
Punishment or chastisement	5	8.5%
Visions	1	1.7%
Candle ignition	1	1.7%
Safe travel	1	1.7%
Returned property	1	1.7%
Wax preservation	1	1.7%
Procuring child or oblate	1	1.7%
Total	59	100%

other contemporary cults, such as censures and visionary experiences.[37] The author of the *Miracula* often took special care to describe pilgrims' experience of illness and impairment, thereby presenting an image of a saint's shrine particularly concerned with the curing of devotees' maladies.

According to the *Miracula*, pilgrims suffering from a wide variety of illnesses found relief at Souvigny (table 4). Those afflicted with some form of paralysis or motor impairment (*contracti*) were predominant, accounting for close to 40 percent of the recorded petitions (twenty of the fifty-one examples). The term *contractus* referred to medieval conceptions of paralysis, whereby blood-starved nerves "contracted" and rendered limbs immobile and contorted.[38] The author of the *Miracula* implied such a view when describing the healing of Bernardus, the cleric from Chartres, who traveled to the tomb on account of the withered nerves and veins that deprived him of all feeling in his leg.[39] The account

---

37. For example, Fleury's collection of Saint Benedict's miracles, written between the ninth and twelfth centuries, spends considerable time focusing on the divine retribution meted out to those who usurped Fleury's material interests. See Rollason, "Miracles of St. Benedict," pp. 84–90. For a new edition and French translation of this important collection, see *Les miracles de Saint Benoît: Miracula sancti Benedicti*, ed. and trans. A. Davril, A. Dufour, and G. Labory (Paris, 2019).

38. P.-A. Sigal, "Comment on concevait et on traitait la paralysie en Occident dans le Haut Moyen Age (V^e-XIIe siècles)," *Revue d'histoire des sciences* 24 (1971): 193–211, at pp. 197–200. Learned medicine in early medieval Europe remains somewhat obscure, featuring a mix of unstable translations of ancient treatises and short miscellanies with few attempts at any comprehensiveness. See P. Horden, "Sickness and Healing," in *The Cambridge History of Christianity*, Vol. 3, *Early Medieval Christianities, c. 600–c. 1100*, ed. T. F. X. Noble and J. M. H. Smith (Cambridge, 2008), pp. 416–32, at pp. 420–24.

39. For what follows, see *MM* 2.7.

Table 4. Distribution of posthumous healing miracles in the *Miracula Maioli*

HEALING MIRACLES	NUMBER OF MIRACLES	PERCENTAGE
Paralysis or contraction	20	39%
Blind or impaired vision	13	25%
Deafness or mutism	6	12%
Lost mind or demon	4	8%
Burning plague	2	4%
Cancer	1	2%
Dropsy	1	2%
Ingrown toenail	1	2%
Fever	1	2%
Accident	1	2%
Unspecified illness	1	2%
Total	**51**	**100%**

of his healing expressed a neurological understanding of paralysis, whereby the restoration of his dead nerves (*emortui nervi*) allowed his motor functions to return. This causal description of Bernardus's disability is unique in the collection, however, as most accounts discuss paralysis in more general terms. In fact, *contractus* could refer to a person with a range of afflictions from "withered" limbs to paraplegia, and the author of the miracle collection used this term interchangeably with paralysis.[40] Several accounts in the *Miracula* provide detailed information regarding the common symptoms of those *contracti* and *paralytici*, who sought relief at the abbot's tomb. The author frequently called attention to the knottiness (*nodositas*) or death-like immobility (*moriens*) of pilgrims afflicted with various degrees of paralysis.[41] In one account, an elderly man from Berry came to Souvigny suffering from a "knot of contraction" (*nodum contractionis*), whereby his torso bent forward onto his knees, while his fingers clenched involuntarily into fists.[42] On another occasion, the *Miracula* linked certain symptoms of paralysis

---

40. The term *paralysis* is so general that it is difficult to infer the actual maladies afflicting such pilgrims. See Finucane, *Miracles and Pilgrims*, p. 104. Even so, hagiographical accounts occasionally provide enough specific information to distinguish among certain types of paralysis, such as hemiplegia, quadriplegia, and paraplegia. See Sigal, "Comment on concevait et on traitait la paralysie," pp. 200–201. Early medieval medical treatises similarly distinguished between partial and full paralysis. See Metzler, *Disability in Medieval Europe*, pp. 73–76.

41. See, for example, *MM* 1.14, 1.22, 2.1, and 2.7.

42. *MM* 1.13. For a similar case, see *MM* 1.15, where the author described a man from Nevers whose body was so bent that his chin touched his knees.

with specific diseases. When a young man from *Eglismons* arrived at Souvigny disfigured by a grave contraction, the *Miracula* described his hands and feet as afflicted with gout (*ciragra* and *podagra*).⁴³ Well into the eleventh century, gout shared a certain association with paralysis, such that medical treatises at times prescribed the same treatment for each.⁴⁴ At the most fundamental level, however, the language surrounding *contracti* seems to have been representative of an attempt to capture the distress of many pilgrims' physical condition. When a poor father had his only daughter brought to Souvigny in the hope of healing her, the author of the *Miracula* lamented that her contracted condition (*contracta*) made her look like a monster (*monstro simillimam*).⁴⁵

The profile of Maiolus presented in the *Miracula* casts the saint as a remarkably effective intercessor for pilgrims suffering from mobility impairments. Even so, the salubrious roads to Souvigny appealed to other types of petitioners as well. Those afflicted with blindness appear as the most prominent beneficiaries after *contracti* (thirteen of the fifty-one examples, or 25 percent of all healings recorded). Their attraction came naturally enough. The saint's earliest hagiographer had interpreted Maiolus's name as a dithematic compound meaning "great eye" (*magnus oculus*).⁴⁶ Ocular analogies of this kind may have influenced the saint's posthumous reputation among prospective pilgrims. Stephana of *Sanctus Iulianus* (Saint-Gérand-de-Vaux, Allier) had planned to appeal to the saints (*auxilium sanctorum*) for a respite from her blindness, but she remained at home lamenting her condition until specific news of Maiolus's reputation for miracles (*famam virtutum*) reached her.⁴⁷

---

43. *MM* 1.14: "Dira paralisis quidam . . . cuius iuuenile corpus foedauerat grauis contractio manuum ac pedum, ita ut manus illius ciragra, pedes autem eius uexarentur infesta podagra." *Eglismons* remains unidentified. The Bollandists proposed *Gliseneufe* (Égliseneuve-d'Entraigues, Puy-de-Dôme), which lies about seventy miles south of Claremont. See *AASS* Maii 2, p. 693, n. *g*.

44. Sigal, "Comment on concevait et on traitait la paralysie," p. 198; and Metzler, *Disability in Medieval Europe*, p. 75. Salter considers *podagra* a more technical Greek term for gout, perhaps indicating specialized medical knowledge on the part of a hagiographer, but the author of the *Miracula* appears to make little descriptive distinction between *podagra* and other forms of "contraction." See Salter, *Saints, Cure-Seekers and Miraculous Healing*, p. 82.

45. *MM* 1.18. Hagiographers occasionally compared especially disfigured cure-seekers in terms of the monstrous, specifically to capture such a person's natural "deficiency." See Metzler, *Disability in Medieval Europe*, p. 154.

46. *Vita brevior sancti Maioli* 1: "Nam Maiolus, ut iocundo laetemur interprete, quasi magnus videtur dici oculus," in *BC*, col. 1736.

47. *MM* 1.4. The location of *Sanctus Iulianus* is contested. Côte identified *Sanctus Iulianus de Vallibus* with the church of Saint-Gérand et Saint-Julien in modern-day Saint-Gérand-de-Vaux, Allier. See L. Côte, *Histoire du prieuré clunisien de Souvigny* (Moulins, 1942), p. 413. This

Stephana recovered her sight after a brief sojourn at Souvigny, which, according to the *Miracula*, came about "because [Maiolus] was a son of light, not a son of darkness."[48] The abbot's special reputation as an *inluminator* appears to have developed quickly after his burial.[49] Already in 994/995, when Hugh Capet visited the abbot's shrine, he interrogated a pilgrim recently healed of his blindness inside the monastic church.[50]

Accounts of divine chastisement appear rarely in the *Miracula* (five of the fifty-nine examples, or around 9 percent), but in this sample, more than half of them (three of the five, or 60 percent) involved some form of blindness.[51] After cursing the sun for burning her, a certain *rustica* lost her sight as a result of her taunt. Persisting in blindness for some time, she was brought to the tomb of Maiolus, where she lamented her diminished condition. Pleased with her penitential display, God removed her curse-caused blindness on behalf of the merits of Maiolus.[52] Other sinners in the *Miracula* invited punishment through irreverence, for failing to respect the Sunday vigil, or by thanking Maiolus insufficiently for his intercession on their behalf.[53] In the context of a divine rebuke, the blindness of such pilgrims took on the character of a "social illness," whereby their misbehavior led to consequences that interrupted their ability to participate fully in society.[54] Sensory

---

is supported by a privilege issued in November 1095 by Pope Urban II on behalf of Souvigny, confirming the abbey's many ecclesiastical properties, including the *ecclesias Sancti Iuliani de Vallibus* in the diocese of Clermont. See *Bullarium sacri ordinis Cluniacensis*, ed. P. Symon (Lyons, 1680), pp. 29–30; and Constable, "Souvigny and Cluny," p. 225. For their part, the Bollandists posited an *oppidum sancti Iuliani* near the banks of the Dordogne in the Limousin. See *AASS* Mai 2, p. 693, n. c.

48. *MM* 1.4: "quia filius lucis et non filius tenebrarum fuit" with reference to 1 Thess. 5.5. Women in particular appear to have benefited from cures for blindness in medieval miracle collections. See Salter, *Saints, Cure-Seekers and Miraculous Healing*, p. 69. Nevertheless, the author appears to insinuate that Stephana doubted the abilities of other saints to restore her vision until hearing of Maiolus's reputation.

49. See *MM* 1.2, where the monastic community at Souvigny praised Maiolus as *inluminator* after he healed a relative of one of the brethren from blindness.

50. *MM* 2.3.

51. *MM* 1.25, 1.30, 2.18, and 2.20.

52. *MM* 1.25.

53. *MM* 2.20. In one instance (*MM* 2.18), a woman from *Magniacum* (Magny-Cours, Nièvre?) received a divine rebuke for her failure to celebrate the vigil of Saint Maiolus's feast, although she did not experience blindness. The Bollandists situated *Magniacum* in the Limousin March (*Marchiae Lemovicinae*) some forty leagues from Souvigny, but this identification is not plausible, because the author of the *Miracula* reported that the pilgrim came to Souvigny "on the next day" (*in crastino*) after falling ill. See *AASS* Maii 2, p. 698, n. q.

54. For more on social illnesses, especially in relation to the works of Gregory of Tours, see R. Van Dam, *Leadership and Community in Late Antique Gaul* (Berkeley, 1985), pp. 264–66; and Sigal, *L'homme et le miracle*, pp. 276–82.

impairments could disrupt an individual's social agency, as the blind had to rely on the help of others for their mobility. Therefore, saints like Maiolus not only restored the physical health of their blind petitioners but also their capacity for social participation. The author of the *Miracula* implied as much when describing blind pilgrims, formerly dependent on escorts for their travel to Souvigny, returning home without a guide (*sine ductore*) after receiving a cure.[55] This relational understanding of illness and health underscores the importance of social networks in the process of medieval cure-seeking.

Attaining the Tomb: Geography, Networks, and Mobility

The cult of Maiolus increased rapidly in popularity after his death in 994 to such an extent that by the 1040s the monastic chronicler Rodulphus Glaber claimed that the abbot's holy reputation attracted pilgrims "from the whole Roman world" (*ex universo Romano orbe*), who departed from Souvigny "blessed by the curing of their many ills" (*diuersarum infirmitatum gratiam sanitatis*).[56] When analyzed in light of data from the miracle collection, however, the geographic scope of the shrine's appeal seems to have been much more modest than Glaber implied. Despite the claim that pilgrims traveled "from the whole Roman world" to Souvigny, petitioners in the *Miracula* made journeys averaging about sixty miles to visit the abbot's tomb. This distance echoes contemporary trends, as most eleventh- and twelfth-century pilgrims traveled anywhere between twenty to sixty miles to reach a shrine.[57]

Although the distances traversed by pilgrims may not have been as great as Glaber had claimed, even a short journey to the tomb of Maiolus would have been arduous for those afflicted with maladies that prevented them from walking or seeing. Wayfarers to shrines seldom traveled alone and most frequently relied on their families and friends for support to reach their goal. The thaumaturgial focus of the abbot's shrine on the relief of motor and sensory impairments accentuated this feature of the *Miracula*, because the saint's devotees were particularly dependent on the assistance of others to travel these distances.

---

55. See, for example, *MM* 1.4 and 1.27.
56. For what follows, see Rodulfus Glaber, *Historiarum libri quinque* 2.7.14, ed. and trans. J. France, in *Rodulphus Glaber: The Five Books of Histories and the Life of St. William* (Oxford, 1989), pp. 76-77.
57. Sigal, *L'homme et le miracle*, pp. 207-209; Finucane, *Miracles and Pilgrims*, pp. 169-70; and Salter, *Saints, Cure-Seekers and Miraculous Healing*, p. 125.

Furthermore, pilgrims of all sorts counted on helpers for spiritual support once they arrived at the shrine and frequently encouraged those accompanying them to join them in soliciting divine intervention. Shrines like the one at Souvigny therefore fostered a series of voluntary associations among pilgrims, monastic communities, and their saints.[58]

The *Miracula* illustrate the importance of social relationships for supplicants in the pursuit of relief from the maladies afflicting them. The greatest obstacle to analyzing the support networks relied on by pilgrims to Souvigny pertains to the equivocal descriptions of family and friends in the miracle collection. Nearly half of the miracles in the collection (twenty-three of the fifty-three cases, or 43 percent) implied that pilgrims had recourse to a guide or a helper of some kind, often merely stating that petitioners "were led" (*ad/ducere fecit* or *adducitur*) to the shrine. When he chose to be more explicit, the author of the *Miracula* described pilgrims as receiving some form of assistance from their *parentes* (eight of the twenty-three cases, or 35 percent). While nominally referring to biological parentage or ancestry, *parentes* acquired a broad valence by the high Middle Ages and could denote a wider network of kinsfolk (*cognatio, consanguinitas, propinqui*) and friends (*amici*).[59] The relationship of these advocates to the pilgrims remains ambiguous in most cases, but some accounts permit more nuanced distinctions. In one instance, for example, the *Miracula* explicitly referred to parents undertaking a pilgrimage with their child to seek a cure on his behalf. In this case, a father and mother (*pater scilicet et mater*) deliberated together about their mute child's welfare before reaching the decision to take him to the shrine at Souvigny.[60] Other accounts of children seeking

---

58. Yarrow, *Saints and Their Communities*, p. 8.
59. D. A. Bullough, "Early Medieval Social Groupings: The Terminology of Kinship," *Past & Present* 45 (1969): 3–18, at p. 12; and A. Guerreau-Jalabert, "La désignation des relations et des groups de parenté en latin medieval," *Archivum Latinitatis Medii Aevi* 46/47 (1988): 65–108, at pp. 81–85. For more on the imprecise language surrounding discussions of the medieval *familia*, see A. Guerreau-Jalabert, "Sur les structures de parenté dans l'Europe médiévale," *Annales: Economies, Sociétés, Civilisations* 36 (1981): 1028–49, at pp. 1030–31.
60. MM 2.10. For more on parental concern for children's physical and material well-being, see J. M. Theilmann, "English Peasants and Medieval Miracle Lists," *The Historian* 52 (1990): 286–303, at pp. 297–98; B. H. Rosenwein, "Circles of Affection in Cluniac Charters," in *Écritures de l'espace social: Mélanges d'histoire médiévale offerts à Monique Bourin par ses élèves et ses amis*, ed. D. Boisseuil et al. (Paris, 2010), pp. 397–415, at pp. 405–408; and E. Van Houts, *Married Life in the Middle Ages, 900–1300* (Oxford, 2019), pp. 128–29. Women specifically appear as caregivers in *miracula* throughout the Middle Ages. See K. Quirk, "Men, Women and Miracles in Normandy, 1050–1150," in *Medieval Memories: Men, Women and the Past, 700–1300*, ed. E. Van

succor at the shrine of Maiolus implied the agency of parents, but the author's imprecise language makes it impossible to distinguish parents from the larger network of family and friends.[61] As these few examples show, however, parents sometimes played a role in transporting their ailing children to the shrine at Souvigny.[62]

Although parents were the most likely family members to offer aid to pilgrims afflicted by illness, the *Miracula* attest to wider networks of support consisting of extended relations of friends and family (*amici et parentes*). In six of the miracles in the collection, kinsfolk of pilgrims appeared alongside their friends as providers of counsel, transportation, votive offerings, and prayers.[63] The author of the *Miracula* undoubtedly had kinsfolk in mind when he described as *parentes* the individuals who carried an elderly man (*decrepitae aetatis*) stricken with a motor impairment (*contractus*) and nearing the end of his life (*aetatis iam fine*) from *villa Briodorensis* to Souvigny.[64] The support rendered to pilgrims by family members in the *Miracula* often paralleled the assistance they received from their friends (*amici*). Throughout the early Middle Ages, formal bonds of friendship (*amicitia*) entailed certain obligations of support and mutual assistance, expressed within a framework that emphasized the social parity of each member.[65] Friends frequently marshaled their social and material resources on each other's behalf, and such reciprocal

---

Houts (London, 2013), pp. 54–62; and L. A. Craig, *Wandering Women and Holy Matrons: Women as Pilgrims in the Later Middle Ages* (Leiden, 2009), pp. 90–97.

61. In one example (*MM* 1.11), there is no mention of anyone accompanying a boy (*puer*) from *villa Cavannis* seeking a remedy for his withered hand, even though this *villa* lay some seventy miles from Souvigny, a journey of several days. On *villa Cavannis*, which seems to have been located between Saint-Gengoux-le-National, Burnand, Sercy, and Savigny, see BB, vol. 3, pp. 239–40 (no. 2032), with D. Poeck, "Laienbegräbnisse in Cluny," *Frühmittelalterliche Studien* 15 (1981): 68–179, at p. 131.

62. Further on children and the miraculous, see R. Finucane, *The Rescue of Innocents: Endangered Children in Medieval Miracles* (London, 1997); D. Lett, *L'Enfant des miracles: Enfances et familles au Moyen Âge (XIIe–XIIIe siècles)* (Paris, 1997); and A. E. Bailey, "Miracle Children: Medieval Hagiography and Childhood Imperfection," *Journal of Interdisciplinary History* 47 (2016): 267–85.

63. *MM* 1.12, 1.13, 1.15, 2.8, 2.19, and 2.20.

64. *MM* 1.13. Located somewhere in the *pagus Biruricus* (Berry), the exact location of *villa Briodorensis* remains elusive. The Bollandists identified this location as Bridiers in the Limousin March (*Marchia Lemovicina*). See *AASS* Maii 2, p. 693, n. f.

65. G. Althoff, *Family, Friends, and Followers: Political and Social Bonds in Early Medieval Europe*, trans. C. Carroll (Cambridge, 2004), p. 66; and S. Gilsdorf, *The Favor of Friends: Intercession and Aristocratic Politics in Carolingian and Ottonian Europe* (Leiden, 2014), p. 52. For more on the concept of *amicitia* in the Middle Ages, see V. Epp, *Amicitia: Zur Geschichte personaler, sozialer, politischer und geistlicher Beziehungen im frühen Mittelalter* (Stuttgart, 1999).

advocacy could take the form of intercessory prayer.[66] In the *Miracula*, we find friends helping their stricken comrades in practical and devotional ways. Such aid could even precede the pilgrimage itself, as when the friends of a certain deaf woman from Marigny regularly employed some form of silent communication (*signorum aliquorum*) whenever they sought to help her in some way (*aliquid utilitatis facere*).[67] Prospective pilgrims likewise appear to have consulted their friends before embarking on a pilgrimage, frequently seeking their advice and gauging their support. After hearing of the many people healed at the shrine of Maiolus, a paralytic man from Nivernais approached both his kinsfolk (*parentibus*) and friends (*amicis*) about his desire to travel to Souvigny.[68] In several cases, friends accompanied pilgrims to the saint's tomb, and the support they offered appears to have echoed that typically expected from *parentes*. Upon reaching the shrine with the help of his family (*parentum*), a boy named Heldinus tarried in the monastic church hoping for a cure to his blindness. The boy's friends and kin (*amici et parentes*) accompanied him into the church, where they offered up successful petitions on behalf of their young companion.[69] Sundry forms of cooperation and intercession coalesced at cult centers like Souvigny, where ailing pilgrims relied on their family members and close associates for consultation, transportation, and prayerful intercession.

Just as family and friends played an important role in their support of impaired adults with a mind toward pilgrimage, married pilgrims seemed to have likewise expected help from their spouses, albeit less frequently than from their kinsfolk. Only two miracles in the *Miracula* explicitly acknowledge the role of spouses in bringing pilgrims to Souvigny.[70] In each case, marital support networks appear to be far more ambiguous than other relationships. In one instance, the *Miracula* referred to the wife of an elderly man with mobility issues (*contractus*), who had already taken her husband to multiple shrines in the hopes that he might secure a remedy. Although essential for hopeful pilgrims, such sustained support undoubtedly burdened families over time. Such was the case in this story, as the pilgrim's wife objected when he petitioned her to lead him to Souvigny, citing the financial distress that his

---

66. Gilsdorf, *The Favor of Friends*, pp. 61–62.
67. *MM* 2.8.
68. *MM* 1.15.
69. *MM* 1.12.
70. *MM* 2.14 and 2.21.

previous (and unsuccessful) pilgrimages had caused. Even though she eventually gave in to his request, the woman abandoned her husband along with their small child en route to the tomb when their pack animals struggled at a river crossing.[71] Often subordinated to their husbands, women faced greater obstacles in opposing the wishes of their spouses. They nevertheless found ways to make shrine pilgrimages, in some circumstances without explicit spousal support.[72] The *Miracula* included the story of a poor woman (*paupercula*) detested (*despecta*) by her husband and her community on account of her chronic paralysis.[73] Resolving to seek the aid of the saint without her spouse's support, the woman made her own arrangements for her transportation to Maiolus's shrine.[74] Her husband refused to assist or accompany his wife to Souvigny and reunited with her only after she had fully recovered thanks to the intervention of the saint.

Impaired pilgrims relied primarily on the assistance of others when embarking on a pilgrimage, but the *Miracula* also provide evidence for the use of personal mobility aids, which augmented the agency of an otherwise immobile petitioner. Throughout the Middle Ages, mobility tools had a decidedly ad hoc character, and people frequently improvised by adapting existing transportation methods to their particular needs.[75] Canes, crutches, and walking sticks remained popular and easily accessible tools throughout the medieval period, as a number of stories in the *Miracula* attest.[76] In one such story, a man named Iterius relied on a pair of hand trestles (*scamellos*) to help him crawl when his disabled knees prevented him from walking.[77] Such tools could provide disabled pilgrims with some degree of mobility, but their use could

---

71. *MM* 2.14. Accounts of spousal disobedience in medieval miracle collection do not appear to have maligned women more than men and many collections present women as faithful and supportive wives. See A. E. Bailey, "Wives, Mothers, and Widows on Pilgrimage: Categories of 'Woman' Recorded at English Healing Shrines in the High Middle Ages," *Journal of Medieval History* 39 (2013): 197–219, at p. 212; and Van Houts, *Married Life in the Middle Ages*, p. 127.

72. Bailey, "Wives, Mothers, and Widows on Pilgrimage," p. 212; and Van Houts, *Married Life in the Middle Ages*, pp. 123–24.

73. *MM* 2.21.

74. On the "ingenious transportation device" (*artificioso illo ingenio transportatorio*) that she had constructed to make her journey, see n. 82, below.

75. I. Metzler, "Have Crutch, Will Travel: Disabled People on the Move in Medieval Europe," in *Travels and Mobilities in the Middle Ages: From the Atlantic to the Black Sea*, ed. M. O'Doherty and F. Schmieder (Turnhout, 2015), pp. 91–117, at p. 107.

76. See, for example, *MM* 1.20, 2.2, 2.7, 2.11, 2.16, and 2.19.

77. *MM* 2.22. See Metzler, "Have Crutch, Will Travel," p. 110.

also inflict further hardships: Iterius's crawling eventually caused the skin on his knees and elbows to develop painful calluses. Several pilgrims acquired pack animals for transport, typically donkeys, oxen, or horses.[78] A paraplegic farmer from *villa Gunduensis* named Durannus had himself tied atop a donkey to prevent a fall during his ride to Souvigny.[79] Other pilgrims traveled in carts with or without the help of draught animals or otherwise made their journey to Souvigny in some form of vehicle (*in vehiculo*).[80] Armannus, the noble *contractus* from the town of Petra, arranged for two oxen and a horse to ferry him to the abbot's shrine on a small litter (*loculum*).[81] Moreover, some pilgrims made use of novel means of transport constructed specifically for their pilgrimage and tailored to their individual needs. One poor woman (*paupercula*) suffering from quadriplegia had an "instrument of conveyance" (*comportaticium . . . instrumentum*) constructed in preparation for her journey to Souvigny. Another women relied on an "ingenious transportation device" (*artificioso illo ingenio transportatorio*) perhaps some kind of wheelchair, upon which she was lifted onto an ox-drawn carriage (*carrusa*) and brought to the tomb of Maiolus.[82] The author of the miracle collection did not describe the device in detail, but he noted that the woman chose to disembark from it and crawl to the saint's shrine after she had arrived in Souvigny.[83] The type of tool or vehicle employed by a medieval pilgrim depended, much like the efficacy of their social networks, on the circumstances surrounding their illness, their personal relationships, and their financial status. As the *Miracula* attest, pilgrims with physical impairments were far from passive. We find them working actively alongside their family and friends to bring about cures for their maladies at shrines like Souvigny.

---

78. *MM* 2.7, 2.11, and 2.14.

79. *MM* 2.11. The location of *villa Gunduensis* remains unidentified. Following the transcription of *Gunduensis* as *Cunduensis* in the *BC*, the Bollandists suggested the episcopal city of Condom-en-Armagnac, Gers, in the Aquitaine as a possible location, even though it lies more than two hundred miles from Souvigny. See *AASS* Maii 2, p. 698, n. *l*.

80. *MM* 1.8, 1.14, 2.17, 2.19, and 2.21.

81. *MM* 2.17. On the possible location of Petra, see n. 25, above.

82. *MM* 2.21.

83. The pilgrim's decision to crawl to the tomb of Maiolus, unassisted by any helper or tool, was likely an expression of humility. Aristocratic pilgrims would often dismount their horses a few miles away from a shrine for similar reasons. See Finucane, *Miracles and Pilgrims*, p. 48. To overcome their mobility impairments, medieval pilgrims crafted many different kinds of transportation devices by improvising from sledges, wheelbarrows, and furniture. See Metzler, "Have Crutch, Will Travel," pp. 102–106.

CHAPTER 6

The *Miracula* provide us with a *tableau vivant* of the thaumaturgic and social activities surrounding a bustling saint's shrine in the town of Souvigny in the early eleventh century. The anonymous author of this miracle collection curated more than four dozen accounts of miraculous episodes at the request of Abbot Odilo to promote the cult of his predecessor, Maiolus of Cluny. His attention to detail allows us to chart the gender ratios of these suppliants, to gauge the appeal of the shrine to individuals from a wide range of social ranks, and to identify several of the pilgrims mentioned by name in the text. Moreover, these stories cast light on the predominantly therapeutic character of the shrine, which cure-seekers sought for relief from motor impairments and blindness. They also provide a clear indication that the appeal of Maiolus's cult was primarily local, rather than international, as Rudolphus Glaber had claimed in his *Five Books of Histories*. The nature of the maladies described in the *Miracula* accounts for the many references to the important role played by family and friends in helping their kinsfolk reach the tomb at Souvigny. More important, the miracle collection also gives us some rare glimpses of the ways that such pilgrims, specifically those with motor impairments, took steps to increase their agency through the use of personal mobility aids of all kinds, from draught animals and carts, to crutches and "ingenious transportation devices."

CHAPTER 7

Lurking with Spiritual Intent

On the Origin and Functions of the Monastic Roundsman (Circator)

The exercise of discipline presupposes a mechanism that coerces by means of observation.

—Michel Foucault, *Discipline and Punish*[1]

Medieval abbots were primarily concerned with the maintenance of discipline within their monasteries. Although modern scholarship has dealt almost exclusively with the external enemies of monastic communities—rapacious secular landowners and quarrelsome bishops, and their encroachment on monastic property and autonomy—more insidious threats could sometimes be found within the walls of the monastery.[2] Monks who succumbed to the temptations of sleep, idle talk, masturbation, and homosexuality were more dangerous to the community than any external enemy. Despite the program of initiation that existed at most monasteries for the indoctrination of new members, there was a recurring fear that some monks would fail to keep up with the rigorous ascetic regime of cenobitic

---

Originally published as "Lurking with Spiritual Intent: A Note on the Origin and Functions of the Monastic Roundsman (*Circator*)," *Revue bénédictine* 109 (1999): 75-89. Reprinted with permission.

1. M. Foucault, *Discipline and Punish: The Birth of the Prison*, trans. A. Sheridan (New York, 1977), p. 170. Although his topic is the prison and not the monastery, Foucault's insightful analysis of the disciplinary uses of enclosure, surveillance, and visibility has informed my understanding of the enforcement of discipline in the monasteries discussed in this chapter.

2. See, for example, B. H. Rosenwein, T. Head, and S. Farmer, "Monks and their Enemies: A Comparative Approach," *Speculum* 66 (1991): 764-96; and A. G. Remensnyder, *Remembering Kings Past: Monastic Foundation Legends in Medieval Southern France* (Ithaca, 1991), pp. 127-34.

life and that their resulting negligence would disrupt the intention and undermine the integrity of the community.³ Monastic legislators tried to cope with this problem by charging certain monks with the duty of patrolling the monastery and reporting in the daily chapter meeting any deviation from the *ordo*. The "roundsman" (*circator*) was a common feature of cenobitic life in the Middle Ages, yet this important and no doubt dreaded official is largely absent from the historical record.⁴ This study attempts to flesh out a functional portrait of the roundsman from the skeletal descriptions of the office found scattered throughout medieval monastic customaries. A fuller understanding of the origin and functions of this official sheds light both on the fears and concerns of monastic legislators and on the strategies they adopted to discourage the most intimate of their potential enemies: the monks of their monasteries.

Already in the sixth century, abbots recognized that their monks required some kind of supervision when not taking part in communal activities like the *opus Dei* and manual labor. In the anonymous *Rule of the Master*, the responsibility of supervision in a large monastery fell to officials known as provosts (*praepositi*), two of whom were placed in charge of every ten monks. These officials were senior members of the community appointed by the abbot to watch over their charges day and night and to reprove any faults they might commit, especially those involving inappropriate speech.⁵ But surveillance was not their only responsibility. The provosts also read the Lesson of the Apostle during the office and the Gospel in the absence of the abbot.⁶ The near-contemporary *Rule of Benedict* also subdivided its community into small groups under the care of officials known as deans (*decani*) but did not specifically define their

---

3. On the Cluniac novitiate, see I. Cochelin, "Peut-on parler de noviciat à Cluny pour les Xe-XIIe siècles," *Revue Mabillon*, n.s. 9 (1998): 17–52.

4. I employ the English "roundsman" for the Latin *circator* throughout this chapter, a term borrowed from David Knowles's translation of the *Decreta Lanfranci* in *The Monastic Constitutions of Lanfranc* (London, 1951), p. 78. The most complete descriptive catalog of sources referring to this official is H. Feiss, "*Circatores*: From Benedict of Nursia to Humbert of Romans," *American Benedictine Review* 40 (1989): 346–79, with whom I differ substantially on several points. In the present study, I attempt to offer a more dynamic portrait of the roundsman by exploring the historical contingencies that challenged and molded the rubrics of the office from the sixth to the twelfth centuries. In addition, there emerges from my reading of the sources a less idealized image of the disciplinary integrity of some large monasteries in the central Middle Ages. This allows me to consider more fully how monastic legislators developed strategies to discourage negligence and harmful behavior within their communities.

5. *RM* 11.27–30.

6. *RM* 46.3–7.

role in the personal supervision of the monks.⁷ At least part of this duty fell to the more experienced monks, the seniors (*seniores*). They were to watch over new members of the community, supervise the activities of the younger monks, and maintain discipline in the absence of the abbot. In addition, the porter was chosen from their ranks.⁸ They were also to make the rounds of the monastery (*circumire monasterium*) during the hours devoted to private reading to ensure that the monks were in fact reading alone in their cells and not idling away the time or telling stories and thus distracting their fellows.⁹ Two general observations can be made from this sixth-century evidence: the supervision of monks seems to have been a constant concern in these early cenobitic communities; and the responsibility of this supervision fell to more experienced monks, but it was not their sole function in the monastery.

The roundsman emerged as a distinct personage in the monastic legislation of the eighth century. It was the age of the mixed rule, when each cenobitic community compiled its own patchwork of customs and liturgical cycles, cut from the fabric of the rules of Benedict and Columbanus (and other sources now impossible to trace) and tailored to fit the needs of each monastery.¹⁰ In the year 666, Bishop Drausius produced a charter instructing the women of the monastery of Saint Mary in Soissons to follow the precepts of both Benedict and Columbanus.¹¹ In the late seventh century, Evroul "used to recite the monastic hours according to the Roman and Gallic customs of St Benedict, and the Irish custom of St Columbanus" at the hermitage he founded in the forest of Ouche in the province of Rouen.¹² A few decades later, Bede related in his *Lives of the Abbots* how Benedict Biscop made frequent peregrinations from his native Northumbria and gathered all of the best things found in the practices of seventeen monasteries for the monks of Wearmouth and Jarrow.¹³

---

7. *RB* 21 and 65. For a discussion of the terms *praepositus* and *decanus* and their divergent meanings in the *RM* and *RB*, see A. de Vogüé, *The Community and Abbot in the Rule of St. Benedict*, trans. C. Philippi and E. R. Perkins, 2 vols. (Kalamazoo, 1988), vol. 2, pp. 257-70.

8. Appointed to watch over new members: *RB* 58.6; supervising monks: *RB* 22.3 and 22.7; maintaining discipline: *RB* 56.3; appointed porter: *RB* 66.1.

9. *RB* 48.17-18.

10. On the spread of the *Rule of Benedict* and the *regulae mixtae*, see F. Prinz, *Frühes Mönchtum im Frankenreich: Kultur und Gesellschaft in Gallien, den Rheinlanden und Bayern am Beispiel der monastischen Entwicklung (4. bis 8. Jahrhundert)*, 2nd ed. (Munich, 1988), pp. 263-92.

11. *PL* 88, cols. 1183-84.

12. M. Chibnall, "The Merovingian Monastery of St. Evroul in the Light of Conflicting Traditions," in *Popular Belief and Practice*, ed. G. J. Cumings and D. Baker, Studies in Church History 8 (Cambridge, 1972), pp. 31-40 (translation at p. 34).

13. Bede, *Historia abbatum* 11, ed. and trans. C. Grocock and I. N. Wood, in *Abbots of Wearmouth and Jarrow* (Oxford, 2013), pp. 46-50.

CHAPTER 7

The roundsman was a product of this age of selective amalgamation. The office seems to have originated during the eighth century when the circumstances at some monasteries necessitated that the general duties assigned to the senior monks in the *Rule of Benedict* be divided among more specialized officials. The paucity of evidence for the internal life of cenobitic communities in this period makes it difficult to determine with certainty what kind of circumstances resulted in such a reorganization of the monastic infrastructure, but it is most probable that the population of monasteries grew large and unmanageable.[14] Whatever the reason, some legislators of this period found it necessary to create new officials endowed with more precise duties. The duty of making patrols or rounds of the monastery to supervise the brethren fell to an official commonly known as the *circator* (and more rarely as the synonymous *circa* and *circinnator*). The title clearly indicates the primary function of the office: to make the rounds of the monastery (*circumire monasterium*).[15]

The earliest evidence for this official comes from the monastery of Monte Cassino. The Lombards had ravaged Benedict's foundation in the late sixth century, but it was refounded in 720. A short list of customs written for the community around 750 provides us with our first glimpse of the monastic roundsman. Monte Cassino had two *circatores* in the eighth century. They patrolled the monastery at all hours to ensure that each monk was in his proper place. If someone was absent, they noted it on a writing board and presented their complaint to the abbot in the chapter meeting where the negligent monk was admonished by the abbot and punished for his misbehavior.[16] They also enforced the strict precepts regarding silence. No words could be uttered in the church except for the divine office and prayer.[17] The

---

14. There was an increase in child oblation between the sixth and ninth centuries, but this was only one aspect of the growth of monasteries during this period. See M. de Jong, *In Samuel's Image: Child Oblation in the Early Medieval West* (Leiden, 1996).

15. A variation of this term *circator* had currency in the late Roman Empire as the title of a soldier who patrolled the perimeter of the camp. See *Dictionnaire d'archéologie chrétienne et de liturgie*, ed. H. Leclercq, 15 vols. (Paris, 1907-53), vol. 3.2, cols. 1691-92, *s.v.* Circitor ou Circuitor. The earliest etymological definition of the term in a monastic context is found in the late tenth-century *Regularis Concordia Anglicae Nationis* 9: "Qui ab officio circuitus sui circa vocatur," ed. and trans. T. Symons, in *The Monastic Agreement of the Monks and Nuns of the English Nation* (London, 1953), p. 56.

16. *Ordo Casinensis I* 8, ed. D. T. Leccisotti, in *Initia consuetudinis benedictinae: Consuetudines saeculi octavi et noni*, ed. K. Hallinger, CCM 1 (Siegburg, 1963), p. 103.

17. On speech prohibitions in early cenobitic communities, see A. G. Wathen, *Silence: The Meaning of Silence in the Rule of Saint Benedict* (Washington, DC, 1973); and S. G. Bruce, *Silence*

roundsmen were quick to note any monks seen laughing or whispering and to punish them when the opportunity arose.[18] Several of these duties are familiar to us from the description of the seniors' duties in the *Rule of Benedict*, but two important innovations immediately distinguish the later official from his sixth-century prototype. First, unlike the seniors, the roundsman was highly specialized. His sole function was to patrol the monastery and to report faults in the chapter. Second, he was the eyes and ears of the entire community. The admonishment of a monk in the *Rule of Benedict* was a private affair; only successive faults resulted in a public reprimand.[19] By the eighth century, however, every disciplinary action was a communal event, sparked by the public accusation of the roundsman. This accusation took place before all the brethren in the daily chapter and punishment was meted out then and there by the abbot. These two innovations remained core attributes of the roundsman's office throughout the Middle Ages.

The roundsman was the product of specific contingencies of the eighth century, but by the early ninth century, he had become part of the received custom of many monasteries. He was present both in the earliest customs of Corbie (dated before 826) and in the list of monastic officials and their duties composed in 835 for Wala, the abbot of Bobbio.[20] Benedict of Aniane made no mention of the *circator* in his *Concordia Regularum* (compiled before 821) and simply reiterated the precept of the *Rule of Benedict* concerning the patrol duty of the seniors.[21] This conformed to his agenda to unify and standardize the divergent monastic traditions of the Carolingian Empire as an agent of the reform instituted by Louis the Pious. The rule of his namesake provided him with the ideal model of cenobitic organization and an authoritative terminology in which to express it. It is most likely that the reformer was using a passage culled from the *Rule of Benedict* to refer to this new, specialized official.

---

and *Sign Language in Medieval Monasticism: The Cluniac Tradition (c. 900–1200)* (Cambridge, 2007), pp. 13–52.

    18. *Ordo Casinensis I* 11, ed. Leccisotti, p. 104.

    19. *RB* 23.

    20. *Consuetudines Corbeienses*, ed. J. Semmler, in *Initia consuetudinis benedictinae*, ed. Hallinger, p. 417; and *Breve memorationis* of Wala of Bobbio, ed. J. Semmler, in *Initia consuetudinis benedictinae*, ed. Hallinger, pp. 420–22.

    21. Benedict of Aniane, *Concordia Regularum* 60.1, *PL* 103, cols. 1178–79. Martène was the first to equate these seniors with roundsmen (*PL* 103, col. 1178, n. *i*). See also *Regula sancti Benedicti Anianensis* 27, ed. J. Semmler, in *Initia consuetudinis benedictinae*, ed. Hallinger, p. 523.

CHAPTER 7

Monastic legislators further elaborated the duties of the roundsman in customaries compiled in the tenth and eleventh centuries at Cluny or within its orbit of influence.[22] This official occupied an important position in the monastic infrastructure as a direct subordinate of the claustral prior. Second only to the abbot and the major prior in authority, the claustral prior was responsible for the maintenance of regular observance and order throughout the entire monastery.[23] He was a vigilant overseer of his charges. He made sure that they conducted themselves with the proper deportment during all their activities. After Compline, he made a round of the monastery along a predetermined route to ensure that the monks were all in the dormitory. In larger communities, however, the claustral prior alone could not ensure the conduct of his charges. He required assistants and first among them were the roundsmen.

The number of *circatores* active in each monastery varied with the size and needs of the community.[24] Many smaller monasteries probably had no need for them at all. Roundsmen are usually mentioned in the customaries of larger, well-established monasteries like Cluny, and they are often referred to in the plural. Two characteristics of cenobitic monasticism during this period may account for the increasingly detailed descriptions of the roundsman and his duties in the surviving books of customs: the increase in vocations throughout the eleventh and twelfth centuries; and the architectural elaboration of monastic complexes during this same period. The evidence from Cluny provides the best material for a case study. The community at Cluny grew from about one hundred monks at the beginning of the abbacy of Saint

---

22. Many of these customaries were composed at Cluny or by monasteries within its range of influence. The following discussion of the roundsman derives largely from descriptions found in Bernard of Cluny, *Ordo Cluniacensis sive Consuetudines*, ed. M. Herrgott in *Vetus Disciplina Monastica* (Paris, 1726), pp. 136-364; Ulrich of Zell, *Consuetudines Cluniacensis*, PL 149, cols. 649-779, both produced at Cluny in the late eleventh century; and William of Hirsau, *Constitutiones Hirsaugienses*, ed. P. Engelbert, CCM 15.1-2, 2 vols. (Siegburg, 2010), written for the monastery at Hirsau before 1200 after the model of Ulrich. For an overview of this material, see I. Cochelin, "Customaries as Inspirational Sources," in *Consuetudines et Regulae: Sources for Monastic Life in the Middle Ages and the Early Modern Period*, ed. C. M. Malone and C. Maines, Disciplina Monastica 10 (Turnhout, 2014), pp. 27-72.

23. For a portrait of the claustral prior from Cluniac sources, see G. de Valous, *Le monachisme clunisien des origins au XVe siècle: Vie intérieure des monastères et organization de l'ordre*, 2 vols. (Paris, 1970), vol. 1, pp. 120-22.

24. *Decreta Lanfranci*: "Numerus eorum sit secundum facultatem loci, et necessitatem rei," ed. Knowles, p. 78.

Hugh (1049) to as many as four hundred a little more than a century later at the death of Peter the Venerable (1156).²⁵

Such growth must have weighed heavily on the claustral prior. The pressures on internal discipline caused by this increase were compounded by the fact that the community was almost always in flux. More experienced and reliable monks were often sent out on missions for the abbot, and new monks were always arriving at the gates. The traffic of personnel between Cluny and the monastery of Hirsau in the Black Forest demonstrates this point. In the later eleventh century, Abbot Hugh of Cluny sent his monk Ulrich to Hirsau to advise its abbot William on the reform of his community. Later, on three separate occasions, William sent some of his monks to Cluny where they stayed for an unspecified period of time to learn and experience the Cluniac *ordo* firsthand as a model for the reform underway at Hirsau.²⁶ The prolonged absence of responsible monks and the introduction of many new monks reared on alien customs must have caused tremendous problems for the claustral prior and necessitated the appointment of a number of roundsmen to assist him in ensuring that all of the monks living at Cluny kept up with the rigorous disciplinary regime for which the monastery had become renowned.

The complex of structures housing the monks and their dependents grew to accommodate the swelling communities. Again, this process is most clearly seen at Cluny, where we can compare the detailed description of Odilo's monastery in the *Liber tramitis* (c. 1040) with the monumental building program executed by Abbot Hugh and well underway at the turn of the twelfth century.²⁷ What strikes the modern

---

25. N. Hunt, *Cluny Under Saint Hugh, 1049–1109* (London, 1967), pp. 82–83. Similar patterns of growth are evident at other contemporary Benedictine houses. See J. Van Engen, "The 'Crisis of Cenobitism' Reconsidered: Benedictine Monasticism in the Years 1050–1150," *Speculum* 61 (1986): 269–304, at pp. 286–77.

26. William, *Constitutiones Hirsaugienses*, prol.: "Circa idem tempus Vodalricus, senior quidam Cluniacensis, nutu dei pro causa monasterii in Alemanniam missus aliquandiu nobiscum mansit. Et quia nobis olim familiarissimus longaque iam experientia in Cluniacensibus disciplinis exercitatus, rogauimus eum, ut suas nobis consuetudines transscriberet ... primo duos ex nostris fratribus atque iterum alios duos, tercio nihilominus duos Cluniacum direximus. Qui tam diligenti examinatione omnia illius ordinis secreta rimati sunt," ed. Engelbert, vol. 1, p. 154.

27. For the description of Cluny during the abbacy of Odilo, see *Liber tramitis aevi Odilonis Abbatis*, ed. P. Dinter, CCM 10 (Siegburg, 1980), pp. 203–206. For reconstructions of the eleventh- and twelfth-century building phases, see K. J. Conant, *Cluny: Les églises et la maison du chef d'Ordre* (Mâcon, 1968), figures 4 and 5. Many monastic complexes underwent expansion

viewer most when looking at the reconstructed layouts of these building phases is not so much the size of the complex as a whole, but the elaborateness of the plan. Apart from Hugh's great basilica, the sheer vastness of which must have evoked wonder, the individual buildings of the monastery were not exceptionally large; taken together, however, they created a veritable warren of hallways and chambers wherein a variety of disciplinary offenses might easily have gone unnoticed and unpunished by the claustral prior. It was the duty of the roundsmen to patrol the complex at all times to discourage such offenses from taking place.

The *circatores* were chosen from the most trustworthy and prudent monks of the community and held their office for an entire year.[28] They had to be zealous and loyal "friends" of the rule.[29] Their role as the accusers of all transgressors meant they had to be above internal factionalism and favoritism of any kind.[30] The primary function of the roundsmen remained the same as that of their eighth-century predecessors: they patrolled the monastery and reported any negligence in the presence of the entire community in the chapter meeting.[31]

---

during this period for a variety of different reasons. See the examples of the extensive building programs at Saint-Philibert in Tournou and Saint-Bénigne in Dijon, discussed in K. J. Conant, *Carolingian and Romanesque Architecture 800–1200* (Harmondsworth, 1979), pp. 141–53.

28. The duration of the office is mentioned only in the ninth-century commentary on the *Rule of Benedict* by Hildemar, *Expositio regulae sancti Benedicti*: "Verumtamen sciendum est, quia decani minores vel circatores pro hoc, quia decani sunt vel circatores, non debent praeesse allis, h. e. non debent praeponi in choro aut in capitulo aut in aliquo loco, excepto si deest abbas aut praepositus aut decanus major; tunc unus illorum debet praeponi, qui teneat locum abbatis; nam ideo dixi, non debere praeponi, quia non est ratio, ut in isto uno anno, cum habent ministerium, superponantur, in altero autem anno, cum non habent ministerium, iterum sedeant inferius in loco, in quo intraverunt," ed. R. Mittermüller, in *Vita et Regula SS. P. Benedicti una cum Expositio Regulae a Hildemaro tradita* (Regensburg, 1880), p. 576. On Hildemar and his commentary, see M. A. Schroll, *Benedictine Monasticism as Reflected in the Warnefrid-Hildemar Commentaries on the Rule* (London, 1941); and P. W. Hafner, *Der Basiliuskommentar zur Regula S. Benedicti: Ein Beitrag zur Autorenfrage karolingischer Regelkommentare* (Munster, 1959).

29. *Consuetudines Floriacenses Antiquiores* 10: "Qui tenacissimus sit propositi monastici, non levis animo sed constans et discipline regularis amicus," ed. A. Davril and L. Donnat, in *Consuetudinum saeculi X/XI/XII monumenta non-Cluniacensia*, ed. K. Hallinger, CCM 7.3 (Siegburg, 1984), p. 17; and Bernard 1.4, p. 144: "Eligantur de totius congregationis religiosioribus et ferventioribus."

30. Bernard 1.4, p. 144: "Qui nec malitiose pro privato odio unquam clamorem de quolibet faciant, nec pro privata amicitia sive pro v.g. cuiuslibet scurrilitatis taceant negligentias quorumcumque"; and William, *Constitutiones Hirsaugienses* 2.16: "Et in his reclamationibus sicut et in omnibus omnino personarum acceptio est devitanda," ed. Engelbert, vol. 2, p. 99.

31. Bernard 1.4, p. 144: "Circuitores monasterii ... certis horis circumeant officinas monasterii observantes negligentias fratrum, et ordinis praevaricationes"; and Ulrich 3.7, col. 741c:

At first glance, their duties seem little different from that of the claustral prior. Indeed, the signs for the roundsman and the claustral prior in the sign language in use during times of silence at the monastery of Hirsau were similar, both involving a rotation of the extended index finger to indicate the rounds they made.[32] But the method and execution of the duties of these specialists, retailored to the needs of rapidly growing monastic communities, clearly distinguished them from their superiors. As noted above, the claustral prior made a round of the monastery at the end of every day, after Compline. His routine was described in some detail in the Cluniac customaries and varied with the layout of each community. In general, his task was to ensure that the monastery was secure for the night. He stayed behind after the monks filed from the church and, with a lantern, he systematically moved through the empty rooms of the monastery until he reached the dormitory. When he was satisfied that everyone was in his bed and quiet, he too retired. Some claustral priors made lesser rounds of the monastery during the day as well, or when the major prior was absent, they replaced him on the rounds that he was accustomed to make between Matins and Lauds.[33] By contrast, the roundsman followed no predetermined route or timetable. In fact, any such structured routine would have undermined their efficiency, as a statement by Ulrich of Zell made clear: "Let them patrol the entire enclosure not once but many times during the day so that there is neither a place nor a time in which any brother, if he should engage in irregular activity, may be unconcerned of the possibility of detection" and punishment.[34] The randomness of their patrols was thus meant to heighten the fear of detection in negligent monks. A *circator* could appear in any part of

---

"Circatorum munus est ut omnes negligentias tam minimas quam majores, quae ullo modo contra ordinem possunt contingere, notent, et in capitulo reclament."

32. William, *Constitutiones Hirsaugienses* 1.5: "Pro signo claustralis prioris praemisso generali (signo prioris) indicem deorsum verte et circumfer quasi girando ... Pro signo circatoris premisso generali signo monachi praedicto modo indicem circumfer," ed. Engelbert, vol. 1, pp. 243 and 244. For more on the use of monastic sign language at Hirsau, see Bruce, *Silence and Sign Language in Medieval Monasticism*, pp. 118-23.

33. Ulrich 3.6, cols. 740-41; William, *Constitutiones Hirsaugienses* 2.15, ed. Engelbert, vol. 2, pp. 92-97; and *Decreta Lanfranci*, ed. Knowles, pp. 76-77.

34. Ulrich 3.7, col. 741c: "Propterea totum claustrum non semel sed multoties in die circumeant, ut nec locus sit nec hora in qua frater ullus securus esse possit, si tale quid [contra ordinem] commiserit, non deprehendi et non publicari." This sentence is repeated almost verbatim in William, *Constitutiones Hirsaugienses* 2.16, ed. Engelbert, vol. 2, p. 97.

the monastery, from the kitchens to the infirmary to the cemetery.[35] Although they were never to leave the monastic complex, the roundsmen were also charged to look out through the gates to see if any of the brethren were wandering around the courtyard or loitering or sitting together gossiping.[36] Only the presence of the abbot or the prior deterred them, for they were ordered to show discretion and avoid the parts of the monastery where their superiors were known to be.[37]

The thought that a *circator* could appear at any moment, from around any corner of the monastery, must have been a strong deterrent to potential transgressors, but it did not prevent violations of the rules from taking place. In fact, it is clear from the customaries that the roundsmen encountered and made public a wide variety of disciplinary offenses. The burden of the ascetic regime of some monasteries weighed heavily on the monks and, when unsupervised, they would often succumb to sleep. The *circator* was ever on the watch for somnolent monks. At Cluny, he began his rounds in the darkness of early morning, after the monks had risen for the prayers before Matins, by going around with a lantern to the beds in the dormitory and checking around all the altars to ensure that no monk was sleeping there. Throughout the day he glided soundlessly through the halls and chambers of the monastery, arousing any sleepers whom they found by uttering a recognized sound or by shining the light of the lantern into their eyes.[38] At Fleury, the roundsman visited the monks individually while they were praying in their cells to ensure that they

---

35. William, *Constitutiones Hirsaugienses* 2.16, ed. Engelbert, vol. 2, pp. 98-99, provides a list of the parts of the monastery that the roundsmen habitually frequented.

36. *Decreta Lanfranci*: "Officinas monasterii nunquam pro hac cura egrediantur, sed per ostia earum prospiciant, si forte aliqui fratres per curiam vadant vagantes, aut stent vel sedeant fabulantes," ed. Knowles, pp. 78-79. See also Bernard 1.4, p. 144.

37. Ulrich 3.7, col. 741c: "Domno abbati et priori ita deferunt circatores ut nequaquam veniant ubi eos noverint esse quia, ut scriptum est: Non est disciplinus super magistrum."

38. *Redactio Wirzeburgensis* 2: "Circator sumpta in monasterio vel in dormitorio absconsa omne dormitorium et necessaria circueat, ne quem fratrum somnolentia depresserit provisurus. Inde rediens secretariae officinam similiter perlustret. Ille vero alter sumpta item quoque apud sanctam Mariam in cripta absconsa cum lumine circueat lectos infirmorum, si forte aliquem somnolentum invenerit excitaturus . . . Et si forte dormientem fratrem invenerit, luminetur oculis suis et si exhibito non inclinaverit, absconsam ante eum ponat. Qui accipiens itidem circuibit et si alium dormientem invenerit, idem faciet . . . Deinde secundum nocturnum sequitur, cuius intervallo idem circator criptas monasterii perlustret et si quem dormientem invenerit notabit," ed. R. Grünewald, in *Consuetudines Cluniacensium antiquiores cum redactionibus derivatis*, ed. K. Hallinger, CCM 7.2 (Siegburg, 1983), pp. 272-73. See also *Decreta Lanfranci*, ed. Knowles, p. 79.

had not fallen asleep. When he found a monk awake and attentive to his prayers, the *circator* himself immediately offered a prayer with his head inclined toward the monk "as though giving thanks for his diligence." But those unfortunates caught sleeping were awakened abruptly by the sound of the roundsman's boot stamping on the floor or by a swift elbow to the ribs.[39] Other lesser offenses occupied his time as well. On his endless rounds, the *circator* often came across books or articles of clothing which had been left behind by negligent monks and had to be presented in the chapter meeting on the following day.[40]

But more shameful offenses are hinted at in the customaries and confirmed by other sources. The roundsmen were instructed to haunt the halls of the monastery by night, lurking with spiritual intent, lanterns hidden beneath their cloaks, to catch negligent monks unawares, for the darkness veiled all manner of offenses.[41] Masturbation and homosexual behavior were especially feared. Odo of Cluny was accused of grave misconduct in the chapter meeting when he took one of the boys of the monastery to the lavatory in the middle of the night, believing that a burning lantern hung nearby would suffice to ensure the innocence of his intention when in fact he should have awoken a third party to accompany them.[42] The tenth-century *Regularis Concordia* specifically warned monks to avoid situations that would arouse suspicion of sexual misconduct: "Not even on the excuse of some spiritual matter shall any monk presume to take with him a young boy alone for

---

39. *Consuetudines Floriacenses Antiquiores* 10: "Illam vero tertio intervallo inchoante subintrat suaviter circator et facta reverentia omnes singillatim fratres excepto abbate intendit, si forte aliquem somnolentum impingat quem ibi dormire contingat. Quem vero vigilantem et psalmis intentum invenerit, se vigilare statim insinuat inclinato contra eum capite et quasi gratias pro sui cura agente ... Quo facto combinalis eiusdem somnolenti fratris aut cubito sibi latus fodit aut attritione pedis excitandi gratia aliquem sonum facit," ed. Davril and Donnat, pp. 18-19.

40. *Regularis Concordia Anglicae Nationis* 9: "Si qua invenerit ibi codicum aut vestimentorum, asportet ea ad capitulum sequentis diei," ed. Symons, p. 56; and *Consuetudines Floriacenses Antiquiores* 10: "Si quod fortasse post Completorium in claustro vel in aliqua officina incaute derelictum reperrerit, aut vestimentum, aut codicem, aut vascula aliqua de refectorio vel cellario sive infirmario educta, recolligit atque in capitulo fratrum recondit," ed. Davril and Donnat, p. 17.

41. *Consuetudines Floriacenses Antiquiores* 10: "Nam velut insidiator spiritalis nocturno solet tempore laternam quam absconsam vocant sub manica accensam portare et sibi tantum lucens negligentias fratrum quasi ex improvise pervestigare nititur," ed. Davril and Donnat, p. 17.

42. John of Salerno, *Vita Sancti Odonis* 33, PL 133, col. 57.

any private purpose, but as the rule commands, let the children always remain under the care of their master. Nor shall the master himself be allowed to be in the company with a boy without a third person as witness."[43] The customaries stressed that the roundsmen frequent those places in the monastery that might harbor any such suspicious activity.[44]

The *circatores* emerge from the monastic legislation of the central Middle Ages primarily as guardians of silence. Monks were rarely permitted to speak to one another in the monastery. Conversation was usually limited to the cloister and even then, the opportunity was often smothered by the weight of the liturgical round. As Ulrich of Zell noted: "Quite often before all of the monks can take their places in the cloister and one of the brethren can utter a single word, the bell for vespers is rung and that is the end of talking."[45] The monks maintained perpetual silence in the church, dormitory, refectory, and the kitchens.[46] Sign language was in use at some monasteries to enable rudimentary communication in these parts of the complex.[47] These prohibitions could not keep monks from talking to one another, and the roundsmen were charged again and again to report anyone they caught conversing without permission. When a *circator* happened upon some brethren talking together, the monks were expected to rise and state whether they had obtained permission to speak. If not, then they could expect reproach on the following day in the chapter meeting.[48] The roundsmen themselves never passed judgment on their charges.

---

43. *Regularis Concordia Anglicae Nationis* 11: "Nec ad obsequium priuatum quempiam illorum nec saltem sub spiritualis rei obtentu solum deducere praesumant, sed uti regula praecipit sub sui custodis uigilantia iugiter maneat; nec ipse custos cum singulo aliquot puerulo sine tertio qui testis assistat migrandi licentiam habeat," ed. and trans. Symons, p. 8. For useful discussions of this issue, see V. A. Kolve, "Ganymede/*Son of Getron*: Medieval Monasticism and the Drama of Same-Sex Desire," *Speculum* 73 (1998): 1014-67; and C. A. Jones, "Monastic Identity and Sodomitic Danger in the *Occupatio* by Odo of Cluny," *Speculum* 82 (2007): 1-53.

44. *Decreta Lanfranci*: "Circumeat omnia altaria in criptis, et quae ex utraque parte chori subtus sunt, caeteraque monasterii loca ubi suspicio poterit esse," ed. Knowles, p. 79.

45. Ulrich 1.18, col. 668: "Saepius namque priusquam omnes in claustro consideant, et aliquis fratrum vel unum verbum faciat, pulsatur signum ad vesperas, et ecce ibi finis loquendi." For a portrait of the cloister as a bustling space, see I. Cochelin, "Monastic Daily Life (c. 750-1100): A Tight Community Shielded by an Outer Court," in *CHMM*, pp. 542-60.

46. Ulrich 2.3, col. 703; and William, *Constitutiones Hirsaugienses* 1.4, ed. Engelbert, vol. 1, pp. 194-96.

47. For more on this custom, see Bruce, *Silence and Sign Language in Medieval Monasticism*.

48. Bernard 1.4, p. 144; Ulrich 3.6, col. 741; William, *Constitutiones Hirsaugienses* 2.16, ed. Engelbert, vol. 2, pp. 97-102; and *Decreta Lanfranci*, ed. Knowles, p. 78.

Even when they encountered monks involved in some breach of discipline, they passed on in silence, simply noting all they had seen and deferring any punitive action to the abbot.[49]

Disciplinary offenses involving communication could in fact take several unexpected forms. The *Life* of Peter, a twelfth-century abbot of the monastery of Cava (Santissima Trinità di Cava dei Tirreni) in southern Italy, contains an episode about a *circa* who, while making his rounds, heard what he presumed to be two monks conversing without permission. But when he approached the transgressors, he was surprised to discover only one, for the guilty monk had been rebuking a demon.[50] Roundsmen were especially watchful in the refectory as well. Although offenses involving speech were probably rare when the entire community gathered to eat, the *circatores* had to be alert to any misuse of the sign language employed by the monks at the table. Signing was a tool for rudimentary communication, but it could easily become a means of conversation. Consequently, monks who were seen making unnecessary signs were reported in the chapter meeting.[51]

The roundsman played a key role in the maintenance of discipline in many large monasteries, and the utility of such an official did not go unrecognized in other religious communities. In the twelfth century, regular canons began to employ *circatores* to police their enclosures.[52] The canons at Springiersbach and Rolduc had multiple roundsmen, and the customs of the order of Saint Victor of Paris contains a chapter clearly lifted from the customs of Cluny detailing the functions of this official.[53] Canons in fact borrowed many features of their adminis-

---

49. *Decreta Lanfranci*: "Circumitores vero nec verbo nec signo ei respondeant, sed modeste pertranseuentes," ed. Knowles, p. 78.

50. *Vita sancti Petri Abbatis Cavensis*: "Forte tunc senior quidam ex more monasterii cum circam faceret, monachum illum a longe quasi cum alio loquentem audivit, et solum inveniens, cum quo fuisset locutus ab eo inquirere studuit. Cui signo eger monachus dixit: Mane dicam tibi. Diluculo igitur circa rediens, ille ei omnia per ordinem enarravit," ed. L. A. Muratori, *Rerum Italicarum Scriptores: Tomus Sextus* (Milan, 1725), cols. 217-28, at col. 224.

51. *Consuetudines Affligenienses* 29: "Quamdiu autem comeditur, intente debent considerare circatores si qui dissoluti sint vel signa superflua faciant," ed. R. J. Sullivan, in *Consuetudines Benedictinae variae (saec. XI-saec. XIV)*, ed. G. Constable, CCM 6 (Siegburg, 1975), p. 149. For some examples of the abuse of monastic sign language, see Bruce, *Silence and Sign Language in Medieval Monasticism*, pp. 161-69.

52. For a full discussion of the twelfth-century canonical sources mentioning the roundsman, see Feiss, "Circatores," pp. 357-61.

53. *Consuetudines canonicorum regularium Springiersbacenses-Rodenses* 12.53 and 39.229, ed. S. Weinfurter, CCCM 48 (Turnhout, 1978), pp. 26 and 122; and *Liber Ordinis Sancti Victoris Parisiensis* 41, ed. L. Jocqué and L. Milis, CCCM 59 (Turnhout, 1984), pp. 194-96.

tration from successful monasteries. Their adoption of monastic *circatores* is but one aspect of the "inter-institutional currents" of reform that molded and reshaped diverse religious communities in the twelfth century.[54]

There is no evidence, however, for the presence of roundsmen in houses of religious women. Their communities, like those of many male monasteries, were probably too small to warrant the adoption of this specialized official. In fact, the duties of the *circator* may have fallen to the abbess. In an early twelfth-century letter written to the abbess Heloise on the spiritual directives and proper organization of monasteries for women, Abelard advised the abbess to "go carefully round her camp, now here, now there, like a watchful and tireless captain" to ensure that violations of rules were not taking place. Unlike the abbot of a large monastery, the abbess relied on no intermediary agents and rooted out offenses on her own. According to Abelard, she should be the first to discover "the evils of her house" and should rebuke and punish all transgressions in private, so that they might not provide bad examples for the rest of the community.[55] In the thirteenth century, abbesses were scrutinized and censured by bishops, who traveled through their dioceses, inquiring into the state of religious houses under their jurisdiction.[56] Because of their slow and arduous perambulations through the countryside, these episcopal visitors also came to be known as *circatores* in the later Middle Ages.[57]

The *circator* survived as an important feature of male cenobitic communities until the end of the medieval period.[58] Although his title changed in some places to "sentinel" (*observator*) or "patroller"

---

54. G. Constable, *The Reformation of the Twelfth Century* (Cambridge, 1996), pp. 88–124, esp. pp. 109–11.

55. Abelard, *Institutio seu Regula Sanctimonialium* 34: "Nunc igitur huc nunc illuc deambulans more providi et impigri ducis castra sua sollicite giret vel scrutetur ne per alicuius negligentiam ei qui tamquam leo circuit quaerens quem devoret aditus pateat. Omnia mala domus sue prior agnoscat ut ab ipsa prius possint corrigi quam a ceteris agnosci et in exemplum trahi," ed. and trans. D. Luscombe, in *The Letter Collection of Peter Abelard and Heloise* (Oxford, 2013), pp. 358–517, at p. 396.

56. For a discussion of the negligences discovered in female monasteries in mid-thirteenth-century Normandy during the visitations of Archbishop Eudes Rigaud of Rouen, see P. D. Johnson, *Equal in Monastic Profession: Religious Women in Medieval France* (Chicago, 1991), pp. 105–33; and A. J. Davis, *The Holy Bureaucrat: Eudes Rigaud and Religious Reform in Thirteenth-Century Normandy* (Ithaca, 2006), pp. 65–103.

57. C. du Cange, *Glossarium mediae et infimae latinitatis*, 10 vols. (Niort, 1883), vol. 2, p. 336, s.v. Circa.

58. For the adoption of the roundsman by the Premonstratensian order, see Feiss, "Circatores," pp. 368–71.

(*explorator*), his fundamental character and function remained the same. From his origin in Carolingian monasticism to his prominence in the central Middle Ages and thereafter, the roundsman held a pivotal place in the monastic infrastructure. Whether haunting the darkened halls of the monastery as the roving eye of the claustral prior or unveiling transgressions in the chapter meeting as the accusing voice of the entire community, the *circator* was a constant and no doubt dreaded presence in the daily lives and imaginations of medieval monks.

Chapter 8

Monastic Sign Language in the Cluniac Customaries

The Cluniac customaries provide a wealth of information about many aspects of monastic ritual and discipline at Cluny and other abbeys in its orbit of influence in the late eleventh century. They are particularly important as sources for the study of monastic sign language. The monks of Cluny were renowned for this use of manual signs in place of spoken words when rules of silence forbade them from speaking.[1] The earliest rules for cloistered men and women made reference to the use of rudimentary signaling devices in those parts of the abbey where speech was forbidden. These signals did not suffice, however, to convey precise information in monastic houses like Cluny that wed the strict disciplinary ideals of the Carolingian reforms with intensive rounds of corporate prayer and liturgical celebration.

Originally published as "Monastic Sign Language in the Cluniac Customaries," in *From Dead of Night to End of Day: The Medieval Customs of Cluny / Du coeur de la nuit à la fin du jour: Les coutumes clunisiennes au Moyen Âge*, ed. S. Boynton and I. Cochelin, Disciplina monastica 3 (Turnhout, 2005), pp. 273-86. Reprinted with permission.

1. See, for example, John of Salerno, *Vita Odonis* 1.32, *PL* 133, col. 57. The achievement of the Cluniacs was also recognized by the monks of the Cistercian Order, who appropriated the custom of sign language from their competitors in the twelfth century. See Conrad of Eberbach, *Exordium magnum cisterciense* 1.6, ed. B. Griesser, CCCM 138 (Turnhout, 1994), pp. 13-14. For more on this development, see S. G. Bruce, "The Origins of Cistercian Sign Language," *Cîteaux: Commentarii cistercienses* 52 (2001): 193-209.

As a result, in the early tenth century, the brethren of Cluny and other Burgundian abbeys developed a sign language—a system of meaning-specific hand signs that allowed them to communicate essential information to each other without countermanding their rules of silence.[2] The best-known source for the history of monastic sign language in the Middle Ages is a descriptive manual of individual sign-forms preserved in the eleventh-century Cluniac customaries of Bernard and Ulrich. The Cluniac sign lexicon, as it is commonly known, described 118 hand signs.[3] Bernard and Ulrich considered this short text to be of such importance that they included identical copies of it in their respective chapters on the instruction of novices.[4] Most studies of monastic sign language have relied heavily on the Cluniac sign lexicon for information about this custom, but they have generally treated it in isolation from other sources for the cloistered life in this period, including the customaries.[5] Such a narrow focus on a single source has resulted in some misleading conclusions about the function of this custom and its range of application in medieval abbeys.[6]

---

2. On the history of monastic sign language in the Middle Ages, see S. G. Bruce, *Silence and Sign Language in Medieval Monasticism: The Cluniac Tradition, c. 900–1200* (Cambridge, 2007).

3. *De notitia signorum*, in Bernard of Cluny, *Ordo Cluniacensis sive Consuetudines*, in *Vetus Disciplina Monastica*, ed. M. Herrgott (Paris, 1726), 1.17, pp. 169-73; and *De signis loquendi*, in Ulrich of Zell, *Consuetudines Cluniacensis*, PL 149, 2.4, cols. 703-705 (this edition is truncated and incomplete). For a modern critical edition of the Cluniac sign lexicon, see W. Jarecki, *Signa Loquendi: Die cluniacensischen Signa-Listen eingeleitet und herausgegeben* (Baden-Baden, 1981), pp. 121-42. See also the comprehensive reviews of Jarecki's edition by G. Constable in *Mittellateinisches Jahrbuch* 18 (1983): 331-33; and by K. Hallinger in *Zeitschrift für Kirchengeschichte* 44 (1983): 145-50. For an English translation of the Cluniac sign lexicon, see Bruce, *Silence and Sign Language in Medieval Monasticism*, pp. 177-82.

4. It is possible that one of the authors copied the sign lexicon from the other or that both copied it from an original document that has since been lost.

5. L. Gougaud, "Le langage des silencieux," *Revue Mabillon* 19 (1929): 93-100; G. van Rijnberk, *Le langage par signes chez les moines* (Amsterdam, 1953); E. Buyssens, "Le langage par gestes chez les moines," *Revue de l'Institut de Sociologie* 29 (1954): 537-45; P. G. Schmidt, "Ars loquendi et ars tacendi: Zur monastischen Zeichensprache des Mittelalters," *Berichte zur Wissenschaftsgeschichte* 4 (1981): 13-19; and L. Bragg, "Visual-Kinetic Communication in Europe Before 1600: A Survey of Sign Lexicons and Finger Alphabets Prior to the Rise of Deaf Education," *Journal of Deaf Studies and Deaf Education* 2 (1997): 1-25.

6. For example, Jarecki has argued that the boundaries of monastic discipline provided the organizing principle for the Cluniac sign lexicon because the first three thematic sections of signs (food, clothing, and the divine office) seem to correspond to the three parts of the monastery (the refectory, the dormitory, and the oratory) in which the *Rule of Benedict* forbade monks from speaking. See Jarecki, *Signa Loquendi*, pp. 21-22. This inference is misleading, however, because the section headings in the sign lexicon seem to indicate that thematic function was more important than spatial association in the organization of its contents. Moreover, as we will see, most signs were not confined in their use to a single part of the abbey.

It is my contention that the Cluniac sign lexicon alone does not tell the full story of this custom. In the words of Canadian novelist Margaret Atwood, "The living bird is not its labeled bones."[7] The Cluniac customaries described many rituals and other activities that monks were to perform in silence and thus provide a rich and untapped descriptive context for the use of sign language among them. A comparative reading of the Cluniac sign lexicon and the customaries of Bernard and Ulrich allows us to reconstruct probable venues for the use of monastic signs and to infer some of their practical applications for the brethren of Cluny. This comparison promises to change the way that historians have imagined interpersonal communication between monks regarding the preparation of food, the maintenance of clothing and tools, and the orchestration of the divine office. In turn, it creates a much more vivid and detailed portrait of daily life in a large medieval abbey like Cluny at the close of the eleventh century.

During the abbacy of Hugh the Great (1049–1109), Cluniac monks wrote down the customs of their abbey, including their precepts on personal silence. Generally speaking, monastic customaries were intended to affirm and encourage the practice of proper customs. To this end, they provided guidelines for the celebration of the divine office, the duties of monastic officials, and the general discipline of the community. The customaries of Bernard and Ulrich instructed monks to avoid unnecessary conversation during the celebration of the divine office and to preserve a perpetual state of silence in the church, the dormitory, the refectory, and the kitchens.[8] The brethren were permitted to converse for only a short amount of time in the cloister after the prayers that followed the chapter meeting, and again in the afternoon after the office of Sext.[9] The duration of this time of speaking (*hora loquendi*) remains uncertain. The term *hora* is misleading, because the length of an hour varied with the season.[10] When Peter Damian visited Cluny in 1063, he noted that the monks spared only half an hour for speaking

---

7. M. Atwood, *The Blind Assassin* (New York, 2000), p. 395.
8. Bernard 1.74, p. 273; and Ulrich 2.3, col. 703.
9. Bernard 2.20, p. 323; and Ulrich 1.12, col. 658. For more on the activities permitted in the cloister, see P. Meyvaert, "The Medieval Monastic Claustrum," *Gesta* 12 (1973): 53–59; repr. in P. Meyvaert, *Benedict, Gregory, Bede and Others* (London, 1977), no. XVI.
10. The season determined the length of an *hora* for medieval monks and the space of time understood by this term was much longer in the summer ("about three hours") than in the winter. See J. Leclercq, "Prayer at Cluny," *Journal of the American Academy of Religion* 51 (1983): 651–66, at pp. 654–55.

(*horae dimidium*), even on the longest days of summer.[11] The customary of Ulrich reminded its readers to keep the conversation period brief and to regulate comportment during the recess.[12] Monks were allowed to converse only in soft voices and to discuss spiritual subjects that did not concern the world outside of the abbey walls.[13] At the sound of the next signal, they should fall silent immediately, their words left unfinished in their mouths as they hurried off to the church for the celebration of Mass.[14] As Ulrich noted, "Quite often before all of the monks can take their places in the cloister and one of the brethren can utter a single word, the bell for Vespers is rung and that is the end of talking."[15]

The monks of Cluny invented a system of nonverbal communication to achieve their ideals of personal silence. The tenth-century *Life of Odo*, written to commemorate the holy life of the second abbot of Cluny, described how they employed a silent language of hand signs that allowed them to communicate without the need for spoken words: "Whenever it was necessary for them to ask for something, they made it known to each other through various signs, which I think grammarians would call *notas* of fingers and eyes. This practice had developed to such an extent among them that I believe, if they lost the use of their tongues, these signs would suffice to signify everything necessary."[16]

Instruction in this sign language was an important aspect of the training of novices, who followed strict rules of silence from the moment they entered the monastic community.[17] According to the customary of Bernard: "It is also necessary that he (the novice) learn with diligence the signs by which he may communicate in a certain manner while remaining silent, because after he has entered the monastery, he

---

11. Peter Damian, *Ep.* 100, ed. K. Reindel, *Die Briefe des Petrus Damiani*, in MGH Die Briefe der deutschen Kaiserzeit 4.1-4, 4 vols. (Munich, 1983-93), vol. 3, pp. 101-15, at p. 105.
12. Ulrich 1.40, col. 686.
13. Ulrich 2.20, col. 709.
14. Ulrich 2.22, col. 710.
15. Ulrich 1.18, col. 668: "Saepius namque priusquam omnes in claustro consideant, et aliquis fratrum vel unum verbum faciat, pulsatur signum ad vesperas, et ecce ibi finis loquendi."
16. John of Salerno, *Vita Odonis* 1.32: "Nam, quoties necessarias ad exposcendum res instabant, toties diversa in invicem ad perficiendum signa, quas puto grammatici digitorum et oculorum notas vocare voluerunt." *PL* 133, col. 57.
17. On the novices at Cluny in the eleventh century, see N. Hunt, *Cluny Under Saint Hugh 1049-1109* (South Bend, 1967), pp. 92-96; and I. Cochelin, "Peut-on parler de noviciat à Cluny pour les Xe-XIe siècles?," *Revue Mabillon* n.s. 9 (1998): 17-52. For more on the entrance of adults into monasteries in this period, see C. de Miramon, "Embrasser l'état monastique à l'âge adulte (1050-1200): Étude sur la conversion tardive," *Annales: Economies, Sociétés, Civilisations* 54 (1999): 825-49.

is rarely permitted to speak."[18] To this end, the customary of Bernard included the monastic sign lexicon to aid the novices in the acquisition of this silent language.

The Cluniac sign lexicon prescribed a core vocabulary of 118 hand signs that novices were expected to commit to memory before their formal consecration as monks. Each entry included the name of the signified item or object, a description of the sign, and often an explanation of the sign-form. The lexicon opened with the sign for bread: "For the sign of bread, make a circle using the thumbs and the index fingers, the reason being that bread is usually round."[19] The sign descriptions were divided into three thematic sections comprising signs for food (*victus*), clothing (*vestitus*), and the divine office (*divinum obsequium*), followed by a miscellaneous fourth section of signs for various kinds of people and monastic officials, actions, qualities, and abstract concepts (*mixtim de personis et rebus et causis*). The signs for food ranged from common foodstuffs like bread, beans, and fish to drinks and spices. They also included signs for items that the monks associated with food, like serving trays and drinking vessels. In the same way, the lexicon mingled signs for clothing with those for bedding and personal tools, like the knife and the sewing kit that monks carried on their belts. The section on the liturgy included signs for chants, hymns, and books used in the church, along with signs for celestial and saintly persons. The lexicon ended with a miscellany that comprised signs for categories of people, a short list of monastic officials, and a string of verbs as well as signs for concepts (like good and bad) and qualities (like quickness and slowness).

Although sign language was the accepted means of communication among Cluniac monks, the customaries of Bernard and Ulrich tell us very little about the use of this custom in the abbey. The reason for this is clear. Monastic signs were so common that it would have been tedious for Bernard and Ulrich to describe the many applications of this custom to their readers, especially those who were already familiar with the practice. Nonetheless, the Cluniac customaries do describe many of the activities and rituals that monks performed in silence. In doing so, they make reference to almost every item mentioned in the

---

18. Bernard 1.17, p. 169: "Opus quoque habet ut signa diligenter addiscat, quibus tacens quodammodo loquatur, quia postquam adunatus fuerit ad conventum, licet ei rarissime loqui."

19. Jarecki, *Signa Loquendi*, p. 121 (no. 1): "Pro signo panis fac unum circulum cum utroque pollice et his duobus digitis, qui secuntur, pro eo, quod et panis solet esse rotundus."

sign lexicon. Reading the sign lexicon in the context of the customaries of Bernard and Ulrich enables us to make inferences about the places in which monastic signs were used, and the range of their applications, yielding two important insights about this custom. First, whenever possible, monastic officials tried to limit sign use among the brethren by finding ways for them to interact without recourse to words or signs. Sign language was an essential part of monastic discipline, but there was an undercurrent of anxiety that monks would abuse this custom through the garrulous use of their hands. Limited opportunities for sign use lessened the possibility of lapses in discipline. Second, the customaries suggest that monastic signs were particularly important as a medium of instruction and reprimand. The master of novices used them to cue and prompt his charges during activities and services that would have been habitual or intuitive for more experienced monks. The following sections of this chapter examine the possible applications and restrictions of the use of sign language in three fundamental aspects of monastic life at Cluny: (1) sustenance, (2) apparel, and (3) the divine office.

Signs for Sustenance

Rules of silence forbade the monks of Cluny from speaking in the kitchens and the refectory, making sign language an important tool in the preparation and orchestration of meals. According to the customaries, the monastic diet was a carbohydrate-rich combination of breads and vegetables, supplemented with wine and high-protein animal products, such as cheese, eggs, and fish.[20] The novices learned thirty-five signs for food and food-related items like bread, eggs and vegetables, fish, millet, cheese and baked goods, milk and honey, fruit, lentils and garlic, drinks, condiments, and serving vessels.[21] It was important for the novices to gain proficiency in these signs because they were expected to use them when they performed kitchen and refectory duties and ate their meals

---

20. On the monastic diet in the late antique and early medieval periods, see G. Zimmermann, *Ordensleben und Lebensstandard: Die Cura corporis in den Ordensvorschriften des abendländischen Hochmittelalters* (Munster, 1973), pp. 37–87; S. Boulc'H, "Le repas quotidien des moines occidentaux du haut Moyen Age," *Revue belge de philologie et d'histoire* 75 (1997): 287–328; K. L. Pearson, "Nutrition and the Early-Medieval Diet," *Speculum* 72 (1997): 1–32; and M. Harlow and W. Smith, "Between Fasting and Feasting: The Literary and Archaeobiological Evidence for Monastic Diet in Late Antique Egypt," *Antiquity* 75 (2001): 758–68.

21. Jarecki, *Signa Loquendi*, pp. 121–27 (nos. 1–35).

130   CHAPTER 8

alongside professed monks. The evidence of the customaries suggests that these signs played a much more significant role in the preparation of meals than they did in the procurement of rations or the consumption of food and drink.

At Cluny and other abbeys, eating habits changed with the seasons and the liturgical significance of the day. Monks ate one meal a day in the winter and two meals in the summer when the days were longer. They ate once on fast days and twice on feast days, irrespective of the season.[22] Their standard meal included two dishes of cooked beans and vegetables and a dish of raw vegetables and fruit. Monks also received a pound of bread every day to eat with their meals. An extra portion was available to them in the evening as well, if their daily ration did not suffice.[23] The standard drink in the abbey was wine. Monks gathered together for a drink between their two meals in the summer or in the evening in place of the second meal during the winter and on fast days.[24] In the early darkness of winter evenings, they drank their wine in the refectory by candlelight.[25] The name of this drink, the *caritas*, suggests that the custom was an outgrowth of the ration increase recommended in the *Rule of Benedict* and allowed at the kind discretion (*per caritatem*) of the abbot. It may have served originally as a supplement to the single meal provided in the winter season because of the harsher climates endured by monks who lived north of the Alps.[26]

It was forbidden for healthy monks to eat the flesh of quadrupeds, but they did consume a daily portion of high protein animal products, like cheese and eggs, as well as large quantities of fish as supplements to their standard meals.[27] On Tuesdays, Thursdays, and Saturdays, Cluniac monks ate the *pitantia*, a plate of four eggs or raw cheese shared between two people. On other days, they ate the *generale*, a more generous helping of five eggs and cooked cheese for each person, often accompanied

---

22. Bernard 2.31 and 2.32, pp. 349–50 and 355.
23. *RB* 39.3–5; and Bernard 1.11, p. 156.
24. Ulrich 1.18, col. 668. Attendance was mandatory, even if the monk chose not to drink. See Ulrich 2.24, col. 712.
25. Bernard 1.74, p. 269. On the evening drink in the winter, see also Bernard 2.32, p. 354.
26. Zimmermann, *Ordensleben und Lebensstandard*, pp 42–44.
27. Archaeological evidence from medieval garbage pits excavated at the abbey of La Charité-sur-Loire suggest that quadrupeds were being eaten in some Cluniac communities, but there is no way to tell whether this consumption amounted to a breach in regular discipline. Sick monks, lay servants, and secular visitors were not required to follow this dietary restriction. Their needs may account for the presence of such remains. See F. Audoin, *Ossements animaux du moyen âge du monastère de la Charité-sur-Loire* (Paris, 1986).

by a serving of fish.[28] On fast days, the more frugal *pitantia* was served irrespective of the day of the week; on feast days, the *generale* or both portions at once.[29] Raw vegetables replaced the cheese and eggs of these dishes during Lent, but the consumption of fish was allowed throughout the fast.[30] In addition, important occasions earned the monks a celebratory repast. When the abbot returned from a journey, monks enjoyed a *generale* of fish with spiced wine.[31] At the abbot's discretion, they could also receive wine flavored with wormwood and honey, especially when the weather was warm.[32] Similarly, on Sundays in the summer months, the abbot allowed the children in the abbey a drink of milk in the evening, an indulgence warranted by the length of the day and the extent of their fast.[33]

The procurement of rations for a large monastic community required detailed conversations among high-ranking officials and complex transactions with people outside of the abbey walls and thus did not involve the use of sign language. The purchase and harvest of fish is illustrative of this point. The cellarer was responsible for obtaining fish, a standard component of the *generale* that was also in high demand on feast days and during Lent, when animal products like eggs and cheese were forbidden. He had an assistant who purchased the catch of local fishermen and oversaw the harvest of fish from rivers and ponds where the abbey had fishing rights.[34] The monks of Cluny primarily ate indigenous river fish, like salmon, pike, and trout as well as eel and lamprey.[35] The cellarer's assistant had permission to leave the abbey after Vespers to conduct his business with the fishermen.[36] It is unlikely that monastic signs played any role in these transactions. The responsibilities of the cellarer's assistant would have absolved him from the rule of silence when he conducted business on behalf of the community. Duties of this kind were assigned to experienced monks with a reputation for

---

28. Ulrich 2.35 and 3.18, cols. 728 and 761.
29. Bernard 1.6, pp. 147–48.
30. Bernard 2.13, p. 302.
31. Bernard 1.1, p. 138.
32. Ulrich 1.30, col. 677. In the twelfth century, Peter the Venerable limited this practice by prohibiting the use of honeyed or spiced wine at Cluny except on Holy Thursday. See *Statuta* 11, p. 50.
33. Bernard 1.27, p. 207.
34. Bernard 1.6, pp. 147–50.
35. Jarecki, *Signa Loquendi*, pp. 123–24, nos. 12 (*salmo vel sturio*), 13 (*lucius*), 14 (*truta*), 10 (*anguilla*), and 11 (*lampreda*), respectively.
36. Bernard 1.6, pp. 149–50.

good judgment, who could be trusted not to abuse the freedom from discipline that accompanied their increased responsibility.[37] Moreover, it is unreasonable to assume that local fishmongers had any knowledge of the silent language of the Cluniac monks.

Signs for sustenance played a much more evident role in the preparation of food than they did in its procurement. Monastic signs were a practical necessity in the abbey kitchens, where a team of monks prepared and orchestrated the communal meals in silence. Six of the brethren served in the kitchens every week on a rotating basis.[38] Some of them cooked vegetables and fish; others arranged food on trays; others carried the trays into the refectory.[39] These monks relied exclusively on signs for specific food items and utensils to perform their duties because spoken words were expressly forbidden at all times during the preparation of food. Because the kitchen crew worked under close supervision in a hectic environment, it was unlikely that they would use monastic signs to express anything other than the concerns of their labors.

In contrast to the kitchens, the strict regulation of mealtimes and food portions minimized the need for sign use in the refectory, where the entire community gathered for meals. No one was allowed to eat outside of the established mealtimes or after Compline.[40] Each monk received the same portions of vegetables and fish and the same amount of bread and wine. The prior kept a strict watch over the portions of the meals and inspected the servings of fish to ensure that the cooks had divided them fairly among the brethren.[41] These mechanisms of control were an aspect of monastic discipline. The strict regulation of food and drink meant that the monks had no choice regarding the content or portions of their meals. This in turn limited the frequency of sign use in the refectory and thereby curbed opportunities for disciplinary negligence when the monks gathered to eat. Offenses involving speech were undoubtedly rare when the entire community gathered for meals in the silence of the refectory, but some monastic officials expressed concern about the misuse of sign language at the table. A monastic customary from the thirteenth century instructed officials explicitly to report

---

37. See, for example, *RB* 31.1–2 and *RB* 66.1–2 on the requisite character of the cellarer and the porter, respectively.
38. Bernard 1.46, p. 236.
39. Bernard 1.46, p. 238.
40. Bernard 1.11, p. 156. Some allowance was made for the sick; see Bernard 1.74, p. 278.
41. Bernard 1.6, p. 148.

monks observed making unnecessary signs while they ate.[42] Signs for condiments were an exception to this rule. Servers roamed the refectory during mealtimes with trays of mustard seed and vinegar. Monks may have used the signs for these food items to attract the attention of the servers and to indicate their choice of condiment.[43]

Signs for Apparel

Sign language was also an important tool for maintaining monastic discipline, particularly in the church and the dormitory, where rules of comportment applied both to the monks' bodies and to the clothing that covered them. Adult novices exchanged their worldly garments for the monastic habit when they entered the abbey.[44] Their new clothing was a symbol of their vow of stability and obedience.[45] The chamberlain supplied monks with their personal apparel. The customaries of Bernard and Ulrich set down detailed inventories of the clothing, bedding, and tools granted to everyone, along with an indication of their number and quality. According to these inventories, each monk received two frocks and two cowls made from inexpensive cloth, two wool tunics, two pairs of trousers, two pairs of shoes, one pair of night shoes with felt to be worn in winter, one pair of night shoes without felt for summer nights, two pairs of boots, three garments (two made from hide and one from fur), one fur cap, five pairs of ankle straps, one wooden clasp (with which they fastened their pants), and one hide belt for their tunics, on which they carried a knife in a sheath, a wooden comb in a sheath, and a sewing kit (needle and thread) in a small case. For their beds, monks also acquired a pillow; an inexpensive blanket made from lamb, cat, polecat, or rabbit; a heavy coat; and a sheet.[46]

---

42. *Consuetudines Affligenienses* 29: "Quamdiu autem comeditur, intente debent considerare circatores si qui dissoluti sint vel signa superflua faciant," ed. R. J. Sullivan, in *Consuetudines Benedictinae variae (saec. XI–saec. XIV)*, ed. G. Constable, CCM 6 (Siegburg, 1975), p. 149.

43. Jarecki, *Signa Loquendi*, pp. 126–27, nos. 30 (*sinapis*) and 31 (*acetum*). On the condiment servers, see Bernard 1.11, p. 156.

44. Bernard 1.15, p. 165.

45. G. Constable, "The Ceremonies and Symbolism of Entering Religious Life and Taking the Monastic Habit, from the Fourth to the Twelfth Centuries," in *Segni e riti nella chiesa altomedievale occidentale, Spoleto, 11–17 aprile 1985* (Spoleto, 1987), pp. 808–16; repr. in G. Constable, *Culture and Spirituality in Medieval Europe* (Aldershot, 1996), no. VII.

46. Bernard 1.5, p. 146; and Ulrich 3.9, col. 752.

The novices learned signs for most of the items on the chamberlain's inventory when they entered the monastery.[47] This suggests that the signs for apparel in the Cluniac sign lexicon reflected their initial allotment of clothing, bedding, and tools.[48] The sign for cowl was an exception.[49] Novices did not receive cowls until their formal consecration as monks.[50] Even so, it was an important sign for them to learn, because it was a common article of clothing and carried the added significance of visually distinguishing the professed monks from the novices. Among the signs for personal apparel, the novices also learned signs for writing tablet and stylus.[51] These items did not appear on the chamberlain's inventory because they were not supplied to monks on an individual basis. Their inclusion reflects the fact that writing and copying were important skills for novices to learn.[52] Monks proficient in these skills applied them at the order of the cantor, the official who instructed the brethren in the production of charters, letters, and other documents relevant to the needs of the monastic community.[53]

The chamberlain and his assistant supplied the brethren with clothing and tools, but their interaction rarely involved the use of signs for apparel. The customary of Bernard instructed the monks to make requests for new items of clothing in the cloister at a time when speaking was permitted.[54] In addition, the chamberlain distributed new articles of clothing to the brethren at certain times of the year. They received a new frock and cowl every year at Christmas and a new hide garment every third year on the feast day of Saint Michael. The chamberlain left

---

47. See Jarecki, *Signa Loquendi*, pp. 127–31 (nos. 36–57).
48. All but three items from the Cluniac sign lexicon were present on the chamberlain's inventory. The three absent items were sleeves, writing tablet, and stylus (Jarecki, *Signa Loquendi*, pp. 128 and 131, nos. 40 and 56–57), all of which are discussed below.
49. Jarecki, *Signa Loquendi*, p. 128, no. 39 (*cuculla*).
50. On the ceremony of consecration at Cluny, see G. Constable, "Entrance to Cluny in the Eleventh and Twelfth Centuries According to the Cluniac Customaries and Statutes," in *Mediaevalia Christiana, XIe–XIIIe siècles: Hommage à Raymonde Foreville de ses amis, ses collègues et ses anciens élèves*, ed. C. É. Viola (Paris, 1989), pp. 335–54; repr. in G. Constable, *The Abbey of Cluny: A Collection of Essays to Mark the Eleven-Hundredth Anniversary of Its Foundation* (Berlin, 2010), pp. 143–62.
51. Jarecki, *Signa Loquendi*, p. 131, nos. 56 (*tabulae*) and 57 (*graphium*).
52. On writing as a component of the training of novices, see Bernard 1.15, p. 166.
53. On the office of the cantor (*armarius*) and his responsibility for book production, see Bernard 1.14, pp. 161–64. For more on the duties of this official, see M. Fassler, "The Office of the Cantor in Early Western Monastic Rules and Customaries: A Preliminary Investigation," *Early Music History* 5 (1985): 29–51.
54. Bernard 1.5, p. 146; and Ulrich 3.9, cols. 752–53.

the new clothes on their beds during mealtimes.[55] Moreover, a system was in place for the monks to have their tunics and trousers repaired without recourse to words or signs. They left worn-out or damaged clothes at a designated place in the abbey, where the chamberlain's assistant collected them and delivered them to the resident tailors. The monks had their names sewn onto their clothes to prevent the inevitable confusion when their items returned from the tailors.[56]

The Cluniac signs for apparel were a useful medium of instruction and reprimand in the silence of the church. During the celebration of the divine office, rules of comportment extended beyond the movements of the body to the clothing that covered it. The customary of Bernard drew attention to the proper manipulation of the frock and its wide sleeves several times in its discussion of personal comportment in the church.[57] The monastic habit was undoubtedly an unwieldly set of unfamiliar garments for most novices. During their indoctrination, they learned to draw the frock back to their elbows and knees to prevent it from hanging over their feet and touching the ground as they bowed in prayer. They were also instructed to gather up the folds of their sleeves with their hands during the regular hours and collect them onto their laps as they sat in the choir. The presence of a sign for sleeves in the Cluniac sign lexicon supports the inference that the signs for apparel had a disciplinary function.[58] Sleeves were a part of the frock and not a separate article of clothing. The customary of Bernard mentioned them only in the context of proper comportment in the church. The master of novices employed this and other signs for apparel to point out and correct improper comportment as he shepherded his charges through ritual activities in the church, where speaking was forbidden.

Signs for apparel had a similar function in the dormitory. With their new clothes, the novices donned a heightened sense of self-consciousness about their bodies. They slept in a communal dormitory, where lanterns burned throughout the night to dissuade suspicious activities.[59] There they learned to dress and undress in such a way that their nudity

---

55. Bernard 1.5 and 2.31, pp. 146 and 351.
56. Bernard 1.5, pp. 146–47. In the twelfth century, two custodians stayed in the dormitory to prevent quarrels resulting from the loss or confusion of clothing. See *Statuta* 69, pp. 99–100.
57. For what follows, see Bernard 1.18, p. 174.
58. Jarecki, *Signa Loquendi*, p. 128, no. 40 (*manicae*).
59. On the fear of sexual misconduct and the strategies for its deterrence in Cluniac abbeys, see chapter 7, above.

remained hidden from their fellow monks. The customary of Bernard instructed all monks to don their cowls in bed before drawing back the blanket when they rose for the Night Office.[60] Likewise, upon returning to bed, they retained their cowls until they drew the blanket up past their elbows. Even in the summer heat, it was forbidden for them to expose more than their feet, arms and head as they slept.[61] The customary of Bernard also warned monks not to rely on the cowl alone to conceal their nakedness when they changed their clothes in the dormitory, advising that a frock or a tunic was also necessary to shield them sufficiently from the eyes of others.[62] These precautions applied to the novices as well. The scrutiny of their master followed their actions in the dormitory. With signs for apparel, he could instruct them to adhere to the rules of comportment and to guard their modesty in the presence of their brethren.

Divine Office

Sign language also replaced spoken words in the church during the divine office. In the eleventh century, the celebration of the liturgy was the primary focus of monastic communities.[63] The recitation of the psalter and the intonation of lessons from the Bible and the works of patristic authorities directed the attention of the brethren to God. The particulars of the services varied considerably from house to house and changed with the liturgical significance of the day and the season.[64] The Cluniacs were renowned for their intense commitment to the divine office, which they expressed in part by the staggering length of their services. We have every indication that the monks considered the duration of the liturgy to be important and necessary to the fulfillment of

---

60. Bernard 1.18, p. 174.
61. Bernard 1.18, p. 175.
62. Bernard 1.18, p. 175.
63. For an invaluable overview of medieval liturgical practices, see D. Hiley, *Western Plainchant: A Handbook* (Oxford, 1993). On the elaboration of liturgical customs in this period, see K. Hallinger, "Überlieferung und Steigerung im Mönchtum des 8. bis 12. Jahrhunderts," in *Eulogia: Miscellanea Liturgica in onore di P. Burckhard Neunheuser O.S.B.* (Rome, 1979), pp. 125-87.
64. Consequently, it has been proven difficult for historians to reconstruct a timetable that represents with accuracy the liturgical obligations of individual monks. Modern reconstructions of monastic timetables are potentially misleading because it is unreasonable to assume that every monk was obligated to take part in all the services. On this point, see Leclercq, "Prayer at Cluny," pp. 651-57.

their holy purpose.[65] They took the utmost care to orchestrate these ceremonies without recourse to speech.

Using hand signs, the cantor directed individual and communal participation in the divine office and the liturgy of the Mass. The brethren took part according to their singing ability and their knowledge of the complex variations of liturgical chants.[66] The intricacies of these services were notoriously difficult to learn, unless one had grown up in the abbey.[67] The novices lacked the familiarity or expertise necessary to play more than a minor role in the divine office. They were forbidden from beginning antiphons, singing the response, and intoning the lesson for the Night Office.[68] Although the novices were not full participants in the services, it was important for them to learn signs for every important aspect of the liturgy because, even as professed monks, they would rely on nonverbal cues from the cantor to guide them through the ceremonies.

Signs for liturgical books facilitated the celebration of the divine office. The most experienced monks could recite common services from memory, but they referred to books for the words to difficult or seldom used antiphons and hymns.[69] In the silence of the church, signs for books announced the need for particular texts. The novices learned to recognize hand signs for common choir books, like antiphonaries, hymnals, and psalters as well as those for texts read during the Mass, like

---

65. See, for example, Ulrich 1.1, col. 645, in which the senior brethren censured a monk in the chapter meeting for curtailing the reading of a lesson. For more on the growth and character of the Cluniac liturgy in this period, see K. Hallinger, "Das Phänomen der liturgischen Steigerungen Klunys (10./11. Jh.)," in *Studia historicoecclesiastica: Festgabe für Prof. Luchesius G. Spätling O. F. M.*, ed. I. Vázquez (Rome, 1977), pp. 183–236; and S. Boynton, "Shaping Cluniac Devotion," in *CCMA*, pp. 125–45. This sentiment changed in the early twelfth century, when Abbot Peter the Venerable made several attempts to shorten the divine office because the monks found it burdensome. He also introduced pauses to the chanting to provide the brethren with time to consider the meaning of the words that they sung. See, for example, *Statuta* 1, 14, 31, 65, and 67, pp. 40–42, 52–53, 66, 96, and 98. On the liturgical reforms of Peter the Venerable, see R. Folz, "Pierre le Vénérable et la liturgie," in *Pierre Abélard—Pierre la Vénérable: Les courants philosophiques, littéraires et artistiques en Occident au milieu du XIIe siècle (Abbaye de Cluny, 2 au 9 juillet 1972)* (Paris, 1975), pp. 143–61.
66. *RB* 47.3; and Bernard 1.14, p. 161.
67. Monastic sign language distinguished between monks who had entered the abbey as adults and those who had been raised there from childhood. See Jarecki, *Signa Loquendi*, p. 136, nos. 80 (*monachus*) and 83 (*monachus qui nutritus est in monasterio*). On the participation of children in the divine office, see S. Boynton, "The Liturgical Role of Children in Monastic Customaries from the Central Middle Ages," *Studia Liturgica* 28 (1998): 194–209.
68. Bernard 1.15, p. 165.
69. Bernard 1.19, p. 178.

missals, the Gospels, and the Epistles.[70] The Cluniac sign lexicon also included a sign for angel as well as signs for saintly persons like apostle, martyr, confessor, and holy virgin.[71] Their close association in the lexicon with the signs for liturgical books and feast days suggests that they had some function related to the commemoration of the saints. The cantor may have employed them to cue the reader to begin the proper text for the Night Office. An entry in a twelfth-century library catalog from Cluny lends weight to this inference, for it described a compilation of lessons for the Night Office that included sections on martyrs, confessors, and virgins.[72]

The use of signs for books extended beyond the precincts of the church. The authority of the *Rule of Benedict* as a legislative document could account for its place in the Cluniac sign lexicon among signs for books used in the divine office, but it had no liturgical function.[73] The abbot or the prior may have employed this sign in the daily chapter meeting to cue the monk who read a chapter of the rule to the assembled community. The presence of a sign for "secular book" suggests that signs for books also had some function in the abbey library.[74] The rhetoric of disdain for ancient authors was common in monastic sources from this period and implicit in the Cluniac sign for a book composed by a pagan author: "For a sign of a secular book that some pagan composed, add to the aforesaid general sign for book that you touch an ear with a finger, just as a dog usually does when scratching with his foot, because a person without faith deserves to be compared with such an animal."[75]

---

70. Jarecki, *Signa Loquendi*, pp. 133–34, nos. 65 (*liber missalis*), 66 (*textus evangelii*), 67 (*liber epistolaris*), 69 (*antiphonarium*), 71 (*hymnarium*), and 72 (*psalterium*).

71. Jarecki, *Signa Loquendi*, p. 135, nos. 74 (*angelus*), 75 (*apostolus*), 76 (*martyr*), 77 (*confessor*), and 78 (*sacra virgo*).

72. L. Delisle, *Inventaire des manuscrits de la bibliothèque nationale: Fonds de Cluni* (Paris, 1884), p. 338 (no. 12). This redaction of the library catalog was probably compiled during the abbacy of Hugh III (1158–1161). On its organization and contents, see V. von Büren, "Le grand catalogue de la bibliothèque de Cluny," in *Le Gouvernement d'Hugues de Semur à Cluny: Actes du Colloque scientifique international* (*Cluny, septembre 1988*) (Mâcon, 1990), pp. 245–63, who argues that the catalog was originally compiled under Abbot Hugh the Great (1049–1109).

73. Jarecki, *Signa Loquendi*, p. 134, no. 70 (*regula*).

74. Jarecki, *Signa Loquendi*, p. 134, no. 73 (*liber secularis quem aliquis paganus conposuit*).

75. Jarecki, *Signa Loquendi*, p. 134 (no. 73): "Pro signo libri secularis, quem aliquis paganus conposuit, premisso generali signo libri adde, ut aurem cum digito tangas, sicut canis cum pede pruriens solet, quia nec inmerito infidelis tali animanti conparatur." Cluniac monks were among the most vociferous of those who expressed their disdain for classical authors. See, for example, John of Salerno, *Vita Odonis* 1.12, *PL* 133, col. 49, in which Odo dreamed that Virgil handed him a vase full of serpents that represented the dangers of his poetry; and

Despite this sentiment, the library at Cluny preserved dozens of volumes of Roman history and poetry.[76] Many of these works were among the books distributed during the Lenten season for personal reading.[77] The customaries of Bernard and Ulrich made no reference to sign use in the library, but a late eleventh-century customary from Hirsau warned its readers against speaking in the chamber where they stored their books unless they had an urgent concern that could not be expressed with signs.[78] This warning clearly implied that sign language was the accepted means of communication in the Hirsau library. Hirsau's dependency on Cluniac customs suggests that this may have been the case at Cluny as well.[79]

The customaries passed over the mundane applications of monastic signs for food, clothing, and the divine office with little comment, but they described in considerable detail the role of this custom in the act of confession. A new concern with sin and its absolution through confession confronted novices as soon as they entered the monastic community. In the tenth and eleventh centuries, an increasing number of Cluniac monks became ordained priests.[80] Frequent confession was essential for monk-priests because absolution from sin was a prerequisite for the celebration of private masses, which took place daily in most

---

Rodulphus Glaber, *Historiarum libri quinque* 2.12.23, ed. and trans. J. France, in *Rodulfus Glaber: The Five Books of Histories and the Life of St. William* (Oxford, 1989), p. 92, where the author reported that demons appeared to a young man in the guises of Virgil, Horace, and Juvenal and compelled him to preach heretical doctrines.

76. The Cluniac library catalog listed works of Virgil, Horace, Terence, Pliny, Sallust, and Cicero. See Delisle, *Inventaire des manuscrits*, pp. 337–73 (appendix I), *passim*. For a discussion of these contradictory tendencies in medieval monastic thought, see J. Leclercq, *The Love of Learning and the Desire for God: A Study of Monastic Culture*, trans. C. Misrahi (New York, 1982), pp. 112–43.

77. In 1040, for example, a monk of Cluny named Peter borrowed a copy of Livy's *Roman History* in this manner. See *Liber tramitis aevi Odilonis abbatis* 2.190: "Petrus *Historiam* Titi Liuii," ed. P. Dinter, CCM 10 (Siegburg, 1980), p. 264. The Lenten custom of distributing books to the brethren for private reading did not involve the use of sign language. For more on this custom, see A. Wilmart, "Le couvent et la bibliothèque de Cluny vers le milieu du XIe siècle," *Revue Mabillon* 11 (1921): 89–124; and K. Christ, "In Caput Quadragesimae," *Zentralblatt für Bibliothekswesen* 60 (1943): 33–59.

78. William, *Constitutiones Hirsaugienses* 2.20, ed. P. Engelbert, CCM 15.1-2, 2 vols. (Siegburg, 2010), vol. 2, p. 129.

79. On the relationship between Hirsau and Cluny and its role in the dissemination of Cluniac signs, see Bruce, *Silence and Sign Language in Medieval Monasticism*, pp. 118–23.

80. The essential works on this topic remain O. Nussbaum, *Kloster, Priestermönch und Privatmesse: Ihr Verhältnis im Westen von den Anfängen bis zum hohen Mittelalter* (Bonn, 1961); and A. Häussling, *Mönchskonvent und Eucharistiefeier: Eine Studie über die Messe in der abendländischen Klosterliturgie des frühen Mittelalters und zur Geschichte der Messhäufigkeit* (Munster, 1973).

abbeys in this period.[81] Because laymen rarely received communion and were not required to confess their sins with nearly the same frequency as monks, it was vitally important for novices to learn how to initiate this personal and highly ritualized interaction with a priest in the silence of the church.[82]

At Cluny, the brethren used sign language to signal their need for confession and absolution. According to the customary of Bernard:

> If he [the novice] needs to go to confession for some transgression, he approaches the priest who is most preferable to him. Standing before him, he draws his right hand from his sleeve and places it upon his chest, because this is the sign for confession.[83]

Once he had signaled his intention, the novice then followed the priest into the chapter room where he prostrated himself on the floor and asked for forgiveness for his sins.[84] The sign for confession warranted such a detailed treatment in the customary of Bernard because, unlike other signs in the Cluniac lexicon, it was directly relevant to the spiritual well-being of the novice and played a pivotal role in his transition from layman to monk.

Like fossil-rich sediments, the Cluniac customaries have preserved the outlines and textures of human activities and religious values from a distant age. They promise to exert a strong and lasting influence on the ways that historians will come to understand the lived experiences and disciplinary concerns of medieval monks. The insight that they provide into the custom of sign language is one such example. The enterprise of recovering and understanding monastic signs has

---

81. On the history of the private mass in the early Middle Ages, see A. Angenendt, "Missa specialis: Zugleich ein Beitrag zur Entstehung der Privatmessen," *Frühmittelalterliche Studien* 17 (1983): 153-221.

82. The decrees of the Fourth Lateran Council (1215) required laypeople to confess their sins and take communion at least once a year (usually at Easter), but lay participation in these activities in the early medieval period was probably much less frequent. On the practice of confession in the early Middle Ages, see A. Murray, "Confession Before 1215," *Transactions of the Royal Historical Society*, 6th ser., 3 (1993): 51-81; and R. Meens, "The Frequency and Nature of Early Medieval Penance," in *Handling Sin: Confession in the Middle Ages*, ed. P. Biller and A. J. Minnis (Woodbridge, 1998), pp. 35-63.

83. Bernard 1.18, p. 175: "Si opus habet ad confessionem pro aliquo excessu venire, accedit ad sacerdotem ad quem potissimum voluerit, et stans ante eum dextram de manica abstractam ponit super pectus, quod est signum confessionis." Compare Jarecki, *Signa Loquendi*, p. 138 (no. 94): "Pro signo infirmarii, qui obsequitur infirmis, pone manum contra pectus, quod significat infirmitatem, quamvis non semper, quia et confessionem significat."

84. Bernard 1.18, p. 175.

always presented interpretative challenges for historians, but the Cluniac customaries have opened new vistas of possibility for the study of this practice. A comparative reading of the Cluniac sign lexicon and the customaries of Bernard and Ulrich has allowed us to infer with renewed confidence the disciplinary contexts that fostered the silent exchange of signs on the hands of the brethren. As this chapter has shown, monastic signs related to food, clothing, and the divine office were essential tools for interpersonal communication in the silence of the abbey. Whenever possible, the monks of Cluny conducted their activities without recourse to words or signs, but in those instances when communication was essential, meaningful gestures allowed them to convey necessary information without countermanding their rules of silence. Owing to the richness of the customaries as sources for monastic history, it is no longer possible to imagine the daily lives of Cluniac monks without picturing the silent language of signs that permitted them to achieve the ideals of their personal discipline.

Chapter 9

The Relics of Cluny

In the early seventeenth century, the Maurist scholars Edmond Martène (1654–1739) and Ursin Durand (1682–1771) traveled together throughout northern Europe, visiting abbeys and cathedrals in search of monastic manuscripts and other primary source materials for a new edition of the *Gallia Christiana*.[1] During their seventeen-day sojourn at Cluny in 1709, Martène and Durand enjoyed full access to the medieval holdings of the monastery, a rapturous experience subsequently recorded in their account of their travels, titled *The Literary Voyage of Two Benedictine Monks of the Congregation of St. Maur*.[2] They remarked enthusiastically on the quality of the manuscripts (*beaux & anciens*), the richness of the charter collection (*une infinité de*

Originally published as "The Relics of Cluny," in *A Companion to the Abbey of Cluny in the Middle Ages*, ed. S. G. Bruce and S. Vanderputten (Leiden, 2021), pp. 322–39. Reprinted with permission.

1. Their journey took place between 1709 and 1713, during which time they visited hundreds of religious communities in France before returning to the abbey of St-Germain-des-Prés in Paris. Many of the documents they collected appeared not only in the *Thesaurus novus anecdotorum*, ed. E. Martène and U. Durand, 5 vols. (Paris, 1717) but also in the new edition of the *Gallia Christiana* published intermittently by the Maurists throughout the eighteenth century (13 volumes between 1715 and 1785).

2. E. Martène and U. Durand, *Voyage littéraire de deux religieux bénédictins de la Congregation de St. Maur*, 2 vols. (Paris, 1717–24), vol. 1, pp. 227–30. For more on this work, see D.-O. Hurel,

titres originaux), and other features of the abbey, including the architecture of its churches and the character of its liturgical celebrations. Martène and Durand also took note of some of the remains of holy persons displayed in the abbey treasury: the head of Saint Jerome; part of the chains of the apostle Peter; and a host of artifacts associated with Abbot Hugh the Great (1049-1109), including a cross of wood covered in silver and backed with ivory; the knife that he carried on his belt; and his robe and scapular, both very large and brown in color.[3]

In all likelihood, this handful of relics did not represent the full collection of holy remains curated by the monks of Cluny since the tenth century. Although Martène and Durand's account presented three of the major categories of saints revered by devout Christians in the Middle Ages (apostles, church fathers, and abbots), it veiled the fact that the veneration of relics was not an important aspect of Cluniac spirituality in the century after the abbey's foundation in 910. Moreover, the attention to the relics of Abbot Hugh would have seemed disproportionate to medieval Cluniacs, who did not promote the cults of their abbots throughout their early history. In short, the relationship between the brethren of Cluny and the "very special dead," that is, those saints whose relics inhabited the altars and crypts in the chapels and churches associated with the great Burgundian abbey, was not unchanging through the Middle Ages.[4]

For much of their early history, in fact, the Cluniacs had what might best be called an ambivalent attitude toward the need for relics in their community, including the holy remains of their very own abbots. As we will see, however, this attitude changed during the abbacy of Odilo (994-1049) when relics became an important feature not only in the devotional regimes of the brethren but also in the lives of the laypeople who lived in proximity to the abbey. During the twelfth and thirteenth centuries, the Cluniacs further enriched their relic holdings by taking

---

"La place de l'érudition dans le *Voyage littéraire* de dom Edmond Martène et dom Ursin Durand (1717 et 1724)," *Revue Mabillon* n.s. 3 (1992): 213-28.

3. Martène and Durand, *Voyage littéraire*, vol. 1, p. 229: "Parmi les reliques qu'on montre dans le tresor, le chef de S. Hierôme est une des plus considerable; une partie des chaînes de S. Pierre, qu'on dit être semblables à celles qui sont à Rome. Le croce de S. Hugue, qui est de bois couvert de feüilles d'argent, dont le dessus est d'yvoire; le coûteau qu'il portoit à la ceinture; sa robe & son scapulaire, qui sont de couleur brune; les manches de la robe ont bien deux pieds de cironference; pour le scapulaire, il est assez large pour couvrir tout les bras, & le capuchin qui y est attaché est tout d'une venue, & comme un sac."

4. For the phrase "very special dead," see P. Brown, *The Cult of the Saints: Its Rise and Function in Latin Christianity* (Chicago, 1981), esp. pp. 69-85.

possession of sacred remains that had migrated to Western Europe from the Holy Land and Constantinople in the hands of their associates and admirers. By the end of the Middle Ages, the great Burgundian abbey boasted an impressive collection of lavishly decorated reliquaries, the contents of which were carefully delineated in two treasure inventories compiled at Cluny in the late fourteenth century. Throughout their history, the cultivated and ever-changing association of the Cluniacs to the remains of the saints underscored not only the enduring importance of the deceased in the monastic imagination but also the degree to which the dynamic of these relationships permeated the walls of the cloister.

Modest Beginnings: The Tenth Century

The earliest brethren of Cluny did not stake their claim to sanctity on the presence and power of holy relics in their community.[5] When Duke William I of Aquitaine founded the abbey in 910 on the site of a Burgundian villa bequeathed to him by his sister Ava, herself an abbess, he provided no indication in his foundation charter that relics would be an important feature of this new monastic house.[6] To be sure, the pious duke pledged to "hand over from my own power to the holy apostles, Peter, namely, and Paul, the possessions that are mine by right," including "the chapel in honor of St. Mary, the mother of God, and of St. Peter, the prince of apostles."[7] Because the earliest Cluniacs produced no texts to promote these cults, it is unclear whether this church housed any significant relics and, if so, where they came from, how they were procured, and what role they may have played in the devotional life

---

5. The cult of relics is such a central component of Christian devotion in the Middle Ages that it requires no lengthy introduction. For orientation, see J. H. M. Smith, "Portable Christianity: Relics in the Medieval West (c. 700–1200)," *Proceedings of the British Academy* 181 (2012): 143–67.

6. For Ava's donation of the villa to William and the duke's foundation charter for the abbey, see BB, vol. 1, pp. 61 (no. 53) and 124-28 (no. 112), respectively. On the distinctive qualities of this charter relative to its Carolingian antecedents, see F. Gross, "Reprise et réinterprétation de la tradition carolingienne dans la charte de fondation de Cluny," *Revue Mabillon*, n.s. 25 (2014): 45–78. On the discrepancies concerning the date of the foundation charter (909 or 910), see G. Constable, "Cluny in the Monastic World of the Tenth Century," in *Il secolo di ferro: Mito e realtà del secolo X (Spoleto, 19–25 aprile 1990)* (Spoleto, 1991), pp. 391–437, repr. in G. Constable, *The Abbey of Cluny: A Collection of Essays to Mark the Eleven-Hundredth Anniversary of its Foundation* (Munster, 2010), pp. 43–79.

7. BB, vol. 1, p. 125 (no. 112): "[N]otum sit quod, ob amorem Dei et Salvatoris nostri Jhesu Christi, res juris mei sanctis apostolis Petro videlicet et Paulo de propria trado dominatione, Clugniacum scilicet villam, cum cortile et manso indominicato, et capella quae est in honore sancte Dei genetricis Mariae et sancti Petri, apostolorum principis."

of the fledgling community. Instead, what distinguished these monks most from their tenth-century contemporaries was their commitment to an *ordo*, a specific idiom of spiritual life enshrined in the abbey's foundation charter.[8] William founded the abbey of Cluny specifically to benefit from the intercessory prayers of the brethren who would live there. As such, he was primarily concerned with the moral disposition of those responsible for this industry of prayer. This is clear from Cluny's foundation charter, which urged the monks specifically "to seek and desire with full commitment and inner order the heavenly way of life" through the program of the cultivation of virtues outlined in the *Rule of Benedict*.[9]

In contrast to the earliest Cluniacs, the brethren of the imperial monastery of Gorze composed numerous texts in the tenth century to promote the cult of Saint Gorgonius, a martyr of Diocletian's persecution whose remains Chrodogang of Metz had imported from Rome to the Moselle Valley when he founded their community in the eighth century.[10] These texts included a collection of the saint's miracles that doubled as a history of Gorze from its foundation to the tenth century, a *passio* of Gorgonius composed by Bishop Milo of Minden (a community that also possessed relics of this saint), as well as two sermons that were read on his feast day at Minden and Gorze.[11] Unlike the brethren of Gorze, whose prestige as a religious community was based in no small part on their promotion of the potent *praesentia* of Saint Gorgonius in their midst, the earliest monks of Cluny forged their reputation by fostering personal virtue in emulation of the angels.

Despite the absence of texts directly promoting the cult of the saints, the Cluniacs slowly and steadily acquired relics of local and international significance over the course of the tenth century. They obtained these relics in a number of ways, although in some cases it is impossible to trace their provenance. The most direct means to acquire relics in

---

8. On this sense of the term *ordo*, see J. Hourlier, "Cluny et la notion d'ordre religieux," in *A Cluny: Congrès scientifique, fêtes et cérémonies liturgiques en l'honneur des saints abbés Odon et Odilon, 9–11 juillet 1949* (Dijon, 1950), pp. 219–26.

9. BB, vol. 1, p. 126 (no. 112): "[C]onversatioque celestis omni desiderio et ardore intimo perquiratur et expetatur."

10. On the abbey of Gorze in this period, see *L'abbaye de Gorze au Xe siècle*, ed. M. Parisse and O. Oexle (Nancy, 1993); and J. Nightingale, *Monasteries and Patrons in the Gorze Reform: Lotharingia, c. 850–1000* (Oxford, 2001).

11. This dossier of texts has been edited and translated by P. C. Jacobsen in *Miracula s. Gorgonii: Studien und Texte zur Gorgonius-Verehrung im 10. Jahrhundert*, MGH Studien und Texte 46 (Hanover, 2009).

the tenth century was to purchase them.¹² The saintly count Gerald of Aurillac, whose exemplary life as a *perfectissimus laicus* Abbot Odo (927–942) narrated as an exhortation to the powerful, was an avid collector of relics, which he obtained from Rome and elsewhere.¹³ On one occasion, the count traded "precious tents and well-conditioned horses, as well as great sums of money" for a tooth of Saint Martial as well as for relics of Saint Martin and Saint Hilary.¹⁴ Gerald allegedly hung these holy riches in his tent while he traveled and later, two years before his death, he deposited them in a newly consecrated church for safekeeping.¹⁵ The monks of Cluny may have purchased relics directly as well, but they also received them indirectly in property donations. In 955, Stephen and Ermengard gave to the brethren the church of Sainte-Marie at Huillaux, which housed the remains of Saint Leotadus.¹⁶ In another case, a donation of land provided the Cluniacs with the opportunity to build a new chapel and adorn it with relics already in their possession. This was the situation with Chevignes, a plot near Mâcon donated by King Rodulph of France in 932 and later "decorated with the holy remains" of Saint Taurinus, although it is not clear how the brethren obtained these relics.¹⁷

In winter 981, the consecration of the abbey church now known as Cluny II provided the occasion for the Cluniacs to install in their new

---

12. This trend began in earnest in the ninth century. See P. Geary, "The Ninth-Century Relic Trade—A Response to Popular Piety?," in *Religion and the People, 800–1700*, ed. J. Obelkevich (Chapel Hill, NC, 1979), pp. 8–19; repr. in P. Geary, *Living with the Dead in the Middle Ages* (Ithaca, 1994), pp. 175–93.

13. Odo of Cluny, *Vita sancti Geraldi* 3.3, ed. A.-M. Bultot-Verleysen, in *Odon de Cluny, Vita sancti Geraldi Auriliacensis: Édition critique, traduction française, introduction et commentaires* (Brussels, 2009), p. 248.

14. Odo of Cluny, *Vita sancti Geraldi* 3.3: "Frequenter enim pro eisdem pigneribus impetrandis, et preciosa tentoria, necnon et corpulentos equos, et multa pecuniarum pondera constat eum dedisse," ed. Bultot-Verleysen, p. 248; trans. G. Sitwell, in *Soldiers of Christ: Saints and Saints' Lives from Late Antiquity and the Early Middle Ages*, ed. T. F. X. Noble and T. Head (University Park, PA, 1995), p. 350.

15. Odo of Cluny, *Vita sancti Geraldi* 1.25, 2.23, and 3.3, ed. Bultot-Verleysen, pp. 172, 226, and 248.

16. BB, vol. 1, pp. 779–81 (no. 825), at p. 780: "Sunt autem ipsę res sytę in comitatu Arvernico, in episcopate Augustidunense; hoc est curs indominicata, quę vocatur Oydellis, cum capella quę est constructa in honore beate Dei genitricis Marię, ubi sanctus Leotadus in corpore quiescit."

17. BB, vol. 1, pp. 773–74 (no. 780), at p. 774: "Atque capellam in honore beatissimi confesoris Christi Taurini, sacratissimi pontifices, fundaverant; super quam oppido deprecati sunt ut eam more precedentium partum et antistitum benediceret, et sacris pigneribus decoraret." The bones of Saint Taurinus are also included in the eleventh-century relic list preserved in the *Liber Tramitis* (see n. 22, below).

high altar their most prized relics: the ashes of the apostles Peter and Paul.[18] In a letter to Abbot Pontius (1109-1122), a Cluniac monk named Hugh of Gournay related the history of this "inestimable treasure" (*thesaurus inestimabilis*), beginning with the discovery of the apostolic ashes in the Roman catacombs by Pope Cornelius in the third century.[19] These precious relics were housed in the Vatican until their translation in a small container (*vasculum*) to the abbey of San Paolo fuori le Mure, which came under Cluniac influence in the early tenth century because of the reforming activities of Abbot Odo.[20] A few decades later, when urban violence caused calamitous unrest in Rome, brethren of this community fled to their spiritual kinsmen in Burgundy, taking with them the container housing the ashes of the apostles. It was allegedly these same Roman relics that Archbishop Hugh of Bourges placed in the new high altar when he consecrated Cluny II on February 14, 981.

Eleventh-Century Gains

The mounting prestige of Cluny under Abbots Maiolus (954-994) and Odilo (994-1049) may account for the increase in the abbey's relic holdings in the decades around 1000, as royal and episcopal patrons made even more extravagant gifts of holy objects to the community. The most important witness to this increase is the *Liber tramitis*. Written around 1030 and modified with additions in the 1040s, the *Liber tramitis* was a record of Cluniac customs composed by an Italian monk named John.[21] In its explanation of the duties of the sacristan, this text described a reliquary in the likeness of the head of Saint Peter (*in imagine sancti Petri*),

---

18. The association of the abbey of Cluny with these apostles was first invoked in William's foundation charter and recognized more widely as early as 928, when a man named Rostangus came to Cluny to pray as "to the threshold of the holy apostles Peter and Paul." See BB, vol. 1, pp. 345-46 (no. 367), at p. 346: "ad limina sanctorum apostolorum Petri et Pauli." On the construction of Cluny II and the influence of its form and style, see K. J. Conant, *Carolingian and Romanesque Architecture, 800 to 1200* (New Haven, 1993), pp. 185-87; and A. Baud, "Archaeology and the Abbey of Cluny," in *CCMA*, pp. 146-72.

19. For what follows, see *Epistola cuiusdam ad domnum [Pontium] Cluniacensem abbatem*, ed. H. E. J. Cowdrey, in "Two Studies in Cluniac History, 1049-1126," *Studi Gregoriani* 11 (1978): 9-395, at pp. 113-17.

20. I. Rosé, *Construire une société seigneuriale: Itinéraire et ecclésiologie de l'abbé Odon de Cluny (fin du IXe-milieu du Xe siècle)* (Turnhout, 2008), pp. 257-69.

21. On the *Liber tramitis* and its relationship to Cluny, see S. Boynton, *Shaping a Monastic Identity: Liturgy and History at the Imperial Abbey of Farfa, c. 1000-1125* (Ithaca, 2006), esp. pp. 106-43.

which was a veritable treasure trove housing more than twenty individual relics:

> In the image of Saint Peter these relics are contained: A piece of the Lord's cross and of the clothing of the Lord's mother Mary and of the very body of Saint Peter the apostle and of the flesh of Saint Jacob the apostle; there are also relics of Saint Stephen the protomartyr and from the bones of Saint Sebastian and Saint Cecilia and of the forty holy martyrs and of Saint George and Saint Innocent and from the bodies of Dionisius and his companions and from their clothes, from the stone of the Lord's tomb and from the rock where the Lord stood when he ascended into heaven and from the Lord's crib and from the tomb of Saint Lazarus, whom the Lord revived and from the rod of Moses. The bones of Saint Taurinus the bishop, the relics of Marcellus, the holy martyr of Chalon-sur-Saône, and the bones of the holy confessors Silvestrus and Agricola, bishops of the city of Chalon-sur-Saône, and many other saints. In a silver container is kept the body of the holy Pope Marcellus and relics from the very body of the holy Pope Gregory and a lock of hair of Saint Maiolus in a glass vial.[22]

Thus, by the early eleventh century, the Cluniacs boasted a collection of holy objects that included relics of Christ's earthly ministry, passion, and ascension, alongside the remains of the holy family, the apostles, and an Old Testament patriarch. In addition to these potent markers of biblical history, the contents of the Saint Peter reliquary delineated the continuity of Christian history from the time of Christ, through the

---

22. *Liber tramitis aevi Odilonis abbatis* 2.189: "De reliquiis sanctorum. In imagine sancti Petri continentur he reliquiae: Portio de cruce domini et de ueste sancta Marie matris domini et de proprio corpore sancti Petri apostoli et de carne sancti Iacobi apostoli; reliquie quoque sancti Stephani protomartyr<is> et de ossibus sancti Sebastiani et sanctae Cecilie et sanctorum quadraginta martyrum et sancti Georgii et sancti Innocentii et de corporibus Dionisii et sociorum eius et de uestibus eorum, de petra sepulchri domini et de lapide ubi dominus stetit quando ascendit in celum et de praesepio domini et de sepulchro sancti Lazari quem dominus suscitauit et de uirga Moysi. Ossa sancti Taurini episcopi, reliquie sancti Marcelli martyris Cabilonensis et ossa sanctorum confessorum Siuestri et Agricole episcoporum Cabilonensis ciuitatis aliorumque plurimorum sanctorum. In capsa argentea continentur corpus sancti Marcelli pape et reliquie de proprio corpore sancti Gregorii pape et portio capillorum sancti Maioli in uase uitreo," ed. P. Dinter, CCM 10 (Siegburg, 1980), pp. 260–61. The reliquary is no longer extant, but the richness of its contents inspired Alain Guerreau to imagine it as "une vraie caverne d'Ali-Baba." See A. Guerreau, "Espace social, espace symbolique: À Cluny au XIe siècle," in *L'ogre historien: Autour de Jacques Le Goff*, ed. J. Revel and J.-C. Schmitt (Paris, 1998), pp. 167–91, at p. 173.

age of the martyrs and the confessors, right up to the past generation, represented by the final relic on the list: a lock of hair of the recently departed Abbot Maiolus.

Although at first glance it is no more than a modest coda to the relic inventory in the *Liber Tramitis*, Maiolus's lock of hair in fact provides the first concrete evidence of the veneration of the remains of a Cluniac abbot at Cluny.[23] Unlike rival monastic houses, the Cluniacs were not especially interested in promoting the cults of their spiritual leaders. In fact, the earliest accounts of the lives of tenth-century Cluniac abbots were composed by Italian authors with only tangential relationships to Cluny: John of Salerno, who wrote the earliest life of Abbot Odo shortly after 942; and an anonymous monk of Pavia, who wrote the earliest life of Abbot Maiolus around 1000.[24] It was only in the early eleventh century that Abbot Odilo took control of the legacy of his predecessor Maiolus, first around the year 1010 by asking a monk named Syrus to compose a new *vita* of the saint in response to Pavia's claim to be the singular recipients of the holy abbot's *potentia*, and then around the year 1033 by writing yet another account of Maiolus's life in his own hand for the liturgical use of the monks of Romainmôtier, a Cluniac dependency in the Pays de Vaud.[25] The redeployment of Abbot Odo's legacy would have to wait until the twelfth century, when Peter the Venerable commissioned a monk named Nalgod to rewrite the *vitae* of some of his tenth-century predecessors.[26]

This ambivalence extended to the bodies of the abbots. After forty years as the spiritual father of Cluny, Maiolus died in 994 in the town of Souvigny while en route to Paris. Contenting themselves with a lock of his hair, the Cluniacs allowed the brethren of their affiliated priory in Souvigny to keep the saint's body, provided that they built

---

23. D. Iogna-Prat, "La saint Maïeul à Cluny d'après le *Liber Tramitis Aevi Odilonis*," in *Saint Mayeul et son temps: Actes du Congrès international de Valensole, 12–14 mai 1994* (Dignes-les-Bains, 1997), pp. 219–32, at p. 220: "Maïeul est le premier saint abbé clunisien." More than a decade before his death in 994, Maiolus was recognized as an especially holy man (*sanctissimus*) in a lay grant dating from 978/979. See D. Iogna-Prat, *Order and Exclusion: Cluny and Christendom Face Heresy, Judaism, and Islam (1000–1150)*, trans. G. R. Edwards (Ithaca, 2003), p. 58 and n. 129.

24. John of Salerno, *Vita Odonis, PL* 133, cols. 43–86; and the anonymous *Vita brevior sancti Maioli*, in *BC*, cols. 1763–82.

25. Syrus, *Vita sancti Maioli*, ed. D. Iogna-Prat, in *Agni Immaculati: Recherches sur les sources hagiographiques relatives à saint Maieul de Cluny (954–994)* (Paris, 1988), pp. 163–285; and Odilo, *Vita sancti Maioli*, in *BC*, cols. 279–90.

26. Nalgod, *Vita sancti Odonis*, in *Acta sanctorum ordinis sancti Benedicti in saeculorum classes distributa*, ed. J. Mabillon, 9 vols. (Paris, 1668–1701), vol. 5, pp. 186–99; repr. in *PL* 133, cols. 85–104.

a tomb worthy of his eminence and recorded any miracles that took place there.[27] At the request of Abbot Odilo, the brethren of Souvigny documented more than fifty miracles attributed to the abbot's holy agency in the early eleventh century.[28] Giles Constable has argued that the Cluniacs did not demand the return of Maiolus's body because the priory at Souvigny was considered to be a part of Cluny through affiliation and thus the holy abbot was for all intents and purposes already at Cluny.[29] Likewise, as early as 1002, Abbot Odilo had dedicated a church to his abbatial predecessor in the monastic complex at Cluny. Although it lacked the abbot's physical remains, this structure may have sufficed to evoke the holy presence of Maiolus in the community. An account of the abbot's death redacted in a twelfth-century lectionary from Cluny hinted at a less conciliatory reason for allowing his body to stay at Souvigny: the threat of violence by locals who did not wish to part with it.[30]

Irrespective of the Cluniacs' ambivalent relationship to the cult of their abbots, the *Liber tramitis* clearly shows that by the eleventh century the brethren had curated a relic collection that was impressive in its breadth and quality. Abbot Odilo seems to have been an aggressive agent in collecting holy objects, not only for the abbey of Cluny but also for his devotional pursuits.[31] In 1024/1025, he established a small priory on land belonging to his family at Lavoûte-Chilhac. Between 1031 and 1049, an anonymous author composed a history of this foundation, including an inventory of the holy objects amassed by Odilo to grace this new community.[32] The abbot of Cluny endowed the place

---

27. On the ambiguous relationship between the priory of Souvigny and its mother-house, see G. Constable, "Souvigny and Cluny," in G. Constable, *The Abbey of Cluny*, pp. 213–34.

28. *Miraculorum sancti Maioli duo libri*, in BC, cols. 1787–1814. For more on this miracle collection, see chapter 6, above.

29. Constable, "Souvigny and Cluny," p. 222.

30. Paris, BnF, Nouvelle acquisition latine 2246, fols. 235–37, at fol. 237r: "De sancto corpusculo Cluniacum transferendo multi libenter procurarent, nisi copiosiores indigenarum manus conglobatae violenter prohiberent." A new edition and translation of this *Vita altera Maioli* (*BHL* 5185) is in preparation.

31. His contemporary, Abbot Richard of Saint-Vanne (1003–1046), whom Odilo knew, did likewise. See S. Vanderputten, *Imagining Religious Leadership in the Middle Ages: Richard of Saint-Vanne and the Politics of Reform* (Ithaca, 2015), pp. 86–87.

32. The text only survives in an eighteenth-century copy by Dom Fonteaneau, who gave it the title *Historia abbreviata fundationis et consecrationis monasterii de la Voulte*. It has been printed with emendations in P.-F. Fournier, "Histoire anonyme de la foundation du prieuré de Lavoûte-Chilhac par Odilon, abbé de Cluny," *Bulletin philologique et historique (jusqu'à 1715) du Comité des travaux historiques et scientifiques* 46 (1958): 103–15, at pp. 106–15. For what follows, I am indebted to the analysis of E. Bozoky, "Les reliques de La Voûte," in *Odilon de Mercœuer, L'Auvergne et Cluny, La "Paix de Dieu" et l'Europe de l'an mil: Actes du colloque de Lavoûte-Chilhac*

with no fewer than ninety relics, primarily those of saints and confessors with a special emphasis on the remains of popes and bishops, many of them (sixty-seven of the ninety) from late antiquity or the Merovingian period. The relics of "modern" saints were represented in much smaller numbers, the most recent being unidentified relics of Maiolus (*reliquiae egregii patris nostri Maioli*). Odilo had obtained these relics from numerous sources. Some, particularly those of saints from the Auvergne, had already been assembled at Cluny by Maiolus. Many others arrived from the formidable holdings of the abbey of Saint-Denis in Paris, which had come under Cluniac control during the first decade of Odilo's abbacy. But the crowning piece of the collection was a fragment of the True Cross, an imperial gift to the abbot of Cluny from the German empress Cunegonde (d. 1033), the devout wife of Emperor Henry II (d. 1024), who had been a close friend of Odilo. It was no doubt because of the majesty of this relic of Christ's Passion that Odilo consecrated his priory at Lavoûte-Chilhac on the feast of the Exultation of the Cross (September 14).[33]

Relics Beyond the Cloister

Medieval monastic communities often deployed their relics in their interaction with laypeople outside of their cloisters, and the Cluniacs were no exception. The collections of monastic customary law compiled at Cluny in the eleventh centuries provided considerable insight into the ways that the brethren of the great Burgundian abbey interacted with the secular world through the use of relics.[34] As Kate Craig has shown, Cluniac relics were often on the move at the turn of the first millennium.[35] On certain days of the liturgical calendar, the brethren made processions with their relics in the company of laymen. For

---

des 10, 11, et 12 Mai 2000, ed. J. Vigier (Nonette, 2002), pp. 175-91. I am grateful to Julia M. H. Smith for drawing my attention to this important source.

33. On the enthusiasm for the cult of the True Cross at Cluny in this period, see D. Iogna-Prat, "La croix, le moine et l'empereur: Dévotion à la croix et théologie politique à Cluny autour de l'an mil," in *Haut Moyen-Age: Culture, Éducation et Société: Études offertes à Pierre Riché*, ed. C. Lepelley et al. (La Garenne-Colombes, 1990), pp. 449-75; repr. in D. Iogna-Prat, *Études clunisiennes* (Paris, 2002), pp. 75-92. A portion of this gift may have found its way into Cluny's Saint Peter reliquary, where a piece of the True Cross held pride of place as the first object listed in the inventory (see n. 22, above).

34. For more on the historical value of the Cluniac customaries, see I. Cochelin, "Discipline and the Problem of Cluny's Customaries," in *CCMA*, pp. 204-22.

35. For what follows, see K. M. Craig, *Mobile Saints: Relic Circulation, Devotion, and Conflict in the Central Middle Ages* (London, 2021), esp. pp. 52-78.

instance, the late tenth-century *Consuetudines antiquiores* described the conventions of a Palm Sunday procession in which laymen marched with banners, followed by *conversi* and monks carrying candles, holy water, censers, crosses, and evangeliaries. There followed two of the brethren bearing a large reliquary (*cassam maiorem*) and two more holding the reliquary in the likeness of Saint Peter (*himmaginem sancti Petri*).[36] On Rogation Days, the monks of Cluny processed with relics carried individually in small golden vessels called *phylacteria*. Fashioned in the shape of crosses, boxes, or brooches, these vessels normally resided on the altars (sometimes hung on poles) when the brethren were not using them in procession.[37]

Relics traveled outside of their sanctuaries for other reasons as well. In the late eleventh century, the Cluniac customary of Bernard detailed the protocols for moving the abbey's relics "whenever because of some urgent need [they] should be carried out of the abbey to some other place."[38] This process involved an elaborate, reverential procession of the entire monastic community to the gates of the abbey (*ad portas castelli*), where those responsible for carrying the relic handed it over to the laypeople (*laici*) entrusted to bear it toward its designated purpose, presumably (although not explicitly) accompanied by a monastic escort. Bernard's description of the ritual did not reveal the necessities that would require moving relics beyond the confines of the abbey, but in another passage concerning processions during the Trinity season, his customary made reference to occasions when "the image of St. Peter or other containers with relics of the saints are sent to some village of ours, for fear of plunders and robberies (as often happens)."[39] Brimming with the *potentia* of the abbey's holy allies, the Saint Peter reliquary was a formidable ward against the myriad of dangers threatening Cluniac dependencies in the eleventh century. It was also a potent ally in settling disputes in the abbey's favor. A charter from the late tenth century finds Garnier, the prior of Cluny, in the town of Valensole, where he accepted

---

36. *Consuetudines Cluniacensium antiquiores (BB1)*, in *Consuetudines Cluniacensium antiquiores cum redactionibus derivatis*, ed. K. Hallinger, CCM 7.2 (Siegburg, 1983), pp. 63–64.

37. On the shape and substance of these *phylacteria*, see K. M. Craig, "Bringing Out the Saints: Journeys of Relics in Tenth- to Twelfth-Century Northern France and Flanders" (PhD diss., University of California at Los Angeles, 2015) pp. 44–45.

38. Bernard 1.56, p. 251: "Quoties aliqua urgente necessitate reliquiae sanctorum extra monasterium alicubi sunt ferendae, hujusmodi effociis sunt prosequendae."

39. Bernard 2.25, p. 336: "Quando imago sancti Petri, vel aliae capsae cum reliquiis sanctorum, ad aliquam villam nostrum mittuntur, pro timore praedarum et rapinarum (ut saepe contingit)," trans. Craig, "Bringing Out the Saints," p. 61.

the promise made by Bishop Helmeradus of Riez to abandon his quarrels against the abbey "before the precious relics of the saints which are contained in the image of Saint Peter."[40] A few years after their dispute had been mediated successfully in the presence of the reliquary, Bishop Helmeradus and his canons initiated a prayer union with Abbot Odilo and the brethren of Cluny.[41]

The relics of the saints did not have to leave their sanctuaries to have a profound influence on the activities of laypeople, especially if they were behaving in ways detrimental to the well-being of the monks. As Lester Little and others have shown, cloistered communities ritually "humiliated" their relics to coax inattentive saints to come to their aid when the interests of the brethren were threatened, especially by rapacious laymen.[42] A liturgical formula from the eleventh-century *Liber tramitis* detailed this procedure, which involved placing a cross, the text of the Gospels, and the relics of the saints on a coarse cloth spread out on the floor before the altar. As the monks prostrated themselves in prayer, a priest recited the request for the saint in question to deliver them from their current distress.[43] Gilo's *Life of Abbot Hugh*, written in the 1120s, related how the humiliation of the relics of John the Baptist at the Cluniac priory of Saint-Jean-Baptiste in Chaveyriat near Lyons caused the saint to strike a layman named Berard of Riotier with blindness until he abandoned the rights that he had unlawfully usurped from the priory.[44] A charter from June 13, 1082, bears witness to Berard's willingness to make amends with the monks by abandoning his illegitimate claims, but without reference to the vengeance of the saint.[45]

---

40. BB, vol. 3, p. 101 (no. 1866): "Venit prafatus pontifex in ecclesiam ejusdem ville, ante preciosa pignora sanctorum que in imagine Sancti Petri continentur, et vuerpivit in presentia domni Varnerii, Cluniacensis prepositi, aliorumque fratrum qui cum eo aderant, omnem querelam quam habebat adversum eos de decimis eorum proprii laboris ac omnis possessionis." The editors have dated this notice to the final years of the abbacy of Maiolus (990-994). On the dates of Prior Garnier and evidence of his activity on behalf of Cluny, see M. Chaume, "Les grands prieurs de Cluny," *Revue Mabillon* 28 (1938): 147-52, at p. 149 (Warnerius III).

41. BB, vol. 4, pp. 201-203 (no. 1990), dated between 993 and 1031.

42. L. K. Little, *Benedictine Maledictions: Liturgical Cursing in Romanesque France* (Ithaca, 1993), esp. pp. 26-30; and P. Geary, "L'humiliation des saints," *Annales: Économies, Sociétés, Civilisations* 34 (1979): 27-42; English translation: P. Geary, "Humiliation of Saints", in P. Geary, *Living with the Dead in the Middle Ages*, pp. 95-115.

43. *Liber tramitis* 2.174, ed. Dinter, pp. 244-47.

44. Gilo, *Vita sancti Hugonis* 49, ed. Cowdrey, in "Two Studies in Cluniac History," pp. 87-88.

45. BB, vol. 4, pp. 748-49 (no. 3592).

154   CHAPTER 9

New Opportunities: The Twelfth Century and Beyond

By all measures, the eleventh century marked the apogee of Cluny's relic collecting ambitions, but the twelfth and thirteenth centuries brought new opportunities for yet more acquisitions, especially from the Holy Land during the age of the crusades.[46] During the abbacy of Pontius (1109-1122), the great Burgundian abbey acquired two substantial relics through a circuitous network of agents and admirers in the East. The first were some remains of Saint Stephen, which came to Cluny by means of the city of Edessa through the agency of Hilduin of Le Puiset.[47] Hilduin was a nobleman related to King Baldwin II of Jerusalem, who had converted to the monastic life and had become prior of a Cluniac dependency called Lurcy-le-Bourg near La Charité-sur-Loire. Like other members of his family, he felt a strong compulsion to journey to the East. Under Abbot Pontius, Hilduin made a pilgrimage to the Holy Land, where he visited Archbishop Hugh of Edessa in the entourage of his royal cousin. This distinguished prelate entrusted the monk with the task of delivering a precious treasure—relics of Saint Stephen—to Cluny, for he held the abbey dear and believed that it had originally been consecrated not only to the apostles Peter and Paul, but also to the protomartyr. Indeed, the monks of Cluny had already acquired some remains of Saint Stephen in the early eleventh century, but this did not dissuade them from welcoming the arrival of these new relics from Edessa upon Hilduin's return to Burgundy in 1120.[48]

Around the same time, the Cluniacs acquired a relic of great antiquity and renown: a fragment of the True Cross allegedly once in the possession of the late antique monastic saint Basil of Caesarea who had enshrined it in a reliquary shaped like a Gospel book (*tabula*).[49] Like the remains of Saint Stephen, this relic of Christ's Passion followed a circuitous route from the Holy Land to Burgundy. In the eleventh century, the *tabula* had belonged to an archdeacon named Mesopotamius,

---

46. For Cluny's participation in the crusading movement, see chapter 10, below.
47. For what follows, see *Quomodo reliquiae beati Stephani protomartyris Cluniacum delatae fuerunt tempore eiusdem Pontii abbatis*, in BC, cols. 565-68; and *Recueil des historiens des croisades: Historiens occidentaux*, 5 vols. (Paris, 1844-95), vol. 5, pp. 317-20.
48. On the presence of Stephen's relics at Cluny in the early eleventh century, see n. 22, above.
49. Basil of Caesarea (329-78) was revered as a saint in the medieval west due to his authority as a monastic teacher whose writings had informed the *Rule of Benedict*. On the history of this relic and its movements, see *Qualiter tabula sancti Basilii continens in se magnam dominici ligni portionem Cluniaceum delata fuerit tempore Pontii abbatis*, in BC, cols. 561-64; and *Recueil des historiens des croisades: Historiens occidentaux*, vol. 5, pp. 295-98.

who brought it from Caesarea to Constantinople to protect it from the incursions of the Seljuk Turks. His wife took possession of the relic after his death. In the early twelfth century, she gave it to Archbishop Maurice of Braga, while he tarried in Constantinople en route back to Spain after the First Crusade. Upon his return, he secretly deposited this "incomparable treasure" (*incomparabili thesauro*) in the abbey of San Zoilo de Cordoba, a Cluniac dependency located in Carrión de los Condes along the Camino de Santiago in northwestern Spain. In 1112, shortly after Pontius became abbot, Maurice translated the *tabula* to Cluny, where it would receive adoration more fitting to its eminence to the benefit of his soul.

It was during the twelfth century that Abbot Peter the Venerable articulated most clearly his understanding of the meaning of relics in his community and why they were worthy of reverence by devout Christians. The context was most likely the anniversary of the translation of the bones of Saint Marcellus to Cluny (January 6). The monks of Cluny had a special fondness for this martyred late antique pope. According to the early eleventh-century *Liber tramitis*, they possessed the remains of his holy body, which they kept in a silver container (*in capsa argentea*).[50] This was very likely the same reliquary that Abbot Hugh requested to be brought to his bedside as he lay dying in 1109.[51] Moreover, Peter was well versed not only with accounts of Marcellus's life and martyrdom but also with the pope's writings, which he quoted verbatim in an undated sermon praising his sanctity.[52] In yet another sermon, ostensibly also about Marcellus, but treating the cult of relics more generally, Peter insisted that the remains of the saints were not comparable to the cadavers of animals, which were worthless and trampled underfoot without a thought.[53] Rather, their holy corpses were divine seeds from

---

50. See n. 22, above.

51. Hildebert of Le Mans, *Vita sancti Hugonis*: "Poro exiturus ex hac Aegypto Dei famulus, B. Marcelli capsam sibi iubet praesentari, pium lachrymis interpellans aduocatum, ut eius conductu, post exilium, patriae redderetur," in *BC*, col. 436. Further on this *vita*, see Cowdrey, "Two Studies in Cluniac History," pp. 27–28.

52. Peter the Venerable, *Sermo de sancto Marcello papa et martyre*, ed. G. Constable, in "Petri Venerabilis Sermones Tres," *Revue bénédictine* 64 (1954): 224–72, at pp. 227–28 (a discussion of Peter's sources) and pp. 255–65 (an edition of the Latin text of the sermon itself).

53. Peter the Venerable, *Sermo cuius supra in honore sancti illius cuius reliquiae sunt in presenti*, ed. Constable, in "Petri Venerabilis Sermones Tres," pp. 265–72, esp. p. 231, where Constable notes: "Marcellus is, nevertheless, nowhere mentioned by name in this sermon, which is rather a general defense and discussion of the practice of the veneration of relics." For a discussion of this sermon in the context of twelfth-century seed metaphors based on 1 Cor. 15, see C. W. Bynum, *The Resurrection of the Body in Western Christianity, 200–1336* (New York, 1995), pp. 176–80.

which immortal bodies would one day generate and live again for all eternity: "Behold whose bodies you venerate, brothers, in whose ashes you exalt, for whose bones you prepare golden sepulchers. They are the sons of God, equal to the angels, sons of the resurrection. Hence you should receive them reverently as sons of God, extol them as equal to the angels with suitable praises, and expect that they will rise in their own flesh as sons of the resurrection."[54] For Peter, the bones of dead saints merited reverence because they pulsed in their reliquaries with the potential of their future resurrection, the proof of which lay in the miracles made manifest to those devout Christians who visited their tombs. Concealed in the darkness of their sepulchers, the saints were not dead; in fact, they already lived with God.

Much like the era of the First Crusade, the brethren of Cluny emerged in the thirteenth century primarily as supporters of expeditions to the East and beneficiaries of their success rather than as active participants.[55] In the aftermath of the conquest of Constantinople in April 1204, European monasteries received a steady stream of Greek relics as gifts from western crusaders returning from the new Latin Empire of the East.[56] In the summer of 1206, the abbey of Cluny welcomed the head of the first-century pope and martyr Saint Clement, a precious relic plundered from the monastery of Theotokos Peribleptos in Constantinople. A Cluniac monk named Rostang provided an unusual narrative of the events that culminated in the arrival of the saint's remains in Burgundy.[57] This text is exceptional because, nested

---

54. "Ecce quorum corpora fratres ueneramini, quorum cineribus exultatis, quorum beatis ossibus aurea sepulchra paratis. Inde eos ut filios Dei reuerenter suscipitis, ut angelis equales paribus laudibus extollitis, ut filios resurrectionis in carne propria resurrecturos speratis." ed. Constable, in idem, "Petri Venerabilis Tres Sermones," p. 269; trans. Bynum, *The Resurrection of the Body*, pp. 178-79.

55. See chapter 10, below.

56. For the arrival of Greek relics in northern Europe as a result of the Fourth Crusade, with an emphasis on female recipients, see A. E. Lester, "What Remains: Women, Relics, and Remembrance in the Aftermath of the Fourth Crusade," *Journal of Medieval History* 40 (2014): 311-28.

57. For what follows, see Rostang, *Narratio exceptionis apud Cluniacum capitis beati Clementis, ex ore Dalmacii de Serciaco, militis, excepta*, in *BC*, cols. 1481-90; repr. in *Exuviae sacrae Constantinopolitanae*, ed. P. Riant, 2 vols. (Paris, 1877-78), vol. 1, pp. 127-40. Riant claimed that the Cluniac manuscript containing this work was "now lost" (*nunc deperditi*), but a medieval witness of this text survives in Paris, BnF, Nouvelle acquisition latine 2483, a compilation of Cluniac privileges and history made in 1480, where it appears on fols. 51v-54r under the title "Incipit tractatus exceptione capitis sancti Clementis pape et martiris ab Constantinopolim in Cluniacum translati, que eddidit magister Rostangno Cluniacensis monachus." This text went unnoticed for so long because it was not listed in the description of the manuscript provided

in his narrative, Rostang purported to reproduce a firsthand account to the sacred theft allegedly told by one of the perpetrators.[58] He related how two Christian soldiers, Dalmase de Sercy and Ponce de Bussière, decided to procure a relic that would bring them glory and praise, after their attempts to travel from Constantinople to Jerusalem had been thwarted due to conditions that made the trip much too dangerous. With the help of an unnamed French priest, these veterans of the Fourth Crusade stole the head of Saint Clement, which they claimed had been treated with disrespect by its Greek custodians. They obtained the relic through subterfuge on Palm Sunday (March 26) in 1206, fled the scene in disguise and evaded capture, venerating the saint's remains in secret until they departed Constantinople in May. After an eventful sea voyage, during which they called on the mercy of Clement to save them from a storm, the knights eventually arrived at the abbey of Cluny, where on July 27, 1206, the brethren joyfully installed the saint's skull in a silver reliquary.

With these slow but steady gains over the course of several centuries, it is not surprising to find that the abbey of Cluny boasted a lavish assembly of relics by the end of the Middle Ages. The magnitude of the Cluniac collection is on display in the two major inventories of treasures compiled by the monks in the late fourteenth century. The first is a discursive list of nearly five hundred precious objects housed at the great Burgundian abbey.[59] Dated August 12, 1382, this inventory included more than two dozen reliquaries, most of which were adorned with gold, silver, and precious stones. These extravagant items housed the remains of the most prestigious relics: items related to Christ's earthy ministry and death (his umbilical cord and foreskin; a fragment of the True Cross; and a piece of his sepulcher); relics of the holy family (the heads of Saint Anne and Saint Elizabeth; a sleeve of the Virgin Mary as

---

by P. Lauer, "Nouvelles acquisitions latines et françaises du Départment des Manuscrits de la Bibliothèque Nationale pendent les années 1932-1935," *Bibliothèque de l'école des chartes* 96 (1935): 205-45, at p. 215 (no. 2483). In light of this discovery, a new edition and translation of the *Tractatus exceptione capitis sancti Clementis* is in preparation.

58. See R. Bartlett, *Why Can the Dead Do Such Great Things? Saints and Worshippers from the Martyrs to the Reformation* (Princeton, 2013), pp. 310-11; and D. M. Perry, *Sacred Plunder: Venice and the Aftermath of the Fourth Crusade* (University Park, PA, 2015), pp. 102-105.

59. The 1382 inventory was originally written in Latin, but it only survives in a French translation prepared in 1792 by Philibert Bouché de la Bertillière for his *Description historique et chronologique de la ville, abbaye et banlieue de Cluny*, now Bibliothèque du Musée d'art et d'archéologie de Cluny, MS 79, pp. 359-92. This inventory has been published by A. Bénet, "Le trésor de l'abbaye de Cluny: Inventaire de 1382," *Revue de l'Art chrétien* 6 (1888): 195-205.

well as a goblet associated with her; and two teeth of John the Baptist); the bones of the fathers of the monastic tradition in Gaul (the head of Saint Jerome; relics of Saint Benedict; and an arm of Saint Maurus); the remains of Cluny's holy abbots (arms and other relics of Abbots Odo and Odilo); and many other relics besides.[60]

Another reckoning of Cluny's relics took place in 1399, when an unnamed monk made an inventory of the contents of the five reliquaries kept on the major altar and in the cloister. Almost a century later, this inventory found a place in a volume of documents related to the history and privileges of the monastery compiled before 1480 at the request of Philippe de Lozier, the Grand Prior of the Order of Cluny.[61] The Cluniac relic inventory of 1399 differs from its predecessor in the eleventh-century *Liber tramitis* in a number of ways: it described the contents of multiple reliquaries rather than just one, some of which were decorated with scenes from the Gospels; the saints represented in these five reliquaries revealed new patterns of devotion among late medieval Cluniacs; and the emphasis on relics of Abbot Hugh the Great suggested that the cult of abbots had developed considerably at Cluny by the later Middle Ages.

While the *Liber tramitis* described the contents of a single large reliquary fashioned in the likeness of the head of Saint Peter, the 1399 inventory detailed the contents of four distinct reliquaries of various sizes kept on the major altar as well as a fifth reliquary located in the cloister specifically as a ward against inclement weather. Like the Saint Peter reliquary, which was a central feature of processions and conflict resolution in the late tenth and eleventh centuries, several of these reliquaries were precious objects in their own right. Although the 1399 inventory made no mention of the Saint Peter reliquary, it did describe a reliquary crafted in the image of Abbot Hugh, which had been "newly made" to hold the relic of his head.[62] Likewise, two of the five reliquaries were decorated with scenes from the Gospels wrought with inlaid

---

60. See Bénet, "Le trésor de l'abbaye de Cluny," pp. 196–97 (nos. 16, 19–23, 26–27, 30, 33–49, 51 and 53).

61. Paris, BnF, Nouvelle acquisition latine 2483, fols. 100r–100v. For an partial description of the manuscript, see Lauer, "Nouvelles acquisitions latines et françaises," p. 215 (no. 2483). On the date of this manuscript, see the inscription on the bottom of fol. 7r: "Iste liber est ecclesiae Cluniacensis ex dono prioris majoris anno Domini millesimo quatercenesimo octuagesimo, mense Augusti."

62. "Caput positum est in ymagine beati Hugonis de nouo facta" (Paris, BnF, Nouvelle acquisition latine 2483, fol. 100r).

silver.[63] Lastly, within the reliquary kept in the cloister as a ward against tempests was a smaller container made of lead (*piris plumbea*), on which was written the names of the Virgin Mary and all of the apostles.

The panoply of saints represented in the 1399 inventory was not only much larger than that of its eleventh-century predecessor but also more expressive of trends in devotion unattested in other sources from this period. The presence of early Christian martyrs is not surprising, but they appear in such great numbers in the 1399 inventory and some of them are obscure or otherwise unknown, like Cyrilla, the daughter of Emperor Decius, that they clearly represent a consciously cultivated constituency of the saints revered at Cluny. Even more striking is the new attention paid to relics of the earliest abbots of the monastery of Luxeuil: Columbanus, Eustace, and Waldebertus. Founded in the late sixth century by the Irish missionary Columbanus (c. 543-615), Luxeuil was one of the oldest monastic foundations in Burgundy.[64] In the twelfth century, Cluny had a copy of the monastic rule composed by Columbanus as well as his sermons (known collectively as the *Instructio de fide*), but otherwise there is no indication that the abbots of Luxeuil enjoyed any special reverence among the Cluniacs.[65] Therefore, their presence in the 1399 inventory may have represented a new trend in devotion at Cluny that had gained traction only in the late Middle Ages.

A final feature of the 1399 inventory is its emphasis on the cult of Abbot Hugh the Great. As we have seen, the Cluniacs did not promote the sanctity of their abbots until the eleventh century and placed little emphasis on the commemoration of their relics. By the later Middle Ages, this aspect of Cluniac devotion appears to have changed, at least with respect to the relics of Saint Hugh, whose body occupied one of the two larger reliquaries on the major altar of Cluny, with the exception of

---

63. "Item in illa parua capsa in qua desuper ab una parte est ystoria argentea qualiter dominus Ihesus intrauit Iherusalim in die ramis palmarum et ab alia parte qualiter in cena fecit mandatum discipulis suis continentur sequentes reliquie" and "Item in alia parua capsa in qua desuper est ystoria argentea illius Euuangelii" (Paris, BnF, Nouvelle acquisition latine 2483, fol. 100r). For a useful discussion of the "semantic instability" inherent in the description of metals recorded in church inventories, see J. S. Ackley, "Re-Approaching the Western Medieval Church Treasury Inventory, c. 800-1250," *Journal of Art Historiography* 11 (2014): 1-37.

64. A. O'Hara, *Jonas of Bobbio and the Legacy of Columbanus* (Oxford, 2018).

65. L. Delisle, *Inventaire des manuscrits de la Bibliothèque nationale: Fonds de Cluni* (Paris, 1994), p. 353 (no. 276): "Volumen in quo continetur regula sancti Columbani, instructio ejusdem de fide."

his head, which had its own reliquary crafted in his image.[66] Moreover, the author of the 1399 inventory was careful to note that the reliquary housing the body of Abbot Hugh contained no other relics. This is in marked contrast to the other reliquaries on the list, which each contained the remains of numerous named saints and, in three cases, many other bones that lacked labels. Hugh the Great's dominance as a central figure of the cult of relics at Cluny persisted until the early eighteenth century, when Martène and Durand observed the many articles that had belonged to the abbot displayed prominently and reverentially in the abbey treasury.[67]

For the century after its foundation in 910, the abbey of Cluny did not place an emphasis on the powerful presence of the remains of the saints in their community as a guarantee of the sanctity of their monastic endeavor. By the turn of the first millennium, however, Abbots Maiolus and Odilo made an effort to curate a collection of relics that grew in stride with the prestige of their abbey, in no small part because of the generous donations of Cluny's many powerful patrons. These relics were not only objects of devotion; the presence of the saints also played an important role in protecting the abbey's dependencies from the depredations of laymen and in facilitating conflict resolutions with the monks' adversaries. Cluny's collection of relics grew in the twelfth and thirteenth centuries, when the age of the crusades opened up new possibilities to obtain holy objects from the East. By the end of the Middle Ages, the Cluniacs housed the most important relics of their collection, especially those associated with Christ's earthly ministry and passion, in priceless reliquaries wrought from the finest materials and decorated with precious stones.

Carefully curated over the course of the Middle Ages, Cluny's relic hoard suffered tremendously during the wars of religion that ravaged Burgundy in the early modern period. The threat to the abbey's treasury was such that the monks made yet another inventory of their relics in the sixteenth century, perhaps in preparation for the strategic dispersal and concealment of the collection to prevent it from being looted by their

---

66. "Et primo in maiori capsa est corpus integrum beati Hugonis abbatis Cluniacensis sine capite, quia caput positum est in ymagine beati Hugonis de nouo facta et in dicta capsa non sunt alie reliquie" (Paris, BnF, Nouvelle acquisition latine 2483, fol. 100r). Only one other abbot of Cluny, Hugh's predecessor Odilo, appeared in the 1399 inventory and then only briefly (Paris, BnF, Nouvelle acquisition latine 2483, fol. 100r: "Item sancti Odilonis").

67. See n. 3, above.

Huguenot adversaries.[68] By the time that Martène and Durand visited the abbey in the early eighteenth century, the collection was undoubtedly much diminished in its size and quality from its height in the late Middle Ages, so vividly described in the treasure and relic inventories of the fourteenth century. Even in their diminished state, however, the relics of Cluny made a deep impression on the Maurist visitors in 1709 and remained an essential feature of monastic devotion at the great Burgundian abbey until its dissolution in 1789. Ultimately, Cluny's lack of popular relics in the eighteenth century may have contributed to its demise, for the community's failure to attract Catholic pilgrims to the abbey gates on the magnitude of Lourdes and Chartres probably accounted for the lack of public outcry when the physical fabric of the great basilica was sold as quarry material and torn down in 1800.[69]

---

68. "Inventaire des reliques conserves en l'abbaye de Cluny dans l'estat quelles étoient avant le pillage de ladite abbaye par Puisaye," in Philibert Bouché de la Bertillière, *Description historique et chronologique de la ville, abbaye et banlieue de Cluny*; now Paris, BnF, Nouvelles acquisitions françaises 4336, pp. 135–57. On the upheavals at Cluny caused by the wars of religion, see M. P. Lorain, *Histoire de l'abbaye de Cluny depuis sa fondation jusqu'à sa destruction à l'époque de la Révolution française* (Paris, 1845), pp. 222–47.

69. J. T. Marquardt, *From Martyr to Monument: The Abbey of Cluny as Cultural Patrimony* (Newcastle, 2007), p. 7: "Never holding the major relics of a popular saint nor recording miracles on the site since the obscure tales of medieval abbots' graves, there was nothing at Cluny to inspire an outcry from Catholic believers, especially the women who made up the largest number of pilgrims, *miraculés*, and new clergy."

Chapter 10

Cluny and the Crusades

What has Cluny to do with the crusades? At first glance, the career of Odo of Châtillon-sur-Marne (c. 1042–1099) appears to provide a clear link between the great Burgundian abbey and the origins of the crusade movement. Odo, later known as Pope Urban II, the author of the First Crusade, had been a high-ranking monk of Cluny, serving in the 1070s as the community's prior, second only to Abbot Hugh the Great, before Pope Gregory VII chose him to be cardinal-bishop of Ostia around 1080 and designated him as one of his possible successors.[1] Even after his election as pope in the spring of 1088, Urban II still identified as a monk of Cluny. In a letter to Abbot Hugh written during the first year of his papacy, Urban II entreated his spiritual father to visit him in Rome or at the very least to send some of his fellow monks from Burgundy: "If [a visit from you] is not possible, at least send some of your sons, my brothers, in whom I may see you, receive

---

Originally published as "Cluny and the Crusades," in *A Companion to the Abbey of Cluny in the Middle Ages*, ed. S. G. Bruce and S. Vanderputten (Leiden, 2021), pp. 306–21. Reprinted with permission.

1. For what follows on the career of Urban II, see A. Becker, *Papst Urban II (1088-1099)*, MGH Schriften 10.1-3, 3 vols. (Stuttgart, 1964–2012), esp. vol. 1, pp. 41–51 on his time as a monk at Cluny; vol. 2, p. 439 on his papal visit to Cluny from October 18-25, 1095; and vol. 3, pp. 414–63 on his esteem for the value and utility of monasticism and his efforts to protect the interests of cloistered communities.

you, recognize the voice of your consolation in the extremely troubling situation I find myself in; send one who will make your love and the warmth of your affection present to me, who will be a sign of kindness toward me from you and all the brothers of our congregation."[2]

For his part, Hugh the Great fostered this sense of comradery and cooperation between Urban II and his monastic home, even urging the pope to consider the Cluniacs as the distant, yet intimate, servants (*domestici*) of his reforming agenda.[3] The marriage of Cluniac monasticism and the author of the crusade movement appeared most vividly in an illumination of Urban II consecrating the high altar of Cluny's new basilica in October 1095, a month before he would preach the First Crusade on November 27 at the Council of Clermont.[4] Surely, given the close ties between Cluny and its prior-turned-pope, spiritual and intellectual currents at the abbey must have played a formative role in the development of Urban II's gambit to win back the city of Jerusalem for Christendom by means of an armed, penitential expedition against the Muslims.

Over the past century, however, the notion that Cluny "made a major positive contribution to the genesis of the Crusading idea" has receded in the wake of studies arguing that the penitential spirituality fostered at Cluny only indirectly "prepared both the world in which it was in contact and its own monks to respond favourably to the Crusade, once it was preached by the pope."[5] Moreover, although historians have

---

2. *Regesta pontificum Romanorum*, ed. P. Jaffé, 2 vols. (Leipzig, 1885–88), vol. 1, p. 658 (no. 5349); repr. in Urban II, *Epistola* 2, *PL* 151, cols. 284–85, at col. 285: "At vero, si id fieri nequit, ut tales de filiis tuis confratribus meis te ad nos mandare non pigeat, in quibus te videam, te suscipiam, tuae consolationis in immensis perturbationibus positus verba cognoscam, qui tuam charitatem tuaeque dilectionis affectum mihi repraesentent, qui qualiter et tu omniumque fratrum nostrorum se habeat congregatio mihi denuntient." The "great disturbances" (*immensis perturbationibus*) no doubt referred to the machinations of the anti-Gregorian antipope Clement III (1080–1100), whose reign overshadowed Urban II's entire career in Rome.

3. *Chronicon sancti Huberti Andaginensis* 84, ed. G. Pertz, MGH Scriptores 8 (Hanover, 1848), pp. 616–17 (dated 1096). For context, see H. E. J. Cowdrey, *The Cluniacs and the Gregorian Reform* (Oxford, 1970), pp. 179–80, who wrote that Urban II "saw in the Cluniac monastic family a principal means for advancing the interests of the Papacy and of reform in France and elsewhere."

4. Paris, BnF, Latin 17716, fol. 91. On this manuscript, which is dated around the year 1200, see S. Boynton, "Music and the Cluniac Vision of History in Paris, Bibliothèque nationale de France, lat. 17716," in *Chant, Liturgy, and the Inheritance of Rome: Essays in Honour of Joseph Dyer*, ed. D. J. DiCenso and R. Maloy (London, 2017), pp. 407–30.

5. H. E. J. Cowdrey, "Cluny and the First Crusade," *Revue bénédictine* 83 (1973): 285–311, at pp. 287 and 291–92; repr. in H. E. J. Cowdrey, *Popes, Monks, and Crusaders* (London, 1984), no. XV. See also D. Iogna-Prat, *Order and Exclusion: Cluny and Christendom Face Heresy, Judaism, and Islam (1000–1150)*, trans. G. R. Edwards (Ithaca, 2002), pp. 323–31.

devoted considerable energy to examining and ultimately downplaying Cluny's role in the First Crusade, the part played by the abbey in subsequent expeditions to the East remains little studied and poorly understood. In this chapter, I offer an assessment of pre-Crusade sources that call attention to the symbolic nature of the martial language employed by Cluniac authors, the unusual attention paid to Islam in some early Cluniac texts, and the fostering of a penitential spirituality in Cluniac circles that may have informed the Crusade movement, albeit indirectly. I then consider the evidence for the abbey's role in promoting and participating in the First Crusade before turning to Abbot Peter the Venerable's support of the failed Second Crusade and his role in planning the aborted 1150 expedition that followed it. I argue that, throughout the age of the crusades, with few exceptions, the Cluniacs emerge as opportunistic beneficiaries of the desire of Western Christians to embark on expeditions to the East rather than as primary instigators of the Crusade movement.

Penance and Preaching on the Eve of the First Crusade

In the two centuries between the foundation of Cluny in 910 and Urban's preaching of the First Crusade in 1095, Cluniac leaders composed texts expressing pious concerns that, with hindsight, appear to have informed the genesis of the Crusade movement. Following a tradition of martial language dating back to late antiquity and informed by the Old Testament, monastic authors often referred to their spiritual struggles in terms of armed combat.[6] At the end of his sermon for the Feast of Saint Benedict, Odo of Cluny (927–942) depicted the holy abbot as a king, whose "vast army of monks" (*tam numerosus . . . exercitus monachorum*) marched under his banner against the hosts of the Devil.[7] A few decades later (c. 1000), the anonymous author of the earliest life of Maiolus of Cluny described the abbot as a "glorious standard-bearer," who marshaled legions of monks "in the camps of lordly observance, ready to fight with all due strength against the insolence of raving iniquity."[8] Moreover, at Cluny and elsewhere, many adult

---

6. On this tradition, see K. A. Smith, *War and the Making of Medieval Monastic Culture* (Woodbridge, 2011).
7. Odo, *Sermo 3 (De sancto Benedicto abbate)*, PL 133, cols. 721–29, at cols. 728–29.
8. *Vita brevior sancti Maioli* 6: "Easque signifer gloriosus secum in dominicae religionis castris fortiter bellaturas contra seuientis nequitiae importunitatem preordinauit," in *BC*, col. 1769.

converts to the cloistered life came from the nobility and most would have had firsthand experience in lethal battles, the sins of which they may have hoped to extirpate by adopting the monastic habit. Starting in the mid-eleventh century, some of these converts to the cloistered life even persisted in wearing their chainmail under their robes as a form of penance.[9] Among them was Abbot Hugh the Great, who as a young man had resisted the military training expected of a scion of a noble class and later as a monk chose to endure the discomfort of wearing armor specifically to atone for the faults of his noble father Dalmatius, whose sudden death by violence had burdened him with the weight of many unconfessed sins.[10]

Deploying martial imagery, whether in hagiography or the liturgy, is not the same, however, as advocating violence against others, even with pious intent.[11] The Cluniacs recruited from the ranks of the nobility, to be sure, but as Hugh the Great's act of penance shows, they repudiated the bloodshed and worldliness of the warrior class. Odo of Cluny's early tenth-century account of the pious life of Count Gerald of Aurillac is a well-trodden example.[12] It was clearly a challenge for Odo to portray a saint who exercised his sanctity in the tumult of the world, rather than retreating from it to the safety of the cloister. Yet Gerald was a warrior

---

9. For a list of examples of *loricati* (mailed ones) between the eleventh and thirteenth centuries, see Smith, *War and the Making of Medieval Monastic Culture*, pp. 201-202.

10. Gilo of Cluny, *Vita Hugonis* 51, ed. H. E. J. Cowdrey, in "Two Studies in Cluniac History, 1049-1126," *Studi Gregoriani* 11 (1978): 13-298, at p. 88; and Renaud of Vézelay, *Vita domni Hugonis* 6, ed. R. B. C. Huygens, in *Vizeliacensia II: Textes relatifs à l'histoire de l'abbaye de Vézelay*, CCCM 42 Suppl. (Turnhout, 1980), p. 41.

11. See J. Leclercq, "Prayer at Cluny," *Journal of the American Academy of Religion* 51 (1983): 651-65, esp. pp. 657-62, written in response to B. H. Rosenwein, "Feudal War and Monastic Peace: Cluniac Liturgy as Ritual Aggression," *Viator* 2 (1971): 129-57.

12. Odo of Cluny, *Vita Geraldi auriliacensis comitis*, ed. A.-M. Bultot-Verleysen, in *Odon de Cluny, Vita sancti Geraldi Auriliacensis: Édition critique, traduction française, introduction et commentaires* (Brussels, 2009). A recent attempt to reinterpret the authorship and date of this *vita* has failed to convince: M. Kuefler, *The Making and Unmaking of a Saint: Hagiography and Memory in the Cult of Gerald of Aurillac* (Philadelphia, 2013). For a firm rebuttal of his thesis, see C. A. Jones, "Odo of Cluny and the Authenticity of the *Vita prolixior prima* of St. Gerald of Aurillac (BHL 3411)," *Analecta Bollandiana* 139 (2021): 289-338. For Odo's expectations of the laity, see F. Lotter, "Das Idealbild adliger Laienfrömmigkeit in den Anfängen Clunys: Odos Vita des Grafen Gerald von Aurillac," in *Benedictine Culture, 750-1050*, ed. W. Lourdaux and D. Verhelst (Leuven, 1983), pp. 76-95; S. Airlie, "The Anxiety of Sanctity: St. Gerald and His Maker," *Journal of Ecclesiastical History* 43 (1992): 372-95; D. Iogna-Prat, "La place idéale du laïc à Cluny: D'une morale statutaire à une éthique absolue," in *Guerriers et moines: Conversion et sainteté aristocratiques dans l'Occident medieval (IXe-XIIe siècle)*, ed. M. Lauwers (Nice, 2002), pp. 291-316, repr. in D. Iogna-Prat, *Études clunisiennes* (Paris, 2002), pp. 93-124; and I. Rosé, *Construire une société seigneuriale: Itinéraire et ecclésiologie d'abbé Odon de Cluny (fin du IXe-milieu du Xe siècle)* (Turnhout, 2008), pp. 457-508.

who, like Saint Martin before him, actively repudiated armed combat.[13] When he was forced to do battle, Gerald allegedly "commanded his men with imperious tones to fight with the backs of their swords and with their spears reversed" and trusted in God to win the day.[14]

It is tempting for historians to locate in this portrait of Gerald an antecedent to the first crusaders, but several factors mitigate against this interpretation. The *Life of Gerald* was not read outside of monastic circles in the tenth century; the primary audience seems to have been those very warriors who had chosen the serenity of the cloister over the turmoil of the world.[15] Moreover, as Carl Erdmann observed long ago, "the real merit of the saint consists in asceticism and *caritas*, just like a monk, and not in warlike deeds . . . Odo's ethic does not as yet extend to holy war."[16] Cluniac hagiographers were, in fact, specific about their literary depiction of the authors of violence: they were always enemies of their abbey. For example, when Odo arrived at the abbey of Fleury sometime in the 930s to reform the community, some of the brethren railed against his presumptive authority and "arming themselves with swords went up on to the roof of the building, as though to hurl stones and missiles on their adversaries from the sky."[17] Odo eventually won them over with his humility, aided in no small part by a vision of Saint Benedict. A few decades later, after Muslim adventurers seized Abbot Maiolus and his entourage as they crossed the Great Saint Bernard Pass en route from Rome to Burgundy in July 972, Cluniac hagiographers portrayed the abbot's captors as unrelenting in their cruelty, which they expressed with violence against their captives.[18] In this case, the Mus-

---

13. B. H. Rosenwein, "St. Odo's St. Martin: The Uses of a Model," *Journal of Medieval History* 4 (1978): 317–31.

14. Odo of Cluny, *Vita sancti Geraldi* 1.8: "Aliquociens autem, cum ineuitabilis ei pręliandi necessitas incumberet, suis imperiosa uoce precepit, mucronibus gladiorum retro actis, hastas inantea dirigentes pugnarent," ed. Bultot-Verleysen, p. 144.

15. As Marcus Bull reminds us, however, the memory of Gerald lived on in the Limousin well into the twelfth century, where legends about him circulated beyond the cloister. See M. Bull, *Knightly Piety and the Lay Response to the First Crusade: The Limousin and Gascony, c. 970–c. 1130* (Oxford, 1993), pp. 227–29, esp. p. 227: "But what is true of the work as pure text need not have applied to popular legends and oral transmissions which contributed to or developed from it."

16. C. Erdmann, *The Origin of the Idea of Crusade*, trans. M. W. Baldwin and W. Goffart (Princeton, 1977), p. 88.

17. John of Salerno, *Vita Odonis* 3.8: "Quorum adventu fratres cognito, sumptis gladiis alii ascenderunt aedificiorum tecta, quasi hostes suos lapidibus et missilibus coelorum iaculaturi." PL 133, col. 81.

18. On the portrayal of these Muslims in Cluniac hagiography, see S. G. Bruce, *Cluny and the Muslims of La Garde-Freinet: Hagiography and the Problem of Islam in Medieval Europe* (Ithaca, 2015), pp. 41–62.

lims' savagery was presented as a hardship brought on by God to test the holy man's saintly forbearance.

For their part, Cluniac leaders generally agitated for peace rather than war, especially in the late tenth century, when the dissolution of local authority increased the vulnerability of monastic communities and their landholdings.[19] Abbot Odilo was instrumental in the early stages of the Peace of God movement, which aimed to protect helpless people and their property from the depredations of the powerful.[20] During the first months of his abbacy, Odilo participated in the Council of Anse (994), where he lobbied successfully for decrees that protected Cluniac property from the violent encroachment of laymen, arguing that "it is not fitting for holy monks that those living in this place should suffer any disturbances from evil or proud men."[21] A few decades later, Odilo also took part in the so-called Truce of God, a measure taken to curtail private warfare among the warrior class by forbidding armed combat between Christians from sunset on Wednesday to sunrise on Monday. In 1041, the abbot of Cluny was one of several prelates who lent their names to an appeal sent by the churches of Gaul to those in Italy to adopt and uphold the truce.[22] The ideal was that "at any time people would feel safe and could do whatever was fitting, free from any fear of enemies and confident in the serenity of peace brought about by the truce."[23] It is telling that the single concrete portrayal of a Cluniac abbot as a military leader in the decades before the First Crusade was in fact a biting satirical caricature of Abbot Odilo, "prince of war," by

---

19. Cowdrey, *The Cluniacs and the Gregorian Reform*, pp. 15–22.

20. See, in general, H. Hoffmann, *Gottesfriede und Treuga Dei* (Stuttgart, 1964); and Bull, *Knightly Piety*, pp. 21–69. See also R. Landes, "Popular Participation in the Limousin Peace of God," in *The Peace of God: Social Violence and Religious Response in France around the Year 1000*, ed. T. Head and R. Landes (Ithaca, 1992), pp. 184–218, at pp. 204–205: "The prominent role Cluny played in all this suggests that, through the Peace and Truce, that order's realized ascetic eschatology had been transferred from the cloister into the *saeculum*."

21. BB, vol. 3, p. 387 (no. 2255): "Non decet sanctis cenobitis in iam dicto loco morantes a malignis vel superbis hominibus aliquas molestias ingeri," with Hoffmann, *Gottesfriede und Treuga Dei*, pp. 45–47; and G. Constable, "Cluny in the Monastic World of the Tenth Century," in *Il secolo di ferro: Mito e realtà del secolo X (Spoleto, 19–25 aprile 1990)* (Spoleto, 1991), pp. 391–437, repr. in G. Constable, *The Abbey of Cluny: A Collection of Essays to Mark the Eleven-Hundredth Anniversary of Its Foundation* (Berlin, 2010), pp. 43–79, at pp. 63–65.

22. *Sacrorum Conciliorum Nova et Amplissima Collectio*, ed. G. D. Mansi, 31 vols. (Florence, 1759–98), vol. 19, col. 593.

23. *Sacrorum Conciliorum*, ed. Mansi, vol. 19, col. 594: "Omni hora securi sint et faciant quidquid erit opportunum ab omni timore inimicorum absoluti et in tranquillitate pacis et istius treuvae confirmati."

Bishop Adalbero of Laon, written to protest what he perceived to be Cluny's tentacular involvement in worldly affairs.[24]

In the past, historians have also looked at Cluniac involvement in the Spanish *reconquista* of the eleventh century as a forerunner of crusading sensibilities, but as Giles Constable has noted "scholars have now abandoned the view that [Cluny] was the primary force" behind this military movement.[25] To be sure, the abbots of Cluny cultivated a strong relationship with the kings of León-Castile, from whom they collected an annual subsidy in exchange for prayers, and thereby exerted a powerful influence on the Iberian peninsula, but evidence for their interest in inciting war against Islam in Spain is scant.[26] Indeed, Abbot Hugh the Great seems to have been much more interested in a pastoral approach to Iberian Muslims. According to the early twelfth-century hagiographer Walter of Doyde, the abbot encouraged Anastasius, a hermit with close ties to Cluny, to venture into Spain in the hope of winning converts to Christianity through preaching and pious example.[27] His mission was unsuccessful, but the hermit may have been the courier of a letter from Hugh the Great to al-Muktadir ibn Hud, the ruler of Saragossa (1049–1082), inviting the monarch to embrace the Christian faith. This missive is now lost, but it inspired a lengthy and condescending rebuttal in Arabic from the scholar Abu al-Wadil Sulayman al-Bājī (d. 1081) on behalf of his royal patron.[28] On the whole, the evidence suggests that Cluny's overtures toward the Muslims of eleventh-century Spain were neither violent nor effectual.

---

24. Adalbero, *Carmen ad Robertum regem*, lines 155–59, esp. lines 155–56: "Militiae princeps ad te nos Oydelo mittit, / Te dominum monachorum bellicus ordo salutat," ed. and trans. C. Carozzi, in *Adalberon de Laon, Poème au roi Robert* (Paris, 1979), p. 12. On this poem, see S. Vanderputten, "Adalbero of Laon's Poem to King Robert (1023–25/7): A Discourse Against Cluniac Reform or a Commentary on Monastic Hypocrisy?" *Early Medieval Europe* 32 (2024): 159–83.

25. G. Constable, "Cluny and the First Crusade," in G. Constable, *Crusaders and Crusading in the Twelfth Century* (Farnham, 2008), pp. 183–96, at p. 189.

26. See the evidence cataloged in Constable, "Cluny and the First Crusade," pp. 189–93. For reevaluations of this relationship and Cluniac influence on Hispanic monasticism in general, see L. K. Pick, "Rethinking Cluny in Spain," *Journal of Medieval Iberian Studies* 5 (2013): 1–17; and the contributions to *Cluniac Culture Across the Iberian Peninsula*, a special issue of the *Journal of Medieval Iberian Studies* (vol. 9.2) edited by J. L. Senra in 2017.

27. Galterius, *Vita Anastasii*, PL 149, cols. 427–32; English translation: "The *Life* of Anastasius of Cluny, Monk and Hermit," trans. S. G. Bruce, in *The Renaissance of the Twelfth Century: A Reader*, ed. A. J. Novikoff (Toronto, 2017), pp. 32–40.

28. On this letter, see S. Cucarella, "Corresponding Across Religious Borders: Al-Bājī's Response to a Missionary Letter from France," *Medieval Encounters* 18 (2012): 1–35, with reference to earlier literature.

For Cluniac monks, Islam was a potential threat to Christianity, but the urgency of this threat was mitigated by Cluny's distance from Muslim principalities. Knowledge of Islamic beliefs was scant in Western Europe, in no small part because there were no Latin translations of the Qur'an before the twelfth century and no opportunity for Christians north of the Pyrenees to engage in direct discourse with Muslim believers. An exception to this was the serendipitous encounter between a Cluniac abbot and a group of Muslims in the late tenth century. Although Maiolus of Cluny crossed the Great Saint Bernard Pass through the Alps in July 972 on his return home to Burgundy from Rome, he was abducted by Islamic adventurers who had been active for decades in and around Provence from their base at La Garde-Freinet.[29] An early account of the abbot's captivity written by Syrus of Cluny (c. 1010) depicted Maiolus as a relentless preacher among his Muslim captors and couched his response to their alleged disparagement of Christianity in martial language: "Like a seasoned warrior, blessed Maiolus immediately seized the shield of faith and, making the case for the Christian religion he pierced the enemies of Christ with the blade of God's word. He attempted to demonstrate with proven and most credible arguments that the one whom they worshipped as God did not have the power to free himself from punishment, let alone to help them in any way."[30] In this passage, Syrus trumpeted the preaching prowess of the abbot of Cluny with images of armed conflict, but the symbolism of this account was not an endorsement for a holy war against Islam. Instead, the hagiographer was tapping into a millennium-old tradition of couching monastic preaching and prayer in terms of spiritual warfare.

Cluniac Participation in the First Crusade

The general prohibition against monks taking part in the First Crusade prevented any of the brethren of Cluny from abandoning their cloister to undertake the journey to the East, but several charters from

---

29. On the evidence for this episode and the tenacity of the story in the Cluniac tradition, see Bruce, *Cluny and the Muslims of La Garde-Freinet*.
30. Syrus, *Vita sancti Maioli* 3.2: "Protinus ergo beatus Maiolus belligerator optimus scutum fidei arripiens, cuspide uerbi dei perfodiebat inimicos Christi, Christiane religionis cultum approbans, et eum quem deum colebant, nec se a supplicio liberare, nec illos in aliquot posse adiuuare certis et euidentissimis adgressus est rationibus demonstrare," ed. D. Iogna-Prat, *Agni Immaculati: Recherches sur les sources hagiographiques relatives à saint Maieul de Cluny (954–994)* (Paris, 1988), pp. 249–50.

the great Burgundian abbey provide direct evidence for the support provided by the Cluniacs to knights on the eve of their departure.[31] Like many other religious communities, the abbey of Cluny made loans to individuals, the terms of which are spelled out in charters. In the eleventh century, it was not uncommon for pilgrims to exchange property for cash to fund their journeys to Jerusalem. After Urban II's sermon at Clermont, aspiring crusaders did the same thing. In April 1096, Achard of Montmerle mortgaged some of his property to Abbot Hugh and the brethren of Cluny in return for cash and supplies necessary to participate in this expedition "against the pagans and the Saracens."[32] According to the terms of the charter, the abbey obtained full ownership of the property when Achard died en route to Jerusalem in 1099.[33] Likewise, in the summer of 1100, a knight named Stephen of Neublens settled his disputes with the abbey and mortgaged some of his properties in exchange for prayers and supplies before departing for the East.[34]

Transactions of this kind took place at Cluniac dependencies as well. In 1097, in return for a fine beast of burden, Robert of Saint Germanus and his eponymous son renewed and amplified a gift that they had made to Sauxillanges, a monastic community near Clermont with an affiliation to Cluny.[35] Whether the abbey was actively supporting the crusading enterprise by making these loans or simply seeking to profit from this new impulse of religious enthusiasm is an open question. According to Giles Constable, "Some of these transactions look like a hard bargain, and they show that Cluny and its dependencies took advantage of the crusade to acquire land by providing money and equipment to participants, but they may have reflected a desire to support the undertaking."[36]

---

31. On the prohibition, see J. Riley-Smith, *The First Crusade and the Idea of Crusading* (Philadelphia, 1986), p. 36. For the examples that follow, see Constable, "Cluny and the First Crusade," and more generally, C. Bouchard, *Sword, Miter, and Cloister: Nobility and the Church in Burgundy, 980–1198* (Ithaca, 1987), pp. 197–99.

32. BB, vol. 5, pp. 51–53 (no. 3703): "ad belligerandum contra paganos et Sarracenos pro Deo."

33. Likewise, Cluny obtained a *mansus* from two brothers who mortgaged it to the monks in 1096 to fund their participation in the crusade and then died on the way to Jerusalem; see BB, vol. 5, p. 59 (no. 3712).

34. BB, vol. 5, pp. 87–91 (no. 3737).

35. H. Doniol, "Cartulaire de Sauxillanges," *Mémoire de l'Académie des sciences, belles-lettres et arts de Clermont-Ferrand*, n.s. 3 (1861): 465–1199, at pp. 1072–73 (no. 905).

36. Constable, "Cluny and the First Crusade," p. 185.

No brethren of Cluny took part directly in the First Crusade, although some well-known crusaders, like Ordo Arpinus, viscount of Bourges, and Eustace III, count of Bolougne, retired to Cluny as monks *after* their return from the East.[37] Moreover, Cluniac monks did not seem to have taken much interest in texts composed by their contemporaries about the expedition, for their twelfth-century library catalog—an expansive list numbering more than five hundred volumes—makes no mention of any of the chronicles or vernacular songs or poems related to the events.[38] Nevertheless, within a generation of the First Crusade, it is possible to discern the presence of individual Cluniacs in the Holy Land. A group of monks that had accompanied Duke Godfrey of Bouillon on the march to Jerusalem established an abbey dedicated to Saint Mary in the Valley of Jehoshaphat.[39] These monks were not affiliated with Cluny, but their second leader was Gilduin of Le Puiset, formerly prior of a Cluniac dependency at Lurcy-le-Bourg, whom William of Tyre described as their "abbot elect" in 1120.[40] Gilduin owed his appointment not to Cluniac influence in the East, but rather to his close relationship to King Baldwin II of Jerusalem: he was the monarch's cousin.[41] As a

---

37. On his career of Odo Arpinus, see J. Shepard, "The 'Muddy Road' of Odo Arpin from Bourges to La Charité-sur-Loire," in *The Experience of Crusading II: Defining the Crusader Kingdom*, ed. P. Edbury and J. Phillips (Cambridge, 2003), pp. 11–28; and G. Constable, "The Three Lives of Odo Arpinus: Viscount of Bourges, Crusader, Monk of Cluny," in G. Constable, *Crusaders and Crusading*, pp. 215–28. On Eustace III, see H. J. Tanner, "In His Brother's Shadow: The Crusading Career and Reputation of Eustace III of Boulogne," in *The Crusades: Other Experiences, Alternative Perspectives*, ed. K. I. Semaan (Binghamton, NY, 2003), pp. 83–99, esp. pp. 89–90, on the epitaph written for him by a monk of Cluny. I am grateful to Nick Paul for alerting me to this evidence.

38. See L. Delisle, *Inventaire des manuscrits de la Bibliothèque nationale: Fonds de Cluni* (Paris, 1884), pp. 337–73 (appendix A: Catalogue de la Bibliothèque de Cluni), with V. von Büren, "Le grand catalogue de la Bibliothèque de Cluny," in *Le gouvernement d'Hugues de Semur à Cluny: Actes du Colloque scientifique international (Cluny, septembre 1988)* (Mâcon, 1990), pp. 245–63. A Cluniac hagiographer named Gilo of Paris, who penned a *vita* of Abbot Hugh in the early 1120s (*BHL* 4007) and later became cardinal bishop of Tusculum, composed a rhymed Latin epic about the history of the First Crusade before he entered the abbey, but it does not seem to have been read at Cluny. See *The Historia Vie Hierosolimitane of Gilo of Paris*, ed. and trans. C. W. Grocock and J. E. Siberry (Oxford, 1997), where the poem is dated to "the first two decades of the twelfth century" (p. xxiv).

39. D. Pringle, *The Churches of the Crusader Kingdom of Jerusalem: A Corpus*, Vol. 3, *The City of Jerusalem* (Cambridge, 2007), pp. 287–305 (no. 337: St. Mary of the Valley of Jehoshaphat), esp. p. 289.

40. William of Tyre, *Chronicon* 12.13, ed. R. B. C. Huygens, in *Guillaume de Tyr, Cronique*, CCCM 63 (Turnhout, 1986), p. 563.

41. On the relationship between Baldwin II and Gilduin, both of whom were descended from Guy I of Montlhéry, see J. Riley-Smith, *The First Crusaders, 1095–1131* (Cambridge, 1997), pp. 169–70.

result of Gilduin's association to Lurcy-le-Bourg, later tradition held that the abbey of Saint Mary was a Cluniac house.[42]

Abbot Pontius of Melgueil was another prelate from Cluny active in the Holy Land in the 1120s.[43] After his abbacy (1109–1122) ended in scandal, Pontius departed for Jerusalem as a pilgrim, despite the prevailing view at Cluny and elsewhere that monks should not travel to the East.[44] In emulation of his uncle Raymond IV of Saint Gilles, a hero of the First Crusade with strong ties to Antioch, Pontius allegedly carried a relic of the Holy Lance into battle against Muslims in 1123.[45] He returned to the West soon thereafter, becoming abbot of Santa Croce di Camese near Vicenza, Italy, in late 1123 or early 1124. He died in a papal prison in 1126 after a failed attempt to usurp by violence the abbacy of Cluny from Peter the Venerable. While Pontius was in the East, he visited the abbey of Mount Tabor located near Nazareth, where he may have been instrumental in forging a connection between this community and Cluny, despite being in exile. The brethren of Mount Tabor identified themselves as Cluniacs as early as the 1130s, when Peter wrote to them to praise their recent adoption of the customs of the great Burgundian abbey, but the precise relationship between Cluny and Mount Tabor remains unclear.[46]

---

42. See the portion of the fifteenth-century *Chronicon Cluniacense* by Francisco de Rivo concerning the abbacy of Peter the Venerable in *BC*, cols. 589–602, at col. 600, with G. Constable, *The Letters of Peter the Venerable*, 2 vols. (Cambridge, MA, 1967), vol. 2, pp. 291–92 (appendix I: Cluniac Houses in the East). For more on this source, see D. Riche, "Un témoin de l'historiographie clunisienne à la fin du Moyen Âge: Le *Chronicon* de François de Rivo," *Revue Mabillon*, n.s. 11 (2000): 89–114.

43. On the career of Pontius, see J. Wollasch, "Das Schisma des Abtes Pontius von Cluny," *Francia* 23 (1996): 31–52.

44. See G. Constable, "Opposition to Pilgrimage in the Middle Ages," *Studia Gratiana* 19 (1976): 123–46; and G. Constable, "Monachisme et pèlerinage au Moyen Âge," *Revue historique* 258 (1977): 3–27; repr. in G. Constable, *Religious Life and Thought (11th-12th Centuries)* (London, 1979), nos. IV and III, respectively. See more generally A. Jotischky, *The Perfection of Solitude: Hermits and Monks in the Crusader States* (University Park, PA, 1995), pp. 1–16; and W. J. Purkis, *Crusading Spirituality in the Holy Land and Iberia, c. 1095–c. 1187* (Woodbridge, 2008), pp. 12–29.

45. Peter the Venerable, *De miraculis libri duo* 2.12, ed. D. Bouthillier, CCCM 82 (Turnhout, 1988), pp. 117–20.

46. Peter the Venerable, *Ep.* 80, ed. Constable, vol. 1, pp. 214–17, at p. 215, with Cowdrey, *Cluniacs and the Gregorian Reform*, pp. 248–49; and B. Hamilton and A. Jotischky, *Latin and Greek Monasticism in the Crusader States* (Cambridge, 2020), p. 193: "There is no evidence that the house was part of the Cluniac Order." Later tradition held, however, that the brethren of Cluny and Mount Tabor were joined in confraternity (*BC*, col. 600).

Peter the Venerable and the Second Crusade

Peter took an active interest in Islam during his abbacy (1122–1156) and was an advocate of the Second Crusade (1145–1149).[47] During a trip to Spain in 1142–1143, the abbot of Cluny hired the services of three Christian scholars who were proficient in Arabic to translate a dossier of Muslim religious texts into Latin, including the Qur'an.[48] Upon his return to Burgundy, Peter composed a short handbook on Muslim beliefs called *A Summary of the Entire Heresy of the Saracens* (*Summa totius haeresis Sarracenorum*) to serve as a prologue to these translations.[49] Intended to discredit the religious beliefs and personal character of Mohammad, this work argued that Islam was nothing less than the sum of all previous heresies. During the 1140s, Peter was eager to find a prominent spokesman to use the "Christian arsenal" (*Christianum armarium*) that he had assembled in Spain to refute at length the truth claims of the Qur'an.[50] His requests to Bernard of Clairvaux went unanswered, so he put the project aside and returned to it only in the mid-1150s, after the failure of the Second Crusade in 1149 underscored the folly of a military solution to the problem of Islam.

In the meantime, Peter began another polemical treatise entitled *Against the Long-Standing Stubbornness of the Jews* (*Adversus Iudeorum inveteratam duritiem*).[51] He was in the process of revising this work when Pope Eugenius III called for a new crusade in 1146 in response to the fall of

---

47. The best overview of the causes and consequences of the Christian expeditions to the East in the late 1140s, as well as the conquest of Lisbon (1147) and the so-called Wendish Crusade (1147), remains J. Phillips, *The Second Crusade: Extending the Frontiers of Christendom* (New Haven, 2007). Virginia Berry was the first to argue that Peter was an active supporter of the Second Crusade: V. Berry, "Peter the Venerable and the Crusades," in *Petrus Venerabilis, 1156–1956: Studies and Texts Commemorating the Eighth Centenary of His Death*, ed. G. Constable and J. Kritzeck (Rome, 1956), pp. 141-62.

48. On this enterprise, see J. Kritzeck, *Peter the Venerable and Islam* (Princeton, 1964), esp. pp. 56-69, on the identity of these scholars. For more on the Latin translation of the Qur'an and its reception in Western Europe, see T. E. Burman, *Reading the Qur'an in Latin Christendom 1140–1560* (Philadelphia, 2007), pp. 60-87.

49. Peter the Venerable, *Summa totius haeresis Sarracenorum*, ed. R. Glei, in *Petrus Venerabilis, Schriften zum Islam* (Altenberge, 1985), pp. 2-22; English translation: *Peter the Venerable, Writings Against the Saracens*, trans. I. M. Resnick (Washington, DC, 2016), pp. 34-50.

50. For the phrase "armarium Christianum," see Peter the Venerable, *Epistola de translatione sua*, ed. Glei, p. 26.

51. Peter the Venerable, *Adversus Iudeorum inveteratem duritiem*, ed. Y. Friedman, CCCM 58 (Turnhout, 1985); English translation: *Peter the Venerable, Against the Inveterate Obduracy of the Jews*, trans. I. M. Resnick (Washington, D.C., 2013).

the county of Edessa in 1144 to Emir Imad ad-Din Zengi, the ruler of Aleppo and Mosul. When the abbot of Cluny received a letter from King Louis VII asking for his support in this endeavor, Peter called the king's attention to those adversaries of Christianity who were much closer to home than the Muslims, namely, the Jews of Western Europe. "What good is it," he asked the king, "to pursue the enemies of the Christian faith in far and distant lands, if the Jews, vile blasphemers and far worse than the Saracens, not far from us but right in our midst, blaspheme, abuse, and trample on Christ and the Christian sacraments so freely and insolently and with impunity?"[52] Although the abbot of Cluny was not advocating violent action against European Jews, he nonetheless encouraged the king of France to burden their communities with the expense of the proposed expedition: "Spare their lives," he wrote, "but take away their money."[53]

Peter simmered with anger for months after the Second Crusade ended in failure.[54] In 1150, with Bernard of Clairvaux, he agitated for a new crusade against the perfidious Greeks who undermined the previous expedition at the cost of many Christian lives, but this idea gained no traction either among the exhausted nobility, who had just returned from the Holy Land, or in the court of Pope Eugenius III, who supported the mission in principle but not in practice.[55] It was in the aftermath of the Second Crusade that the abbot of Cluny returned to his Muslim project. In the final year of his life (1156), he composed a long treatise refuting the truth claims of Islam titled *Against the Sect of the Saracens* (*Contra sectam Saracenorum*).[56] Scholars have made much of Peter's conciliatory, modern-sounding approach toward his imagined Muslim audience in this treatise, especially his pacifist claim: "I do

---

52. Peter the Venerable, *Ep.* 130: "Sed quid proderit inimicos Christianae spei in exteris aut remotis finibus insequi ac persequi, si nequam blasphemi, longeque Sarracenis deteriores Iudaei, non longe a nobis, sed in medio nostri, tam libere, tam audacter, Christum, cunctaque Christiana sacramenta impune blasphemauerint, conculcauerint, deturpauerint?," ed. Constable, vol. 1, pp. 327-30, at p. 328. On this letter, see Y. Friedman, "An Anatomy of Anti-Semitism: Peter the Venerable's Letter to Louis VII, King of France (1146)," *Bar-Ilan Studies in History* 1 (1978): 87-102.

53. Peter the Venerable, *Ep.* 130: "Reseruertur eis uita, auferatur pecunia," ed. Constable, vol. 1, p. 330.

54. See, for example, Peter's language in *Ep.* 162 (written to King Roger II of Sicily around 1150), ed. Constable, vol. 1, pp. 394-95; and vol. 2, pp. 206-207 on the date of the letter.

55. G. Constable, "The Crusading Project of 1150," in G. Constable, *Crusades and Crusading in the Twelfth Century*, pp. 311-20.

56. Peter the Venerable, *Contra sectam Saracenorum*, ed. Glei, pp. 30-244; trans. Resnick, pp. 51-159.

not attack you, as some of us often do, with arms but with words, not with force but with reason, not out of hatred but out of love."[57] But the prologue of the treatise, which explains its rationale to a Christian audience, quickly dispels any notion that the abbot of Cluny was tolerant or open-minded about Islam. Peter's recourse to reason in his final rapprochement with the Muslims was a last-ditch effort to make his case against the authenticity of the prophet Mohammad with words, in a world in which the strength of Christian arms had failed. It is almost certain that no medieval Muslim ever read it.

A recently discovered twelfth-century poem speaks to an abiding interest in the purpose and value of Christian warfare at twelfth-century Cluny. During Peter the Venerable's abbacy, an unknown Cluniac poet composed a verse retelling of a popular prose exemplum about two warring dukes and a mysterious army of dead souls sent by God to intervene in their conflict.[58] The plot of the exemplum is as follows. A pious duke of Sardinia named Eusebius devoted the income of an entire town to suffrages for the dead, until his rival, a Sicilian tyrant named Ostorgius, captured the town by treachery. Despite being outmatched, Eusebius and his follows pledged to fight back against Ostorgius, even if it meant that they would die in the attempt. Suddenly, an army clad in brilliant white appeared to fight on Eusebius's behalf. Frightened by the sudden appearance of this radiant host, Ostorgius returned the captured town to Eusebius and paid back twice the amount that he had wrongfully seized. When asked their identity, an emissary from the white army revealed that they were legions of Christian souls rescued from torment by Eusebius's generosity, who had been sent by God to fight on his behalf. The exemplum claimed that it was none other than Abbot Maiolus of Cluny who had reported this tale, for he was allegedly a witness to these events while he was being held captive by Ostorgius during a visit to Sardinia to inspect Cluniac monasteries.[59]

While the exemplum of the warring dukes underscored the benefits of prayer for the dead among the Christian nobility, a Cluniac poet

---

57. *Contra sectam Saracenorum* 1.24: "Aggredior inquam vos, non, ut nostri saepe faciunt, armis sed verbis, non vi sed ratione, non odio sed amore," ed. Glei, p. 62.

58. For what follows, see *The Relatio metrica de duobus ducibus: A Twelfth-Century Cluniac Poem on Prayer for the Dead*, ed. and trans. C. A. Jones and S. G. Bruce (Turnhout, 2016), esp. pp. 173–80 for an edition of the prose exemplum. There is an English translation of the exemplum by C. A. Jones in *The Penguin Book of the Undead: Fifteen Hundred Years of Supernatural Encounters*, ed. S. G. Bruce (New York, 2016), pp. 154–60.

59. Modern historians concur that the two dukes and Maiolus's alleged visit to Sardinia are fictional.

recast this 1,500-word narrative into a much longer and more complex 827-line poem that amplified a theme absent in the original: the value of war and the moral conduct of warriors, both on and off of the battlefield.[60] At the beginning of the poem, the character of Maiolus denounced the practice of warfare in a long speech that chided the powerful for indulging recklessly in their wrath to the detriment of common people.[61] Warfare incited a kind of madness in those who participate in it. This rashness may be forgivable in hotheaded youths, but it was reprehensible for older men to wage wars because their advanced age should give them "mild dispositions" (line 133: *mansuetas mentes*). Later in the poem, Maiolus conflated the love of battle and unbridled lust in his condemnation of "the vain knight" who "clanks in his armor and secretly whinnies after married women, whose rape is his motive for bridling his excellent mount" (lines 307–308: *Vanus eques tinnit nuptasque latener adhinnit, / rapto pro quarum falerant equum sibi clarum*). The tyrant Ostorgius represented the worst of these violent tendencies. He was a man "disloyal as the wind, both unjust and bloody" (line 334: *Perfidus ut uentus, uir iniquus uirque cruentus*).

The hero Eusebius was not entirely blameless either. He also came under censure from Maiolus for his part in past conflicts, but in a lengthy speech, he espoused a different rationale for the use of his armor, his weapons, and his mount: "Every one of these we purchase in vain if we do not fight to the death to defend the wretched and give aid to widows: this is the ultimate purpose of my bearing arms." (lines 430–32: *Singula mercamur frustra nisi digladiamur / pro defensandis miseris uiduisque iuuandis: hęc est armorum finalis causa meorum*). Eusebius's speech resonated with a sentiment expressed several decades earlier in Baldric of Bourgueil's *History of Jerusalem* (*Historia Ierosolimitana*, composed c. 1105).[62] In Baldric's retelling of Urban II's preaching at the Council of Clermont (1095), the pope lashed out at Christian warriors who have deformed the knighthood of Christ (*militiam*) into wickedness (*malitiam*). Among their crimes was their predation on young children and widows. Eusebius's ultimate purpose for fighting on behalf of the weak presented a vision of Christian knighthood inspired by the ideals of the

---

60. For what follows, see *The Relatio metrica de duobus ducibus*, ed. Jones and Bruce, pp. 23–29.

61. *Relatio metrica*, lines 121–33, ed. Jones and Bruce, p. 82.

62. Baudric of Bourgueil, *Historia Ierosolimitana* 1, ed. S. Biddlecombe (Woodbridge, 2014), p. 9.

First Crusade set in direct juxtaposition with the crimes of the wicked knights condemned by Urban II.

In addition to promoting the martial piety of Eusebius, the *Relatio*-poet portrayed Ostorgius and his entourage as infidels who had usurped a holy place. Eusebius's town, the source of his funds for providing ceaseless suffrages for the dead, is nothing less than a "city of God" (lines 390 and 499), which was a common term for Jerusalem at this time.[63] Raging against Ostorgius's capture of this town, Eusebius claimed that his outrage was justified "since this loathsome court reigns . . . in my city as the Jebusites did in Jerusalem" (lines 498–99: *quia regnat curia vilis / regnat in urbe Dei uelut in Solima Iebusei*). It is striking that Urban II had also evoked the Jesubite occupation of Jerusalem several decades earlier when preaching about the Muslim capture of Jerusalem: "We say this, brothers . . . so that you would attack and drive out the Turks who are currently there, more abominable than the Jebusites."[64] In this way, the *Relatio*-poet appropriated an ancient analogue for the occupation of the holy city, rendering Ostorgius and his entourage as the equivalent of the Muslims and, by extension, Eusebius and his followers as the equivalent of crusaders.

After the death of Peter the Venerable in 1156, the Cluniacs had little involvement in the affairs of the East for the rest of the century, either as active participants or as armchair critics. An exception was the mission of a Cluniac prior named Thibaud of Vermandois, who traveled through Sicily and Constantinople en route to the Holy Land in 1170 or soon thereafter. Letters of recommendation written on his behalf by King Louis VII of France and the exiled Thomas Becket explained that Thibaud had been chosen "to look after the needs of the famous church of Cluny in the east" (*Procurat autem necessitates nobilis ecclesiae Cluniacensis in Oriente*).[65] During this visit, the prelate was instrumental in the foundation of a new Cluniac house at Palmaria in the vicinity of Haifa.[66] Thibaud eventually returned to Europe, where he was

---

63. See Tobit 13:11: "Hierusalem civitas Dei castigavit te Dominus in operibus manuum tuarum."

64. Baudric of Bourgueil, *Historia Ierosolimitana* 1: "Hec ideo, fratres, dicimus, ut [. . .] Turcos qui in ea sunt, nefandiores quam Iebuseos, impugnetis et expugnetis," ed. Biddlecombe, p. 9.

65. See *Recueil des historiens des Gaules et de la France* (Paris, 1738–1904), vol. 16, pp. 149–51 (no. 451: *Ludovici ad Manuelem, Imperatorem C. P.*; and no. 452: *Ludovici ad Guillelmum II, Siciliae Regem*) and p. 407 (no. 244: *Thomae ad Margaretam, Siculorum Reginam*), all of which are dated 1169. The quotation is on p. 151.

66. H. E. Mayer, *Bistümer, Klöster und Stifte im Königreich Jerusalem*, MGH Schriften 26 (Stuttgart, 1977), pp. 403–405; and B. Z. Kedar, "Palmarée: Abbaye clunisienne du XIIe siècle en Galilée," *Revue bénédictine* 93 (1983): 260–69.

promoted as abbot of Cluny (1179–1183) and then cardinal bishop of Ostia (1183–1188). The dependency of Palmaria, about which little is known, disappeared from the historical record soon after its affiliation with Cluny, most likely because of the hostile climate following the disastrous Christian defeat by the forces of Saladin at the nearby Battle of Hattin in July 1187.

Not even the loss of Jerusalem, which prompted the Third Crusade (1189–1192), roused the interest of any contemporary authors associated with Cluny. It may have been the case that the opposition to pilgrimage by monks voiced repeatedly by Peter the Venerable and many of his contemporaries had a lasting impact on monastic practice by the late twelfth century. According to this teaching, the good works that the brethren undertook in their abbeys were more efficacious in saving their souls than visits to holy places. This attitude did not prevent the slow and steady trickle of eastern relics into Burgundy, however.[67] During the abbacy of Pontius (1109–1122), Cluny acquired relics of Saint Steven and a fragment of the True Cross through the agency of admirers in the East. Nearly a century later, in the aftermath of the Fourth Crusade (1204), the brethren obtained the head of Saint Clement, which had been liberated from the monastery of Theotokos Peribleptos in Constantinople by two Christian knights.

For most of the twentieth century, scholars have held the conviction that the monks of Cluny were directly involved in crusading expeditions to Spain and to the East, if not as primary actors, then at the very least as spiritual sponsors. Odo's *Life of Gerald of Aurillac*, Maiolus's verbal sparring with the Muslims of La Garde-Freinet, Odilo's participation in the Peace of God movement, Hugh the Great's sponsorship of the hermit Anastasius's mission to Spain, and not least Pope Urban II's Cluniac origins were all viewed as symptomatic of Cluny's formative role in preparing and promoting the ambitions of the First Crusade. Beginning with a revisionist article published in 1973, H. E. J. Cowdrey called into question this received tradition by arguing that the Cluniacs had much less to do with the crusades than previous historians had maintained.[68] To be sure, the brethren of Cluny played a leading role in the formation of a penitential spirituality for laypeople, but they were not crusaders. The great Burgundian abbey certainly benefited from new contacts in the East following the establishment of the crusader

---

67. For what follows, see chapter 9, above.
68. Cowdrey, "Cluny and the First Crusade."

kingdoms in the aftermath of the First Crusade. Cluniac prelates like Pontius of Melgueil made pilgrimages to the Holy Land and established important contacts with monastic communities, but the abbots of Cluny never adopted a sustained policy of eastern expansion for the *ordo Cluniacensis*. Serendipity seems to have played a stronger role than planning in these relationships.

Although scholars have downplayed the role of the Cluniacs in the crusade movement, they have paid considerably more attention to the Muslim project of Peter the Venerable.[69] Peter stood alone among twelfth-century prelates for his interest in refuting the truth claims of the prophet Mohammad based on a reading of Muslim religious texts in Latin translation. It is doubtful that his polemical rapprochement to Islam in the aftermath of the failed Second Crusade reached the ears of his imagined Muslim interlocutors, but the Latin translation of the Qur'an that he commissioned during his visit to Spain in the early 1140s became an important tool for missionaries to Islamic principalities in North Africa and the East from the thirteenth century onward.[70] It would be naïve to believe on the basis of the conciliatory prologue to his treatise *Against the Sect of the Saracens* that Peter approached Islam with an attitude of tolerance; however, his work stands out in the era of the early crusades for the depth of its engagement with Muslim religious texts and for its reasoned approach to a rival system of belief based on primary source research.

---

69. See Iogna-Prat, *Order and Exclusion*; and Bruce, *Cluny and the Muslims of La Garde-Freinet*.
70. Burman, *Reading the Qur'an in Latin Christendom*.

CHAPTER 11

Nunc homo, cras humus
A Twelfth-Century Cluniac Poem on the Certainty of Death

Between the abbacies of Odo (927-942) and Peter the Venerable (1122-1156), monks of Cluny composed thousands of lines of Latin verse on moral and devotional themes. Odo's 5,580-line *Occupatio* and Bernard of Cluny's 2,966-line *De contemptu mundi* are the most outstanding examples of the ambition and virtuosity of Cluniac poets in this period.[1] Although considerably more modest in scale, a hitherto unpublished seventy-two-line poem added at the end of an eleventh-century manuscript in the Médiathèque de l'Agglomération troyenne in Troyes (MAT 918; provenance unknown) adds to this impressive corpus of religious verse. Despite the historical importance of Troyes MAT 918, which preserves one of the oldest exemplars of Odo of Cluny's *Collationum tres libri*, an early tenth-century treatise on the

---

Originally published as *"Nunc homo, cras humus*: A Twelfth-Century Cluniac Poem on the Certainty of Death (Troyes, Médiathèque de l'Agglomeration troyenne 918, fols. 78v-79v)," *Journal of Medieval Latin* 16 (2006): 95-110. Reprinted with permission.

1. There is no comprehensive study of monastic poetry in Europe from the tenth to the twelfth centuries. For a general discussion that refers to the work of Cluniac poets, see M. Manitius, *Geschichte der lateinischen Literatur des Mittelalters*, 3 vols. (Munich, 1911-31), vol. 2, pp. 20-27 ("Odo von Cluni"); and vol. 3, pp. 780-83 ("Bernardus Morlanensis"). A new edition and translation of Odo's prolix and difficult poem by C. A. Jones will soon replace the standard edition by A. Swoboda, *Odonis Abbatis Cluniacensis Occupatio* (Leipzig, 1900). On the poems of Bernard of Cluny, see n. 4, below.

virtues and the vices, the anonymous poem on its final folios has escaped critical attention.[2] The theme of the poem is the vanity of earthly glory in the face of the certainty of death. The poet marshaled a long series of arresting and unsettling metaphorical analogues for human mortality to convey this theme. His message was clear: without exception, all mortals will eventually succumb to the embrace of death, irrespective of the greatness of their deeds, the loftiness of their thoughts, or their station in life. Undoubtedly directed at a monastic audience, the poem encouraged the defeat of pride and the cultivation of humility. In this chapter, I provide a diplomatic edition and prose translation of the Troyes poem. I also explore the possibility that this short piece was composed by Bernard of Cluny, the early twelfth-century author of *De contemptu mundi*.

The Character of the Troyes Poem

The Troyes poem includes seventy-two lines of hexameter verse. The first forty-eight verses are written in a difficult and complex hexameter line involving both internal and tailed rhymes (*tripertiti dactylici caudati*) in couplets.[3] This meter is relentlessly dactylic. The avoidance of spondees in all but the last foot of the line makes it in effect accentual. The opening lines of the poem illustrate the cadence of this meter at work:

> O caro carnea, iam modo glarea, post breue uermis.
> Nunc homo, cras humus, istud enim sumus. Unde superbis?
> O caro lubrica, mentibus unica gloria cecis.
> Igniculus febris est tibi funebris. Unde superbis? (lines 1–4)

---

2. The contents of Troyes MAT 918 include the following: (1) Odo of Cluny, *Collationum tres libri* (fols. 1r–78r); and (2) the anonymous poem under consideration here (fols. 78v–79v). See *Catalogue général des manuscrits des bibliothèques publiques des départments*, 7 vols. (Paris, 1849–85), vol. 2, p. 380 (no. 918). Odo's treatise was first printed in *BC*, cols. 159–262; repr. in *PL* 133, cols. 517–638. There is no modern edition of this work. The editor of the *Catalogue général des manuscrits* called the short poem that followed Odo's treatise "Anonymi carmen heroicum de carnis corruptibilitate" (vol. 2, p. 380), but it has no title in the manuscript and does not appear in the standard reference work for medieval verse: H. Walther, *Initia Carminum ac Versuum Media Aevi Posterioris Latinorum: Alphabetisches Verzeichnis der Versanfänge mittellateinischer Dichtungen* (Gottingen, 1959).

3. See D. Norberg, *Introduction to Latin Versification*, trans. G. C. Roti and J. de la Chapelle Skubly (Washington, DC, 2004), pp. 60–61, for a discussion of this metrical feature.

The tone of the poem changes markedly, however, at line 49, where the poet switches to leonine hexameter. Unlike the first half of the poem, these lines allow spondees in the first four feet, which has the effect of slowing the verse. While carrying on the same themes, the pace of these lines is much more ominous than the first part of the poem:

> Cerne quid es, quid eris. Modo flos, cras fex morieris.
> Flos es. Eris fames. Homo nunc, cras non homo fies.
> Qui bona carnis habes uis scire quid est homo? Tabes.
> Fex quid amas feces tibi? Clamans busta putresces. (lines 52-55)

After twenty-two lines of leonine verse, the poet concludes with a rhymed couplet in dactylic hexameter that summarizes his thoughts on the inevitability of death:

> Intereunt et, ut amnis, eunt omnes cito gentes.
> Praetereunt et dispereunt peritura sequentes. (lines 71-72)

The deployment of these meters to the theme of contempt for the world calls to mind the work of Bernard of Cluny, a poet best known for epic works of devotional verse, biblical paraphrase, and caustic satire. Little is known about the life of Bernard other than his name and his poems. He was a Cluniac monk, who flourished in the middle decades of the twelfth century. He dedicated his major work, *De contemptu mundi*, to Abbot Peter the Venerable (1122-1156), and a shorter satire, *De octo vitiis*, to Pope Eugenius III (1145-1153).[4] The latter work concluded with a plea to the pope to protect the monks of Cluny from the adversities assailing them.[5] It is unclear, however, what monastic house Bernard

---

4. The *De contemptu mundi* was edited most recently by H. C. Hoskier in *De Contemptu Mundi, A Bitter Satirical Poem of 3000 Lines Upon the Morals of the Twelfth Century by Bernard of Morval, Monk of Cluny (fl. 1150): Re-edited with Introduction and Copious Variants from All the Known Manuscripts* (London, 1929). Unfortunately, this edition overlooked an important thirteenth-century manuscript witness, as noted by C. D'Evelyn, "A Lost Manuscript of the *De contemptu mundi*," *Speculum* 6 (1931): 132-33. For an English translation of the poem, which suggests several emendations to Hoskier's Latin text, see R. E. Pepin, *Scorn for the World: Bernard of Cluny's De Contemptu Mundi: The Latin Text with English Translation and an Introduction* (East Lansing, MI, 1991). There is a thorough review of this translation by J. Mann in *Journal of Medieval Latin* 4 (1994): 163-69. For an edition of Bernard's *De octo vitiis*, see *Bernardi Cluniacensis carmina de trinitate et de fide catholica, De castitate servanda, In libros regum, De octo vitiis*, ed. K. Halvarson (Stockholm, 1963), pp. 97-138. This poem has been translated into English in R. E. Pepin, "*De octo vitiis*: A Satire by Bernard of Cluny," *Allegorica* 18 (1997): 31-99.

5. Bernard of Cluny, *De octo vitiis*, lines 1365-99, ed. Halvarson, in *Bernardi Cluniacensis carmina*, pp. 137-38.

called home. Manuscript copies of his poems refer to him variously as *Bernardus Morlanensis, Bernardus Morlacensis*, and *Bernardus Morvalensis*. This variety of names has prompted historians to propose as his place of origin the town of Morlas in the county of Bigorre, Morlaix in Brittany, the château of Murles in Montpellier, and Morval, a village in the Jura.[6] Since the solution to the problem of his origins is unlikely to be found without the emergence of new evidence, scholars of the poet have been content to call him Bernard of Cluny.[7]

Bernard was a prolific author, who composed no fewer than five substantial poems in hexameter.[8] These included verses on religious themes, like the 1,402-line *De trinitate et fide catholica*, the 523-line *De castitate servanda*, and a 1018-line paraphrase of the Book of Kings titled *In libros regum*.[9] He is best known, however, for two works of satire: *De contemptu mundi* and *De octo vitiis*. Bernard's *De contemptu mundi* has attracted the lion's share of critical attention in the past century.[10]

---

6. For a summary of these hypotheses, see A. Wilmart, "Grands poèmes inédits de Bernard le Clunisien," *Revue bénédictine* 45 (1933): 249-54, at p. 249.

7. This appellation is confusing as well, because there were many monks named Bernard living and writing at Cluny in the decades around 1100. See K. Hallinger, "Klunys Bräuche zur Zeit Hugos des Grossen (1049-1109): Prolegomena zur Neuherausgabe des Bernhard und Udalrich von Kluny," *Zeitschrift der Savigny-Stiftung für Rechtsgeschichte: Kanonistische Abteilung* 45 (1959): 99-140, at pp. 137-38, n. 100.

8. *Dictionnaire d'histoire et de géographie ecclésiastiques*, 31 vols. to date (Paris, 1912-), vol. 8, cols. 699-700, *s.v.* Bernard de Morlaix, where the author misleadingly supported the identification of the poet with the eleventh-century author of the *Consuetudines Cluniacenses*, who was also called Bernard (see n. 7, above); *Lexikon für Theologie und Kirche*, ed. M. Buchberger et al., 10 vols., 2nd ed. (Freiburg, 1957-65), vol. 2, col. 246, *s.v.* Bernard de Morlas; *Lexikon des Mittelalters*, ed. Robert Auty et al., 9 vols. (Munich, 1977-99), vol. 1, pp. 2001-2002, *s.v.* Bernard von Morlas; Manitius, *Geschichte der lateinischen Literatur des Mittelalters*, vol. 3, pp. 780-83; F. J. E. Raby, *A History of Christian-Latin Poetry from the Beginnings to the Close of the Middle Ages* (Oxford, 1927), pp. 315-19 and 481; and Wilmart, "Grands poèmes inédits de Bernard le Clunisien," pp. 249-54.

9. These poems have been edited by K. Halvarson in *Bernardi Cluniacensis carmina*, pp. 7-96. A collection of verses in praise of the Virgin known collectively as the *Mariale* has also been associated with him. See the edition by G. M. Dreves under the heading "Bernhardus Morlanensis, Monachus Cluniacensis, um 1140," *Analecta Hymnica* 50 (1907): 423-83, where the editor notes that these poems have also been attributed to Anselm of Bec and Bernard of Clairvaux (p. 424).

10. The most comprehensive study of this poem is a series of articles by G. J. Engelhardt, "The *De contemptu mundi* of Bernardus Morvalensis, Part One: A Study in Commonplace," *Mediaeval Studies* 22 (1960): 108-35; G. J. Engelhardt, "The *De contemptu mundi* of Bernardus Morvalensis, Part Two: A Study in Commonplace," *Mediaeval Studies* 26 (1964): 109-42; and G. J. Engelhardt, "The *De contemptu mundi* of Bernardus Morvalensis, Part Three: A Study in Commonplace," *Mediaeval Studies* 29 (1967): 243-72. Other useful studies include R. C. Petry, "Medieval Eschatology and Social Responsibility in Bernard of Morval's *De contemptu mundi*," *Speculum* 24 (1949): 207-17; R. Bultot, "La doctrine du mépris du monde chez Bernard le

This 2,966-line poem treats numerous topics in three books. Book 1 details the rewards awaiting the blessed, the splendors of Heaven, the Second Coming, and the terrors of Hell, before repudiating the vanity of the world and announcing the Last Judgement. Books 2 and 3 present a general satire of various social classes and a lament for moral ills in the tradition of Roman satirists like Juvenal and Horace.[11] Portraits of bishops, women, and the city of Rome were particularly scathing. Bernard displayed his literary virtuosity by sustaining a demanding rhymed meter (*tripertiti dactylici caudati*) for the entire poem. Moreover, he adorned many of his verses with alliteration and other repetitions of sound and form. His long diatribe against sinful women (2.445-598) provides the most memorable examples of these poetic devices: "Foemina sordida, foemina perfida, foemina fracta" (2.445); "Foemina res rea, res male carnea, vel caro tota" (2.457); and especially the couplet "Foemina foetida, fallere fervida, flamma furoris / Prima peremptio, pessima portio, praedo pudoris" (2.509-510). The poem was popular with monastic readers, surviving in fifteen manuscripts from the thirteenth and fourteenth centuries. Less well known was Bernard's *De octo vitiis*, a satirical poem on the vices comprising 1,399 verses of leonine hexameter. After a short introduction that laments the emptiness of earthly pleasures, Bernard warns his readers about the dangers of the eight vices and presents a portrait of a world enthralled by them. Although its themes overlapped considerably with *De contemptu mundi*, this poem did not enjoy the same popularity in the Middle Ages. It survives in only a single manuscript from the thirteenth century.[12]

The Authorship of the Troyes Poem

There are many strong textual parallels between the anonymous Troyes poem and the satirical works of Bernard of Cluny, particularly in the first section of forty-five lines composed in *tripertiti dactylici caudati*.

Clunisien," *Le Moyen Âge* 70 (1964): 179-204 and 355-376; K. Giocarinis, "Bernard of Cluny and the Antique," *Classica et Mediaevalia* 27 (1966): 310-48; and R. E. Pepin, "Heaven in Bernard of Cluny's *De contemptu mundi*," in *Imagining Heaven in the Middle Ages: A Book of Essays*, ed. J. S. Emerson and H. Feiss (New York, 2000), pp. 101-17.
   11. Giocarinis, "Bernard of Cluny and the Antique."
   12. Vatican City, Biblioteca Apostolica Vaticana, Reg. Lat. 134, fols. 52r-61v. See Wilmart, "Grands poèmes inédits de Bernard le Clunisien," pp. 249-54; and Halvarson, *Bernardi Cluniacensis carmina*, pp. 5-6.

Twenty-nine of these lines mirror or echo verses from Bernard's repudiation of worldly vanities in *De contemptu mundi* (*DCM*) 1.719–993.[13] For example,

Troyes anon. 1	O caro carnea, iam modo glarea, post breue uermis.
Bernard, *DCM* 1.739	O caro carnea jam, modo glarea, *postmodo* vermis.
Troyes anon. 2	Nunc homo, cras humus, istud enim sumus. Unde superbis?
Bernard, *DCM* 1.740	Nunc homo, cras humus, istud enim sumus. Unde superbis?
Troyes anon. 4	Igniculus febris est tibi funebris. Unde superbis?
Bernard, *DCM* 1.908	Igniculus febris est tibi funebris; unde *tumescis*?
Troyes anon. 5	O caro candida, post breue fetida uel stabularis.
Bernard, *DCM* 1.737	O caro candida, post breve foetida *plenaque fecis*.
Troyes anon. 7	Cras hominem sinis, in cineres cinis extenuaris.
Bernard, *DCM* 1.794	*Esse quod es* sinis; in cineres cinis extenuaris.
Troyes anon. 8	Cur morulas paro? Cara iaces caro. Fex es, humaris.
Bernard, *DCM* 1.793	Cur morulas paro? Cara *jacens* caro, fex es, humaris.

In addition to these direct parallels, seven lines in the first section of the Troyes poem were drawn from the same repertoire of short metrical phrases as verses in Bernard's *De contemptu mundi*. For example:

Troyes anon. 6	Nunc rosa, cras fimus et fimus infimus. Ad quid amaris?
Bernard, *DCM* 1.738	*Flos modo, mox* fimus, et fimus infimus, *unde tumescis*?

---

13. See the notes to the text for a full commentary on all parallels with Bernard of Cluny's work.

| Troyes anon. 10 | Regia pectora, lactea corpora conputruere. |
| Bernard, *DCM* 1.804 | *Collaque* lactea, *brachia cerea* computruere. |

| Troyes anon. 31 | Corporis omnia quomodo somnia conspiciuntur. |
| Bernard, *DCM* 1.993 | *Mundus et* omnia quomodo somnia *vana recedunt*. |

Verbal affinities with Bernard of Cluny's satirical work continue in the second half of the Troyes poem, where nine of the lines composed in leonine hexameter bear a striking resemblance to verses from the opening section of Bernard's *De octo vitiis* (DOV), lines 6–188, on the emptiness of earthly pleasures. For example:

| Troyes anon. 51 | Mente, manu, uerbis? Quid, terra cinisque, superbis? |
| Bernard, *DOV* 101 | Mente, manu uerbis quid, terra cinisque, superbis. |

| Troyes anon. 60 | Carnis dulcedo uermis putris immo putredo. |
| Bernard, *DOV* 93 | Carnis dulcedo *quid sit, uis scire*? Putredo. |

| Troyes anon. 66 | Culpa cito transit, sed crux, crux illa remansit. |
| Bernard, *DOV* 116 | Culpa cito transit sed *perpes pena* remansit. |

These instances of parallel lines and verbal echoes are too numerous and extensive to be coincidental. The Troyes poem was clearly related to Bernard of Cluny's satirical work, but the nature and direction of this relationship are open to question. It is possible that the anonymous Troyes poet flourished in the eleventh or early twelfth century, well before the literary career of Bernard. If so, his verses may have provided a model for the Cluniac poet, who later incorporated them and expanded on their sentiment in *De contemptu mundi* and *De octo vitiis*. Alternatively, the Troyes poem could have been the product of an imitator of Bernard, who digested and recast the content of that poet's longer pieces as a short work with greater thematic unity. Neither of these hypotheses is entirely convincing, however. First, there is no evidence from the poem or the manuscript to suggest that the Troyes poet predated Bernard of Cluny. Although Troyes MAT 918 is almost certainly an eleventh-century manuscript, the poem written on its final folios cannot be dated definitively on paleographical grounds and could have easily been added in the twelfth century or later. Second, although Bernard once boasted that he was renowned for his verses, the survival of *De octo vitiis* in only a single manuscript suggests that it was not well known by his contemporaries.[14]

---

14. Bernard of Cluny, *De contemptu mundi*, prol.: "Inter contemporaneos meos fama bene versificandi mihi licet immerito circumvolabat," ed. Pepin, p. 6.

This makes it unlikely that the poem circulated widely enough to influence potential imitators outside of Bernard's innermost circle of readers and listeners.

Given the available evidence, it is reasonable to infer that the Troyes poem was an original work of Bernard of Cluny. This attribution would explain both the numerous parallels between this work and *De contemptu mundi* as well as its author's familiarity with Bernard's little-known *De octo vitiis*. While there is no indication in the large corpus of Bernard's poetry that he routinely cannibalized his own verses in this way, this fact alone does not preclude the attribution of this work to him. It would also be rash to conclude that the Troyes poem was simply a pastiche or an empty literary exercise in comparison to Bernard's much longer verses on similar themes. *De contemptu mundi* and *De octo vitiis* were both complex works that treated a number of disparate topics relevant to their broader theme of contempt for the world. In contrast, the Troyes poem provided its monastic readers with a poetic distillation of a single current of Bernard's thought: the emptiness of worldly glory in the face of the certainty of death. Like his longer satirical works, this poem was written in the service of virtue. The beauty of its meter and the literary devices employed by its author played an important role in the reader's contemplation of the poem's theme. As Bernard explained in his preface to *De contemptu mundi*: "Wherefore it happens that while a reader is enticed by the form of the verses, by the melodiousness of the words, he is incited towards and made ready for the practice of the things which either he read or heard. And while he contemplates the elegance of the words, let him practice their virtue."[15]

The Troyes poem was a pointed and concise meditative tool for monks. The virtuosity of its author enhanced the power of the poem by embedding its message firmly in the contemplative mind of readers and listeners alike. Understood in this way, the inclusion of the poem in Troyes MAT 918 appears to be more purposeful than accidental. The theme of the poem was a fitting complement to Odo of Cluny's *Collationum tres libri*. In this treatise, the second abbot of Cluny presented the sin of pride as the root of avarice and malice, two of the worst evil tendencies that afflicted the will of powerful men in tenth-century society.[16] The Troyes poem used vivid images of rot and decay to remind

---

15. Bernard of Cluny, *De contemptu mundi*, prol.: "Quo fit ut dum specie versuum dum sonoritate verborum lector allicitur, ad exhibitionem eorum quae vel legerit vel audierit accendatur et accingatur. Et dum verborum elegantiam considerat efficaciam exerceat," ed. and trans. Pepin, pp. 4-7 (translation slightly modified).

16. See, for example, Odo of Cluny, *Collationes tres libri* 3.25, PL 133, cols. 608-609: "Ne igitur, o principes, comminationes istae vos maneant, si potentes estis humiliamini sub potenti

its monastic readers that death would inevitably reduce to dirt and ash everything that provoked pride in humankind.

Principles of the Edition

The Troyes poem was written in a single column with no rubrication. There are numerous abbreviations, which increase toward the end of the work. The scribe used very few punctuation marks, but he capitalized the first word in every line. Some errors occurred in the transcription process. In several instances, the scribe dropped letters from words without using an abbreviation mark (line 41: *mobis* for *morbis*; line 44: *canea* for *carnea*; line 47: *fatus* for *flatus*, and *uapo* for *uapor*). In four cases, he omitted words from a line (line 33: *uolatilis*, which he wrote in the margin; line 35: *nascitur*, which he added interlinearly; line 47: *breuis*, which went uncorrected in the manuscript, but the reading is probable from Bernard, *De contemptu mundi* 1.855; and line 65: *error abit*, which was written in the margin). He also misread the rare classical name *Senocratis* as *Senoeratis* (line 19). Moreover, given the regularity of rhyming couplets throughout the poem, it is very likely that the scribe left out two lines: one after line 33 (to rhyme with *punctum*) and another after line 44 (to rhyme with *cenum*).

The present edition adopts the orthography of the manuscript (for example, line 22: *artaque* for *arctaque*; and line 34: *mondo* for *mundo*), silently expands abbreviated words according to classical norms, and follows modern principles of punctuation. The first letter of proper names has been capitalized. The correction of scribal errors is signaled with square brackets.

Troyes, Médiathèque de l'Agglomeration troyenne 918, fols. 78v–79v.

[78v]   O caro carnea, iam modo glarea, post breue uermis.
        Nunc homo, cras humus, istud enim sumus. Unde superbis?
        O caro lubrica, mentibus unica gloria cecis,
        Igniculus febris est tibi funebris. Unde superbis?

---

manu Dei; mementote qualia vitia vicinius potentiam comitentur. Solent enim potentes superbire, de temporalibus gaudere, et ut sit quod abundanter expendant, vel habeant, solent aliena concupiscere." For a helpful discussion of this passage, see B. H. Rosenwein, *Rhinoceros Bound: Cluny in the Tenth Century* (Philadelphia, 1982), pp. 66–72.

5	O caro candida, post breue fetida uel stabularis.
	Nunc rosa, cras fimus et fimus infimus. Ad quid amaris?
	Cras hominem sinis. In cineres cinis extenuaris.
	Cur morulas paro? Cara iaces caro. Fex es, humaris.
	Regia funera siue cadauera perge uidere!
10	Regia pectora, lactea corpora conputruere.
	Pontificalia denique pallia mors sibi sternit,
	Regia culmina, regia fulmina subdita cernit.
	Nunc ubi curia sceptraque Iulia? Cesar, abisti.
	Tu quoque grandior orbe potentior ante fuisti.
15	Qui cinis es modo, tantus eras homo quantus et orbis.
	Vi tibi subditus extitit anbitus urbis et orbis.
	Gentibus, urbibus, et dominantibus es dominatus.
	Ecce, tuus uigor et furor et rigor est nece stratus!
	Arida Socratis atque Senocratis ossa tenentur.
20	Vox anime Plato, iusticie Cato, puluis habentur,
	Plenaque roboris illius Hectoris, illius ossa
	Que minus eminet unica continet artaque fossa.
	Ille probissimus illeque maximus ille uir ille
	Quid modo cernitur aut fore dicitur? Urna fauille.
25	Flos Helene fuit et species ruit Absalon illa.
	Ad breue floruit. Ecce qui aruit estque fauilla.
	Flaua uel aurea, quae per eburnea colla uolabat,
	Cesaries iacet et cor et os tacet. Unde tonabat?
	Ibimus, ibimus atque redibimus. Ad quid? Ad urnam.
30	Sceptra iacent ibi. Mors cathedram sibi subdit eburnam.
[79r]	Corporis omnia quomodo somnia conspiciuntur.
	Crassa sed arida, blanda sed hispida quaeque feruntur.
	Vita uolubilis atque uolatilis est quasi punctum.
	Nulla manentia, cuncta fluentia sunt bona mondo.
35	Ad breue nascitur et cito frangitur eius arundo.
	Gloria terrea, gloria uitrea, uitrea plane,
	Tempore uoluitur atque resoluitur eius inane.
	Quomodo flumina cerne uolumina currere rerum!
	Orbis onor ruit et fugit et fluit orbe dierum.
40	Est resolubilis, immo uolubilis orbis, ut orbis
	Illius omnia, peste ruentia, tabida mo[r]bis.
	Gloria terrea, res uaga, res rea, res fugitiua.
	Maneque prospera sero fit aspera, mortua uiua.
	Ca[r]nea gloria, carnis et omnia, carne uigente

45	Sunt quasi stantia, deficientia deficiente.
	Quid caro debilis aut quid inutilis est homo? Cenum.
	F[l]atus homo levis atque uapo[r breuis] ad breue paret.
	Paret et enitet, illico delitet, occidit, aret.
	Ergo quid inflaris, qui nasceris ut moriaris?
50	Quid tumidum spiras? Quid concipis et paris iras
	Mente, manu, uerbis? Quid, terra cinisque, superbis?
	Cerne quid es, quid eris. Modo flos, cras fex morieris.
	Flos es, eris sanies. Homo nunc, cras non homo fies.
	Qui bona carnis habes uis scire quid est homo? Tabes.
55	Fex quid amas feces tibi? Clamans busta putresces.
	Putresces busto qui rides ore uenusto.
	Post animal fies uermis. Quid plus? Putrefies.
	Flebis qui gaudes, damnabere qui scelus audes.
	Qui meretricaris audi, qui luxuriaris,
60	Carnis dulcedo, uermis putris, immo putredo,
[79v]	Ve tibi, ue tibi, ue, si perdis tempus oliue,
	Si pro flore b[r]eui perdis bona perpetis eui!
	Qui bona carnis amas, flammis nutris tibi flammas.
	Peccas momento, sed penam stare memento.
65	Pena stat, error abit; quos hic ligat, illa ligabit.
	Culpa cito transit, sed crux, crux illa remansit.
	Sicut equus uel uile pecus cur stas homo cecus?
	Cur queris, cur flenda geris, qui cras morieris?
	Stercus, humus, cinis, aura sumus caro, fex. Homo sumus.
70	Cur igitur caro diligitur, quae cras sepelitur?
	Intereunt et, ut amnis, eunt omnes cito gentes.
	Praetereunt et dispereunt peritura sequentes.

O carnal flesh, now already dirt, a worm soon thereafter. Today a man, tomorrow earth, for that is what we are. Why are you so proud? O fleeting flesh, sole glory to clouded minds, the heat of a mild fever is deadly to you. Why are you so proud? [5] O beautiful flesh, after a while you will become rotten or vile. Today a rose, tomorrow dung, the lowest dung. Why are you loved? Tomorrow, you cease to be a man. You are reduced, an ash into ashes. Why do I delay? Dear flesh, you lie still. You are worthless remains, ready for burial. Go and watch the stately funerals and the bodies of kings! [10] Princely hearts and pallid corpses have rotted together. In the end, death lays low pontifical palliums. It also sees royal crowns and imperial powers overthrown. Where are the senate and Julian sceptres now? Caesar, you have gone. You were once stronger and more powerful than anyone in the world. [15] You were once a very great man, as great as the world, and now you are only ashes. The extent of the city and of the world was subject to you by force. You vanquished nations, cities, and rulers. Behold, your strength and rage and toughness have been laid low by death! Of Socrates and Xenocrates dry bones remain. [20] Plato, the voice of the soul, and Cato, the mouth of justice, are dust, as are the bones of Hector, once full of strength. A lonely, narrow grave, something less exalted, holds them. That man most upright, and that one most powerful, that one, and that one, what is he seen to be now or said to be? An urn for ashes. [25] The glamor of Helen is a thing that was, and the beauty of Absalom has perished. It flourished briefly. See in what way it has withered up and is a cinder. The yellow or golden hair that used to fly from his white neck lies still. His heart and voice fall silent. How could he boast? We will go, we will go, but we will return. To what? To the urn. [30] There sceptres lie. Death subjects the ivory throne. All bodily things are as dreams: they move, massive but dry, enticing but foul. Life is as swift and fleeting as a moment. Worldly goods flow away until nothing remains. [35] The reed of life is short-lived and quickly broken. Worldly glory is a fragile glory, as fragile as glass. Its emptiness spirals down and dissolves in time. Watch the course of events rush past like rivers! Worldly honor tumbles and flees and flows away with the circuit of days. [40] This fleeting world quickly dissolves, for everything in it succumbs to sickness and is laid low by pestilence. Worldly glory is doubtful and suspect and elusive. The good hopes of morning turn to peril by evening; the living eventually yield to death. The glory of the flesh and everything related to it persists while the flesh lives but dies along with it. What is feeble flesh or useless man? Merely dirt. Man is a soft breath and a fleeting mist that exists only for a short time. He appears and shines forth, then skulks off, perishes, and withers away. Therefore, why are you so proud when you are born only to die? [50] Why are you swollen with pride? Why do you conceive and beget anger and act upon it with your mind, hands, and words? How can you be proud when you are earth and ash? Understand what you are and what you will become. Today a flower, tomorrow you will die and become worthless remains. You are a bloom, but you will be corruption. Today a man, tomorrow nothing. You who have in mind the delights of the flesh, do you want to know the condition of man? Decay. [55] Dregs yourself, why do you long for dregs? A corpse, you will rot, crying out as you do. You who laugh with your beautiful mouth will molder in the grave. Once a living being, you will become a worm. What more? You will putrefy. You who rejoice will weep. You who dare to commit evil deeds will be condemned. Take heed, whoremonger and debaucher! [60] You, sweetness of the flesh, worm, rotten or rather rottenness, woe to you, woe to you, woe, if you lose the time of the olive, if you forsake the blessings of eternal life for a brief bloom! You who love the delights of the flesh feed with fire the flames awaiting you. It takes only a moment to sin, but bear in mind that punishment for it endures. [65] The punishment remains after the transgression departs. The former entangles sinners now. The latter waits to ensnare them. The act of sin passes quickly away, but the torment, the torment has remained. Why do you stand there, blind man, like a horse or some lowly beast? Why do you, who will die tomorrow, seek out and do those things that ought to bring tears? We are dung, dirt, ash, a breath, flesh, empty remains. We are mortal men. [70] Therefore, why is the flesh beloved, which will lie buried tomorrow? All nations die and, like a river, are quickly gone. They pass by and disappear, following things bound to perish.

Notes to the Text

The following abbreviations appear in this section: *DCM* = *De contemptu mundi*; and *DOV* = *De octo uitiis*.

1. Compare Bernard, *DCM* 1.739, where *postmodo* replaces *post breue* as the final dactyl.
2. Bernard, *DCM* 1.740.
4. Compare Bernard, *DCM* 1.908, where *tumescis* replaces *superbis* at the end of the line.
5. Compare Bernard, *DCM* 1.737, where the words *plenaque faecis* replace *uel stabularis*. For the use of *stabularis* as an adjective meaning "vile" or "beastly" (literally, "belonging to a stable"); see *DCM* 3.174 and 3.238.
6. Compare Bernard, *DCM* 1.738: *Flos modo, mox fimus, et fimus infimus. Unde tumescis?*

7. Compare Bernard, *DCM* 1.794, where the words *Esse quod es* replace *Cras hominem*.
8. Bernard, *DCM* 1.793.
10. A possible echo of Bernard, *DCM* 1.804, which is similar in content and where the words *lactea* and *conputruere* appear in proximity, with *conputruere* closing out the line.
11. A verbal resonance: Bernard, *DCM* 2.261 and 2.262 both commence with the word *pontificalia*.
12. Another possible resonance: *Regia culmina* are the first two words of Bernard, *DCM* 2.273.
13. Compare Bernard, *DCM* 1.937: *Nunc ubi curia pompaque Iulia? Caesar, obisti.*
14. Compare Bernard, *DCM* 1.938: *Te truculentior orbe potentior ipse fuisti*. At some point, the scribe or a later reader of MAT 918 changed the word *Te* to *Tu*.
15. Bernard, *DCM* 1.943.
16. Compare Bernard, *DCM* 1.944, where *an* replaces *ui* as the first word in the line.
17. Compare Bernard, *DCM* 1.928, where the word *est* replaces *es*.
19. Compare Bernard, *DCM* 1.911: *Quid tibi grammatis? Arida Socratis ossa tenentur*. The abbreviated word *Senoeratis* is probably *Senocratis* (Ξενοκράτης), but the scribe did not recognize the name and mistakenly wrote <e> for <c>. The abbreviation over the <e>/<c> very likely stands for "ra" (compare line 13, where the scribe uses the same mark to abbreviate the last syllable of the word *sceptra*). Xenocrates of Chalcedon (396–314 BCE) was an academic philosopher and successor of Plato.
20. Bernard, *DCM* 1.912.
21. Compare Bernard, *DCM* 1.909, where the words *quid tibi* replace *plenaque* as the first dactyl.
22. Compare Bernard, *DCM* 1.910, where *et* replaces *que* as the first word in the line.
23. Compare Bernard, *DCM* 1.787, where the words *ille potissimus* replace *illeque maximus*.
24. Compare Bernard, *DCM* 1.611: *Quid modo noscitur aut fore cernitur illa favilla?*
25. Although this line has no parallels in Bernard's other poems, the figure of Absalom, the rebellious son of King David, is mentioned twice in *DCM* (1.57 and 1.917) and numerous times in Bernard's verse paraphrase of the biblical Book of Kings (*In libros regum*, lines 343–409, passim).

27. Compare Bernard, *DCM* 1.799: *Flava vel aurea, quam per eburnea colla rotabas.*
28. Compare Bernard, *DCM* 1.800, where *tonabas* replaces *tonabat* as the last word in the line.
29. Compare Bernard, *DCM* 1.961, where *imum* replaces *urnam* as the last word in the line.
30. A later corrector of the manuscript, ignoring the dominant meter, altered *iacent* to *iacentur* and then had to expunge *mors* to preserve the (now nonconforming) meter.
31. Some verbal resonances: Bernard, *DCM* 2.702 also begins with the words *corporis omnia*. In addition, Bernard twice uses the word *conspiciuntur* to end a line (*DCM* 1.1000 and *DOV* 6).
33. Compare Bernard, *DCM* 1.897, where the word *immo* replaces *atque*.
34. Compare Bernard, *DCM* 1.987: *Cuncta fluentia, nulla manentia sunt bona mundo.*
36. Bernard, *DCM* 1.989.
37. Compare Bernard, *DCM* 1.990, where *illico tollitur* replaces *tempore uoluitur* at the beginning of the line.
38. Bernard, *DCM* 1.979.
39. Compare Bernard, *DCM* 1.980, where *honos* replaces *onor* as the second word in the line.
40. Bernard, *DCM* 1.975. Bernard also uses the words *orbis ut orbis* to conclude *DOV* 29.
41. Bernard, *DCM* 1.976.
42. Another possible resonance: Bernard, *DCM* 1.985 and 1.989 also begin with the words *gloria terrea*.
44. Bernard, *DCM* 1.763.
45. Bernard, *DCM* 1.764.
46. Compare Bernard, *DCM* 1.761, where the word *labilis* replaces *debilis*.
47. Bernard, *DCM* 1.855. The scribe of Troyes MAT 918 mistakenly omitted the letter *r* and the word *breuis* after *uapo*.
48. Compare Bernard, *DCM* 1.856, where the words *herba fit* replace *occidit*.
51. Bernard, *DOV* 101.
52. A possible resonance: Bernard, *DOV* 33 shares the verbal unit *modo flos cras*.
53. Another verbal parallel: Bernard, *DOV* 124 also ends with the phrase *non homo fies*.

57. Compare Bernard, *DOV* 123: *Post animal uermis, post uermem puluis inhermis.*
58. Bernard, *DCM* 3.127 also concludes with the words *scelus audes*.
60. Compare Bernard, *DOV* 93: *Carnis dulcedo quid sit, uis scire? Putredo.*
61. Bernard, *DOV* 113: *Ue tibi, ue tibi, ue, qui perdis tempus oliue.* The phrase *tempus oliue* is obscure. It may be a reference to the land of plenty promised to the faithful in Deut. 8:7–8: "Dominus enim Deus tuus introducet te in terram bonam, terram rivorum, aquarumque et fontium, in cujus campis et montibus erumpunt fluviorum abyssi: terram frumenti, hordei ac vinearum, in qua ficus, et malogranata, et oliveta nascuntur."
62. Compare Bernard, *DOV* 114, where *qui* replace *si* as the first word in the line.
63. A possible echo of Bernard, *DOV* 130, where the words *amas, tibi,* and *flammas* appear in proximity, with *tibi flammas* closing out the line.
65. Compare Bernard, *DOV* 120, where *mors manet* replaces *pena stat* as the first words in the line. The phrase *error abit* appears in the same position of the line in Bernard, *DOV* 1244.
66. Compare Bernard, *DOV* 116, where the words *perpes pena* replace *crux crux illa*.
69. A possible verbal resonance: the words *aura sumus* also appear in Bernard, DOV 53.

CHAPTER 12

Abbot Peter the Venerable's Two Missions to England (1130 and 1155/1156)

Peter the Venerable, the ninth abbot of Cluny, who ruled the great Burgundian monastery from 1122 until his death in 1156, understood the didactic potential of ghost stories. In a treatise on miracles written in the 1140s, he related several tales of hauntings that took place at Cluny to warn his audience about the punishments awaiting sinners in the afterlife and to promote the power of Cluniac prayer to relieve their suffering and to speed their souls to heaven.[1] These kinds of stories were not subtle. Time and again, the spirits of the dead appeared to Cluniac monks to beseech their prayers to remedy the otherworldly pain that they had earned for a host of mundane sins: a nobleman's love of plundering, a bishop's fondness for laughter. The prayers of the community never failed these sinners, whose apparitions almost always returned to the abbey one last time to give the brethren thanks before departing for heaven.

Originally published as "Abbot Peter the Venerable's Two Missions to England (1130 and 1155/1156)," *Anglo-Norman Studies* 40 (2018): 91–105. Reprinted with permission.

1. Peter the Venerable, *De miraculis libri duo* 1.9–11, ed. D. Bouthillier, CCCM 83 (Turnhout, 1988), pp. 34–42; trans. S. G. Bruce, in *The Penguin Book of the Undead: Fifteen Hundred Years of Supernatural Encounters*, ed. S. G. Bruce (New York, 2016), pp. 100–107.

It should not surprise us, then, that the earliest account of Peter the Venerable's life and miracles featured a ghost story. Composed in the late twelfth century by Rodulphus de Sully, the twelfth abbot of Cluny (1173-1176), this short *vita* survives in no medieval manuscripts; we owe its preservation to the industry of the Maurists, who copied it in the eighteenth century.[2] The ghost story told by Rodulphus de Sully was unusual because the specter in question was a king of England, none other than King Henry I (1100-1135).[3] According to this miracle, the ghost of the monarch appeared upon a black horse "as though alive" (*quasi vivus*) to one of his own soldiers in England. He was accompanied by a great multitude of mounted knights. "Are you not my lord king?" asked the soldier in amazement, "Are you not dead?" "Truly, I am dead," replied the specter, "and my death would have been eternal, if Lord Peter, the abbot of Cluny, with his brethren had not come to my aid." The ghost of Henry I ordered the soldier to make haste to Lewes priory, a Cluniac dependency in Southover, East Sussex.[4] He was told to relate the ghost's tale to the brethren who lived there and bid them to send a letter to Abbot Peter at Cluny requesting prayers of intercession on his behalf. When Peter received the letter, he marshaled all of the resources of prayer at his disposal throughout all of his dependencies (*per totum orbem in suis domibus*) to help the soul of the dead king, who appeared once more, this time to the abbot and many others, to thank them for securing his release from otherworldly punishment. This story of King Henry's ghost took its place among a litany of lesser miracles that Rodulphus de Sully had allegedly learned through the accounts of devout men or had seen himself (*quod virorum religiosorum relatione didici, aut ipse vidi*), none of which managed to convince anyone to recognize the ninth abbot of Cluny as a saint.[5] Even so, with this miracle,

---

2. Rodulphus de Sully, *Vita Petri Venerabilis abbatis Cluniacensis*, ed. E. Martène and U. Durand, in *Veterum Scriptorum et Monumentorum Historicorum, Dogmaticorum, Moralium, Amplissima Collectio*, 9 vols. (Paris 1724-33), vol. 6, cols. 1187-1202 (*ex ms. Silviniacensis monasterii*, now lost); repr. in *PL* 189, cols. 15-28.

3. For what follows, see Rodulphus, *Vita Petri Venerabilis* 13, ed. Martène and Durand, vol. 6, col. 1198; repr. in *PL* 189, col. 25: "Quem ut miles vidit, obstupuit, et magna voce clamare coepit: Nonne tu es dominus meus rex? Ego, inquit, sum. Nonne mortuus es? Vere, inquit, mortuus, et morti aeternae deputatus fuissem, nisi dominus Petrus abbas Cluniacensis cum suis subvenisset."

4. On the founding of Lewes priory, see n. 17, below.

5. D. Knowles, "Peter the Venerable," *Bulletin of the John Rylands Library* 39 (1956): 132-45, at p. 145: "Peter was never officially canonized, and although his contemporary biographer relates incidents in his life that might be considered near-miracles, neither these, nor the record of his actions, nor the witness of his letters, ever convey to us the authentic touch of

Peter's hagiographer underscored an important aspect of the abbot's career: his relationship to the Anglo-Norman monarchs who ruled during his abbacy, most notably Henry I, but also Stephen (1135–1154) and Henry II (1154–1189).

In this chapter, I investigate the commerce between Cluny and the English crown through an examination of Peter the Venerable's two visits to England—the first in 1130 and the second in 1155 or early 1156. During the central Middle Ages, it was not unusual for abbots of Cluny to travel widely throughout France and as far away as Spain and Italy to reform distant abbeys, to protect the interests of their far-flung dependencies, and to serve as powerbrokers for religious and secular powers. Before Peter's abbacy, however, no Cluniac abbot had ever ventured to England. I attempt to provide a "cost analysis" of these missions, that is, to explain the circumstances that led Peter to believe that it was worth both his time and his effort to travel so far afield in the interests of his community, to identify the English agents who fostered relationships with Cluny in this period, and to gauge precisely what the abbot of Cluny hoped to gain by undertaking these visits. In both instances, Peter must have been prompted to travel by some urgent need, because he did not travel well. As Giles Constable noted, he suffered from malaria and chronic bronchitis and "for most of his adult life he was in delicate, if not poor, health."[6] Even so, as we will see, the potential gains of these visits in terms of capital and influence clearly outweighed the risks, whether they were carried out with the blessing of the sitting king, as was the case in 1130, or in covert opposition to him, as was the case in 1155 or 1156.

From William the Conqueror to Henry I

The relationship between the abbey of Cluny and the English crown began during the reign of William the Conqueror (1066–1087). After the conquest, in the decade between 1066 and 1076, King William allegedly made overtures to Abbot Hugh the Great (1049–1109) to enlist the support of Cluny in establishing and overseeing new monastic communities in England.[7] The evidence for their interaction comes primarily from early twelfth-century sources related to the cult of Abbot Hugh,

---

sanctity, the direct vision, the imperative call, the glimpse of a life that re-enacts in its own idiom the life of Christ."

6. G. Constable, *The Letters of Peter the Venerable*, 2 vols. (Cambridge, MA, 1967), vol. 2, pp. 247–51 (appendix B: The Health of Peter the Venerable), at p. 247.

7. For what follows, see F. Barlow, "William I's Relations with Cluny," *Journal of Ecclesiastical History* 32 (1981): 131–41, repr. in F. Barlow, *The Norman Conquest and Beyond* (London,

which were eager to portray the relationship in ways that favored the saint.[8] With a posture of humility that amazed his barons (*satrapae*), William requested the gift of confraternity (*donum societatis*) from the great Burgundian abbey and received in response a visit from a legate named Warmund, who was at that time the abbot of the Cluniac priory of Déols near Châteauroux in Berry and later archbishop of Vienne.[9] Once this relationship had been confirmed (the terms of which are not explained), William sent a extravagant gift to Abbot Hugh: an exquisite golden cope embroidered with electrum and pearls and fringed with tiny golden bells. His queen, Mathilda of Flanders, sent an equally impressive chasuble (*planetam dignissimam*) as a complement to her husband's gift.[10]

Another tradition preserved in the hagiography of Hugh the Great asserted that William the Conqueror wrote to the abbot of Cluny requesting six of his best monks to serve as his advisers and to receive appointments as his prelates (*rectores*) in postconquest England. In return, the king offered to pay one hundred pounds of silver annually for each of the monks in recognition of the cost of the loss of such worthy individuals to the monastic community.[11] Although the king made the request "in the spirit of friendship and grace" (*sub titulo amicitiae et gratiae*), Abbot Hugh was offended by the offer and made his anger plain in his response, which the hagiographer preserved verbatim in the narrative. First, the abbot flatly refused the king's request on the grounds that he could not take part in a monetary transaction of this kind, which smacked of the sin of simony. Moreover, he was unwilling to send any of his monks "into perdition" (*in perditionem*) at any cost, because he was responsible for the well-being of their souls. William

---

1983), pp. 245–56; and A. Kohnle, *Abt Hugo von Cluny (1049–1109)* (Sigmaringen, 1993), pp. 191–93.

8. The Cluniacs produced no fewer than six accounts of the life and miracles of Abbot Hugh the Great in the early twelfth century. On their complex genealogy, see F. Barlow, "The Canonization and Early Lives of Hugh I, Abbot of Cluny," *Analecta Bollandiana* 98 (1980): 297–334, repr. in Barlow, *The Norman Conquest and Beyond*, pp. 257–95; and D. Iogna-Prat, "Panorama de l'hagiographie abbatiale clunisienne (v. 940–v. 1140)," in *Manuscrits hagiographiques et travail des hagiographes*, ed. Martin Heinzelmann (Sigmaringen, 1992), pp. 77–118, at pp. 97–102, repr. in D. Iogna-Prat, *Études clunisiennes* (Paris, 2002), pp. 35–74, at pp. 52–57.

9. For what follows, see *Alia miraculorum quorundam S. Hugonis relatione MS. collectore monacho quodam, ut videtur Cluniacensi* (BHL 4013), in *BC*, cols. 447–62, at col. 453. On the career of Warmond, see D. N. Huyghebaert, "Un légat de Gregoire VII en France: Warmond de Vienne," *Revue d'Histoire Ecclésiastique* 40 (1944–45): 187–200, at pp. 188–90.

10. These royal gifts are also described in Gilo, *Vita sancti Hugonis abbatis* 15 (BHL 4007), which was composed before Christmas 1121. See H. E. J. Cowdrey, "Two Studies in Cluniac History, 1049–1126," *Studi Gregoriani* 11 (1978): 5–298, at pp. 64–65.

11. *Alia miraculorum quorundam S. Hugonis*, in *BC*, cols. 453–54.

was naturally not pleased with this reply, but his anger eventually gave way to an understanding of Hugh's reasoning.

It is important to note that King William and Abbot Hugh did not meet in person to propose, negotiate, and conclude these alliances. Instead, they commended their intentions to formal proxies and their precious gifts to trusted couriers. Indeed, there would have been little reason for the abbot of Cluny to venture into Normandy, where his monastery had no formal dependencies but plenty of informal influence from local prelates who had spent formative time at the great Burgundian abbey.[12] Orderic Vitalis named two of them: Robert of Grandmesnil, later abbot of Saint Evroul, who spent time as a novice at Cluny and successfully sought Hugh's permission to bring a monk named Bernefrid back with him to Normandy to instruct the brethren in Cluniac customs; and Mainerius, who had spent a year in training at Cluny before he became first the prior and later the abbot of Saint Evroul.[13] The only evidence that Hugh the Great ever visited Normandy appeared in the early twelfth-century *vita* of the hermit Anastasius composed by Walter of Doydes.[14] According to this account, the abbot of Cluny was in the vicinity of Mont Saint Michel around 1067 while "travelling with many of his monks for the purpose of visiting monastic houses and exhorting the brethren who were serving God in many remote places."[15] There he heard news about the hermit living on an island in the English Channel. After several days of conversation, Anastasius agreed to accompany the abbot back to Cluny to "provide an example of excellent conduct to the rest of the monks."[16] Unfortunately, we have no other source to corroborate Hugh's travels in Normandy.

---

12. D. Knowles, *The Monastic Order in England: A History of its Development from the Times of St. Dunstan to the Fourth Lateran Council, 940–1216*, 2nd ed. (Cambridge, 1963), pp. 83–88.

13. Orderic Vitalis, *Historia Ecclesiastica* 3, ed. and trans. M. Chibnall, in *The Ecclesiastical History of Orderic Vitalis*, 6 vols. (Oxford, 1969–80), vol. 2, pp. 74 and 96. On the careers of these prelates, see V. Gazeau, *Normannia monastica*, 2 vols. (Caen, 2007), vol. 2, pp. 275–76 (Robert [de Grandmesnil]) and 278–80 (Mainier d'Échauffour).

14. For what follows, see Galterius, *Vita sancti Anastasii*, PL 149, cols. 423–32; English translation: "The Life of Anastasius of Cluny, Monk and Hermit," trans. S. G. Bruce, in *The Twelfth-Century Renaissance: A Reader*, ed. A. J. Novikoff (Toronto, 2017), pp. 32–40. See also Kohnle, *Abt Hugo von Cluny*, pp. 191 and 301 (no. 79), where this encounter is dated around 1067.

15. Galterius, *Vita Anastasii* 4: "Venerabilis abbas, Hugo nomine, qui Cluniacensi monasterio eodem tempore praeerat, ad revisenda coenobia, exhortatione fratrum, qui per diversa loca et longe remota Deo deserviebant, cum multis fratribus exivit." PL 149, col. 428.

16. Galterius, *Vita Anastasii* 4: "Et multum rogavit ut Cluniacum secum adiret, ubi et votum suum complere posset, et exemplum bonae conversationis caeteris fratribus daret." PL 149, col. 428.

Pious English barons had better fortune than William the Conqueror in cultivating long-lasting relationships with the Cluniacs in the late eleventh century, but their efforts could also be hampered when they were unable to meet personally with the abbot. The establishment of Lewes priory in Southover, East Sussex, is a well-documented example.[17] The foundation chronicle for Lewes tells how Earl William I de Warenne and his wife Gundreda tarried at Cluny in 1076 when the conflict between Henry IV and Gregory VII prevented them from making their intended pilgrimage to Rome. They were allegedly so impressed by the conduct of the brethren that they decided to establish a Cluniac priory on their estates in England. Unfortunately, Hugh the Great was absent during their stay, so William de Warenne waited until his return to England to send a letter to the abbot requesting two, three, or four monks for the proposed foundation.[18] Hugh demurred at first. "This would be especially hard for us," he replied, "because of the distance of your foreign land and mostly because of the sea."[19] The earl would have to send to Cluny not only a copy of his grant of the church of Saint Pancras as proof of his intentions and the solvency of the fledging community but also the king's confirmation of it, before Hugh relented and dispatched three monks to Lewes with Lanzo as their first prior.

The death of William the Conqueror in 1087 brought to the throne his son William II, also known as William Rufus (1087–1100). An able general, but by most monastic accounts a ruler lacking in personal virtue and Christian piety, William Rufus was primarily remembered by the Cluniacs for his contempt for Archbishop Anselm, who weathered his exile from England at Lyon and Cluny, and for the fatal and fitting accident that killed the king unshriven at the age of forty while he was on a hunting expedition. According to an account composed by Eadmer and repeated by Cluniac authors, several days before the king's death, Abbot Hugh the Great revealed to Anselm in the presence of many startled witnesses that he had experienced a vision of the king being prosecuted before the throne of God, judged unfavorably, and

---

17. B. Golding, "The Coming of the Cluniacs," *Anglo-Norman Studies* 3 (1980): 65–77; and Kohnle, *Abt Hugo von Cluny*, pp. 193–96.

18. Hugh was traveling in Germany and Italy in the fall and early winter of 1076 as a power broker in the conflict between the emperor and the pope. See Kohnle, *Abt Hugo von Cluny*, pp. 308–309 (nos. 126–27).

19. BB, vol. 4, pp. 689–96 (no. 3561), at p. 690: "Sed sanctus abbas prius valde nobis fuit durus ad audiendum peticionem nostram, propter longinquitatem aliene terre et maxime propter mare."

cast into hell.[20] The brethren of Cluny were not alone in their disdain for William Rufus; a chorus of monks and churchmen reported signs and portents that foretold in no uncertain terms the unhappy fate awaiting the impious king.[21]

The ascent of King Henry I (1100-1135) to the throne of England heralded a new season in the relationship between Cluny and the crown, a bountiful spring after a short, harsh winter.[22] After Henry I's death in 1135, twelfth-century authors remembered the king as a generous benefactor of the great Burgundian abbey. Writing at Bec in the 1140s, Robert of Torigni compiled a list of Henry's many gifts to Cluny, including the financial burden of building "a major part" of Cluny III, the reconstruction of the abbey's massive Romanesque church initiated by Hugh the Great in 1088 and finally completed under Peter the Venerable in 1130.[23] Likewise, in the late twelfth century, Walter Map deployed his trademark hyperbole to praise the monarch for "completing from the foundations" (*perfecit a fundamentis*) the new church at Cluny after the structure built by King Alfonso VI of León-Castile (1065-1109) had completely collapsed and for endowing the abbey handsomely "to keep the fabric in good condition" (*ad conseruandam operis indempnitatem*).[24]

These fond recollections of the king's generosity to Cluny have all the benefits of hindsight. Henry I's support of the abbey began early in his career, to be sure, but as a trickle rather than a torrent. Throughout the first twenty years of his reign, the king not only confirmed modest grants made by his barons to Cluny and its daughter houses on the continent but also made his own gifts and confirmed and augmented the property and rights of the growing number of Cluniac dependencies

---

20. Anselm's exile began in October 1097; William Rufus died on August 2, 1100. For accounts of Hugh's vision, see Eadmer, *Vita sancti Anselmi* 46-47, ed. and trans. R. W. Southern, in *The Life of Anselm, Archbishop of Canterbury by Eadmer* (London, 1962), pp. 123-24; and Gilo, *Vita sancti Hugonis abbatis* 15, ed. Cowdrey, in "Two Studies in Cluniac History," pp. 65-66.

21. See the evidence marshalled in F. Barlow, *William Rufus* (London, 1983), pp. 426-30.

22. For what follows, see D. Lohrmann, "Pierre le Vénérable et Henri Ier, roi d'Angleterre," in *Pierre Abélard—Pierre le Vénérable: Les courants philosophiques, littéraires et artistiques en occident au milieu du XIIe siècle (Abbaye de Cluny, 2 au 9 juillet 1972)* (Paris, 1975), pp. 191-203; and C. W. Hollister, *Henry I* (New Haven, 2001), pp. 412-57.

23. Robert of Torigni, *Gesta Normannorum Ducum* 8.32, ed. and trans. E. Van Houts, in *The Gesta Normannorum Ducum of William of Jumièges, Orderic Vitalis, and Robert of Torigni*, 2 vols. (Oxford, 1995), vol. 2, pp. 254-55.

24. Walter Map, *De nugis curialium* 5.5, ed. and trans. M. R. James, in *Walter Map, De nugis curialium: Courtiers' Trifles*, rev. ed. (Oxford, 1983), pp. 436-39. Walter is probably referring to the rebuilding that took place after the collapse of the vaulting of the nave in 1125.

both large and small in England.[25] Henry's most generous gesture, which made such an impression on his contemporaries and later chroniclers, did not take place until May 10, 1131. The setting was the king's court in Rouen, where a host of northern abbots and churchmen had convened to throw their support behind Pope Innocent II, whose candidacy had been challenged in Rome by the antipope Anacletus II.[26] Innocent II's chief supporters in attendance included monastic leaders like Bernard of Clairvaux, Geoffrey of Chartres, Suger of Saint-Denis, and possibly Peter the Venerable, as well as leading prelates, including King Henry's close friend and confidant, the powerful archbishop Hugh of Rouen.[27] Innocent had obtained recognition as the legitimate pope by the Holy Roman Emperor Lothar III the previous year, but it was nonetheless important to him to gain the support of the king of England as well.

The Rouen convocation was by all accounts a success, for Henry I deigned to recognize Innocent II as the legitimate pope. But it was an especially memorable event for the Cluniacs in particular, because it was on this occasion that the English king offered their mother abbey in perpetuity an annual gift of one hundred marks of silver drawn from the income of farms in London and Lincoln.[28] Henry was clear in his instructions that forever more "his officers shall annually bring the 100 marks with the rest of the rents to his exchequer and they shall there be delivered to the agent of the abbey."[29] Innocent II confirmed the king's gift to Cluny in Rouen, and upon his return to England, the king reconfirmed the gift twice later that same year, first at Northampton and later at Woodstock.[30] The timing of the king's gift to Cluny,

---

25. Hollister, *Henry I*, pp. 415–18 provides a convenient summary of the evidence.

26. On the causes of the papal schism and its outcome, with attention to the insinuations circulated about Ancletus II's alleged Jewish ancestry, see M. Stroll, *The Jewish Pope: Ideology and Politics in the Papal Schism of 1130* (Leiden, 1987).

27. Peter was absent from Cluny at the time of the meeting in Rouen, but there is no direct evidence that he attended it. See Constable, *Letters of Peter the Venerable*, vol. 2, pp. 257–69 (appendix D: Chronology and Itinerary of Peter the Venerable), at p. 259.

28. *Regesta Regum Anglo-Normannorum 1066–1154*, ed. H. W. C. Davis, C. Johnson, and H. A. Cronne, 3 vols. (Oxford, 1913–68), vol. 2, p. 248 (no. 1691). Hollister called it "one of the largest gifts of [the king's] life," surpassed only by a comparable gift to Fontevrault (*Henry I*, p. 416 with n. 264).

29. *Calendar of Documents Preserved in France, Illustrative of the History of Great Britain and Ireland*, Vol. 1, *AD 918–1206*, ed. J. H. Round (London, 1889), pp. 507–508 (nos. 1387 and 1389). The quotation is a paraphrase of the charters from Hollister, *Henry I*, p. 417.

30. The pope's confirmation: *Regesta Regum Anglo-Normannorum*, ed. Davis, Johnson, and Cronne, vol. 2, p. 248 (no. 1691); and *Calendar of Documents Preserved in France*, p. 508 (no. 1388). The king's reconfirmations in England: *Regesta Regum Anglo-Normannorum*, ed. Davis,

CHAPTER 12

indeed, his tenacious interest in the great Burgundian abbey throughout his reign, has never been adequately explained. It is unclear whether Peter the Venerable actually attended the Rouen convocation in person, but he may not have felt the need to do so, if he had already spent the time and energy to broker the royal gift to his abbey beforehand. We may be able to glimpse his agency in laying the groundwork for the king's generosity in the months before the meeting in Rouen in the evidence for the abbot's unprecedented visit to England only one year earlier, in the spring of 1130.

Peter's First Mission to England (1130)

The abbots of Cluny traveled extensively in the tenth, eleventh, and early twelfth centuries as agents of monastic reform, as protectors of the interests of their communities in far-flung locales, and as brokers of peace at the highest levels of medieval society. Peter the Venerable did so too. Despite his frequent bouts of poor health, he made several trips over the Alps into Italy and spent an entire year on a visit to Spain (1142–1143).[31] Unlike his predecessors, however, he also ventured into England on at least two occasions. His first visit took place in the spring or early summer of 1130.[32] Cluniac sources from this period made no direct mention of this voyage, but Manuscript E of the *Anglo-Saxon Chronicle* did.[33] The so-called *Peterborough Chronicle* was copied after a fire in 1116 destroyed the abbey of Peterborough, including many of its precious manuscripts.[34] Working from an exemplar written in Kent, a Peterborough scribe copied the chronicle until the year 1121. Over the next decade, this scribe added updates

---

Johnson, and Cronne, vol. 2, pp. 252 and 254 (nos. 1713 and 1721), and *Calendar of Documents Preserved in France*, p. 507 (no. 1386).

31. On Peter's fragile health, see n. 6, above. The abbot's itinerary has been reconstructed in Constable, *Letters of Peter the Venerable*, vol. 2, pp. 256–69, which is superior to the study by D. van den Eydne, "Les principaux voyages de Pierre le Vénérable," *Benedictina* 15 (1968): 58–110.

32. J.-P. Torrell and D. Bouthillier, *Pierre le Vénérable et sa vision du monde: Sa vie, son oeuvre, l'homme et le demon* (Leuven, 1986), pp. 54–56.

33. In a letter to Henry of Blois, Peter mentioned that he had tarried in England "the previous year." See *Ep.* 49, ed. Constable, vol. 1, pp. 148–50, at p. 150. Constable dated this letter to 1131 on the basis of the 1130 visit recorded in the *Peterborough Chronicle* (*Letters of Peter the Venerable*, vol. 2, pp. 131 and 259).

34. Oxford, Bodleian Library, Laud Misc. 636; with N. R. Ker, *Catalogue of Manuscripts Containing Anglo-Saxon* (Oxford, 1957), pp. 424–26 (no. 346); and *The Anglo-Saxon Chronicle: A Collaborative Edition*, Vol. 7, *MS. E, A Semi-Diplomatic Edition with Introduction and Indices*, ed. S. Irvine (Cambridge, 2004), pp. xiii–xvii.

of events important to his community until 1131. Twenty years later, a second scribe concluded the chronicle with news and events up to the year 1154.

Peter the Venerable's visit to Peterborough in 1130 warranted mention in the *Peterborough Chronicle* because it raised alarm among the local brethren, who feared that the abbot's close friend and ally, Henry of Blois, abbot of Glastonbury and bishop of Winchester, was going to hand over control of their community to Cluny. The entry for 1130 reads as follows:

> After him [Henry] came the abbot of Cluny, named Peter, to England, by the king's leave, and was received everywhere whithersoever he came with much worship. To Peterborough he came, and there Abbot Henry promised him that he would get him the monastery of Peterborough that it might be subject to Cluny. But it is said for a proverb, "The hedge abides that fields divide." May God Almighty frustrate evil counsels. Shortly after this the abbot of Cluny went home to his own country.[35]

The monks of Peterborough had every reason to be alarmed. They were already deeply dissatisfied with their current abbot, Henry of Angély (1128–1133), who was a Cluniac.[36] As bishop of Soissons in the late eleventh century, this wayward character had been accused of simony and made amends by taking the monastic habit at Cluny. There Henry rose to the rank of prior. Owing to his kinship with the king of England and the count of Poitou, he became abbot of Saint-Jean d'Angély near Saintes (1104–1131) and a papal legate to England (1123).[37] In 1128, King Henry I appointed him as abbot of Peterborough. The abbey's annalist did not mince words in his portrait of this predatory prelate, whose arrival was heralded by nocturnal appearances of the terrifying Wild Hunt and whose abbacy was likened to a drone

---

35. *Anglo-Saxon Chronicle*, a. 1130, ed. Irvine, in *The Anglo-Saxon Chronicle*, pp. 131–32; trans. B. Thorpe, in *The Anglo-Saxon Chronicle According to the Several Original Authorities*, 2 vols. (London, 1861), vol. 2, p. 227. A mid-twelfth-century Latin epitome of the *Peterborough Chronicle* reported Peter's visit without the disdain of the chronicler. See Hugo Candidus, *Chronicon*, ed. W. T. Mellows, in *The Chronicle of Hugh Candidus, A Monk of Peterborough* (London, 1949), p. 102.

36. For what follows, see C. Clark, "This Ecclesiastical Adventurer: Henry of Saint-Jean d'Angély," *English Historical Review* 84 (1969): 548–60.

37. Henry of Angély was the second cousin of King Henry I. See Clark, "This Ecclesiastical Adventurer," p. 554.

fattened by the labor of his worker bees.[38] Henry's tenure lasted only until 1132, when the king stripped him of his office and banished him from the kingdom, but he was the sitting abbot at the time of Peter's visit to Peterborough.

Despite the negative posture of the *Peterborough Chronicle* toward the Cluniacs, it is possible to glean some important information about the nature of Peter the Venerable's visit to England in 1130. First, the annalist tells us that Peter had obtained the king's permission to come to England, which implies some kind of formal contact between the abbot and the royal court. Second, the notice that Peter was "received everywhere whithersoever he came with much worship" indicates that his visit to England was not limited to Peterborough; his ambit was clearly wider, although how much wider it is impossible to say. Unfortunately, the myopic character of the *Peterborough Chronicle* with its focus on the concerns of one local community of beleaguered monks provides no information to illuminate the question that interests us the most: the reason (or multiple reasons) for the abbot of Cluny's visit to England in the first place.[39]

Several decades ago, David Knowles proposed that Peter's mission to England in 1130 was in some way related to the "reform chapter" of Cluniac priors that convened at the great Burgundian abbey on March 13, 1132.[40] "It is not stated what his business was [in England]," Knowles wrote, "but it is natural to suppose that it was some kind of survey preparatory to his summons to Cluny of all the priors of the order in 1132."[41] The Norman chronicler Orderic Vitalis attended this meeting at Cluny and reported the vector of Peter's program of reform: "He imposed new fasts on his subject monks and took away times for conversation and various supports of bodily infirmity, which the moderate mercy of reverend

---

38. *Anglo-Saxon Chronicle*, a. 1127, ed. Irvine, in *The Anglo-Saxon Chronicle*, p. 129. On the Wild Hunt, see J.-C. Schmitt, *Ghosts in the Middle Ages: The Living and the Dead in Medieval Society*, trans. T. L. Fagan (Chicago, 1998), pp. 93–122, esp. p. 109 on Peterborough.

39. For a firm rebuttal to Lohrmann's hypothesis ("Pierre le Vénérable et Henri Ier," p. 197) that Peter was in England to bring not only Peterborough but also Glastonbury and Reading under Cluniac control, see Hollister, *Henry I*, pp. 429–30.

40. On the relationship between this Cluniac chapter and the General Benedictine chapter that proceeded it in 1131 and took place in the archdiocese of Reims, see S. Vanderputten, "The First 'General Chapter' of Benedictine Abbots (1131) Reconsidered," *Journal of Ecclesiastical History* 66 (2015): 715–34, at pp. 722–28.

41. Knowles, *The Monastic Order in England*, p. 157. Other scholars have repeated his hypothesis. See, for example, J. A. Green, *Henry I, King of England and Duke of Normandy* (Cambridge, 2006), p. 208.

fathers had previously allowed them."[42] These new rules were met with considerable resistance by the assembled priors, who balked as much at their novelty as at their severity, prompting the abbot of Cluny to abandon his most severe precepts out of consideration for the shortcomings of the brethren of his extended community. But if laying the groundwork for the Cluniac General Chapter was in fact Peter's primary reason for traveling to England in 1130, then his trip was in vain, because there is no record that any representatives from Cluniac houses in England attended the meeting in Burgundy in 1132.

Peter's motive for traveling across the English Channel must have involved an issue so important that he was convinced that his personal presence was necessary to effect its resolution. Given his poor health, the abbot would not have risked leaving the pressing demands of his office to undertake an arduous voyage unless he felt that the possible outcome of the trip outweighed the risks attendant with it. The fact that he made this voyage only a year before King Henry I made one of the largest gifts of his reign to the abbey of Cluny in revenue rather than in landholdings cannot be ignored. The negotiation of this gift in person was very likely the primary purpose for the abbot's voyage. If, however, Peter did make the journey to England to argue the case in person for the need and benefits of a perpetual fund for Cluny from the king, the question remains why he thought it was an auspicious time to do so and who, if anyone, helped him to broker the grant with the king. The answers to these question lie in the intensification of the relationship between members of Henry I's immediate family and the abbey of Cluny in the years leading up to Peter's visit.

King Henry I's sister Adela and her son Henry of Blois both nurtured close relationships with Cluny during the abbacies of Peter's predecessors Hugh the Great (1049–1109) and Pontius of Melguiel (1109–1122). Upon assuming the abbacy in 1122, Peter the Venerable would have recognized that Adela and Henry were the members of the king's immediate family most likely to influence his decision to endow Cluny with a perpetual fund. Adela was a formidable woman active in the highest level of Anglo-Norman politics.[43] This daughter of William the

---

42. Orderic Vitalis, *Historia Ecclesiastica* 13.13: "Ille uero subiectis auxit ieiunia, abstulit colloquia, et infirmi corporis qaedam subsidia quae illis moderata patrum hactenus permiserat reuerendorum clementia," ed. Chibnall, vol. 6, pp. 426–27.

43. For an exhaustive evaluation of Adela's life and influence, see K. A. LoPrete, *Adela of Blois: Countess and Lord (c. 1067–1137)* (Dublin, 2007).

Conqueror married Count Stephen of Blois and Chartres, with whom she had several children, including the future King Stephen and Henry of Blois. Her influence on her brother Henry I was strong. Early in his reign, she played a key role in reconciling the king with Archbishop Anselm, from whom he had been estranged.[44] Her decision to enter the Cluniac nunnery of Marcigny in Burgundy around the year 1120 put her in proximity to Peter the Venerable, both physically and spiritually.[45] Their relationship was such that the abbot of Cluny addressed a letter of condolence to Adela in early 1136 after the death of her royal brother on December 1, 1135.[46] Later, after her death in 1137, Peter cast Adela as a witness to a wonder in his treatise on miracles, calling her "lord Adela, sister of the king of England, once countess of Blois, now a humble handmaiden of Christ."[47]

Adela's son, Henry of Blois, exerted a comparable influence on King Henry I during the last decade of his reign, but his ties to Cluny were arguably even closer than those of his mother.[48] Born around 1098, Henry spent his childhood as a monk at the great Burgundian abbey, an institution to which he remained fiercely loyal and generous throughout his life, even when his activities were far from monastic in tenor or substance.[49] Little is known about his life until 1126, when his royal uncle promoted him from head of the modest Cluniac priory of Montacute in Somerset to the abbacy of Glastonbury, one of the richest monasteries in the realm. Three years later, the king nominated Henry of Blois to be the bishop of Winchester, but with the pope's permission, he retained his abbacy as well.[50] He held both of these positions until

---

44. LoPrete, *Adela of Blois*, pp. 174–77.
45. LoPrete, *Adela of Blois*, pp. 405–18.
46. Peter the Venerable, *Ep.* 15, ed. Constable, vol. 1, p. 22 (the letter); and vol. 2, pp. 103–105 (the date).
47. Peter the Venerable, *De miraculis* 1.26: "At nominata soror domnam Adelam regis Anglici sororem prius Blesensem comitissam, nunc humilem Christi ancillam adiens, ei uniuersa narrauit," ed. Bouthillier, p. 81.
48. The best modern study remains L. Voss, *Heinrich von Blois, Bischof von Winchester (1129–1171)* (Berlin, 1932). For a recent assessment of Henry, see E. King, "Henry of Winchester: The Bishop, the City and the Wider World," *Anglo-Norman Studies* 37 (2014): 1–24.
49. See the resignation of David Knowles on this issue expressed in D. Knowles, "Henry of Blois, Bishop of Winchester 1129–71," *Winchester Cathedral Record* 41 (1972): 28–36, at p. 33: "How far Henry was a monk at heart throughout his life is a matter beyond the ken of an historian." Neil Stratford was less equivocal: "Il est avant tout et toujours un moine de Cluny." See N. Stratford, "Un grand clunisien, Henri de Blois," in *Cluny 910–2010: Onze siècles de rayonnement*, ed. N. Stratford (Paris, 2010), pp. 238–44, at p. 242.
50. On these appointments, see J. le Neve, *Fasti Ecclesiae Anglicanae 1066–1300: II. Monastic Cathedrals*, ed. D. Greenway (London, 1971), p. 85; and D. Knowles, C. N. L. Brooke, and V. C.

his death in 1171. These appointments, which launched Henry to the highest levels of wealth and power in Anglo-Norman England, demonstrate clearly the trust placed in this young man by his uncle, who had no sons of his own to promote to positions of ecclesiastical and secular prominence. All evidence points to a close friendship between Henry of Blois and Peter the Venerable. Other than one frosty missive of 1131, when the abbot of Cluny chided Henry for not taking the abbey's side more aggressively in a quarrel with the brethren of La Charité-sur-Loire in their bid to cast off the yoke of their motherhouse, Peter expressed himself in the warmest possible terms to the Anglo-Norman prelate in letter after letter, at one point even asking Henry to consider being buried at Cluny.[51]

The influence of these high-ranking allies in the royal family may not have been enough, however, to secure the generous royal gift that Peter the Venerable hoped to broker for the security of his abbey's future. Some historians have associated King Henry I's gift with a request from Cluny for cash "toward the cost of the great building work at Cluny," but by the time of Peter's visit to England in 1130, the lion's share of this labor had already been completed.[52] To be sure, the collapse of the vaulting in the nave of the massive church known as Cluny III in 1125 was a disappointing setback in a construction project begun by Abbot Hugh the Great in 1088, but the consecration of the new church in October 1130 suggests that the repairs were largely finished by the time Peter went to England. In fact, it may well have been the looming completion of that formidable undertaking, as well as other internal reforms undertaken by the new abbot in the aftermath of the divisive departure of his predecessor Pontius of Melguiel, that convinced the English king that Cluny under Peter's proven stewardship was worth an investment of this magnitude in perpetuity. The timing was thus auspicious for Peter to make his bid for a royal gift. Henry I was in the south of England in the spring of 1130 when the abbot of Cluny was at Peterborough. The king spent Easter (March 30) in Woodstock, about eighty miles southwest of Peterborough, and he frequented several of

---

M. London, *The Heads of Religious Houses: England and Wales, 940–1216* (Cambridge, 1972), pp. 51 and 121.

51. Peter the Venerable, *Ep.* 49 (the frosty missive) and *Ep.* 60 (the proposal to bury Henry at Cluny), ed. Constable, vol. 1, pp. 148–50 and 190–91. In the end, Henry chose to be buried at Winchester.

52. Green, *Henry I*, p. 210.

his royal estates in Oxfordshire in April.⁵³ He then moved on to Windsor, where Henry of Blois joined him.⁵⁴ It seems plausible, then, that Peter met with the king either on his own in Oxfordshire or in Henry's company at Windsor sometime in the late spring.⁵⁵

By all accounts, Peter the Venerable's gambit paid off when in the late winter of the following year King Henry announced his annual gift to Cluny at the convocation at Rouen, where it was immediately confirmed by Pope Innocent II. The king's generosity was not forgotten by the Cluniacs. After Henry's death in 1135, Peter consoled Adela of Blois with the promise that "[f]or the eternal salvation of the dead king we have established many things which the Cluniacs have never done for anyone before."⁵⁶ Nor did the passage of time tarnish the abbot's admiration of Henry's investment in Cluny's future. Toward the end of his life, Peter praised the king's generosity in the strongest possible terms: "Among all the kings of the Latin west, who for the last three hundred years have testified their affection for the church of Cluny ... Henry, king of the English and duke of Normandy, has surpassed all others in his gifts and has shown more than an ordinary share of love and attachment to [Cluny]."⁵⁷

Even Peter's hagiographer, Rodulphus de Sully, had kind words to say about the king. This is most apparent not in the ending of the ghost story (with which we began), which cleaves closely to the conventions of the genre, but rather in its beginning, which emphasized the relationship between the king and the abbey with the following words: "Concerning the older King Henry of the English, it is known to many how many good things he brought to Cluny."⁵⁸ Rodulphus then took pains to stress that Henry was a man of character, despite the return of his restless soul. Unlike other sinners who appeared in monastic ghost stories, the king was not suffering in the afterlife because of his proclivity

---

53. W. Farrer, *An Outline Itinerary of King Henry the First* (Oxford, 1920), pp. 130–31 (esp. nos. 607 and 609).

54. Farrer, *An Outline Itinerary of King Henry*, p. 131 (no. 610).

55. It is unclear when Peter came back to France. He had certainly returned by September 1130, when he greeted Pope Innocent II in Saint Gilles. See Constable, *Letters of Peter the Venerable*, vol. 2, p. 259.

56. Peter the Venerable, *Ep*. 15: "Pro regis defuncti aeterna salute tanta constituimus, quanta nunquam Cluniaci pro alio constituta sunt," ed. Constable, vol. 1, p. 22.

57. BB, vol. 5, pp. 532–34 (no. 4183), at pp. 532–33; trans. Hollister, *Henry I*, p. 413.

58. Rodulphus, *Vita Petri Venerabilis* 13, ed. Martène and Durand, vol. 6, col. 1198; repr. in *PL* 189, col. 25: "De rege Anglorum Henrico seniore multis notum est quanta bona Cluniaco contulerit."

for particular sins, but simply "because the powerful suffer torments powerfully" (*quia potentes potenter tormenta patiuntur*) as a result of the responsibilities attendant to their lofty station among the living.[59] It was thus fitting that the king of England would turn for help in death to the abbey that he had endowed so generously in life.

Peter's Second Mission to England (1155/1156)

After the passing of King Henry I in 1135, his nephew Henry of Blois became the most important advocate in England for the Cluniacs.[60] Time and again, the letters of Peter the Venerable bear witness to this prelate's agency in securing and maintaining financial support for his childhood home. It was Henry who brokered the abbey's relationship with his brother, King Stephen (1135-1154), and witnessed the new monarch's replacement of Henry I's annual gift of one hundred marks in cash with a manor in Letcombe-Regis, which yielded a comparable amount.[61] It was Henry who on several occasions sent thousands of silver marks to his brethren in Burgundy to help pay down the abbey's mounting debts.[62] Indeed, in a letter written in 1135, Peter expressed his relief and gratitude for Henry's financial intervention, which allowed the monks of Cluny to buy back some liturgical vestments that were being held as collateral by Jewish moneylenders in Mâcon.[63] It was Henry who applied the financial acumen and administrative skills that he had honed in his reform of Glastonbury to a survey of Cluny's patrimony and a reckoning of its worth and solvency.[64]

---

59. Rodulphus, *Vita Petri Venerabilis* 13, ed. Martène and Durand, vol. 6, col. 1198; repr. in *PL* 189, col. 25. The sentiment is biblical in origin. See Wisd. of Sol. 6:7: "Exiguo enim conceditur misericordia potentes autem potenter tormenta patientur."

60. Voss, *Heinrich von Blois*, pp. 108-21; and Knowles, *Monastic Order of England*, pp. 286-93, which focuses on Henry of Blois's promotion of Cluniac monks to prominent positions in England.

61. Peter the Venerable, *Ep.* 60, ed. Constable, vol. 1, pp. 190-91. Constable was inclined to see this grant as "positive evidence of [Stephen's] bid for Cluniac support" (*Letters of Peter the Venerable*, vol. 2, p. 256). Stephen also founded several abbeys that followed Cluniac observances, but were otherwise free from Cluniac control. The most important was Faversham in Kent (1148), which served as a mausoleum for Stephen, his wife, and his son. See Hollister, *Henry I*, pp. 428 and 441.

62. Conveniently summarized by Voss, *Heinrich von Blois*, pp. 114-15 and 118.

63. Peter the Venerable, *Ep.* 56, ed. Constable, vol. 1, pp. 177-78.

64. BB, vol. 5, pp. 475-82 (no. 4132). The classic study of Cluny's economy based on Henry's fiscal account is G. Duby, "Le budget de l'abbaye de Cluny entre 1080 et 1155: Economie domaniale et économie monétaire," *Annales: Économies, Sociétés, Civilisations* 7 (1952): 155-71; repr. in G. Duby, *Hommes et structures du moyen âge: Recueil d'articles* (Paris, 1973), pp. 61-82, but

Henry of Blois successfully lobbied for Cluniac interests and redirected moveable wealth to Burgundy throughout the tumultuous two decades of the Anarchy (1135–1153), but the precarious peace that the prelate helped to negotiate at Winchester Cathedral in the summer of 1153 would result in his three-years-long self-imposed exile to the great Burgundian abbey in 1155. Like many other powerful lords of the twelfth century, Henry was an energetic sponsor of building projects, but to the surprise and dismay of his contemporaries, this abbot-cum-bishop built many fortifications.[65] In its entry for the year 1138, the Winchester chronicle listed no fewer than six castles that Henry built on the sites of manors owned by the cathedral at Wolvesey (Winchester), Taunton (Somerset), Downton (Wiltshire), Merdon and Bishop's Waltham (Hampshire), and Farnham (Surrey).[66] It was these fortifications, built to maintain the prelate's security in the perilous political climate of the civil war, that cast suspicion on Henry as a threat to royal authority once peace had been achieved. Indeed, in accordance with the Treaty of Winchester (1153), King Henry II (1154–1189) set about consolidating his power in England and Normandy by confiscating and demolishing any privately owned castles that could be used to destabilize his new regime. Following a policy of fortress control that remained consistent throughout his reign, the king "seized castles as a legal pretext as well as in response to rebellions in his greater domains."[67] Several barons rose up in revolt against this policy, but they were all defeated and their fortifications impounded or destroyed. Faced with the new king's aggressive posture in regard to his fortifications, Henry took the path of least resistance. Instead of actively contesting Henry II's command to relinquish his castles, the prelate quietly gathered a large quantity of moveable wealth and secretly fled to the abbey of Cluny. It was Henry's act of subterfuge that brought the aged abbot of Cluny to England for a second and final time.

---

this topic demands fresh inquiry. On Henry's reforms at Glastonbury, see N. E. Stacy, "Henry of Blois and the Lordship of Glasonbury," *English Historical Review* 114 (1999): 1–33.

65. M. W. Thompson, "Recent Excavations in the Keep of Farnham Castle, Surrey," *Medieval Archaeology* 4 (1960): 81–94; and E. Mason, "The Purposeful Patronage of Henry of Blois," *Medieval History* 3 (1993): 30–50, at pp. 42–43.

66. *Annales de Wintonia*, s.a. 1138, ed. H. R. Luard, in *Annales Monastici*, Vol. 2, *Annales Monasterii de Wintonia (A.D. 519–1277) and Annales Monasterii de Waverleia (A.D. 1–1291)* (London, 1865), p. 51.

67. J. D. Hosler, *Henry II: A Medieval Soldier at War, 1147–1189* (Leiden, 2007), pp. 171–93, esp. pp. 185–87.

A number of different sources attest to Peter the Venerable's second voyage to England, including the abbot's writings, which firmly situate the visit in 1155 or early the following year, in any case shortly before his death at Cluny on December 25, 1156.[68] In a late addendum to his treatise on miracles, which Peter began writing in the mid-1140s, the abbot related an account of a wonder performed by his tenth-century predecessor Maiolus. Peter had a particular fondness for stories about Maiolus, claiming that more legends were told about his virtues throughout all of Europe than about any other saint in Christendom besides the Virgin Mary.[69] To this fund of miracles, Peter added the story of a dead boy at Souvigny, whom the holy abbot had miraculously restored to life, and remarked that at the time he was writing, Maiolus had been dead for 162 years.[70] Given that the fourth abbot of Cluny had died in 994, Peter must have been writing this addendum in 1156. In the following chapter, written at the same time, the abbot explicitly stated that he had recently returned from his second trip to England, which thus most likely occurred in 1155 or early 1156.[71]

A letter of Peter of Poitier, a monk of Cluny who served for many years as Peter the Venerable's trusted notary, also mentioned the abbot's second voyage to England.[72] It is well known that Peter the Venerable commissioned a Latin translation of the Qu'ran and other religious and historical Islamic texts during his sojourn in Spain in 1142/1143.[73] The abbot's outspoken aim was to create a "Christian arsenal" (*armarium Christianum*) for European intellectuals who could use this newly translated knowledge to refute the truth claims of Mohammad and his followers. In 1143, Peter wrote to Bernard of Clairvaux, inviting him to undertake this task, but he received no answer. The project lay fallow until the aftermath of the disastrous Second Crusade (1045–1049) and

---

68. For what follows, see Constable, *Letters of Peter the Venerable*, vol. 2, p. 268; and Torrell and Bouthillier, *Pierre le Vénérable et sa vision du monde*, pp. 57–59, esp. p. 57, n. 38, where the hypothesis of D. van den Eydne ("Les principaux voyages de Pierre le Vénérable," pp. 89–94) that Peter took this trip to England in late 1148 is convincingly dismissed on the basis of the evidence cited later in this chapter

69. Peter the Venerable, *De miraculis* 2.32, ed. Bouthillier, p. 162.

70. Peter the Venerable, *De miraculis* 2.32, ed. Bouthillier, p. 162.

71. Peter the Venerable, *De miraculis* 2.33: "Eo enim anno quo de Anglia secondo redii, illud me audisse contigit," ed. Bouthillier, p. 164.

72. On the identity and role of Peter of Poitiers, see Constable, *Letters of Peter the Venerable*, vol. 2, pp. 331–43 (appendix Q: Peter of Poitiers).

73. For what follows, see S. G. Bruce, *Cluny and the Muslims of La Garde-Freinet: Hagiography and the Problem of Islam in Medieval Europe* (Ithaca, 2015), pp. 70–99, with reference to earlier literature.

the death of Bernard in 1153 prompted Peter to turn his attention to Islam once again. While the abbot of Cluny was abroad on his second trip to England, Peter of Poitiers set to work outlining a treatise against Islam for his master. In a remarkable letter sent from Cluny to England, Peter of Poitiers stated with frustration that he had prepared a first draft of the treatise outline (*capitula*) and had sent it to England in the hands of a monk named John, who somehow lost it en route.[74] This accident forced Peter of Poitiers to rewrite the outline from scratch, but it also provided him with the opportunity to make improvements to it before sending it again to England. This time, however, he took the precaution of making a second copy for himself.

The Norman chronicler Robert of Torigni spoke most plainly about the purpose of Peter the Venerable's second voyage to England. In the year 1155 of his continuation of Sigebert of Gembloux's *World Chronicle*, Robert reported that King Henry II had decided not to invade Ireland at the request of his mother, the empress Mathilda. The only other noteworthy event of that year read as follows: "Bishop Henry of Winchester, having first sent out money via the abbot of Cluny, departed from England without the king's license and rather stealthily. As a result, Henry ravaged his castles."[75] What is most remarkable about this entry is not Henry's desire for secrecy as he fled the country, but rather the personal role played by Peter the Venerable in smuggling the bishop's movable wealth from Winchester to Cluny. Many religious communities and shrines housed portable wealth like gold, silver, and precious stones in the twelfth century, and Cluny was no exception, but its movement from place to place entailed significant risk, especially from the threat of bandits or pirates.[76] The sum of wealth that Henry snuck out of England must have been great indeed, if the abbot of Cluny felt the need to accompany it personally across the English Channel. It may have been the case that Peter traveled with a large enough retinue that Henry's *thesaurus* would have been both well guarded and well concealed on the

---

74. Peter of Poitiers, *Epistola* 4, ed. R. Glei, in *Petrus Venerabilis, Schriften zum Islam* (Altenberge, 1985), pp. 228–39; trans. I. M. Resnick, in *Peter the Venerable, Writings Against Islam* (Washington, DC, 2016), pp. 163–71.

75. Robert of Torigni, *Chronica*, s.a. 1155: "Henricus episcopus Winthoniensis, clam premisso thesauro suo per abbatem Cluniacensem absque licentia regis et quasi latenter recessit ab Anglia. Ideo rex Henricus omnia castella eius pessundedit," ed. and trans. T. Bisson, in *The Chronography of Robert of Torigni*, 2 vols. (Oxford, 2020), vol. 1, pp. 194–95.

76. For examples of cash donations to religious houses and their vulnerability to theft, see E. Cownie, *Religious Patronage in Anglo-Norman England, 1066–1135* (Woodbridge, 1998), pp. 51–52, 75, and 77; and, more generally, Hollister, *Henry I*, pp. 454–57.

journey, but in the end there is no way to know. After many years of Henry's support, the abbot of Cluny finally had the chance to return the favor by offering the bishop (and his wealth) a safe haven in Burgundy during the early years of the reign of the new king of England.

The exact timing of Peter the Venerable's second visit to England is open to question, but given the covert nature of the transfer of Henry of Blois's treasure to Cluny, it most likely took place at a time when King Henry II was preoccupied with military campaigns, a frequent feature of the early years of his reign.[77] The king held a great council of Wallingford on April 10, 1155, and then spent the summer suppressing the rebellion of Hugh de Mortimer with sieges at Cleobury, Wigmore, and Northbridge.[78] Henry II remained in England throughout the autumn and early winter, but in January he departed for Dover and from there to Picardy. He then spent the first six months of 1156 campaigning in Anjou against his brother Geoffrey, where he laid siege to castles at Mirebeau, Chinon, and Loudon. Peter's movements in this period are not as well documented as Henry's. The abbot was in Soissons in June 1155, where he met with King Louis VII about a matter concerning the abbey of Vézelay, but he may have ventured to England later that summer.[79] His whereabouts in the fall and early winter are unknown. Upon his return from England, he tarried at the monastery of Reuil on the Marne before returning to Cluny, but it is impossible to date this visit with any precision.[80] For his part, Henry of Blois would have been especially savvy about his departure from England. The summer of 1155 and the winter of 1156 would have been ideal times to move his treasure in secret from Winchester to Cluny, for on both occasions the king was preoccupied with military campaigns to consolidate his rule in England and France.

Peter the Venerable's two trips to England in 1130 and 1155/1156 were similar in purpose, but different in character. In 1130, the time was auspicious for the abbot of Cluny to lobby King Henry I for a perpetual gift to his monastery, for several reasons. The aging king had favored the great Burgundian abbey and its English dependencies in the past. Peter had cultivated the friendship of two influential members of the

---

77. Hosler, *Henry II*.
78. For what follows, see R. W. Eyton, *Court, Household, and Itinerary of King Henry II* (London, 1878), pp. 12–18.
79. Constable, *Letters of Peter the Venerable*, vol. 2, p. 268.
80. Peter the Venerable, *De miraculis* 2.33, ed. Bouthillier, p. 164.

royal family: Henry I's sister Adela, by then a Cluniac nun of Marcigny, and his nephew Henry of Blois, a powerful prelate who had spent his childhood at Cluny. In a world in which abbots communicated primarily by letters and proxies, Peter's decision to embark for England speaks to his understanding that the negotiation of a large perpetual gift for his abbey required him to make his case in person before the king that Cluny was worth the investment. In the end, he was successful.

By 1155, the political climate had changed. The abbey of Cluny had found an especially rare and excellent benefactor in Henry of Blois, whose bountiful gifts and loans did much to keep the great Burgundian monastery solvent in the 1130s and 1140s. When Henry decided to flee from England to Cluny with his moveable wealth during the early years of the reign of King Henry II, Peter the Venerable decided once again to make the voyage across the English Channel. Unlike his first journey, undertaken with a king's permission, this latter visit was a covert expedition to shepherd the fugitive prelate's treasure from Winchester to Cluny. Peter's personal role in this adventure is open to question, but his intention was clear. His abbey would surely benefit from this portion of Henry of Blois's wealth, but even more important, the abbot of Cluny was repaying a debt of friendship to one of his oldest and dearest allies, a generous bishop in need of a safe haven when the tide of royal politics had turned against him.

CHAPTER 13

Curiosity Killed the Monk
The History of an Early Medieval Vice

A twelfth-century chapter book for nuns (Admont, Benediktinerstift, Codex 567; hereafter Admont 567) preserves a warning to curious monks.[1] On fol. 46v, situated as a prologue to the *Rule of Benedict*, a line drawing depicts a young man, most likely a monk, ascending a ladder (figure 1).[2] As he reaches the top rung, the monk stretches out his hand toward his goal, a framed portrait of Jesus Christ, the author of his salvation. Arranged in columns on either side of the ladder are two lists written in Latin (table 5). On the left-hand side, the scribe has written down the twelve steps of humility cribbed from the seventh chapter of the *Rule of Benedict*. According to the rule, "Wherefore, brothers, if we wish to reach the highest peak of humility and if we desire to attain quickly that heavenly exaltation towards which we climb by means of the humility of this life, we must set up for

---

Originally published as "Curiosity Killed the Monk: The History of an Early Medieval Vice," *Journal of Medieval Monastic Studies* 8 (2019): 73-94. © Brepols Publishers n.v., Turnhout, Belgium. Reprinted with permission.

1. For a description of the manuscript, see J. Wichner's handwritten *Catalogus codicum manu scriptorum Admontensis* (Admont, 1889), p. 228. On the twelfth-century scriptorium at Admont, with an emphasis on the prevalence of female scribal labor (although not on the production of this particular manuscript), see A. Beach, *Women as Scribes: Book Production and Reform in Twelfth-Century Bavaria* (Cambridge, 2004), pp. 65-103.

2. Wichner gave this drawing the title "Gradus duodecim perfectionis et corruptionis monachorum" (*Catalogus codicum*, p. 228).

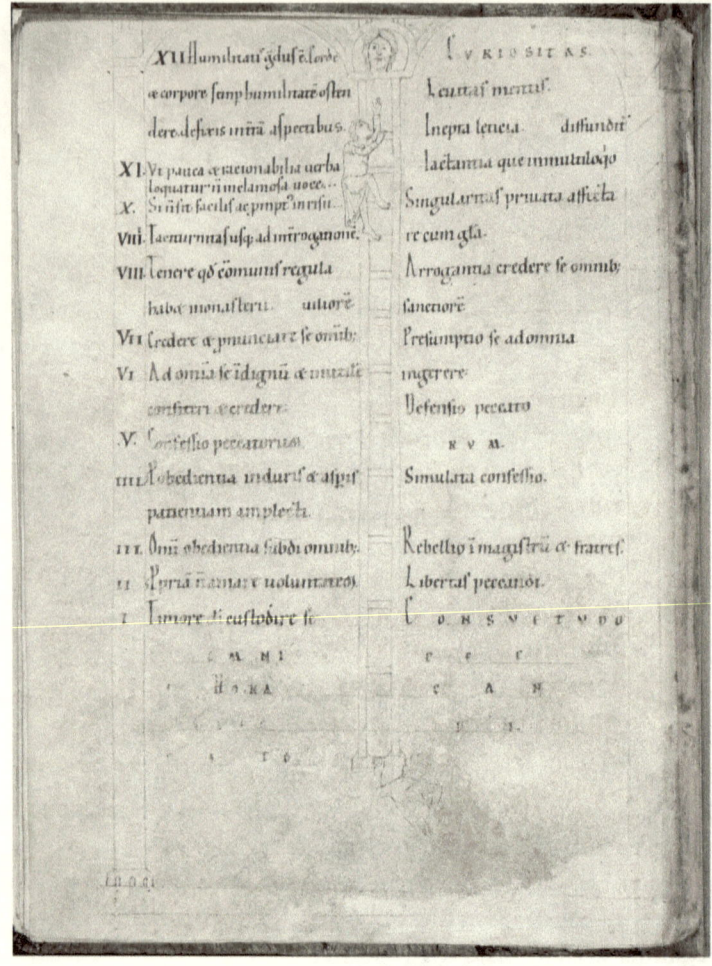

Figure 1. Admont, Benediktinerstift, Codex 567, fol. 46v. Permalink: https://manuscripta.at/diglit/AT1000-567/0094.

our ascent the ladder that Jacob saw in his dream, on which the angels appeared to him, descending and ascending."[3]

On the opposite side of the ladder is a list of dangerous distractions that threaten to hinder the monk's ascent to Christ. These include levity of mind (*leuitas mentis*), foolish merriment (*inepta laeticia*), boasting

---

3. *RB* 7.5–6, with reference to Gen. 28:12: "Unde, fratres, si summae humilitatis uolumus culmen adtingere et ad exaltationem illam caelestem, ad quam per praesentis uitae humilitatem ascenditur, uolumus uelociter preuenire actibus nostris ascendentibus scala illa erigenda est, quae in somno Iaco apparuit, per quam ei descendentes et ascendentes angeli monstrabantur." trans. C. White, in *The Rule of Benedict* (New York, 2008), p. 22.

Table 5.   Gradus duodecim perfectionis et corruptionis monachorum (Admont, Benediktinerstift, Codex 567, fol. 46v)

XII. *Humilitatis gradus est corde et corpore semper humilitate ostendere defixis in terram aspectibus.*	The twelfth step of humility is to express humility always with heart and body with eyes fixed on the ground.	[1] *Curiositas.*	Curiosity.
XI. *Ut pauca et racionabilia uerba loquatur non in clamosa uoce.*	The eleventh step, that one speaks only a few well-chosen words in a quiet voice.	[2] *Leuitas mentis.*	Levity of mind.
X. *Si non sit facilis ac promptus in risu.*	The tenth step, not to laugh easily and quickly.	[3] *Inepta laeticia.*	Foolish merriment.
VIIII. *Taciturnitas usque ad interrogationem.*	The ninth step, silence unless asked a question.	[4] *Iactantia que in multiloquio diffunditur.*	Boasting, which is spread by talking too much.
VIII. *Tenere quod comunis regula habet monasterii.*	The eighth step, to do what the common rule of the monastery upholds.	[5] *Singularitas priuata affectare cum gloria.*	Selfishness, to strive after your own aims with glory.
VII. *Credere et pronunciare se omnibus uiliorem.*	The seventh step, to believe and proclaim to everyone that he is quite lowly.	[6] *Arrogantia credere se omnibus sanctiorem.*	Arrogance, to believe yourself to be holier than all.
VI. *Ad omnia se indignum et inutilem confiteri et credere.*	The sixth step, to confess and to believe that he is unworthy and useless in every way.	[7] *Presumptio ad omnia ingerere.*	Presumption, to complain about everything.
V. *Confessio peccatorum.*	The fifth step, confession of sins.	[8] *Defensio peccatorum.*	Self-justification.
IIII. *Pro obedientia in duris et asperis patientiam amplecti.*	The fourth step, to embrace suffering for obedience in harsh and adverse conditions.	[9] *Simulata confessio.*	Feigned confession.
III. *Omni obedientia subdi omnibus.*	The third step, to submit to everyone with full obedience.	[10] *Rebellio in magistrum et fratres.*	Revolt against teacher and brethren.
II. *Propriam non amare uoluntatem.*	The second step, not to love one's own will.	[11] *Libertas peccandi.*	Freedom to sin.
I. *Timore Dei custodire se omni hora peccato.*	The first step, with the fear of God to guard oneself against sin at all times.	[12] *Consuetudo peccandi.*	Habit of sinning.

(*iactantia*), selfishness (*singularitas*), conceit (*arrogantia*), presumption (*presumptio*), self-justification (*defensio peccatorum*), and feigned confession (*simulata confessio*). The cultivation of these sins eventually leads to open revolt against teacher and brethren (*rebellio in magistrum et fratres*). Forsaking his community, the rebel monk embraces the freedom to sin (*libertas peccandi*) and then falls headlong into the habit of doing so (*consuetudo peccandi*), abandoning completely any remaining pretenses of his cloistered life.

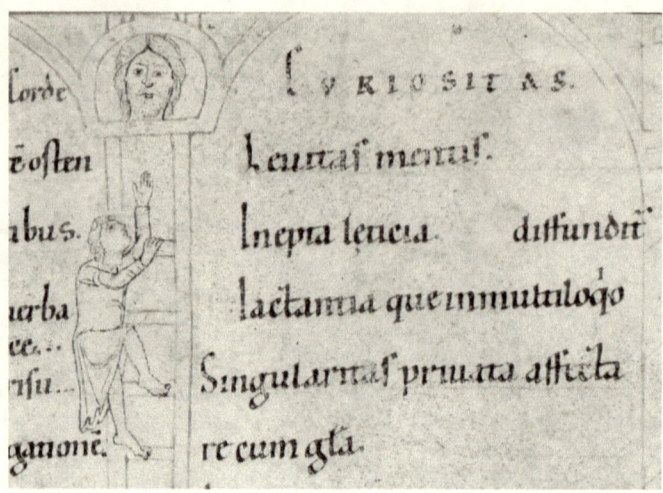

FIGURE 2. Admont, Benediktinerstift, Codex 567, fol. 46v (detail). Permalink: https://manuscripta.at/diglit/AT1000-567/0094.

The gateway sin in this litany of monastic vices is curiosity (*curiositas*) (figure 2). The pride of place given to curiosity in this twelfth-century diagram invites inquiry, for two reasons. First, the peril of curiosity on the diagram has no analogue in the precepts of the sixth-century *Rule of Benedict*, to which it provides a figural preface. Benedict's little handbook for monks emphasized the cultivation of the virtues of obedience, silence, and especially humility, as the left column of the diagram attests. In contrast, the *Rule of Benedict* includes very little discussion of monastic vices, with the exception of a chapter on punishments for faults, in which the author singled out stubbornness, disobedience, and pride as the most dangerous sins in a communal context.[4] Strikingly, curiosity receives not a single mention. Second, the notion that curiosity is a life-threatening vice is completely at odds with contemporary valorization of inquisitive thinking as a positive human attribute that is essential to the acquisition of knowledge and skills. It is without question the driving force behind humanistic and scientific inquiry. In a classic essay written in 1939, Abraham Flexner, the founding director of the Institute for Advanced Study in Princeton, New Jersey, extolled curiosity with these words: "Curiosity, which may or may not eventuate in something useful, is probably

---

4. *RB* 23.

the outstanding characteristic of modern thinking. It is not new. It goes back to Galileo, Bacon, and to Sir Isaac Newton, and it must be absolutely unhampered."[5] Given the lack of attention to curiosity as a perilous trait in the *Rule of Benedict* and the value that we place on inquisitiveness as a constructive personal attribute, the prominent place of *curiositas* on the list of vices marshaled on this twelfth-century diagram as a hinderance to a monk's ascent to Christ begs the question: Why does curiosity kill the monk?

Prompted by this image, in this chapter, I investigate the meaning and use of the word *curiositas* in early medieval monasticism from the fourth to the twelfth centuries.[6] This chapter begins with the deployment of the term in Roman literature and its subsequent redeployment in the Christian tradition by patristic authors. It then shows how compilers of florilegia for cloistered communities imported the word into the monastic tradition. With this introduction in place, I examine the diagram in Admont 567. First, I identify the list of vices as a précis of Bernard of Clairvaux's treatise *On the Steps of Pride and Humility* (*De gradibus superbiae et humilitatis*), composed in the early 1120s. Then I show how the Cistercian abbot developed a theory of monastic praxis that implicated curiosity as the root of the most disruptive sins in medieval cloisters. Bernard's authority on matters of virtue and vice assured that other Cistercian authors would repeat his promotion of curiosity as the gateway to pride, a fact most evident in Galand of Reigny's *Parabolarium*, a collection of forty-two edifying stories written in the early twelfth century. As we will see, however, curiosity was not exclusively a Cistercian concern in this period. The writings of Peter the Venerable of Cluny, most notably the statutes that he composed to govern the far-flung dependencies of his abbey, likewise betray an uneasiness about dangerous distractions in the cloister, very likely informed by Cistercian discourse on the subject. Finally, I turn to the double monastery of Admont, where the manuscript was made, to examine the threat of curiosity in the context of the sinful potential of male and female interaction. Curiosity, it seems, was an even graver threat to nuns than it was to monks.

---

5. A. Flexner, *The Usefulness of Useless Knowledge* (Princeton, 2017), p. 57.

6. In an article published in 1990, Jean Leclercq signaled his intention to "devote a study to the use of the word [*curiositas*] in the authors of the early Middle Ages," but unfortunately his death in 1993 prevented him from doing so. See J. Leclercq, "*Curiositas* and the Return to God in St Bernard of Clairvaux," *Cistercian Studies* 25 (1990): 92–100, at p. 92, n. 2.

Late Ancient Origins

The word *curiositas* did not have a long pedigree in Roman antiquity.[7] It was coined by Cicero in a letter to his friend Atticus in the waning days of the Republic, but its use was a rarity in Latin literature until the second century CE, when Apuleius employed the word a dozen times in his ribald novel *The Golden Ass*.[8] Deriving from *curiosus*, the adjective of the substantive *cura* ("care" or "attention"), *curiositas* was central to the theme of Apuleius's story, for it was the inquisitiveness of his main character, Lucius, about knowledge of the magical arts that resulted in his metamorphosis into a donkey.[9] For their part, late Roman Christians appropriated the word in the second century and articulated its meaning primarily in the context of the perils of seeking knowledge of God beyond what had already been revealed in the Christian scriptures. For example, Jerome accused the builders of the Tower of Babel of the sin of pride incited by their curiosity to speak directly to God: "For after people had migrated from the east and receded from the true light, at that time they constructed a tower of their impiety against God. Then, they constructed the vanities of their teachings, longing with a forbidden curiosity to penetrate into heaven's heights."[10]

The sin of curiosity entered the monastic tradition through the writings of Augustine, John Cassian, and Gregory the Great. Augustine warned that curiosity presented as grave a threat to Christians as the

---

7. For overviews of the history of the word and its meaning, see A. Labhardt, "*Curiositas*: Note sur l'histoire d'un mot et d'une notion," *Museum Helveticum* 17 (1960): 206-24; H. A. Oberman, *Contra vanam curiositatem: Ein Kapital der Theologie zwischen Seelenwinkel und Weltall* (Zurich, 1974); and R. Newhauser, "Towards a History of Human Curiosity: A Prolegomenon to Its Medieval Phase," *Deutsche Vierteljahrsschrift für Literaturwissenschaft und Geistesgeschichte* 56 (1982): 559-75.

8. Cicero, *Ad Atticum* 2.12.2 (April 19, 59 BCE), in *M. Tullius Cicero: Epistulae ad Atticum*, ed. D. R. Shackleton Bailey, 2 vols. (Stuttgart, 1987), vol. 1, p. 68.

9. On its use by Apuleius, see P. G. Walsh, "The Rights and Wrongs of Curiosity (Plutarch to Augustine)," *Greece and Rome* 35 (1988): 73-85; *Apuleius Madaurensis Metamorphoses Book IX: Text, Introduction, and Commentary*, ed. B. L. Hijmans Jr. et al. (Groningen, 1995), pp. 362-79 (appendix III: *Curiositas*); and J. DeFilippo, "*Curiositas* and the Platonism of Apuleius' *Golden Ass*," in *Oxford Readings of the Roman Novel*, ed. S. J. Harrison (Oxford, 1999), pp. 269-89.

10. Jerome, *Epistula* 21.8 (*Ad Damasum*): "Nam postquam moti sunt homines ab oriente et a uero lumine recesserunt, tunc aduersum deum inpietatis suae aedificauere turrem, tunc dogmatum superbias confinxerunt uolentes curiositate non licita in ipsius caeli alta penetrare," ed. I. Hilberg, CSEL 54 (Leipzig, 1910), p. 119. The word *curiositas* occurs only once in the Latin Vulgate, when God instructed Moses and Aaron to prohibit the Ko'hathites from entering the sanctuary because of their curiosity to look upon the holy objects there, lest they die. See Num. 4:20: "Alii nulla curiositate videant quae sunt in sanctuario priusquam involvantur alioquin morientur."

sins of pride and lust.¹¹ The curious were those who indulged excessively in their own senses, but like fish swimming through the depths of the sea, they tried without success to grasp the vast emptiness of everything that flowed past them.¹² Looking outward, the curious were also more likely to take an excessive interest in the faults of others, while neglecting their own transgressions, thus imperiling their salvation. For his part, John Cassian emphasized the capacity of curiosity to erode the communal bonds of cloistered communities. Inquisitiveness lapsed into sin when the monk dwelt too long on the doings of his brethren.¹³ Gregory the Great's understanding of curiosity as a sin was informed by both of these traditions, but he had the genius to distill his concern into a pithy phrase—"the sin of curiosity is grave indeed" (*grave namque curiositatis est vitium*)—that was repeated by generation upon generation of Christian authors throughout the Middle Ages.¹⁴

In early medieval Europe, Christian ideas about the dangers of curiosity circulated most widely in western monastic communities not through the individual treatises of church fathers like Augustine, Cassian, or Gregory the Great, but rather in compendia of patristic knowledge, like the encyclopedic works of Isidore of Seville, and in anonymous yet influential florilegia, like the eighth-century *Book of Sparks* (*Liber scintillarum*).¹⁵ In his *Books of Synonyms* (*Synonymorum libri*), Isidore reminded his readers to avoid the kind of curiosity that compelled them to "look into the character of others, while unmindful of your own."¹⁶ Later in the same work, he extended this warning to excessive inquisitiveness about forbidden knowledge: "Let there be in you no curiosity for knowing hidden things. Beware of investigating things remote from human sense.

---

11. The bibliography on Augustine's concerns about the dangers of curiosity is vast. For a useful summary with reference to earlier literature, see N. J. Torchia, "Curiosity," in *Augustine Through the Ages: An Encyclopedia*, ed. A. D. Fitzgerald (Grand Rapids, MI, 1999), pp. 259–61.

12. Augustine, *Confessiones* 5.3.4: "et curiositates suas sicut pisces maris, quibus perambulant secretas semitas abyssi," ed. J. J. O'Donnell, in *Augustine: Confessions*, 3 vols. (Oxford, 1992), vol. 1, p. 47.

13. On Cassian and *curiositas*, see M. Carruthers, *The Craft of Thought: Meditation, Rhetoric, and the Making of Images, 400–1200* (Cambridge, 1998), pp. 82–84.

14. Gregory the Great, *Homiliae in Euangelia* 36.4, ed. R. Étaix, CCSL 141 (Turnhout, 1999), p. 335.

15. The repackaging of the equivocal claims of patristic authors like Augustine and Gregory as binding maxims in florilegia is an important aspect of what made them authoritative in the first place. On this important point, see J. Keskiaho, *Dreams and Visions in the Early Middle Ages: The Reception and Use of Patristic Ideas, 400–900* (Cambridge, 2015).

16. Isidore, *Synonymorum liber* 2.52: "Nulla curiositas animum tuum capiat . . . nec, oblitus tuorum morum, alienos perquiras." *PL* 83, col. 857. For more on this work, see C. Di Sciacca, *Finding the Right Words: Isidore's "Synonyma" in Anglo-Saxon England* (Toronto, 2008).

Leave as a secret what you have not learned from Scriptures."[17] In the decades around 700, a monk named Defensor from the abbey of Saint Martin at Ligugé near Poitiers drew heavily from the work of Isidore in a chapter on the dangers of curiosity in his collection of maxims and proverbs known as the *Book of Sparks*. After compiling a list of brief extracts from the Bible, Augustine, Jerome, Ambrose, and Gregory the Great, Defensor concluded his chapter with nine sentences draw from the mouth of Isidore, including a direct warning: "Curiosity is a dangerous presumption."[18] In the ninth century, Hincmar of Reims employed a vivid metaphor to underscore the risks attendant with this vice: "A curious man who investigates the affairs of another often causes his own misfortunate, like a hound that follows the tracks of a boar or a stag wisely at first, but then dies by the teeth or horn of the one it pursues."[19]

In the late eleventh century, Anselm of Bec reformulated these traditions about the dangers of curiosity in the context of the excessive zeal for new learning that he witnessed both in monasteries and beyond their walls. In his treatise *On Likenesses* (*Liber de humanis moribus per similitudines*), Anselm characterized curiosity as "the eagerness to pursue those things which there is no use in knowing."[20] He applied his imagination to the manifold expressions of inquisitiveness that could harm monks and identified forty-four different kinds of curiosity (*genera curiositatis*) to avoid.[21] Among them was astronomical inquiry, "the numbering, measuring, and considering by how much the sun and moon are distant from Earth, or how great the sun and the moon are in size."[22]

---

17. Isidore, *Synonymorum liber* 2.71: "Nulla autem sit tibi curiositas sciendi latentia. Cave indagare quae sunt a sensibus humanis remota. Praetermitte, quasi secretum, quod Scripturae auctoritate non didicisti." *PL* 83, col. 861.

18. Defensor, *Liber scintillarum* 70: "Curiositas periculosa praesumptio est," ed. D. H. M. Rochais, CCSL 117 (Turnhout, 1957), p. 212. For a positive reappraisal of this work, which has often been dismissed by scholars as derivative and unimaginative, see Y. Hen, "Defensor of Ligugé's *Liber Scintillarum* and the Migration of Knowledge," in *East and West in the Early Middle Ages: The Merovingian Kingdoms in Mediterranean Perspective*, ed. S. Esders et al. (Cambridge, 2019), pp. 218-29.

19. Hincmar, *De cavendis vitiis et virtutibus exercendis* 3: "Et saepe dum curiosus quisque quae sunt aliena investigat, suam molestiam excitat, sicut canis apri vel cervi sagaciter vestigia insequens, consecuti dente vel cornu perit." *PL* 125, col. 886.

20. Anselm, *Liber de humanis moribus per similitudines* 26: "Curiositas est studium perscrutandi ea, quae scire nulla est utilitas," ed. R. W. Southern and F. S. Schmitt, in *Memorials of St. Anselm*, Auctores Britannici Medii Aevi 1 (London, 1969), p. 47.

21. Anselm, *Liber de humanis moribus* 26-36, ed. Southern and Schmitt, pp. 47-50.

22. Anselm, *Liber de humanis moribus* 28: "ut cum aliquis enumerat et mensurat et considerat, quantum sol et luna distent a terra vel quam magna sint ipsa luminaria," ed. Southern and Schmitt, p. 48.

Anselm was criticizing a long history of lunar and stellar observation by monks that dated back hundreds of years to Bede and reached its fruition around the turn of the first millennium in Lotharingia, which "served as an important seed-bed for new scientific ideas and practices that had trickled into Christian Europe thanks to contacts with the Muslim-dominated parts of the Iberian peninsula."[23] Among these monastic scientists in Lotharingia was Walcher of Malvern, whose use of an astrolabe to calculate the exact time of a lunar eclipse in 1092 has been widely recognized as a significant milestone of observational science.[24] Anselm would not have approved, but as we will see, his ideas about curiosity did not have the same purchase in the monastic tradition as those of his near contemporary, Bernard of Clairvaux.

Cistercian Curiosity

Despite its absence from the *Rule of Benedict*, the sin of curiosity was a well-established vice by the early twelfth century because of the authoritative proscriptions of Augustine, John Cassian, and Gregory the Great, which were echoed by early medieval authors and disseminated widely in monastic florilegia. Drawing on these traditions, Bernard of Clairvaux elevated curiosity to a new status among the vices in his treatise *On the Steps of Pride and Humility* (*De gradibus superbiae et humilitatis*), which is the source of the litany of vices to the right of the line drawing of the ascending monk in Admont 567.[25] Written in the early 1120s, this treatise was addressed to Geoffrey of Roche-Vanneau, Bernard's cousin and companion during his entry to Clairvaux, who was the first abbot of Fontenay (1113–1118) and later became prior of Clairvaux (1118–1126) and bishop of Langres (1138–1168).[26] It was at his request that Bernard prepared this treatise on the degrees of humility outlined in the seventh chapter of the *Rule of Benedict*. The work falls into two parts: the first part (§1–11) on the virtue of humility and the second part (§12–22) on the corresponding sin of pride. The treatise was immensely popular both

---

23. Walcher of Malvern, *Walcher of Malvern, "De Lunationibus" and "De Dracone": Study, Edition, Translation, and Commentary*, ed. and trans. C. P. E. Nothaft (Turnhout, 2017), p. 15.
24. See C. P. E. Nothaft, *Scandalous Error: Calendar Reform and Calendrial Astronomy in Medieval Europe* (Oxford, 2018), pp. 80–85 ("Walcher of Malvern and the Tipping Point of Latin Astronomy").
25. Hereafter *De gradibus* in the notes. For the Latin edition, see *SBO*, vol. 3, pp. 13–59.
26. On the date of *De gradibus*, see *SBO*, vol. 3, pp. 3–4.

during Bernard's lifetime and after his death, surviving in sixty-nine manuscripts from the twelfth and early thirteenth centuries alone.[27]

Like Augustine before him, Bernard's treatise wedded the sin of pride with that of curiosity, but the abbot of Clairvaux amplified its significance, devoting more words to this particular vice than to any of the others associated with pride.[28] Although Benedict's humble monk always assumed a posture that signaled the submission of his heart and his body with his head bowed and his eyes fixed on the ground whether he was sitting, walking, or standing, the bearing of Bernard's curious monk betrayed his intention: he could not help but to raise his head, to roam with his eyes, and to perk up his ears.[29] Only under certain circumstances could the monk raise his eyes without fault, for example, out of necessity for the welfare of himself or one of his brethren.[30] In most cases, however, any prideful searching was comparable to the ancient transgressions of Dinah and Eve, and even the Devil, each of whom, Bernard explained, had succumbed to the lure of curiosity. In the Book of Genesis, Dinah was a daughter of Jacob, who was raped by Shechem the Hivite when she went out on her own "to see the women of that country."[31] What purpose did it serve Dinah to venture forth alone, Bernard asked, other than to satisfy her "hateful curiosity" (*otiosam curiositatem*)? Not only did Dinah's inquisitiveness bring ruin upon herself, but it also brought ruin on everyone around her, including her brothers, who ignored a peace treaty brokered by their father and murdered the Hevites for the offense against their sister. Eve, too, was a thrall to curiosity, when her wandering eyes spied the fruit of the tree of the knowledge of good and evil.[32] According to Bernard, the Devil increased her "interest" (*curam*) while arousing her taste for the

---

27. Bernard promoted *De gradibus* during his lifetime, recommending it first among his shorter works to Cardinal Peter in *Ep.* 18. See *SBO*, vol. 3, p. 3.

28. For what follows, see R. Newhauser, "The Sin of Curiosity and the Cistercians," in *Erudition at God's Service: Studies in Medieval Cistercian History*, ed. J. R. Sommerfeldt (Kalamazoo, MI, 1987), pp. 71–95; and, more generally, Leclercq, "*Curiositas* and the Return to God," pp. 92–100.

29. Compare *RB* 7.63: "Monachus . . . ubicumque sedens, ambulans uel stans inclinator sit semper capite defixis in terram aspectibus"; and *De gradibus* 10.28: "Si videris monachum, de quo prius bene confidebas, ubicumque stat, ambulat, sedet, oculis incipientem vagare, caput erectum, aures portare suspensas, e motibus exterioris hominis interiorem immutatum agnoscas," in *SBO*, vol. 3, p. 38.

30. *De gradibus* 10.29: "Tu quoque si locum, tempus et causam considerans, tua vel fratris necessitate oculos levas, non solum non culpa, sed et plurimum laudo," in *SBO*, vol. 3, p. 39.

31. Gen. 34:1: "ut uideret mulieres regionis illius."

32. Gen. 3:1–6. For what follows, see *De gradibus* 10.30, in *SBO*, vol. 3, pp. 39–40.

fruit; he sharpened her "curiosity" (*curiositatem*) while prompting her desire. As a result, she took the fruit and surrendered paradise. Like Dinah, Eve's curiosity led not only to her ruin, but to the fall of the entire human race, for it placed "a heavy yoke upon all of your sons down to the present day."[33] The Devil was clearly instrumental in arousing Eve's curiosity, but he too was the victim of his own thirst for knowledge. His sin was to attempt to comprehend secrets that belonged only to God. In the end, the Seraphim cast down the rebel angel, who fell from truth because of his inquisitiveness, drawn by his eyes to what he desired illicitly and yearned for presumptively.[34] Through these ancient examples, Bernard warned his readers that the threat of curiosity lay in seeking knowledge beyond yourself: "Keep to yourself lest you fall from yourself," he wrote, "if you tread among the great and wonderous things above you."[35]

Bernard's elevation of curiosity as a key accomplice to pride among the sins most likely to threaten the well-being of human souls soon found expression in the works of other Cisterican authors of the twelfth century, including but not limited to the line drawing of the ascending monk found in Admont 567. The most important of these was Galand of Reigny, an admirer of Bernard who wrote a handbook of spiritual and moral instruction for monks sometime in the late 1130s or 1140s. Known as the *Parabolarium*, Galand's manual conveyed its lessons in the form of parables, that is, pithy allegorical stories with a moral point.[36] These stories covered a range of concerns from theological topics like the doctrine of atonement to practical concerns like the distinction between cloistered monks and obedientiaries, those officials who held special offices that gave them autonomy and freedom of movement within the abbey. Galand devoted a long chapter to a conversation among the vices (*De colloquio vitiorum*), ten in number, each of which he personified as a woman in the tradition of Prudentius's *Psychomachia*. One by one, the vices praised their unique capacity to lead human beings into sin. The chief among them and the last to speak was pride, who boasted: "Who, other than me, cast Lucifer from Heaven? Who

---

33. *De gradibus* 10.30: "grave iugum super omnes filios tuos usque in hodiernum diem," in *SBO*, vol. 3, p. 40.

34. *De gradibus* 10.35 and 10.38, in *SBO*, vol. 3, pp. 43 and 45.

35. *De gradibus* 10.31: "Sta in te, ne cadas a te, si ambulas in magnis et in mirabilibus super te," in *SBO*, vol. 3, p. 40.

36. Galand of Reigny, *Parabolarium*, ed. and trans. C. Friedlander, J. Leclercq, and G. Aciti, in *Galand of Reigny: Parabolarium*, SC 378 (Paris, 1992).

evicted humankind from paradise? For I am the font and origin of all evil; I am the spark of every sin."[37] Speaking directly before pride, however, and thus second in rank among the ten assembled vices was curiosity herself. After she entered the conversation unbidden, the other sins demanded to know her authority for taking such an exalted place among them. She replied in this way:

> My role is . . . to examine and learn about whatever goes on and wherever it goes on, whether great or small, not pertaining to me whatsoever nor having any use for me . . . While I occupy the minds of men with such trifles, I divert them from the investigation of what is true and useful, so that, while they seek what is shallow, they forsake what is necessary and waste the time given to them for acquiring eternal life on things which are not useful for that task. And why do I make them investigate others' sins while they neglect their own? Because the more they censure those sins, the more they forget their own.[38]

Inspired by the abbot of Clairvaux, to whom the *Parabolarium* was dedicated, Galand was the first Latin author to personify the sin of curiosity as a woman and to place her so prominently in the cohort of vices inherited by medieval Christians from late antique monastic authorities.

Curiosity and Discipline in Twelfth-Century Monastic Polemic

Once the early Cistercians had promoted curiosity as the deputy vice of pride, it did not take them long to level the charge of inquisitiveness against their monastic rivals, most notably the Cluniacs. In his *Justification to Abbot William* (*Apologia ad Guillelmum abbatem*) written around 1125, Bernard assailed the brethren of Cluny for adorning their church

---

37. Galand, *Parabolarium* 16.10: "Quis enim, nisi ego, Luciferum de caelo proiecit? Quis hominem de paradiso? Denique ego fons et origo totius mali, ego initium omnis peccati," ed. Friedlander, Leclercq, and Aciti, p. 286.

38. Galand, *Parabolarium* 16.9: "'Meum,' inquit, 'est rumoribus audiendis vacare et quidquid ubicumque fit, magnum vel modicum, eitiam nihil ad me pertinens, etiam nihil commodi habens, perscrutari ac discere . . . Talibus nugis dum mentes hominum occupo, a veri et utilis inquisitione averto ut, cum superflua quaerunt, necessaria relinquant et tempus aeternae vitae acquirendae datum, in non profuturis expendant. Quid quod aliorum peccata, propriis neglectis, eos discutere facio? Quae quo magis insequuntur, eo plus suorum obliviscuntur'," ed. Friedlander, Leclercq, and Aciti, p. 284; trans. Newhauser, "The Sin of Curiosity," p. 72 (modified).

with gold ornaments and rich decorations, especially the distracting images (*curiosas depictiones*) that "divert the attention of those who are praying and thereby impede their devotion."[39] Likewise, a generation later, the Cistercian Idung of Prüfening criticized the Cluniacs in his *Dialogue Between Two Monks* (*Dialogus duorum monachorum*) not for the curiosity of their eyes, but rather for the inquisitiveness of their ears (*aurium curiositas*), which abandoned necessity and utility in their desire to hear "many large bells of different tones and of such great size that two monks together can barely sound them because of their great weight."[40] By defining the sin of curiosity in terms of an inordinate love of *vanitates ac superfluitates* that distracted devout Christians from the pursuit of their salvation, the early Cistercians criticized the luxuries of the Cluniacs as proof that their roving senses—their wandering eyes and their perked-up ears—undermined their allegedly hallowed way of life.

Bernard of Clairvaux composed his *Justification to Abbot William* in the early years of the abbacy of Peter the Venerable, when lingering loyalties to Peter's predecessor Pontius of Melgueil divided the monastic community at Cluny, leading to rebellion and violence.[41] It took several years for Peter to regain control over his house. The culmination of this effort was the convocation of an unprecedented general chapter meeting in 1132, which brought hundreds of Cluniac priors and monks to the great Burgundian abbey. On this occasion, Peter issued a series of administrative decrees aimed at introducing a stricter way of life in Cluny's dependencies, including the imposition of new fasts and the curtailing of time set aside for conversation in the cloister. According to the Norman chronicler Orderic Vitalis, who attended the meeting, Peter met with resistance from his brethren and later softened his position, but during the first two decades of his abbacy, he managed to introduce

---

39. Bernard, *Apologia ad Guillelmum abbatem* 12.28: "Curiosas depictiones, quae dum in se orantium retorquent aspectum, impediunt et affectum," in *SBO*, vol. 3, p. 104. For more on the theme of Bernard's concern with visual excess in churches, see C. Rudolph, *"The Things of Greater Importance": Bernard of Clairvaux's "Apologia" and the Medieval Attitude Toward Art* (Philadelphia, 1990).

40. Idung of Prüfening, *Dialogus duorum monachorum* 1.40: "Multas diversi soni et tam diversi ponderis campanas, ut aliquam earum propter nimium pondus eius vix duo monachi pulsare possint, non requirit necessarues usus, sed aurium curiositas," ed. R. B. C. Huygens, in *Le moine Idung et ses deux ouvrages: "Argumentum super quatuor questionibus" et "Dialogus duorum monachorum"* (Spoleto, 1980), p. 107. On the positive role of church bells in medieval Christian communities, see J. H. Arnold and C. Goodson, "Resounding Community: The History and Meaning of Medieval Church Bells," *Viator* 43 (2012): 99–130.

41. On the tumultuous abbacy of Pontius, see J. Wollasch, "Das Schisma des Abtes Pontius von Cluny," *Francia* 23 (1996): 31–52.

many modifications to Cluniac customs.⁴² In 1146/1147, the abbot of Cluny codified these changes in a collection of seventy-six legal statutes (*statuta*) introduced by a preface.⁴³ Most of these statutes lacked temporal markers, so it is unclear when exactly they were written, but each of them included a rationale for the changes made to Cluniac custom, which provides valuable insight into the abbot's thinking.

Scholars have not been able to agree about the impetus behind Peter the Venerable's reforming activities. Were the statutes an answer to Cistercian critiques of Cluniac customs or were they simply expressive of twelfth-century trends in Benedictine monasticism?⁴⁴ The fact that the abbot of Cluny made mention of the danger of *curiositas* in several of his rationales for statutes that specifically addressed customs that had been condemned by Bernard of Clairvaux suggests that at least some of this legislation was indeed responsive to Cisterican criticisms of the Cluniacs. The abbot of Clairvaux was a keen observer of the details of contemporary religious life and he did not mask his disdain for any aspect of monastic custom that strayed from the letter of the *Rule of Benedict*. In his *Justification to Abbot William*, Bernard complained at length about the opulent garments worn by some monks, when Benedict's rule had specifically instructed them to purchase the cheapest possible clothing. Harkening back to the community of the apostles, where all goods were shared according to need and no one coveted anything for themselves "in the manner of a child" (*pueriliter*), Bernard wrote, "Obviously, where only that which was needed was allowed, nothing superfluous was sanctioned there, how much less anything curious, how much less anything sumptuous."⁴⁵ Certainly, no one there ever sought to wear a garment of silk (*galabrunum*) or satin (*isembrunum*); certainly, no one there enjoyed the luxury of a catskin coverlet for their bed (*lectulum opertorium cattinum*) or a multicolored bedspread (*discolor barricanus*).⁴⁶

---

42. Orderic Vitalis, *Historia ecclesiastica* 13.13, ed. and trans. M. Chibnall, in *The Ecclesiastical History of Orderic Vitalis*, 6 vols. (Oxford, 1969–80), vol. 6, pp. 426–27.

43. On the formative place in the statutes in the legislative history of Cluny, see G. Melville, "Action, Text, and Validity: On Re-Examining Cluny's *Consuetudines* and Statutes," in *From Dead of Night to End of Day: The Medieval Customs of Cluny / Du coeur de la nuit à la fin du jour: Les coutumes clunisiennes au moyen âge*, ed. S. Boynton and I. Cochelin, Disciplina monastica 3 (Turnhout, 2005), pp. 67–84.

44. *Statuta*, pp. 22–24, with J.-P. Torrell and D. Bouthillier, *Pierre le Vénérable et sa vision du monde: Sa vie, son oeuvre, l'homme et le demon* (Leuven, 1986), pp. 38–39.

45. Bernard, *Apologia* 10.24: "Sane ubi tantum quod opus erat accipiebatur, ibi procul dubio nihil otiosum admittebatur, quanto magis nihil curiosum, quanto magis nihil superbum," in *SBO*, vol. 3, p. 101.

46. Bernard, *Apologia* 10.24, in *SBO*, vol. 3, p. 101.

In the late 1140s, Peter the Venerable issued a set of statutes that specifically prohibited the kinds of clothing, furs, and bedding that Bernard had criticized two decades earlier in his *Justification to Abbot William*.[47] In particular, the abbot of Cluny forbade his monks from wearing fabrics made of silk (*galabrunum*) and satin (*isembrunum*), using the very same, very rare Latin terminology for these materials that Bernard had used.[48] Likewise, Peter did not permit his brethren to wear garments made from cat hide or any other exotic fur that they had been accustomed to wear.[49] Lastly, they should avoid the use of bedspreads that were dyed red or decorated in any fashion or otherwise ornate in any way.[50] Moreover, in the rationale for each of these amendments to Cluniac customs, Peter echoed Bernard's concern that these items were not only superfluous to the religious life but also dangerously distracting to the devout monk. Again and again, he railed against "the shameful and disgraceful curiosity" (*inhonesta ac turpis curiositas*), "the significant and damnable curiosity" (*notabilis et damnabilis curiositas*), and "the condemnable curiosity" (*damnata curiositas*) aroused by the use of these kinds of clothing, fur, and bedding in the abbey.[51]

In the later Middle Ages, long after the controversy between the Cistercians and the Cluniacs had ended, monastic preachers returned time and again to the theme of curiosity as a dangerous distraction for monks. To take one example, in a popular *exemplum* told and retold by Jacques de Vitry (c. 1160/1170–1240), Stephen of Bourbon (c. 1180–1261), and many others, a hermit complained loudly that Adam should have resisted tasting the fruit of the tree of the knowledge of good and evil and thus spared humankind its unfortunate fate.[52] To teach the hermit a lesson, one of his companions placed a mouse under a bowl and forbade him to look underneath it. When he was alone, the hermit could not resist his own curiosity. He lifted the bowl and quickly realized his folly when the mouse scurried away. When his companion returned, he rebuked the hermit with the following words: "You blamed Adam because he so lightly transgressed the command, but you have

---

47. *Statuta* 16–18 and 70, pp. 54–56 and 100.
48. *Statuta* 16, p. 54.
49. *Statuta* 17, p. 55.
50. *Statuta* 18, p. 56.
51. *Statuta* 16–18, pp. 54–56.
52. For a summary of the story and a discussion of its enduring influence down to the modern period, see *The Exempla or Illustrative Stories from the "Sermones Vulgares" of Jacques de Vitry*, ed. T. F. Crane (London, 1890), p. 139.

transgressed it even more lightly."[53] Chastened in this way by his inability to bridle his inquisitiveness, the hermit's anger for Adam turned to pity. The message of the story was clear: curiosity was such an alluring and dangerous temptation that it had caused the Fall of Man.

Curiosity and Cloistered Women at Twelfth-Century Admont

Given the authority and influence of Bernard of Clairvaux, the sin of curiosity became an important feature of Benedictine discourse in the twelfth century, but the artistic expression of *curiositas* as the gateway sin on the litany of vices prefacing the *Rule of Benedict* in Admont 567 suggests that the community at Admont had a preoccupation with the threat posed by monastic inquisitiveness. Founded in 1074 as an exclusively male house by Archbishop Gebhard of Salzburg (1060-1088), Admont became a double monastery with adjacent male and female communities sometime between 1116 and 1120 under the influence of the Hirsau reforms initiated by Abbot Wolfhold (1115-1138).[54] Wary of the dangers posed by the proximity of their female counterparts, the monks of Admont kept the nuns locked in their enclosure at all times. When a fire roared through the community in 1152, they had to break down the locked door to free them.[55] From Abbot Irimbert's account of this event, we learn that a single tripled-locked door provided access to the female community. The keys to these locks were distributed between the *magistra* who oversaw the women and two of the senior brethren. Under normal circumstances, the nuns used this portal twice: once to enter their community upon their profession and once again to leave upon their death. Their interaction with the outside world took place primarily through a small window.

Despite their separation, the monks and nuns of Admont interacted frequently on intellectual projects, including the production of manuscripts. As the research of Alison Beach has shown, Admont's female religious were active both as scribes and as authors of documents of practice, like charters, as well as letters, biblical exegesis, saints' lives, and

---

53. The translation is from Crane, *The Exempla or Illustrative Stories*, p. 139.
54. On the early history of Admont, see Beach, *Women as Scribes*, pp. 66-68.
55. For a breathless account of this disaster, which destroyed many of the buildings at Admont, see Irimbert, *De incendio monasterii sui ac vita et moribus virginum sanctimonialium Parthenonis Admontensis narratio*, ed. B. Pez, in *Bibliotheca ascetica antiquonova*, 12 vols. (Regensburg, 1723-25), vol. 8, pp. 455-64. For more on the career and writings of Irimbert, see J. W. Braun, "Irimbert von Admont," *Frühmittelalterliche Studien* 7 (1973): 226-323.

even a chronicle of world history.[56] Their scribal industry often involved direct commerce with the monks, as was the case when Abbot Irimbert dictated his commentary on 4 Kings to two sisters who, excused from their regular duties, "continually and diligently transcribed on tablets what was spoken by me" (*que continue ac dilgenter transcriberent, que a me dicta in tabulis excipi potuissent*).[57] Rubrication in a surviving Admont manuscript suggests that nuns named Irmingart and Regilind were also instrumental in either transcribing or copying Irimbert's commentaries on Ruth and Judges 19-21.[58] Despite working in "segregated scriptoria" behind a triple-locked door, the women of Admont clearly played an active role in the intellectual life of their male counterparts.[59]

The strict claustration of the Admont nuns did not prohibit sanctioned interaction with their male counterparts, but this commerce between the sexes may have caused anxiety about the dangers of inquisitiveness that provided the context for the creation of the line drawing in Admont 567.[60] This image is especially poignant if we consider that the manuscript was likely made for, and perhaps even created by, the nuns. The contents of Admont 567 strongly suggest that this manuscript was, in fact, the nuns' chapter house book.[61] It included Usuard's martyrology (fols. 1r-44r); a profession formula in German for the nuns of Admont (fol. 44v); a letter of Pope Innocent II to the nuns of Admont (fol. 45r-v); the line drawing of a monk ascending to Christ (fol. 46r); the *Rule of Benedict* (47r-86v); and an unpublished homiliary (fols. 87r-141v). In addition to the inclusion of the profession formula and the letter of Innocent II to the nuns, the manuscript's copy of the *Rule of Benedict* has been modified in three places to inflect the work for an audience of women. The interlinear insertion of *sororibus* above the

---

56. Beach, *Women as Scribes*, pp. 72-77.
57. Braun, "Irimbert von Admont," p. 320; trans. Beach, *Women as Scribes*, p. 86.
58. Admont, Benediktinerstift, Codex 17. See Beach, *Women as Scribes*, pp. 86-87.
59. A. Beach, "Claustration and Collaboration Between the Sexes in the Twelfth-Century Scriptorium," in *Monks and Nuns, Saints and Outcasts: Religion in Medieval Society*, ed. S. Farmer and B. Rosenwein (Ithaca, 2000), pp. 57-75, at p. 66.
60. For examples of the complexities and anxieties involved in the close proximity of male and female religious in twelfth-century double monasteries, see A. Beach, *The Trauma of Monastic Reform: Community and Conflict in Twelfth-Century Germany* (Cambridge, 2017), pp. 73-92. More generally on concerns about the pastoral care of cloistered women by men, see F. Griffiths, *Nuns' Priests' Tales: Men and Salvation in Medieval Women's Monastic Life* (Philadelphia, 2018).
61. *Krone und Schleier: Kunst aus mittelalterlichen Frauenklöstern*, ed. J. Frings (Munich, 2005), p. 323 (no. 214), where the manuscript is called "ein typisches Kapiteloffiziumsbuch mit den Texten für die täglichen Lesungen im Nonnenkapital."

words *infirmis fratribus* (fol. 69r), the addition of *et sorores* above the word *fratres* (fol. 75v), and the modification of *monacho* to *monache* (fol. 77r) are all indicative of female use.

If Admont 567 was, in fact, the chapter house book of the nuns of Admont, what implication does it have for the line drawing of the climbing monk, if the scribe or artist or audience was female rather than male? In his treatise on pride and humility, Bernard of Clairvaux singled out the agency of two biblical women (Dinah and Eve) in examples about the dangers of curiosity with consequences both for the women and for the men proximate to them. The Cistercian abbot's warning about inquisitiveness applied even more readily to the nuns of Admont than to the monks, because as Dinah and Eve showed, women were allegedly more susceptible to curiosity than men. This lesson was apparently not lost on the women of Admont, who had access to Bernard's treatise in a twelfth-century manuscript of the abbot's works (Admont, Benediktinerstift, Codex 380, fols. 50r–78v). This book had been copied by one of their male counterparts, a monk of Admont named Fridricus, who identified himself in a colophon as *Admuntensi claustro monasteriensi oblatus* (fol. 182v).[62] Bernard's promotion of *curiositas* as a sin comparable to pride that implicated women even more so than men may have inspired the unknown scribe of Admont 567, who was perhaps a woman, to render this table of virtues and vices with the line drawing of the climbing monk prominently in the nun's chapter book. This served as a firm reminder for the nuns of Admont to guard their modesty and act humbling in their interactions with their neighboring brethren, lest the lure of inquisitiveness doom both them and the men with whom they enjoyed intellectual commerce. For, as Admont 567 reminded its female readers, curiosity not only killed the monk, but the nun as well.

Despite the absence of curiosity as a concern in the sixth-century *Rule of Benedict*, which emerged as the authoritative statement on the organization and operation of cloistered communities from the ninth century onward, there was unanimity among early medieval authors that inquisitiveness was a dangerous distraction for monks to pursue. In late antiquity, patristic authors like Augustine and Gregory the Great called attention to the dangers of curiosity for Christians and warned

---

62. Wichner, *Catalogus codicum*, pp. 175–76; and M. Mairold, *Die datierten Handschriften in der Steiermark außerhalb der Universitätsbibliothek Graz bis 1600*, 2 vols. (Vienna, 1988), vol. 1, p. 173 and vol. 2, fig. 405.

that inquiry into the sins of others could cause individuals to overlook their own faults and thus jeopardize their salvation. In the early Middle Ages, compilers of patristic florilegia for monastic audiences confected their collections with carefully curated excerpts from the writings of the church fathers and honed the message that curiosity was a grave threat to the communal life. During the eleventh century, Anselm provided monastic readers with the longest and most detailed list of dangerous lines of inquiry, including lunar and stellar observation, but it was Bernard of Clairvaux's early twelfth-century treatise *On the Steps of Humility and Pride* that captured the monastic imagination and dominated the discourse on the sin of curiosity for the rest of the Middle Ages. Bernard's treatise was copied dozens of times in the decades after its composition, including at the double monastery of Admont, where its contents inspired the line drawing of the monk ascending a ladder to Christ in the nuns' chapter book, Admont 567. As this drawing clearly shows, the humble monk was not hindered in his climb to Heaven if he kept his sights firmly on Christ, but if for any reason his eyes roved in curiosity, especially toward the women cloistered nearby, he could easily begin a descent from grace that would ultimately result in rebellion against his community and the loss of his salvation.

Chapter 14

The Dark Age of Herodotus
Shards of a Fugitive History in Early Medieval Europe

The *Histories* of Herodotus of Helicarnassus (c. 485–425 BCE), one of the earliest known works of historiography in the western tradition, were not read during the European Middle Ages.[1] Writing in the Ionic dialect of Greek, Herodotus set out to explain why the Persian Empire went to war with the city-states of Greece in the early fifth century BCE. He was well known in antiquity as "the father of history," but after a millennium of currency, knowledge of his *Histories* withered in the fifth century CE with the disappearance of Greek as a living language in Western Europe and the rise of providential Christian histories. This much is well known, but it does not explain how a twelfth-century monk knew a story from Herodotus's *Histories*. In a

---

Originally published as "The Dark Age of Herodotus: Shards of a Fugitive History in Early Medieval Europe," *Speculum* 94 (2019): 47–67. Reprinted with permission.

1. The standard critical edition of Herodotus remains *Herodoti Historiae*, ed. C. Hude, 3rd ed., 2 vols. (Oxford, 1927), cited hereafter by book and chapter. *The Landmark Herodotus: The Histories*, ed. R. B. Strassler (New York, 2009) boasts excellent maps, rich annotations, and useful ancillary essays. The literature on the narrative techniques, historical method, and ancient reception of Herodotus is enormous. Modern scholars remain indebted to F. Jacoby's masterful survey, which laid the groundwork for all future study, in *Paulys Realencyclopëdie der classischen Altertumswissenshaft*, ed. W. Kroll, Supplementband 2 (Stuttgart, 1913), cols. 205–520 (*s.v.* Herodotos); repr. in F. Jacoby, *Griechische Historiker* (Stuttgart, 1956), pp. 7–164.

polemical letter written in the late 1130s, Abbot Peter the Venerable of Cluny (1122–1156) retold an historical anecdote first attested in the *Histories*, when he compared the impudence of a heretical Christian sect known as the Petrobrusians to the arrogance of King Cyrus the Great, the founder of the Achaemenid Empire who lived in the sixth century BCE:

> But perhaps you have resolved to emulate in rivalry the audacious pride of King Cyrus, who wanted to avenge a beloved horse that had been swallowed up by the mighty river which is called the Ganges [*sic* for Gyndes]. The king raged against the river and, interrupting the crossing that he was going to make with his foot-soldiers, he fulfilled his promises. Dividing the mighty swells of the waves into three hundred and more channels, the proud king diminished the river's pride and, diverting through many channels a waterway whose vastness would scarcely have respected even a flotilla of ships, he made that river, as he put it, crossable without getting one's feet wet.[2]

Although ancient Greeks and Romans would have recognized the story of King Cyrus's vengeance against the Gyndes River from Herodotus, it is unclear how a Christian abbot of the twelfth century learned this ancient tale, for Peter knew no Greek and the *Histories* were not available in the Latin language until the fifteenth century, when the early Italian humanist Lorenzo Valla (c. 1406–57) applied his formidable energy to translating both Herodotus and Thucydides at the request of Pope Nicholas V (1447–1455).[3] How can we explain the cultural currency of this story for the abbot of Cluny when it was written

---

2. Peter the Venerable, *Contra Petrobrusianos* 121: "Sed forte uos animosam Cyri regis arrogantiam emulati imitari proposuistis, qui, absorbtum maximo flumine, qui Ganges dicitur, dilectum equitem ulcisci cupiens, exarsit in flumen, et peruium se peditibus facturum comminans, impleuit promissa. In trecentos enim et eo amplius alueos tumentes undarum moles dispartiens, superbiam fluminis superbus imminuit, et per plures tramites unius magnitudinem deriuans, naualem uix pompam dignantem, siccis, ut dixerat, pedibus fluuium meabilem fecit," ed. J. Fearns, CCCM 10 (Turnhout, 1968), pp. 71–72. Compare Herodotus 1.189. The river in question was not the Ganges, as Peter falsely remembered the story, but the Gyndes, a tributary of the Tigris (perhaps the Diyala River in modern Iraq). For more on the fluidity of this river's name in Latin sources, see n. 58 below.

3. E. B. Fryde, "Some Fifteenth-Century Latin Translations of Ancient Greek Historians," in E. B. Fryde, *Humanism and Renaissance Historiography* (London, 1983), pp. 87–99. See also P. Burke, "A Survey of the Popularity of Ancient Historians, 1450–1700," *History and Theory* 5 (1966): 135–52, on the earliest printed editions of ancient historians and their early modern audiences.

more than sixteen hundred years before he was born in a language he did not understand?

Studies of the transmission and reception of Greek and Roman literature in medieval Europe flourished throughout the twentieth century and have shown no signs of abating.[4] The pivotal role played by monastic communities as the primary agents in the preservation of ancient texts is a commonplace in academic literature and in popular conceptions of the Middle Ages.[5] Scholars who lend their industry to the analysis of medieval manuscripts containing works originally written by Greek and Roman authors invariably find themselves reading over the shoulders of early medieval monks, who painstakingly copied voluminous texts by hand as an expression of their ascetic discipline. The time and expense required to construct and transcribe a vellum manuscript in the early Middle Ages was so prohibitive that monks did not have the leisure to copy texts that they were not going to read again and again. In most cases, classical works survived the end of antiquity because monastic readers admired their beauty of expression and found ways to repurpose their content for Christian readers. Evidence for the consumption of ancient texts in early medieval abbeys takes many forms, from laconic marginal notations in the manuscripts to the composition of glosses and commentaries that direct the reader to the Christian meaning of their pagan content to the imitation of the style and vocabulary of classical authors in works written by medieval monks. From Augustine's tearful response to Dido's suicide in Virgil's *Aeneid* in the fourth century to Gabriel Harvey's bloody-minded rumination on the *Histories* of Livy in the early seventeenth century, there can be no doubt, that ancient literature exerted an enormous influence

---

4. M. R. James, *The Wanderings and Homes of Manuscripts* (London, 1919) is an early example, rich with illuminating anecdotes. *Texts and Transmission: A Survey of the Latin Classics*, ed. L. D. Reynolds (Oxford, 1983) remains indispensable. L. D. Reynolds and N. G. Wilson, *Scribes and Scholars: A Guide to the Transmission of Greek and Latin Literature*, 4th ed. (Oxford, 2014) provides an excellent up-to-date introduction, even for nonspecialists. For a case study, see S. O'Sullivan, "Glossing Vergil and Pagan Learning in the Carolingian Age," *Speculum* 93 (2018): 132–65.

5. See, for example, B. Bischoff, *Manuscripts and Libraries in the Age of Charlemagne*, trans. M. Gorman (Cambridge, 1994), esp. 134–59 ("Benedictine Libraries and the Survival of Classical Literature"). An egregious exception is S. Greenblatt, *The Swerve: How the World Became Modern* (New York, 2011), which unconvincingly dismisses the participation of early medieval monks in the transmission of Lucretius's poem *De rerum natura* to trumpet the role of Italian humanists like Poggio Bracciolini as the "true" discoverers of this text. See the pointed review by M. W. Herren in *Journal of Medieval Latin* 22 (2012): 295–301, esp. p. 298, on Greenblatt's uninformed depiction of monastic literary habits.

on the intellectual and cultural formation of Christian readers in premodern Europe.[6]

Despite the ascendence of providential history in the Christian tradition, which obviated the relevance of the *Histories* for medieval readers, stories originally told by Herodotus survived into the Latin Middle Ages like flower petals pressed into the pages of a book. In this chapter, I offer a case study of the reception history of the Herodotean echo preserved in Peter the Venerable's treatise against the Petrobrusians. After examining the ambivalent reputation of Herodotus's *Histories* among Greek and Roman readers, I turn to the abbot of Cluny and work to unspool his tale of the vengeance of King Cyrus back through history from the twelfth century to its sources in Roman antiquity, a period when the pragmatics of reading on papyrus scrolls and the pedagogical habits of Roman schools fragmented the *Histories* into a myriad of literary shards. The reception history of Herodotus, I argue, is the history of the trajectory of these literary shards, how the whims and designs of late antique authors of historical epitomes and compendia carried them into the Latin Middle Ages, and how medieval readers redeemed them for purposes far removed from their ancient source. Peter the Venerable was certainly not the only medieval author to deploy a story originally told by Herodotus in this fashion. A sounding of a wide range of texts composed between the sixth and the eleventh centuries reveals that shards of the *Histories* entered the medieval literary tradition in numerous ways, most often through the agency of late Roman intermediaries. Long after the *Histories* had lost their currency in Western Europe, indeed long after the name Herodotus had lost its association with the writing of history, these ancient stories endured as new readers rediscovered them and wrought new meanings from them.

Father of History, Father of Lies

Herodotus has not fared nearly as well as other ancient Greek authors in the western tradition. Ancient readers were ambivalent at best, devouring and denouncing the *Histories* in equal measure for centuries after their composition in the early fifth century BCE.[7] Herodotus's younger

---

6. See, respectively, S. MacCormack, *The Shadows of Poetry: Vergil in the Mind of Augustine* (Berkeley, 1998); and L. Jardine and A. Grafton, "'Studied for Action': How Gabriel Harvey Read His Livy," *Past & Present* 129 (1990): 30–78.

7. On the reception of Herodotus in the Greek and Roman traditions, see A. Momigliano, "The Place of Herodotus in the History of Historiography," *History* 43 (1958): 1–13, repr. in A. Momigliano, *Studies in Historiography* (London, 1966), pp. 127–42; K.-A. Riemann, *Das*

contemporary Thucydides (d. c. 395 BCE) was the first to call into question his rival's methodology, in particular by raising doubts about his reliability when writing about events in the past that he had not witnessed and narrating the customs of peoples whose languages he did not understand. He clearly had Herodotus in mind when he debased those "prose chroniclers, who are less interested in telling the truth than in catching the attention of the public, whose authorities cannot be checked, and whose subject-matter, owing to the passage of time, is mostly lost in the unreliable streams of mythology" (1.21).[8] In contrast, Thucydides's participation in the long conflict between Athens and Sparta invested his account, the *History of the Peloponnesian War*, with the reliability of eyewitness testimony. Despite his disparagements, Thucydides was clearly indebted to Herodotus's *Histories*, in particular for information on the Persian Wars, but also in his habit of offering commentary on the motivations of the historical figures who populate his text.[9]

For all of the criticism leveled against the reliability of his sources, the influence of Herodotus on ancient Greek historians was profound, especially in the early Hellenistic period.[10] The influence of Herodotus on Roman authors was no less great, beginning in the later Republic, when the Roman rout of the Macedonians at Pydna (168 BCE) and the sack of Athens by Sulla (86 BCE) surrendered troves of Greek literary plunder to the West. The barbs of Thucydides and many other detractors held firm, however. To readers of ancient Greek, the *Histories* had a superficial charm, to be sure, but Herodotus was not a trustworthy historian; he was always suspected of being a spinner of tall tales, a liar. In the preface to his treatise *On the Laws*, Cicero captured the ambivalent assessment of the *Histories* that the Romans had inherited from the Greeks when he praised Herodotus as the "father of history" (*patrem historiae*) and at the same time likened him to Theopompus (d. c. 315

---

herodoteische Geschichtswerk in der Antike (Munich, 1967); J. A. S. Evans, "Father of History or Father of Lies: The Reputation of Herodotus," *Classical Journal* 64 (1968): 11–17; and S. Hornblower, "Herodotus' Influence in Antiquity," in *The Cambridge Companion to Herodotus*, ed. C. Dewald and J. Marincola (Cambridge, 2006), pp. 306–18.

8. Thucydides, *The Peloponnesian War*, trans. R. Warner (Baltimore, 1954), p. 24.

9. P. A. Stadter, "Thucydides as 'Reader' of Herodotus," and R. V. Munson, "Persians in Thucydides," in *Thucydides and Herodotus*, ed. E. Foster and D. Lateiner (Oxford, 2012), pp. 39–66 and 241–77, respectively, with ample references to earlier literature on this topic.

10. See O. Murray's brilliant revisionist essay "Herodotus and Hellenistic Culture," *Classical Quarterly* 22 (1972): 200–13; and J. Priestley, *Herodotus and Hellenistic Culture: Literary Studies in the Reception of the Histories* (Oxford, 2014), pp. 109–56.

BCE), an early Hellenistic imitator of Herodotus who was frequently censured by ancient authors for his long-winded digressions, his "endless bullshitting" (*innumerabiles fabulae*).¹¹ A little more than a century later, Plutarch (c. 46–120 CE) openly attacked the reliability of the *Histories* and the character of its author in a shrill treatise entitled *On the Malice of Herodotus*.¹²

Just as early twentieth-century poets and authors from T. S. Eliot to H. P. Lovecraft trawled the twelve volumes of Sir James Frazer's *The Golden Bough: A Study in Magic and Religion* to inspire and inform their literary enterprises, so too did Roman writers, pagan and Christian alike, mine the rich veins of the *Histories* for all manner of precious material.¹³ Historians from Fabius Pictor to Livy to Ammianus Marcellinus actively borrowed "narrative excerpts and structural elements" from the work of Herodotus.¹⁴ Seneca found in the *Histories* a rogues' gallery of ancient Persian kings—Cambyses, Dares, Cyrus, and others—whose occasions of wrath he retold with therapeutic purpose in his treatise *On Anger*.¹⁵ For Pliny the Elder, Herodotus was an authority

---

11. Cicero, *De legibus* 1.1.5: "Quippe cum in illa ad veritatem Quinte <cuncta> referantur, in hoc ad delectationem pleraque; quamquam et apud Herodotum patrem historiae et apud Theopompum sunt innumerabiles fabulae," ed. K. Ziegler (Freiburg, 1979), pp. 22–23. Theopompus was the author of a notoriously verbose history of Philip II (the *Philippica*), which borrowed extensively from Herodotus. See M. R. Christ, "Theopompus and Herodotus: A Reassessment," *Classical Quarterly* 43 (1993): 47–52.

12. Plutarch, *De Herodoti malignitate*, ed. P. A. Hansen (Amsterdam, 1979). On Plutarch's use of Herodotus, see J. P. Hershbell, "Plutarch and Herodotus: The Beetle in the Rose," *Rheinisches Museum für Philologie* 136 (1993): 143–63. On the treatise in the context of ancient literary criticism, see J. M. Marincola, "Plutarch's Refutation of Herodotus," *Ancient World* 25 (1994): 191–203.

13. J. G. Frazer, *The Golden Bough: A Study in Magic and Religion*, 3rd ed., 12 vols. (London, 1906–15) was a voluminous comparative study of ancient and modern religion and mythology. In his notes to *The Waste Land* (1922), Eliot called it a "work of anthropology ... which has influenced our generation profoundly." Likewise, Frazer's book is among the "mythological and anthropological source-books" found on the desk of the doomed Professor George Angell in Lovecraft's short story "The Call of Cthulhu" (1928), in H. P. Lovecraft, *The Call of Cthulhu and Other Weird Stories*, ed. S. T. Joshi (New York, 1999), pp. 139–69, at p. 142. For more on the influence of Frazer's study in creative circles, see J. B. Vickery, *The Literary Impact of The Golden Bough* (Princeton, 1973).

14. For a summary of the evidence, see I. Samotta, "Herodotus and Thucydides in Roman Republican Historiography," in *Thucydides and Herodotus*, ed. Foster and Lateiner, pp. 345–73 (quotation at p. 373); and J. Matthews, *The Roman Empire of Ammianus* (London, 1989), esp. p. 14: "In such passages, Ammianus stands square as a Greek historian in the tradition of Herodotus—whom he names in this very context (22.15.28); travelling widely, curious in everything he sees, eager for information about it."

15. See n. 66 below for a summary of the passages in Seneca's treatise that transmitted episodes from Herodotus into the Latin tradition.

242   CHAPTER 14

on the culture of monstrous peoples, in particular the one-eyed Arimaspians who waged a relentless war against the winged gold-hoarding griffins of their northern homeland.[16] Knowledge of the *Histories* was also part of the literary repertoire of the Christian author Tertullian. In his denial of the charge that the followers of Christ drank the blood of infants, this second-century apologist drew on his memory of Herodotus to argue that it was in fact pagans and not Christians who had a long and abhorrent history of consuming human blood in ritual contexts.[17]

It was in the eastern Mediterranean, where Greek remained the dominant language for more than a millennium, that the *Histories* endured most successfully. Papyrus fragments from Roman Oxyrhynchus (modern el-Bahnasa, Egypt) and Dura-Europos (near Salhiyé, Syria) speak to the allure of Herodotus among the middle-class inhabitants of prosperous eastern trade towns in the second and third centuries and confirm the impression of a wide currency left by the historical and literary debts recorded above.[18] Most of these fragments were short excerpts from the early books of the *Histories*, in all likelihood used as school texts to introduce advanced students to the dialect of Herodotus and a selection of his exemplary stories.[19] The sands of Egypt have shared other secrets about the reception of Herodotus in this period as well: remnants of a commentary on book 1 of the *Histories* by Aristarchus of Samothrace (fl. second century BCE); scraps of a dramatic performance based on Herodotus's story of Gyges and the wife of Candaules; and the ruins of a private letter recounting a journey up the Nile to visit a temple in the city of Syrene, which the writer, informed by the *Histories*, identified as the source of the river.[20] Borrowings from the

---

16. Pliny, *Naturalis historiae libri XXXVII* 7.2, ed. K. Mayhoff, 6 vols. (Stuttgart, 1967–70), vol. 2, pp. 4–5, drawing on Herodotus 3.116, who doubted the existence of one-eyed men.

17. Tertullian, *Apologeticum* 9.1: "De sanguinis pabulo et eiusmodi tragicis ferculis legite, necubi relatum sit (est apud Herodotum, opinor), defusum brachiis sanguinem ex alterutro degustatum nationes quasdam foederi conparasse," ed. J. E. B. Mayor (Cambridge, 1917), p. 32 (remembering Herodotus 4.70).

18. S. R. West, "The Papyri of Herodotus," in *Culture in Pieces: The Proceedings of a Conference in Honour of Professor Peter Parsons*, ed. D. Obbink and R. Rutherford (Oxford, 2011), pp. 69–83. On the Dura fragment, see C. B. Welles, "Fragments of Herodotus and Appian from Dura," *Transactions and Proceedings of the American Philological Association* 70 (1939): 203–12.

19. The history of Roman education in Egypt is unusually vivid, due to the evidence of the papyri. See R. Cribiore, *Gymnastics of the Mind: Greek Education in Hellenistic and Roman Egypt* (Princeton, 2001), esp. pp. 127–59, on books and writing implements.

20. The commentary of Aristarchus: *The Amherst Papyri*, ed. B. P. Grenfell and A. S. Hunt, 2 vols. (London, 1900–1901), vol. 2, pp. 3–4 (no. 12) and plate III; with Priestly, *Herodotus and*

Histories echoed for centuries throughout Byzantine literature, from the letters of Libanius of Antioch (c. 314-93) to the classicizing history of Laonikos Chalkokondyles (c. 1430-90), who has been called "the ornate Herodotus of the new Persian Conquest."[21]

In contrast, the early fifth century marked the beginning of an apparent dark age for Herodotus in the West. Ausonius of Bordeaux (c. 310-c. 395) and Jerome of Stridon (c. 347-420) belonged to the last generation of Latin speakers who read the *Histories* in Greek.[22] Ausonius's claim to own "the eight books of Thucydides, the nine of Herodotus" is not necessarily an empty boast, given that his social network had strong ties to the eastern book trade, but according to Richard Green, even if Ausonius was fortunate enough to possess these treasures, "It can nowhere be demonstrated that he used them."[23] This is not the case for his near contemporary, the Christian scholar Jerome. Like Ausonius, Jerome was a native speaker of Latin who learned Greek as a young man, and a sifting of his letters and biblical commentaries quickly uncovers his personal familiarity with many ancient Greek authors, including

---

Hellenistic Culture, pp. 223-29. The lost play: *The Oxyrhynchus Papyri*, 87 vols. to date (London, 1898-2023), vol. 23, pp. 101-104 (no. 2382). The ruined letter: Papyrus 854 (first-century), in *Greek Papyri in the British Museum*, 7 vols. (London, 1893-1974), vol. 3, pp. 205-206; with A. Deissmann, *Licht vom Osten: Das Neue Testament und die neuentdeckten Texte der hellenistisch-römischen Welt*, 4th ed. (Tübingen, 1923), p. 141, n. 9 (with reference to Herodotus 2.28).

21. Libanius, *Ep.* 1036, ed. R. Foerster, in *Libanii Opera*, 12 vols. (Leipzig, 1903-63), vol. 11, pp. 160-62, but compare *Ep.* 615 (ed. Foerster, vol. 10, pp. 566-67), where it is clear that the orator was not above criticizing Herodotus on occasion. On the extent of Libanius's knowledge of classical Greek literature, see A. F. Norman, "The Library of Libanius," *Rheinisches Museum für Philologie* 107 (1964): 158-75. On Chalkokondyles as an "ornate Herodotus," see W. Miller, *Essays on the Latin Orient* (London, 1921), p. 237. For a welcome reevaluation of his work, see A. Kaldellis, *A New Herodotos: Laonikos Chalkokondyles on the Ottoman Empire, the Fall of Byzantium, and the Emergence of the West* (Washington, DC, 2014). The earliest surviving Greek manuscript of the *Histories* is Florence, Laurentianus 70.3, which dates to the tenth century, but arrived in Florence much later. See B. Hemmerdinger, *Les manuscrits d'Hérodote et la critique verbale* (Genoa, 1981), esp. pp. 86-93.

22. Augustine of Hippo (354-430 CE) probably knew Greek as well, but he did not value the ancient Greek historians to the same degree as Ausonius and Jerome and provided no evidence that he had ever read them. See P. Courcelle, *Late Latin Authors and Their Greek Sources*, trans. H. E. Wedeck (Cambridge, MA, 1969), pp. 149-223, esp. p. 166, n. 19, about the danger of presuming Augustine's knowledge of ancient Greek sources for stories that were in "the public domain of Latin literature."

23. Ausonius, *Ep.* 8.32: "ὀκτὼ Θουκυδίδου, ἐννέα Ἡροδότου," ed. R. Green, in *The Works of Ausonius* (Oxford, 1991), p. 201; and R. Green, "Greek in Late Roman Gaul: The Evidence of Ausonius," in *"Owls to Athens": Essays on Classical Subjects Presented to Sir Kenneth Dover*, ed. E. M. Craik (Oxford, 1990), pp. 311-19, at p. 318. On the career of Ausonius and his ties to Constantinople, see H. Sivan, *Ausonius of Bordeaux: Genesis of a Gallic Aristocracy* (London, 1993), esp. pp. 74-93, on his intellectual milieu.

Herodotus.²⁴ Unlike Ausonius and other late Roman readers, however, Jerome studied the *Histories* not for the prestige of mastering the charming prose of the "father of history," but rather for the historical information that Herodotus provided about the Persian kingdom during the time of the Babylonian captivity of the ancient Israelites.²⁵ With his combination of scholarly industry and linguistic virtuosity in the service of sacred scripture, Jerome was "the defender of a new Hellenism that developed in the shadow of the cross."²⁶

But it was not to last. The political dissolution of the Western Roman Empire over the course of the fifth century resulted in the collapse of the state-funded system of education throughout most of Western Europe.²⁷ Familiarity with Greek survived among the elite classes for another few centuries in the Western Mediterranean, but only in those cultural outposts that had close contact with Constantinople, like the old imperial capital of Ravenna, the abbey of Vivarium in southern Italy, and the cities of Byzantine North Africa.²⁸ A century after Jerome's death, Boethius (d. 526) and Cassiodorus (d. 585) may have surpassed the biblical scholar's proficiency in Greek, but they could not rival the breadth of his knowledge of the distant past, for the intellectual ambitions that influenced their reading of Greek literature in sixth-century Italy did not place the same importance on Herodotus and other early historians of the ancient Near East.²⁹

After the sixth century, manuscripts of texts written in ancient and patristic Greek were almost impossible to acquire in the Latin West, especially north of the Alps, primarily because of the disappearance of

---

24. For a masterful summary of the evidence, see Courcelle, *Late Latin Writers and Their Greek Sources*, pp. 48-127, esp. pp. 79-81, on his knowledge of Herodotus.

25. See, for example, Jerome, *In Adbiam prophetam* 1.15, *PL* 25, cols. 1097-1118, at col. 1110. For more examples, see the index of H. Hagendahl, *Latin Fathers and the Classics: A Study on the Apologists, Jerome, and Other Christian Writers* (Stockholm, 1958).

26. Courcelle, *Late Latin Writers and Their Greek Sources*, p. 48.

27. See H. I. Marrou, *A History of Education in Antiquity*, trans. G. Lamb (New York, 1956), pp. 299-313, on state support for education during the Roman Empire; and p. 344 on the date of its demise: "This system [of Roman education] must have disappeared with the great invasion and the catastrophes that marked the beginning of the fifth century."

28. Italy: M. McCormick, "The Imperial Edge: Italo-Byzantine Identity, Movement, and Integration, A.D. 650-950," in *Studies on the Internal Diaspora of the Byzantine Empire*, ed. H. Ahrweiler and A. E. Laiou (Washington, DC, 1998), pp. 17-52, at pp. 22-23. North Africa: J. Conant, *Staying Roman: Conquest and Identity in North Africa and the Mediterranean, 439-700* (Cambridge, 2012), pp. 244-46.

29. Courcelle, *Late Latin Writers and Their Greek Sources*, pp. 273-330 (Boethius) and 331-409 (Cassiodorus).

spoken Greek as a language of proficiency in Western Europe.[30] Despite the poverty of resources, some early medieval monks made the effort to teach themselves Greek because it was the sacred language of the community of the apostles, but with few exceptions, their efforts were more symbolic than successful.[31] Some northern abbeys, like Saint Gall, fostered the study of Greek by collecting bilingual manuscripts, but these texts were biblical rather than classical, the Psalter and the Gospels being the most common among them.[32] With many years of dedicated study, however, a motivated student with access to even these limited resources could pool a modest reservoir of Greek vocabulary and obtain a working knowledge of Greek grammar.[33] This was certainly the case for the Venerable Bede (d. 735), whose hard-won proficiency in Greek was the reward for countless hours spent poring over grammars and plodding through interlinear texts, including a bilingual *Acts of the Apostles* originally written in sixth-century Sardinia.[34]

Despite the waning knowledge of Greek in the early medieval West, fragments of ancient Greek texts found their way into monastic libraries, smuggled in by the conceit of Roman and late antique authors eager

---

30. G. Cavallo, "La circolazione dei testi greci nell'Europa dell'alto medioevo," in *Rencontres de cultures dans la philosophie médiévale: Traductions et traducteurs de l'antiquité tardive au XIVe siècle; Actes du Colloque international de Cassino 15–17 juin 1989*, ed. J. Hamesse and M. Fattori (Louvain and Cassino, 1990), pp. 47–64. I have excluded from this discussion the abundant evidence for the knowledge of Greek patristic literature available in Latin translation in early medieval abbeys, a topic in need of further attention. See A. Siegmund, *Die Überlieferung der griechischen christlichen Literatur in der lateinischen Kirche bis zum zwölften Jahrhundert* (Munich, 1949); and S. G. Bruce, "The Lost Patriarchs Project: Recovering the Greek Fathers in the Medieval Latin Tradition," *Religion Compass* 14 (2020): 1–8.

31. For an excellent overview, see M. W. Herren, "Pelasgian Fountains: Learning Greek in the Early Middle Ages," in *Learning Latin and Greek from Antiquity to the Present*, ed. E. P. Archibald, W. Brockliss, and J. Gnoza (Cambridge, 2015), pp. 65–82.

32. B. M. Kaczynski, *Greek in the Carolingian Age: The St. Gall Manuscripts* (Cambridge, 1988).

33. Herren, "Pelasgian Fountains," p. 74: "When we extend the notion of writing beyond alphabetical literacy to the ability to express one's thoughts in correct Greek, or something resembling it, the quantity of evidence shrinks exponentially." This seems to have been the case in early medieval Ireland, where the evidence points to the monastic use of written texts to achieve "some passive knowledge [of Greek] and at best very basic reading ability." See also P. Moran, "Greek in Early Medieval Ireland," in *Multilingualism in the Graeco-Roman Worlds*, ed. A. Mullen and P. James (Cambridge, 2012), pp. 172–92 (quotation at p. 191).

34. A. C. Dionisotti, "On Bede, Grammars, and Greek," *Revue bénédictine* 92 (1982): 111–41; and K. M. Lynch, "The Venerable Bede's Knowledge of Greek," *Traditio* 39 (1983): 432–39, both offer positive assessments of Bede's proficiency in Greek. For the manuscript in question (Oxford, Bodleian Library, Laud Gr. 35), see *CLA*, vol. 2, p. 37 (no. 251), but note the editor's caveat: "Bede, in his commentary on Acts, uses a text in remarkable agreement with this unique MS., but it should be noted that no marginalia in Anglo-Saxon script occur." On its later pedigree, see James, *The Wanderings and Homes of Manuscripts*, p. 21.

to impress their readers with the breadth of their learning.[35] Lactantius, Servius, Jerome, Macrobius, Priscian, Boethius, and Isidore preserved many hundreds of Greek words between them, which delighted Carolingian compilers of Greek word lists and confounded early medieval scribes, who routinely elided the alien words or botched the unfamiliar letter forms.[36] At the abbey of Saint-Amand-les-Eaux in the ninth century, it would have been possible to hear in a "malicious little satire" attributed to Seneca the Younger (d. 65) the ancient language of Homer and Euripides, provided that one knew how to pronounce the Greek letters.[37] In the early Roman Empire, this kind of casual familiarity with Greek literature united elite Romans around the Mediterranean rim, whose shared education in Greek and Latin classics created a cultural homogeneity that engendered friendship and solidarity among its participants.[38] As late as the fourth century, Libanius of Antioch could broker a successful relationship with an educated governor by first addressing him with a verse from Homer's *Odyssey*.[39] Centuries later, in the northern world of Carolingian Europe, the same words had lost all resonance of their previous cultural capital, because most learned Christians had long since turned a deaf ear to the literary heritage of ancient Greece. Very few monks at ninth-century Saint-Amand-les-Eaux had the hard-won expertise necessary to extract meaning from these relics of Homeric Greek. For most early medieval readers, the

---

35. In addition to Courcelle, *Late Latin Authors and their Greek Sources*, see W. Berschin, *Greek Letters and the Latin Middle Ages: From Jerome to Nicholas of Cusa*, trans. J. C. Frakes (Washington, DC, 1988).

36. See, for example, J. C. Frakes, "The Knowledge of Greek in the Early Middle Ages: The Commentaries on Boethius' *Consolatio*," *Studi Medievali*, 3rd ser., 27 (1986): 23–43, which includes discussion of the corruption of Boethius's Greek passages by some early medieval scribes and the ingenuity and frustration of Carolingian readers in their attempts to decipher these texts. For another example, see M. W. Herren, "The Humanism of John Scottus," in *Gli Umanesimi Medievali: Atti di II Congresso dell' "Internationales Mittellateinerkomitee" (Firenze, Cretosa del Galluzzo, 11–15 settembre 1993)*, ed Claudio Leonardi (Florence, 1998), pp. 191–200, at pp. 194–96.

37. See, for example, Valenciennes, BM 411, fols. 93v, 94v–95r, and 100r, reproducing Greek passages in Seneca, *Apocolocyntosis* 4.35 (Euripides), 5.19, 5.23, 5.25, and 11.3 (Homer), ed. P. T. Eden (Cambridge, 1984), pp. 34, 36, and 48; and *Texts and Transmission*, pp. 361–62 (The Younger Seneca), quotation at p. 361. This biting parody of the emperor Claudius's thwarted attempt to obtain deification in the afterlife was known in the Latin manuscript tradition as the *Play on the Death of Divine Claudius* (*Ludus de morte divi Claudii*).

38. The unsurpassed study, which ranges from ancient Greece to the sixth century CE, remains Marrou, *A History of Education in Antiquity*, esp. pp. 255–64, on the knowledge of Greek in the Roman world.

39. P. Brown, *Power and Persuasion in Late Antiquity: Towards a Christian Empire* (Madison, WI, 1992), pp. 35–70 ("*Paideia* and Power"), esp. p. 40, on the Libanius anecdote.

Greek characters were simply indecipherable, like constellations viewed from unaccustomed latitudes.

Cassiodorus played a pivotal role in sealing the fate of the *Histories* in the early medieval West. A successful bureaucrat in the Ostrogothic kingdom, he found himself on the wrong side of Justinian's war of reconquest in Italy (535–554).[40] His hopes of reconciliation smothered, Cassiodorus retired to his estates in southern Italy around 554, where he established monastic communities at Vivarium near the sea town of Squillace and composed the *Institutes*, a treatise on Christian and secular learning that would become one of the most important touchstones for monastic pedagogy in the Middle Ages.[41] Vivarium was one of the last great outposts for the transmission of Greek history into Latin at the end of antiquity.[42] There Cassiodorus assembled an *équipe* of bilingual monks with the time and resources to undertake translation projects too daunting for individuals to tackle alone.[43] Unlike Jerome, who valued the *Histories* of Herodotus for the information they conveyed about the ancient kingdoms of Persia and Egypt, Cassiodorus applied the industry of his scriptorium only to those histories that revealed and explained the agency of God in human affairs: the *Antiquities* of Josephus; the triumphalist ecclesiastical histories of the fourth and fifth centuries (Eusebius, Socrates, Sozomen, and Theodoret); the Latin historians Orosius (d. c. 420) and Marcellinus Comes (d. 534); and the chronicles of Eusebius as translated into Latin by Jerome and furthered by his continuators up to the time of Justinian.[44]

---

40. For a reassessment of his career in Italy, see M. S. Bjornlie, *Politics and Tradition Between Rome, Ravenna and Constantinople: A Study of Cassiodorus and the Variae* (Cambridge, 2013).

41. Cassiodorus, *Institutiones*, ed. R. A. B. Mynors (Oxford, 1937); English translation: Cassiodorus, *Institutes of Divine and Secular Learning and On the Soul*, trans. J. W. Halporn (Leeds, 2004), pp. 103–233. J. J. O'Donnell, *Cassiodorus* (Berkeley, 1979), pp. 177–222, remains a useful point of departure on the foundation of Vivarium and its relationship to monastic culture in sixth-century Italy. On the medieval reception of the work of Cassiodorus, see L. W. Jones, "The Influence of Cassiodorus on Medieval Culture," *Speculum* 20 (1945): 433–42, esp. pp. 436–38, on the *Institutiones*.

42. Rome and Monte Cassino are also likely centers of transmission in this period, but neither locale produced a work as influential or as enduring as Cassiodorus's *Institutiones*.

43. Three monks are singled out as translators of Greek in the *Institutiones*: Epiphanius (1.5.2 and 1.5.4), Bellator (1.6.6), and Mutianus (1.8.3 and 2.5.1).

44. Cassiodorus, *Institutiones* 1.17, ed. Mynors, pp. 55–57. See also A. Momigliano, *The Classical Foundations of Modern Historiography* (Berkeley, 1990), pp. 132–52. On the manuscripts produced at Vivarium and their fate, see F. Troncarelli, *Vivarium: I Libri, Il Destino* (Turnhout, 1998).

In the sixth century, the brethren of Vivarium participated in a great winnowing of Greek sources for ancient history, an event with far-reaching consequences for the literary culture of the Latin Middle Ages. Despite the currency of Herodotus among Procopius and other sixth-century historians active in Constantinople, the events described by these venerable storytellers had no place in the monastic curriculum envisioned by Cassiodorus, whose taxonomy of "Christian history" was strict and exclusive.[45] The cultural program enshrined in the *Institutes* jettisoned all accounts of the past that did not conform with the providential histories of Christian triumph. Departing from the imperial capital, Cassiodorus and his friends abandoned a millennium-old tradition of historical writing in Greek. They took with them to Vivarium only a few Greek manuscripts of Josephus and the early church historians, a handful of precious gems to adorn the new raiment of Christian historiography that they tailored for the Latin readers of the West. Without a second thought, they left Herodotus and his *Histories* behind.

Stygian Channels

How then did Peter the Venerable know this story of Herodotus, a historian whose writings the ages had long since devoured by the twelfth century? As a child oblate at the abbey of Sauxillanges in the last decade of the eleventh century, Peter was nurtured on a curriculum of Christian and secular learning informed by the *Institutes* of Cassiodorus.[46] His familiarity with ancient literature, impressed in his memory at an early age, left a discernable imprint on all of his subsequent writings. Unlike his abbatial predecessors, Peter self-consciously compiled and published his written correspondence to communicate his authority to his Cluniac brethren, while also composing two volumes of miracle stories as well as lengthy treatises against what he perceived to be the three most pressing threats to Christendom in his time: heresy, Judaism, and

---

45. A. Kaldellis, *Procopius of Caesarea: Tyranny, History, and Philosophy at the End of Antiquity* (Philadelphia, 2004), pp. 24-38 (on Procopius's classicism) and 62-93 (on the influence of Herodotus on the *Persian Wars*).

46. Rodulphus de Sully, *Vita Petri Venerabilis abbatis Cluniacensis* 1, ed. E. Martène and U. Durand, in *Veterum Scriptorum et Monumentorum Historicorum, Dogmaticorum, Moralium, Amplissima Collectio*, 9 vols. (Paris, 1724-33), vol. 6, cols. 1187-1202, at cols. 1189-90; repr. in *PL* 189, cols. 15-28, at col. 17. J.-P. Torrell and D. Bouthillier, *Pierre le Vénérable et sa vision du monde: Sa vie, son oeuvre, l'homme et le démon* (Leuven, 1986) remains the fullest study of the abbot's life and thought.

Islam.[47] Taken together, this corpus provides a valuable index of the ancient authors that the abbot of Cluny had his disposal, both through the recollection of texts he had studied as a boy and through his familiarity with the dozens of manuscripts that preserved the work of pagan authors in Cluny's impressive library.

Alongside frequent allusions to important Christian texts that most monks knew from memory, like the *Rule of Benedict* and the writings of Pope Gregory the Great, three ancient authorities are conspicuous throughout the works of Peter the Venerable: Virgil, Ovid, and Horace.[48] The abbot's writings also betray his familiarity with a wide range of historical sources. Among them were the works of Josephus and Eusebius, who had both been sanctioned by Cassiodorus in the *Institutes*. Peter's familiarity with Roman history, however, shows considerably more breadth than these canonical works. He nourished an active interest in ancient historians opining about the wars and intrigues of the waning days of the Roman Republic, including Sallust's *Jurgurthine War* and his account of the conspiracy of Cataline, Lucan's *Civil War*, and the *Gallic Wars* of Julius Caesar.[49]

It is clear, however, that Peter the Venerable did not read the *Histories* of Herodotus, at least not in a form that we would have recognized. Even though the Greek text of this most ancient historian had disappeared from Western Europe by the end of antiquity, two aspects of Roman reading culture conspired to preserve parts of his work for medieval readers: (1) the unruly length of the *Histories* in a society that read literary texts on scrolls; and (2) its wide circulation as a school text,

---

47. D. Iogna-Prat, *Order and Exclusion: Cluny and Christendom Face Heresy, Judaism, and Islam (1000–1150)*, trans. G. R. Edwards (Ithaca, 2002); and S. G. Bruce, *Cluny and the Muslims of La Garde-Freinet: Hagiography and the Problem of Islam in Medieval Europe* (Ithaca, 2015), pp. 70-99.

48. M. Manitius, "Zu Petrus' von Cluni patristischen Kenntnissen," *Speculum* 3 (1928): 582-87, although long out of date, was the first to trace Peter's knowledge and use of early Christian authors like Cyprian, Tertullian, Ambrose, Hilary of Poitiers, Paulinus of Nola, Augustine, Gregory the Great, and Bede. Peter's debt to Roman authors is clear from the indices of citations compiled by the modern editors of his works.

49. Peter's interest in Roman history was not unusual in the twelfth century, and most of these works were accessible in Cluny's library. See L. Delisle, *Inventaire des manuscrits de la Bibliothèque nationale: Fonds de Cluni* (Paris, 1884), pp. 337-73 (appendix A: Catalogue de la Bibliothèque de Cluni, a twelfth-century inventory of 570 volumes), p. 370: "Volumen in quo continetur Salustius de bello Catiline et Jugurthe" (no. 516); p. 372: "Volumen in quo continetur bellorum civilium narrator Lucanus" (no. 548) and "Volumen in quo continentur Sedulius, et Salustius de Catilinario bello et Jugurthino" (no. 559). Caesar's *Bellum gallicum* was well attested in twelfth-century library inventories, but it is inexplicably absent from Cluny. See V. Brown, "Latin Manuscripts of Caesar's *Gallic War*," in *Palaeographica diplomatica et archivistica: Studi in onore di Giulio Battelli*, 2 vols. (Rome, 1979), pp. 105-57, esp. pp. 106-107.

which students digested in small chunks rather than reading in toto. By the height of the Roman Empire, few people would have read the *Histories* from start to finish. The sheer bulk of Herodotus's narrative—many times that of Homer's *Iliad*—made the text much too unwieldy to peruse with ease on papyrus scrolls.[50] With the exception of luxury book rolls made for elite patrons, most ancient readers would have encountered the *Histories* partitioned into smaller units.[51] Almost half of the surviving papyri of Herodotus are from book 1, as are most of the citations of the *Histories* by pagan and Christian authors in late antiquity, which suggests that many readers encountered the first book of the *Histories* as a discrete text.[52] Moreover, Roman schools fostered the dismemberment of sprawling works like the *Histories* into exemplary episodes or discrete set pieces, which were easier for students to rehearse and digest. Broken down into inconspicuous vignettes, the *Histories* survived into an era dominated by the triumphalist narratives of the early Church historians. Unlike other classical works, which early medieval monks copied for their style or content, the reception history of Herodotus in the Latin Middle Ages requires the analysis of the trajectories of dozens of literary shards that were carried into the medieval period discretely embedded in texts that were only tangentially related to the *Histories*. The abbot of Cluny's analogy between Cyrus's anger at the Gyndes River and the futility of heretical doctrines is one such example. It remains to trace the passage of this particular shard back to its source in antiquity.

In his treatise against the Petrobrusians, Peter the Venerable rehearsed from memory a story about King Cyrus that he had learned not directly from Herodotus's *Histories*, but rather from the *Seven Books of History Against the Pagans* by Orosius (c. 385–c. 418).[53] The little we

---

50. Only one example among the more than forty surviving papyri fragments is a page from a codex; the overwhelming majority are fragments of scrolls or book rolls. See West, "Papyri of Herodotus," p. 74, n. 22.

51. For evocative introductions to "book roll culture" in Roman antiquity, see W. A. Johnson, *Readers and Reading Culture in the High Roman Empire: A Study of Elite Communities* (Oxford, 2010), pp. 17–22; and G. W. Houston, *Inside Roman Libraries: Book Collections and their Management in Antiquity* (Chapel Hill, 2014), pp. 5–7.

52. West, "Papyri of Herodotus," p. 71.

53. Orosius, *Historiarum adversum paganos libri septem* 2.6.2-6, ed. M.-P. Arnaud-Lindet, in *Orose, Histories (contre les paiens)*, 3 vols. (Paris, 1990–91), vol. 1, pp. 95–96; English translation: *Orosius, Seven Books of History Against the Pagans*, trans. A. T. Fear (Liverpool, 2010), p. 83. In the following paragraph, I am indebted to Fear's comprehensive summary of Orosius's life and itinerary. After decades of dismissing him as a shallow compiler of historical materials overshadowed by the towering intellect of his contemporary Augustine of Hippo, historians have begun to appreciate the rhetorical prowess of the *Seven Books of History* as a work of late antique

know about the life of Orosius suggests that he was a combative personality who was deeply involved in the theological controversies of his day. The barbarian incursions into his native Spain around 410 exiled him to North Africa, where his writings against the Priscillians made a strong impression on Augustine. On the bishop's recommendation, Orosius traveled eastward to visit Jerome in Bethlehem and attended a synod in Jerusalem (July 28, 415) where he argued in vain against the Pelagian heresy. He returned to North Africa in 416 as the courier of some recently discovered relics of the protomartyr Stephen. Political turmoil in his homeland prevented him from delivering the relics to the bishop of Braga, so he deposited them in a church on the island of Minorca. He disappeared abruptly from the historical record in 418, the circumstances of his early death unknown. Orosius wrote his *Seven Books of History* sometime during this itinerant exile from Spain, but it is difficult to reconstruct how he went about the considerable research required to assemble so much historical material while twice traversing the length of the Mediterranean and participating actively in theological debate.

Unlike the ecclesiastical histories written by Eusebius and Rufinus, Orosius set out to compose a providential history encompassing the ancient civilizations of Persia, Greece, and Rome. His aim was unabashedly polemical. After the sack of Rome by Alaric and the Visigoths in the summer of 410, there was a groundswell of pagan criticism blaming Christianity for the misfortunes besetting the Roman Empire. Augustine responded to these pagan critics, many of whom were refugees from Rome who had been displaced to North Africa, in the first books of his magisterial *On the City of God Against the Pagans*.[54] He also asked Orosius to compile an account of all of the calamities that human beings had suffered in ancient times to illustrate that "the days gone by were as fraught as the present, and all the more horribly wretched as they were further from the salvation of the True Religion."[55] The result is a long

---

historiography. See H. Inglebert, *Les romains chrétiens face à l'histoire de Rome: Histoire, christianisme et romanités en occident dans l'antiquité tardive (IIIe–Ve siècles)* (Paris, 1996), pp. 507–92; A. H. Merrills, *History and Geography in Late Antiquity* (Cambridge, 2005), pp. 35–99; and P. Van Nuffelen, *Orosius and the Rhetoric of History* (Oxford, 2012).

54. For important insight about the genre and composition of this work, see P. Brown, *Augustine of Hippo: A Biography*, 2nd ed. (Berkeley, 2000), pp. 297–311 (chapter 27: "*Magnum opus et arduum*: Writing the 'City of God'").

55. Orosius, *Historiarum adversum paganos libri septem*, prol. 14: "Nanctus sum enim praeteritos dies non solum aeque ut hos graues, uerum etiam tanto atrocius miseros quanto longius a remedio uerae religionis alienos," ed. Arnaud-Lindet, p. 9; trans. Fear, p. 33.

litany of disasters and misfortunes, natural and political, from the time of the ancient Persians down to the present day. Needless to say, this made for grim reading. Despite its formidable length and baleful content, Orosius's compendium was one of the most widely read narratives of ancient history in the Middle Ages. Surviving in more than two hundred manuscripts, it was ubiquitous in the monastic libraries of early medieval Europe.[56] Like many other monks, Peter read his Orosius with the blessing of Cassiodorus, who sanctioned the *Seven Books of History* in the chapter of the *Institutes* devoted to "Christian historians."[57]

Although there are no direct verbal parallels between Peter's treatise and Orosius's history, the narrative correspondence leaves no room for doubt that Orosius was the source for the abbot's knowledge of the story of King Cyrus's vengeance (table 6). Peter botched the name of the river, calling it the Ganges instead of the Gyndes, but otherwise his recollection of the episode was fairly accurate.[58] In the twelfth century, the abbey of Cluny possessed a venerable manuscript of the *Seven Books of History* that had been copied in Burgundy at the end of the eighth century (Paris, BnF, Latin 9665).[59] It is unclear how this precious relic of the Carolingian age found its way to Cluny, but this was very likely the manuscript that Peter had perused in advance of writing his treatise against the Petrobrusians. Although the abbot made no other allusions to the *Seven Books of History* in his extant writings, a seventeenth-century library catalog from Cluny hints strongly at his abiding interest in

---

56. J. M. Bately and D. J. A. Ross, "A Check List of Manuscripts of Orosius' *Historiarum Adversum Paganos Libri Septem*," *Scriptorium* 15 (1961): 329–34; and J. N. Hillgarth, "The *Historiae* of Orosius in the Early Middle Ages," in *De Tertullien aux Mozarabes, Tome II: Antiquité tardive et Christianisme ancient (VIe–XIe siècles): Mélanges offerts à Jacques Fontaine*, ed. L. Holtz and J.-C. Fredouille (Paris, 1992), pp. 157–70. Before the year 1000, it had been rendered into Old English and also into Arabic, a distinction that made it the only early medieval Latin text directly available to Muslim readers. The Old English translation has been edited and translated by M. R. Godden as *The Old English History of the World: An Anglo-Saxon Rewriting of Orosius* (Cambridge, MA, 2016). On the Arabic tradition of this text, see C. C. Sahner, "From Augustine to Islam: Translation and History in the Arabic Orosius," *Speculum* 88 (2013): 905–31.

57. Cassiodorus, *Institutiones* 1.17.1: "Orosius quoque, Christianorum temporum paganorumque collator, praesto vobis est, si eum legere volueritis," ed. Mynors, p. 56.

58. The frequent reference to the Ganges River in India by classical authors may account for the abbot's slip. See, for example, Vergil, *Georgics* 2.137, ed. R. A. B. Mynors, in *P. Vergili Maronis Opera* (Oxford, 1969), p. 50; and Ovid, *Metamorphoses* 2.249 and 4.21, ed. G. Lafaye, 2 vols. (Paris, 2007–2008), vol. 1, pp. 45 and 96, both of which were well-known to Peter. Early medieval scribes confused the name as well. At least two Carolingian manuscripts of Orosius call the river Ganges (*gandes* or *ganges*) instead of Gyndes. See *Orose, Histories*, ed. Arnaud-Lindet, p. 95, note to chapter 6.2.

59. *CLA*, vol. 7, p. 52 (no. 702); and Delisle, *Inventaire des manuscrits*, pp. 182–84 (no. 108) and p. 338 (no. 20: "Volumen in quo continetur historia Pauli Orosii").

Table 6. Narrative correspondence between Orosius's *Historiarum adversum paganos libri septem* and Peter the Venerable's *Contra Perobrusianos*

OROSIUS, *HISTORIARUM ADVERSUM PAGANOS LIBRI SEPTEM* 2.6.2–6, ED. ARNAUD-LINDET, VOL. 1, PP. 95–96.	PETER THE VENERABLE, *CONTRA PETROBRUSIANOS* 121, ED. FEARNS, PP. 71–72
Cyrus, ut dixi, cunctis aduersum quos ierat perdomitis, Assyrios et Babylonam petit, gentem urbemque tunc cunctis opulentiorem; sed impetum eius Gyndes fluuius, secundae post Euphraten magnitudinis, intercepit. Nam unum regiorum equorum candore formaque excellentem, transmeandi fiducia persuasum qua per rapacem alueum offensi uado uertices attollebantur, abreptum praecipitatumque merserunt. Rex iratus ulcisci in amnem statuit, contestans eum qui nunc praeclarum equitem uorauisset feminis uix genua tinguentibus permeabilem relinquendum. Nec peragendo segnior: totis copiis perpeti anno Gynden fluuium per magnas concisum deductumque fossas in quadringentos sexaginta alueos comminuit. Eo opere praedoctis fossoribus, etiam Euphraten longe ualidissimum et mediam Babyloniam interfluentem deriuauit, ac sic meabilibus uadis siccum etiam patentibus aluei patrtibus iter fecit, cepitque urbem; quam uel humano opera exstrui potuisse uel humana uirtute destrui posse utrumque paene incredibile apud mortales erat.	Sed forte uos animosam Cyri regis arrogantiam emulati imitari proposuistis, qui, absorbtum maximo flumine, qui Ganges dicitur, dilectum equitem ulcisci cupiens, exarsit in flumen, et peruium se peditibus facturum comminans, impleuit promissa. In trecentos enim et eo amplius alueos tumentes undarum moles dispartiens, superbiam fluminis superbus imminuit, et per plures tramites unius magnitudinem deriuans, naualem uix pompam dignantem, siccis, ut dixerat, pedibus fluuium meabilem fecit.

Orosius's work, listing two manuscript copies: the Carolingian exemplar, written by scribal hands outstanding in their proficiency and distinctive in their antiquity (*optimae et antiquae manus*); and another, now lost, "written at the request of Abbot Peter of Cluny" (*Scriptus est codex jussu Petri, abbatis Cluniacensis*).[60]

The recovery of this shard of Herodotus does not end with Orosius, however. Unlike his learned contemporaries Ausonius and Jerome, the exiled Spanish priest probably knew no Greek.[61] It is thus highly unlikely that he had consulted the *Histories* of Herodotus directly as an authority on the kings of ancient Persia. Rather, Orosius drew selectively from the work of earlier Latin authors for the information

---

60. Delisle, *Inventaire des manuscrits*, p. 384 (nos. D and E).
61. Orosius's knowledge of Greek authors cited in the *Seven Books of Histories* (Plato, Polybius, Josephus, and others) came from Latin intermediaries like Livy and Jerome's translation of Eusebius's *Chronicle*. See Courcelle, *Late Latin Writers and their Greek Sources*, p. 209, n. 4.

related in the first books of his history.⁶² His main source for the Achaemenid kings seems to have been an epitome of the lost *Philippic History* of the Augustan historian Pompeius Trogus written in the third century by Marcus Junianus Justinus.⁶³ Like Orosius's *Seven Books of History*, Justinus's epitome was popular in the Middle Ages as a compendium of historical information, but the story of King Cyrus's vengeance does not feature in this work, so Orosius must have read it elsewhere.⁶⁴

Seneca's first-century treatise *On Anger* is the most likely candidate as Orosius's source for this tale. This work of Stoic philosophy presented a therapeutic argument for "cutting anger out of our minds or at least to rein it in and curb its fury."⁶⁵ Despite its apparent benefits, especially when directed toward enemies, this unruly passion ultimately hindered the cultivation of the qualities that make us human. Making his case from historical examples, Seneca adorned his treatise with portraits of ancient figures who succumbed to their wicked frenzies or demonstrated admirable self-control when confronted with the anger of others. Several of these he rendered into Latin from stories he had read in the *Histories* of Herodotus: King Cambyses's calculated murder of the son of an adviser who had counseled him against drinking too much; the restraint of poor Harpagus, who was served the flesh of his children at the table of King Asyages, whom he had displeased; the royal cruelty of Darius and Xerxes, the slayers of the sons of noblemen who had begged for their boys to remain behind when the Persian army marched on campaign; and last, the folly of King Cyrus, who waged a war against a river with resources that he should have employed against his enemies in the field.⁶⁶ In contrast to the narrowing horizons of Orosius's world, Seneca lived in an age when the Roman Empire was ruled by a Latin

---

62. For the argument that Orosius made creative use of his sources rather than copying them without thoughtful intervention, see Van Nuffelen, *Orosius and the Rhetoric of History*, pp. 93–114.

63. Justin, *Epitoma historiarum Philippicarum Pompei Trogi*, ed. O. Seel (Stuttgart, 1972).

64. Reynolds, *Texts and Transmission*, pp. 197–99 (Justinus).

65. Seneca, *De ira* 3.1.1: "Iram excidere animis aut certe refrenare et impetus eius inhibere." ed. L. D. Reynolds, in *Dialogorum Libri Duodecim* (Oxford, 1977), pp. 39–128, at p. 93. For an insightful commentary on this treatise, see M. C. Nussbaum, *The Therapy of Desire: Theory and Practice in Hellenistic Ethics* (Princeton, 1994), pp. 402–38.

66. Cambyses: *De ira* 3.14, ed. Reynolds, pp. 105–106 (compare Herodotus 3.34–36); Harpagus: *De ira* 3.15, ed. Reynolds, pp. 106–107 (compare Herodotus 1.108–19); Darius: *De ira* 3.16.3, ed. Reynolds, p. 108 (compare Herodotus 4.84); Xerxes: *De ira* 3.16.4, ed. Reynolds, p. 108 (compare Herodotus 7.38); and Cyrus: *De ira* 3.21.1–4, ed. Reynolds, pp. 111–12 (compare Herodotus 1.189).

class that displayed its knowledge of Greek language and literature as an emblem of its right to govern others.

Seneca's treatise *On Anger* and his other moral essays (known collectively in the manuscript tradition as the *Dialogues*) were not widely read in the early Middle Ages.[67] Late antique Christian apologists like Lactantius certainly knew this Stoic treatise, as did Orosius and another Spaniard, Martin of Braga, who assembled an epitome of it in the late sixth century.[68] Thereafter, Seneca's moral essays disappeared until the eleventh century, when monks of Monte Cassino produced a manuscript of them under the direction of Abbot Desiderius (1058-1087). Even then they were largely unknown north of the Alps until the thirteenth century. The library of Cluny possessed two copies of the popular apocryphal correspondence between Seneca and the apostle Paul, but Peter and his brethren do not seem to have known any of his authentic works.[69] Seneca's treatise *On Anger* introduced the story of King Cyrus into the Latin tradition in the early imperial period, but the abbot of Cluny owed his knowledge of this episode from Herodotus to the popularity of its intermediary—Orosius's *Seven Books of History*—among early medieval readers in Northern Europe.

Fugitive Pieces

It is doubtful that Peter the Venerable knew that the *Histories* of Herodotus were the original source of the vignette about the vengeance of King Cyrus that he had read in the work of Orosius. In the late republic and the early empire, Herodotus's ubiquity as a curricular author and his status as the "father of history" had ensured his fame among the lettered elite as the indisputable progenitor of an important genre of Greek and Latin literature, but his authority and notoriety receded

---

67. For what follows, see L. D. Reynolds, "The Medieval Tradition of Seneca's Dialogues," *The Classical Quarterly* 18 (1968): 355-72; and *Texts and Transmission*, pp. 357-65 (The Younger Seneca), at pp. 357-60.

68. Lactantius, *De ira Dei liber*, ed. C. Ingremeau, in *Lactance, La colère de Dieu*, SC 289 (Paris, 1982). On the "parity between Stoic and Christian ethics" in Martin of Braga's work, see M. L. Colish, *The Stoic Tradition from Antiquity to the Early Middle Ages*, 2 vols. (Leiden, 1985), vol. 2, pp. 297-302 (quotation at p. 297). Martin's epitome has been edited by C. Torre in *Martini Bracarensis de ira: Introduzione, testo, traduzione e commento* (Rome, 2008).

69. Delisle, *Inventaire des manuscrits*, pp. 342 (no. 88) and 347 (no. 169). For an edition of these letters, see *Epistolae Senecae ad Paulum et Pauli ad Senecam*, ed. L. B. Palagi, in *Epistolario apocrifo di Seneca e san Paolo* (Florence, 1985). For more on the adoption of Seneca in the Christian tradition, see A. Momigliano, "Note sulla leggenda del cristianesimo di Seneca," *Rivista storica italiana* 62 (1950): 324-44.

markedly in the Latin Middle Ages.[70] This process was well underway in the seventh century, when Isidore of Seville divested Herodotus of his time-honored place as the world's first historian by putting forward even older authorities, both Christian and pagan.[71] According to Isidore, the first author of history among the Christians was without doubt the patriarch Moses, because he wrote about the beginning of the world (*de initio mundi*) in the book of Genesis. Among the pagans, the eyewitness account of the Trojan War allegedly written by Dares the Phrygian, the priest of Hephaestus named in Homer's *Iliad*, was also demonstrably older than the *Histories*.[72] Isidore even went so far as to demote Herodotus among historians of ancient Greece, ranking him second in his *Chronica* to Pherecydes of Athens, the "first writer of histories" (*historiarum primus scriptor*).[73]

Medieval readers like Peter the Venerable may have lost touch with the historical Herodotus, but they never lost interest in reading about ancient history. Writing at the end of antiquity, Orosius and other authors of historical epitomes and compendia played a vital role in the transmission of Greek and Roman history into the abbeys of Western Europe, including stories culled directly and indirectly from the *Histories* of Herodotus. The tale of King Cyrus's vengeance against the Gyndes River is one such example, but there are many more shards of the *Histories* embedded in the works of early medieval authors, the trajectories of which demand inquiry and recovery.[74] The discovery of the "sword of Mars" that convinced Attila the Hun of his divine right to rule and the ecology of the giant gold-hoarding ants of India are two of many popular tales in the medieval Latin tradition that trace their origin to Herodotus. Like the analogy of King Cyrus in Peter's treatise against the Petrobrusians, these fugitive pieces of the Herodotean tradition

---

70. For what follows, see F. Racine, "Herodotus' Reputation in Latin Literature from Cicero to the Twelfth Century," in *Brill's Companion to the Reception of Herodotus in Antiquity and Beyond*, ed. J. Priestly and V. Zali (Leiden, 2016), pp. 192–212, esp. pp. 203–205.

71. Isidore, *Etymologiarum sive Originum Libri XX* 1.42.2, ed. O. Spevak, in *Isidore de Séville, Étymologies, Livre I: La grammaire* (Paris, 2020), p. 217.

72. This fictional history by Dares was in fact in late antique forgery, but medieval readers took it at face value. On the popularity of Dares's account of the Trojan War in the Middle Ages, see L. F. D'Arcier, *Histoire et géographie d'un mythe: La circulation des manuscrits du* De excidio Troiae *de Darès le Phrygien* (Paris, 2006); and F. Clark, *The First Pagan Historian: The Fortunes of a Fraud from Antiquity to the Enlightenment* (Oxford, 2020).

73. Racine, "Herodotus' Reputation," p. 205.

74. For a catalog of literary and artistic iterations of stories involving King Cyrus from Herodotus to Shakespeare (although with no mention of Peter the Venerable), see A. M. Young, *Echoes of Two Cultures* (Pittsburgh, 1964), pp. 1–58.

underscore the importance of Roman intermediaries as transmitters of Greek texts to medieval readers, illustrate the tenacity of stories from the *Histories* in the Latin Middle Ages, and show clearly how medieval authors repurposed these tales to make new claims for new audiences who were wholly unfamiliar with the work of Herodotus.

Writing in the middle of the sixth century, Jordanes introduced a shard from Herodotus into the Latin tradition in his history of the Goths, commonly known as the *Getica*.[75] According to Jordanes, a shepherd discovered a strange sword when he noticed one of his flock limping from a wound in its hoof. Following the trail of blood, he found the half-buried weapon and brought it to Attila. The leader of the Huns rejoiced, for he recognized it as "the sword of Mars, always esteemed sacred among the kings of the Scythians" and marked its discovery as a sign that "he had been appointed ruler of the whole world and that through the sword of Mars supremacy in all wars was assured to him."[76] The kernel of this story first appeared in the *Histories* (4.62), where Herodotus remarked that the Scythians worshipped the god of war in the form of a sword, which they elevated on a platform made out of brushwood. Generations of later authors, pagan and Christian alike, repeated the story, first from Herodotus and then from one another.[77] By the fourth century, learned readers like Jerome identified the ferocity of the Huns with the savagery of the Scythians.[78] The embellishment of the shepherd's discovery of the sword was the invention of Priscus of Panium, a Greek diplomat who represented Emperor Theodosius II at the court of Attila in 448/449 CE. He wrote a personal account of his diplomatic mission to the Huns in Greek, but the work has survived only in fragments braided into the work of later historians and compilers. Jordanes's *Getica* preserved no fewer than seven portions of the lost history of Priscus, all of which concern the Huns,

---

75. On the *Getica*, see W. Goffart, *The Narrators of Barbarian History (A.D. 550–800): Jordanes, Gregory of Tours, Bede, and Paul the Deacon* (Princeton, 1988), pp. 20–111; and S. Ghosh, *Writing the Barbarian Past: Studies in Early Medieval Historical Narrative* (Leiden, 2016), pp. 39–68.

76. Jordanes, *Getica* 35: "Gladius Martis . . . sacer apud Scytharum reges semper habitus . . . Quo ille munere gratulatus, ut erat magnanimis, arbitratur se mundi totius principem constitutum et per Martis gladium potestatem sibi concessam esse bellorum," ed. T. Mommsen, MGH Auctores antiquissimi 5.1 (Berlin, 1882), pp. 105-106. The translation is by C. C. Mierow, *Jordanes: The Origins and Deeds of the Goths in English Version* (Princeton, 1908), p. 57.

77. For the influence of Herodotus 4.62 on later authors and on the story of Attila and the sword of Mars in particular, see J. O. Maenchen-Helfen, *The World of the Huns: Studies in their History and Culture* (Berkeley, 1973), pp. 278–80.

78. Jerome, *Ep.* 77.8-9, ed. I. Hilberg, CSEL 55.2 (Vienna, 1912), pp. 45-47.

including the circumstances surrounding the discovery of the sword of Mars.[79] Building on the foundation laid in antiquity by Herodotus, medieval chroniclers and nineteenth-century Hungarian scholars alike constructed myths of national origins that identified the ancient Scythians and Attila's Huns as the putative ancestors of the people of Hungary.[80]

Yet another shard from the *Histories* found its way into an Old English sunshine prognostication formula preserved in two manuscripts from the decades around 1100.[81] This text, which offered predictions of good fortune based on the appearance of sunshine during the twelve days of Christmas, reads as follows: "If the sun shines on the fourth day, then the camels will bear off much gold from the ants which then must guard the treasure." Although the promise of abundance is clear, the relationship between the camels and the ants is enigmatic without knowledge of the Herodotean story on which it was based. In his description of India, Herodotus related the gambit of a tribe who used camels to steal the gold that accumulated around the burrows of giant man-eating ants (3.102-105). At the hottest time of the day, when the ants were underground, the Indians arrived on the scene with a female camel that has recently given birth, as well as two male camels. They promptly loaded the female camel with gold. When the ants emerged to stop them, the female camel ran with extraordinary speed to return to its nursing young, carrying the rider and the gold to safety, while the monstrous insects overtook and devoured the slower male camels. Like other stories from the *Histories*, the anecdote about the gold-hoarding ants of India did not reach Anglo-Saxon England directly. Its circuitous route of transmission began in the first century, when Pliny the Elder introduced the story into the Latin tradition in a chapter devoted to ant ecology in his encyclopedic *Natural History* (11.36). Pliny's account later informed the report of the widely read *Etymologies* of Isidore of Seville, who relocated the ants from India to Ethiopia, remarked on their size and covetousness, but

---

79. Jordanes, *Getica* 35: "Gladius Martis inventus . . . quem Priscus istoricus tali refert occasione detectum," ed. Mommsen, p. 105.

80. G. Klaniczay, "The Myth of Scythian Origin and the Cult of Attila in the Nineteenth Century," in *Multiple Antiquities, Multiple Modernities: Ancient Histories in Nineteenth-Century European Cultures*, ed. G. Klaniczay, M. Werner, and O. Gecser (Frankfurt, 2011), pp. 185-212.

81. For what follows, see M. Cesario, "Ant-Lore in Anglo-Saxon England," *Anglo-Saxon England* 40 (2011): 273-91. On this genre more generally, see L. S. Chardonnens, *Anglo-Saxon Prognostics, 900–1100: Study and Texts* (Leiden, 2007); and M. Cesario, "The Shining of the Sun in the Twelve Nights of Christmas," in *Saints and Scholars: New Perspectives on Anglo-Saxon Literature and Culture in Honour of Hugh Magennis*, ed. S. McWilliams (Woodbridge, 2012), pp. 195-212.

failed to mention any camels.[82] Around the year 1000, the story seems to have entered the Anglo-Saxon tradition by yet another route, through its inclusion in *The Wonders of the East*, a fanciful treatise on the flora and fauna of Babylon, India, Ethiopia, and other distant locals.[83] Originally written in Greek during late antiquity, this text circulated in Northern Europe in Latin and Old English translations, some of which boasted fanciful illuminations of the story of the giant ants and the stratagem that allowed the Indians to steal their gold.[84]

Like Peter the Venerable, the medieval audiences of the *Getica* of Jordanes and the Old English *Wonders of the East* were unaware of the fact that the tales that they were reading about the discovery of the sword of Mars or the use of camels to outwit giant gold-hoarding ants had their origin in the inquiries of an ancient Greek historian whose centuries-long fame as the "father of history" had long since dwindled. Even so, the declining fortune of Herodotus's reputation and the usurpation of his place as the first writer of history did nothing to diminish the currency of his stories, long after the language of the *Histories* became unintelligible in the West. Translated into Latin at the height of the Roman Empire, these shards of ancient history found a durable medium that would ensure not only their survival but also their frequent and creative reuse for more than a millennium.

History in Shards

The tenacity of these ancient tales complicates our understanding of the Latin Middle Ages as a "dark age" for the "father of history" and speaks eloquently to the enduring charm and utility of Herodotean episodes in the western tradition, long after the *Histories* were lost. Their persistence challenges our presumptions about the survival of classical literature in the early Middle Ages in important ways, not least by forcing us to look beyond the evidence of surviving manuscripts and direct citations when we consider the influence of ancient authors in medieval Europe and beyond. The survival of Herodotus's *Histories*, one of the foundational authors of our discipline, has always been taken for granted, but it was

---

82. Isidore, *Etymologiarum sive Originum Libri XX* 12.3.9, ed. J. André, in *Isidore de Séville, Étymologies, Livre XII: Des animaux* (Paris, 1986), p. 131.
83. *Wonders of the East (Old English Text)* 9, ed. and trans. A. Orchard, in *Pride and Prodigies: Studies in the Monsters of the Beowulf-Manuscript* (Toronto, 1995), pp. 184–203, at p. 190.
84. A. J. Ford, *Marvel and Artefact: The "Wonders of the East" in Its Manuscript Context* (Leiden, 2015), esp. pp. 60–102 on London, British Library, Cotton Tiberius B V/1.

never guaranteed. As this chapter has shown, its transmission into the Latin West depended on a complex matrix of intellectual and ideological processes. Attention to the changing pragmatics and technologies of reading and writing in the study of reception history is essential for the recovery of the afterlife of ancient texts, especially when concrete evidence of their dissemination and influence does not survive.

As a model for reconstructing the reception history of texts, the concept of "shards" provides a useful vocabulary for the pragmatic disarticulation and creative redeployment of written materials of any genre across all time periods and areas of the world. In this chapter, I have concentrated on the fugitive history of a seminal ancient Greek text in the Latin Middle Ages, but this same inquiry could be made about the trajectory of the shards of ancient and medieval texts preserved in a myriad of later medieval and early modern works: *The Histories of the Kings of France and the Turkish House of Ottoman*, written in Hebrew by the Jewish physician Joseph HaCohen (d. c. 1575); *The Perfumed Breeze from the Tender Branch of al-Andalus, with Mention of Its Vizier, Lisān al-Dīn ibn al-Khatīb*, composed in Arabic by the itinerant Moroccan antiquarian al-Maqqarī (d. 1632) during his residence in Damascus; the encyclopedic *Yamato Honzō* compiled by the Japanese polymath Kaibara Ekiken (1630-1714) on the model of Chinese pharmacopoeias; the "carnival funhouse" of texts redacted and assembled in the *Bee-Hive* of the gifted polymath Francis Daniel Pastorius (1651-c. 1720); and even the *Commonplace Book* kept by the young Thomas Jefferson (1743-1826), the first entries of which are short snippets from the *Histories* of Herodotus.[85] In each of these works, we can observe premodern authors in the process of constructing meaning from the reordering of disparate sources of written information, from the purposeful deployment of so many shards of history.

Modern technologies of writing and social interaction have only amplified these millennium-old habits of deploying extracts and digests of historical information for contemporary use. Public platforms like

---

85. HaCohen: M. Jacobs, *Islamische Geschichte in jüdischen Chroniken: Hebräische Historiographie des 16. und 17. Jahrhunderts* (Tübingen, 2004), pp. 185-220 ("Ha-Kohens Darstellung islamischer Geschichte"); al-Maqqarī: S. F. Adil, "Memorializing al-Maqqarī: The Life, Work, and Worlds of a Muslim Scholar" (PhD diss., University of Chicago, 2015); Ekiken: F. Marcon, *The Knowledge of Nature and the Nature of Knowledge in Early Modern Japan* (Chicago, 2015), pp. 72-110; Pastorius: A. Grafton, "The Republic of Letters in the American Colonies: Francis Daniel Pastorius Makes a Notebook," *American Historical Review* 117 (2012): 1-39 (quotation at p. 6); and Jefferson: *Jefferson's Literary Commonplace Book*, ed. D. L. Wilson (Princeton, 1989), esp. p. 23 (nos. 1-3) on Herodotus.

Facebook and Twitter allow us to compile on our "walls" and "feeds" the digital equivalent of medieval florilegia and early modern commonplace books, crowded with inspirational quotations, historical aphorisms, and news digests. The sum of these shards of information is a staggering public testimony of innumerable personal uses of the past, each "a patterned picture of remembered things said and done in past times and distant places."[86] For medieval readers as much as for modern ones, the criterion for the reuse of pithy stories from antiquity was not their truth value, but their usefulness. Shards of history persist in literary traditions long after their authors and origins have been forgotten so long as an individual can relate them "with some reasonable degree of relevance and harmony to his idea of himself and of what he is doing in the world and what he hopes to do."[87]

---

86. C. L. Becker, "Every Man His Own Historian," *American Historical Review* 37 (1932): 221–36, at p. 229.

87. Becker, "Every Man His Own Historian," p. 229.

Epilogue
A Treasure of Secrets

This book collects and lightly updates fourteen articles on topics in the religious and cultural history of early medieval monasticism between the tenth and twelfth centuries with a focus on the abbey of Cluny. In this epilogue, I provide some context for the composition of these chapters, which were published over the course of two decades (1999-2023) and informed directly or indirectly by my graduate studies at Princeton University under the direction of Professor Giles Constable (1929-2021). Despite their thematic coherence, these chapters were not conceived as a group from the outset. Many of them were written in preparation for the books that I was writing or editing about the history of Cluny. Others were singular studies prepared at the invitation of editors, who presented me with ideas that I found exciting and worthwhile to pursue. Several were the result of serendipity, when an unexpected detail on a manuscript page or an odd phrase in a printed text raised a question that demanded further inquiry. One chapter was the first step toward a book project that failed to materialize. Ultimately, all of these chapters were written to satisfy my curiosity about questions that came to mind as I read monastic sources from the early Middle Ages both in print and in manuscript. What can a ransom note written by a tenth-century abbot tell us about the religion of his captors? What does a lexicon of monastic hand signs reveal about daily life in a medieval abbey? What kinds of people went on pilgrimage to the shrine of a Cluniac saint in the early eleventh century? Why did a line drawing in a twelfth-century manuscript implicate *curiosity* as a life-threatening vice? How did an abbot of Cluny learn an anecdote originally told by the ancient Greek historian Herodotus?

I never expected to become a historian of medieval monasticism. When I arrived at Princeton University to begin my doctorate in History in the fall of 1994, I was intent on studying the material culture of ancient Christianity (what the Germans called *christliches Archäologie*). I had discovered premodern history belatedly, as I was finishing a bachelor's degree in psychology at York University in Toronto in the late 1980s. When I had started college, my goal upon graduation was to become a fireman or a paramedic. Junior-year electives in prehistoric archaeology, the history of Christianity, and medieval civilization changed all that. These encounters with the distant past stirred an interest in premodern history informed up to that point by fantasy motifs prevalent in popular culture, from Dungeons & Dragons and the films of Ray Harryhausen to J. R. R. Tolkien's Middle Earth and Robert E. Howard's Hyborian Age. To do this work well, I would have to start from scratch, a luxury afforded by understanding parents and a university tuition that I could pay on my own with the earnings of summer labor jobs.

In 1989, I began studying Latin and Greek and leapt with little preparation into ancient and medieval history seminars offered by York University's exceptional faculty. In 1992/1993, I spent a year abroad at the Ruprecht Karls-Universität in Heidelberg, where I learned German by studying for the *Latinum* (Germany's national Latin examination). During that year, I visited Rome for the first time, where I was left spellbound by the late ancient sarcophagi in the Vatican Museum. Equally inspiring was Peter Brown's seminal essay "Relics and Social Status in the Age of Gregory of Tours," especially his evocation of Gregory's world as a place dense with tombs.[1] I spent my summers during college working as a gravedigger at the McCowan Road Cemetery in Scarborough, which kindled my curiosity in premodern funerary culture. When I visited Princeton in the spring of 1994, I was certain about what

---

1. P. Brown, "Relics and Social Status in the Age of Gregory of Tours," in P. Brown, *Society and the Holy in Late Antiquity* (Berkeley, 1982), pp. 222–50, at p. 223: "They stood in the shady corners of the great basilicas, in crypts, scattered in the great dormitory suburbs of the dead outside the town, or they lay hidden in the brambles of some deserted village."

my academic future held. During a long walk with Peter Brown, I spoke breathlessly about my passion for late antique visual culture, especially gold glass, catacomb paintings, and early Christian sarcophagi. After listening patiently, he assured me that the Princeton faculty could teach me other things as well.

As it turns out, Peter was right. Although I had the eagerness of a new convert, I had neither the specialist's eye nor the technical training in art history necessary to do advanced research in late antique funerary culture, so I explored other avenues of historical inquiry. A seminar on medieval monasticism offered by John Fleming and Giles Constable provided me with a new calling. I was excited by the research possibilities offered by the study of monastic communities, about which I knew little, but I was equally won over by Gile's warmth and kindness. Giles was a faculty member at the School of Historical Studies at the Institute for Advanced Study, a mile and a half from the Princeton campus, but I learned that Ernst Kantorowicz had established a precedent for an Institute faculty member to serve as the advisor of a Princeton History dissertation.[2] All I needed was a topic that was worthy of Giles.

I owe my dissertation subject to a suggestion from Richard C. Hoffmann, one of my advisers at York University. While visiting my parents in Canada over Christmas in 1995, Rich took me out to lunch and offered a solution to my dilemma. Familiar with my interest in visual culture and mindful that the topic should appeal to Giles, he suggested that I explore the sign language of the monks of Cluny. He had encountered the Cluniac sign lexicon on his endless search for evidence of medieval pisciculture; as it turns out, the silent language of the monks had signs for many kinds of fish. There was, however, no full-length study of this monastic custom. I was intrigued and proposed to Giles a dissertation exploring the rationales for religious silence in early medieval monasticism, the origin and use of hand signs at the abbey of Cluny to curtail harmful speech in the community, and the spread and adaptation of this custom both among Cluniac dependencies and among other monastic orders. Giles liked the topic and agreed to serve as my advisor.

From that point onward, I divided my time between Dickinson Hall, where William Chester Jordan and I met weekly to translate the Cluniac

---

2. That student was Robert Benson (1925–96), who accompanied Kantorowicz when he moved from Berkeley to the Institute for Advanced Study in 1951 and completed his doctorate in History at Princeton under the aegis of Joseph Strayer in 1958. See R. E. Lerner, *Ernst Kantorowicz: A Life* (Princeton, 2017), pp. 369–72.

sign lexicon, a short but obscure document describing more than one hundred hand signs taught to the novices as part of their training to become monks, and the Institute for Advanced Study, where Giles and I convened to discuss the progress of my research. In preparation for writing about Cluniac sign language, Giles advised me to read through the two massive compilations of customary law compiled at the great Burgundian abbey in the late eleventh century. The task was formidable. In addition to the sign lexicon, Bernard of Cluny's *Ordo Cluniacensis* and Ulrich of Zell's *Consuetudines Cluniacensis* contained the rubrics for rituals and liturgical celebrations, the standards of comportment expected during worship and mealtimes, the duties of specialized officials in the abbey, and a myriad of other directives for the organization and operation of a religious community numbering several hundred individuals. In short, these voluminous texts provided innumerable details about the contexts in which the Cluniacs employed their silent language of hand signs.

Although the customaries offered an abundance of information about monastic life in the eleventh century, they were not the only sources relevant to my research. Giles also lent to me his copy of the *Bibliotheca Cluniacensis*, an indispensable treasure trove of primary source materials related to the history of Cluny published in 1618. There I found accounts of the lives of the community's holy abbots, from Odo (927–942) to Hugh the Great (1049–1109), which were replete with anecdotal evidence about many aspects of the cloistered life in this period, including the value of silence and the use of sign language among the brethren. Like the customaries, the study of Cluniac hagiography was in its infancy in the 1990s and virtually unknown in North America. Pioneering work by H. E. J. Cowdrey and Dominique Iogna-Prat had brought to light specific aspects of these literary traditions, but as Iogna-Prat's 1992 catalog of abbatial saint's lives from Cluny made plain, many important texts languished unedited and unread in centuries-old manuscripts housed in European libraries.

Although Giles introduced me to the untapped riches of source materials from eleventh-century Cluny that were essential for reconstructing the lived experiences of the brethren, he offered little guidance about how to read these texts beyond the straightforward advice of paying attention to the ways in which conventions of genre limited the use of customaries and hagiography as historical sources. My method of reading medieval sources developed primarily in emulation of his published work, particularly his magnum opus, *The Reformation of the Twelfth Century*, which appeared in 1996. In the introduction to this book, Giles laid out the challenges of using texts written by medieval monks as historical sources and offered a method of interpretation centered on the identification of tensions, contradictory tendencies, and other discernable changes in the textual record that signaled moments of agency and intention.[3] As his book demonstrates, recognizing these minor changes required an expansive knowledge of the textual evidence, without which it would be easy to miss the little ripples that heralded shifts of seismic significance. This approach to medieval texts informed all my subsequent studies, from the adaptation of the Cluniac sign lexicon to the rewriting of abbatial hagiography to the transmission of ancient stories in medieval reading communities.

My first published article was the result of questions raised as I read through the monastic customaries for the first time to build the context for the value of religious silence and the use of monastic sign language among the Cluniacs. The policing of these customs was at the forefront of my mind. How did monks reconcile the use of hand signs in place of speech and how did they prevent the brethren from misusing them and thereby undermining their spiritual integrity? As I worked my way through the customaries, I kept coming across references to an official called the "roundsman" (*circator*), who patrolled large abbeys at random times to catch monks who took part in illicit activities, from talking or signing when it was forbidden to engaging in sexual commerce with their fellow brethren. I would never have conceived of writing a short history of this official without the encouragement of Teofilo Ruiz, who spent the 1997/1998 academic year at Princeton as a Visiting Professor of Distinguished Teaching. Although I was still a graduate student, he recommended that I try to publish an article, nothing long or ambitious, but something to have in hand for the job market. With this advice in mind, I wrote "Lurking with Spiritual Intent: A Note on the Origins and Function of the Monastic Roundsman (*Circator*)," which appeared in 1999 (§ 7).

The Cluniac customaries proved to be fertile ground for the study of monastic sign language. They not only preserved the only surviving evidence for the forms of individual signs, but also provided abundant information about the devotional and practical contexts in which the

---

3. G. Constable, *The Reformation of the Twelfth Century* (Cambridge, 1996), pp. 1–43.

monks employed their silent language.[4] At the invitation of Susan Boynton and Isabelle Cochelin, I contributed an article titled "Monastic Sign Language in the Cluniac Customaries" to a groundbreaking collection of essays published in 2005 on the use of the Cluniac customaries as historical sources, titled *From Dead of Night to End of Day: The Medieval Customs of Cluny / Du coeur de la nuit à la fin du jour: Les coutumes clunisiennes au Moyen Âge* (§ 8). With the publication of this article, I entered a fruitful dialogue with an international community of scholars at work in the United States, Canada, France, and Germany.

Another publication from this time had nothing to do with the history of silence and sign language, but instead it resulted from an unexpected discovery that I made in an eleventh-century manuscript in France. In the summer of 2003, Anne E. Lester's research on Cistercian convents in late medieval Champagne took us to the city of Troyes. While she worked in the departmental archives, I explored the manuscript holdings of the Médiathèque de l'Agglomération troyenne (formerly the Bibliothèque municipale). I was excited to discover in the library's manuscript catalog an eleventh-century copy of Odo of Cluny's *Collationes*, an early tenth-century treatise on the virtues and the vices. As I leafed through this manuscript, I noticed that a later scribe had copied out a hitherto unstudied seventy-two-line poem on the final two folios. The theme of this poem was the emptiness of worldly glory in the face of the inevitability of death, a topic treated at much greater length by the twelfth-century poet Bernard of Cluny in his poem *De contemptu mundi*. With the help of Drew Jones, whom I met at the University of Notre Dame in 2004, I produced an edition and translation of the poem, examined its tone and content, and made the case for its date, authorship, and audience. The results appeared in 2006 as "*Nunc homo, cras humus*: A Twelfth-Century Cluniac Poem on the Certainty of Death" (§ 11).

As sometimes happens, the idea for my second book, *Cluny and the Muslims of La Garde-Freinet*, arose from a discovery that I made while researching my first book on silence and sign language.[5] While I was writing my dissertation, I read through all the saints' lives produced at Cluny or in its orbit of influence, from Odo of Cluny's early

---

4. S. G. Bruce, *Silence and Sign Language in Medieval Monasticism: The Cluniac Tradition, c. 900-1200* (Cambridge, 2007).
5. S. G. Bruce, *Cluny and the Muslims of La Garde-Freinet: Hagiography and the Problem of Islam in Medieval Europe* (Ithaca, 2015).

tenth-century *Life of Gerald* to Rodulphus de Sully's late twelfth-century *Life of Peter the Venerable*. My goal was to find incidental references to the discipline of silence or the practice of sign language at Cluny and its dependences that would inform my research. I made some welcome discoveries, but I also stumbled across an incident that became the topic of my second book. While reading the many accounts of the life of Abbot Maiolus, I noticed a recurring anecdote about his abduction in the Alpine Passes by Muslim adventurers from La Garde-Freinet (modern Saint-Tropez, in Provence). This story piqued my interest for two reasons. First, I was eager to learn why Muslims were active in the Alps in the late tenth century and why they kidnapped an abbot of Cluny. Second, I noticed that the details of the story changed with each retelling in ways that suggested its value as an historical source for the ways that Cluniac monks thought about Islam between the years 1000 and 1150. My first notes on this new project date from the late 1990s, several years before Monique Goullet applied terminology coined by the literary theorist Gérard Genette to talk about the rewriting of hagiography (*réécriture hagiographique*) as a literary occasion that demanded historical inquiry.[6] As her study confirmed, the choices made by medieval authors who rewrote hagiographical narratives offered opportunities to examine their intention for rewriting and to reconstruct the context that informed their interventions.

Only one source for the abduction of Maiolus in the summer of 972 boasted any immediacy to the event: a short ransom note that the abbot allegedly sent to Cluny from captivity to request payment for the release of him and his entourage, which was preserved in two of the earliest accounts of the kidnapping. Saturated in language borrowed from the Psalms, Maiolus's ransom note characterized his Muslim captors as "the hordes of Belial." I was certain that the abbot's evocation of this ancient and infamous name was no coincidence, so I set about to explore the long history of its dark associations in the hope that it might provide insight into Maiolus's perception of his abductors. Pursuing this topic also provided me with the opportunity to conduct preliminary research into the presence of the Muslim community in Provence in the tenth century and to reconstruct the arteries of pilgrim and merchant traffic

---

6. M. Goullet, *Ecriture et réécriture hagiographiques: Essai sur les réécriture de Vies de saints dans l'Occident latin medieval (VIIIe-XIIIe s.)* (Turnhout, 2005); and G. Genette, *La littérature au second degré* (Paris, 1982); English translation: G. Genette, *Palimpsests: Literature in the Second Degree*, trans. C. Newman and C. Doubinsky (Lincoln, 1997).

over the Alpine Passes that drew these "entrepreneurs" to the mountain heights in search of treasure and human chattel. The resulting article, "An Abbot Between Two Cultures: Maiolus of Cluny Considers the Muslims of La Garde-Freinet," appeared in 2007 (§ 3).

The rewriting of the lives of Maiolus also provided an occasion to investigate the motivations of the hagiographers who composed them. In his foundational study of the cult of Maiolus, Dominique Iogna-Prat had argued that an anonymous *Life of Maiolus* (BHL 5180) believed by the Bollandists to have been a redaction of Syrus of Cluny's early eleventh-century account (BHL 5177/79) was, in fact, the earliest life of the abbot.[7] Moreover, internal evidence suggested that it had most likely been written by a monk of Pavia. In a study of the composition of this saint's life, I took this argument further in three ways: by fleshing out the relationship between Maiolus and the Ottonian royal family, whose court was in Pavia, to provide the context for the impetus behind the author's initiative; by examining how the author of the *vita* used biblical typology to present his fellow citizens as the special recipients of the saint's power by comparing Pavia with the ancient cities of Sidon and Tyre; and by showing how the Pavian claim on the holy patronage of Maiolus spurred the Cluniacs to write their own account of his life, which excised the local details that rooted the abbot's activities in Pavia (thereby revoking their claims on a special relationship with him) and initiating a new tradition of "in-house" abbatial hagiography at Cluny that would endure for a century and a half. "Local Sanctity and Civic Typology in Early Medieval Pavia: The Example of the Cult of Abbot Maiolus of Cluny" was published in 2010 (§ 5).

Although many of the chapters in this book were published in advance of the projects they informed, some were salvaged from the cutting-room floor after those projects were finished. Such was the case with the chapter titled "Clandestine Codices in the Captivity Narratives of Maiolus of Cluny." A recurrent feature in the story of Maiolus's abduction was the role played by books that he carried on his person "in the fold of his cloak" (*sub amictu suo*) in his interaction with his Muslim captors. I rarely travel without a book in hand, so I was intrigued to learn more about the manuscripts that this tenth-century prelate carried with him on his frequent journeys. Unfortunately, the topic was too tangential to the argument of my book on Cluny and Islam to

---

7. D. Iogna-Prat, *Agni Immaculati: Recherches sur les sources hagiographiques relatives à saint Maieul de Cluny (954–994)* (Paris, 1988), pp. 20–29.

warrant an extended discussion of it there. Thankfully, a call for papers for a conference at Pacific University on "The Material World of the Middle Ages" held in October 2016 provided me with the impetus to develop the topic further. The article was published the following year in a Festschrift in honor of Gernot R. Wieland, who was Michael Herren's successor as the editor of the *Journal of Medieval Latin* from 2011 to 2016 (§ 4).

The writings of Peter the Venerable also provided fertile ground for research long after the publication of *Cluny and the Muslims of La Garde-Freinet* in 2015. An invitation from Liesbeth van Houts to present a paper at the Fortieth Battle Conference on Anglo-Norman Studies held in Paris in July 2017 allowed me to compare the motivations behind Peter's two missions to England in 1130 and 1155/1156 (§ 12). This was new territory for me. This research required me to digest a formidable amount of historiography on the political history of twelfth-century England to make sense of the abbot's motivations for undertaking not one, but two, journeys across the English Channel, the first as a young abbot in need of political patronage and the second as an ailing elder statesman acting against the king's interest to help a close friend in need. Giles was very much on my mind as I conducted this research, which relied on his edition of Peter the Venerable's letters. By coincidence, on my way to Paris, I tarried in Cambridge for a few days, where a sudden rainstorm sent me scurrying into G. David Bookseller on Saint Edward's Passage. As I browsed the used books while waiting out the storm, I stumbled across a treasure: a copy of *The Letters of Peter the Venerable* that had belonged to the eminent British medievalist Christopher N. L. Brooke (1927–2015). Giles and Christopher had met in Cambridge as students in the late 1940s and remained lifelong friends. On the first page of the edition, a dedicatory inscription in Giles's familiar handwriting read "For Christopher with best wishes from Giles 15/ix/67." I was two days old when he wrote it. I bought the books and later brought them to Princeton to show Giles. Two months before his death, he made an addendum to the dedication: "And now for Scott Bruce 14/xi/20."

Giles had a fondness for Peter the Venerable as a person that I did not share. One of the aspects of his life that we did not agree on was his view of Muslims. While Giles gave the Cluniac abbot the benefit of the doubt that his conciliatory writings about Islam were sincere, I saw them as a disingenuous last-ditch effort to appeal to Muslims readers only after the might of Christian armies had failed against them. It was equally difficult for me to spend time with Peter's invectives against Jews and heretics, but the effort of doing so brought its own rewards. In the summer of 2014, I was reading the Latin edition of the abbot's treatise against the Petrobrusian heretics in the Corpus Christianorum edition by James Fearns, when I came across a striking analogy. Peter compared the senselessness of the Petrobrusians' belief system to the futility of the ancient Persian monarch Cyrus, who punished a river for drowning his favorite horse. Although Fearns dutifully noted the source of this anecdote as the *Histories* of Herodotus, he offered no explanation for Peter's knowledge of this ancient story. Perplexed by the currency of this tale in twelfth-century Europe, centuries after knowledge of Greek had been lost in the Latin west, I set out to discover the abbot's source for this Herodotean episode, while at the same time tracing the history of the survival of ancient Greek history in the western tradition. The results of this inquiry, which took me from the fifth century BCE to eighteenth-century America, appeared in 2019 as an article titled "The Dark Age of Herodotus: Shards of a Fugitive History in Early Medieval Europe" (§ 14).

Not every project succeeds, however. After I had published *Cluny and the Muslims of La Garde-Freinet* in 2015, I was free to pursue a new book-length research topic. By this point in my career, I had spent considerable time with early medieval manuscripts, most of which were florilegia (miscellanies) made up of many different texts. It struck me that these compilations were analogous to the mixtapes that I made as a teenager in the 1980s. I would often curate collections of songs united by a common theme and record them on cassette tapes. One of the joys of making these tapes was the creation of new meanings through the synergy of songs that belonged to different eras or genres. In the same way, medieval compilers sometimes copied different kinds of texts together in groupings that raised questions about their function for contemporary readers. I noticed that the *Rule of Benedict*, the most important handbook for the practice of cenobitic monasticism in the Middle Ages, rarely appeared alone in its manuscript context. I conceived of a book project to explore the ways in which texts copied alongside Benedict's rule may have inflected its meaning and function, which I called "Reinventing the *Rule of Benedict* in Medieval Monasticism (ca. 600–1600)." My encounters with manuscripts containing the *Rule* in European libraries or with microfilms consulted at the Hill Museum and Monastic Library in Saint John's, Minnesota, suggested to me that medieval readers interacted with this fundamental text with a much wider range of expectations than modern scholars had supposed: devotional, administrative, commemorative, pastoral, and otherwise. The reception history of the *Rule*, I planned to argue, was characterized not by a sense of reverence that rendered its meaning static and unchanging across the centuries, but rather by a creative pragmatism that allowed medieval readers to harness the text of the *Rule of Benedict* to a variety of possible functions.[8]

I soon abandoned this book project to pursue other ventures, but my initial inquiry produced a case study that illustrated what we stand to gain by examining the *Rule of Benedict* in its manuscript context. In a twelfth-century compilation made for the nuns of Admont, a scribe prefaced a copy of Benedict's rule with a line drawing of a monk ascending a ladder to Heaven. On one side, he wrote a list of virtues; on the other, a list of vices. My eye was initially drawn to the illustration, but what piqued my interest was the word at the top of the list of vices: "curiosity" (*curiositas*). Why, I wondered, did the scribe single out "curiosity" as a dangerous vice and upon what authority did he make this claim? It was especially strange to me because the *Rule of Benedict* made no mention of curiosity at all. This inquiry resulted in an article titled "Curiosity Killed the Monk: The History of an Early Medieval Vice," which appeared in 2019 (§ 13).

Between 2015 and 2020, I also had the opportunity to write four articles for various handbooks and collaborative histories of medieval monasticism. These were not research papers, but rather syntheses of scholarship about specific topics. In each case, I strived to produce a study that would have benefited me when I was a student. An invitation to contribute an article on "The Benedictines" for *The Oxford Handbook of Christian Monasticism* (2020) allowed me to explore the early history of the *Rule of Benedict* and its rise to prominence in the Carolingian period, to define the term "Benedictine" and interrogate its utility when applied to monastic communities in the Middle Ages, and to pinpoint three overlooked topics of research in the Benedictine tradition that deserve more attention from the next generation of historians, namely, the activities of Benedictine monks in the later Middle Ages, the application of the *Rule of Benedict* in female communities, and the history of monastic poetry (§ 1). In the same vein, an offer to write an article on "Sources for the History of Monasticism in the Central Middle Ages

---

8. For a Carolingian example, see S. G. Bruce, "Textual Triage and Pastoral Care in the Carolingian Age: The Example of the *Rule of Benedict*," *Traditio* 75 (2020): 127–41.

(c. 800–1100)" for *The Cambridge History of Medieval Monasticism in the Latin West* (2020) provided me with the occasion not only to introduce readers to the three most abundant kinds of sources for the study of medieval monasticism (charters, rules and customaries, and hagiography) but also to draw attention to the importance of material sources, like manuscripts, reliquaries, and archaeological remains, for our study of the monastic past (§ 2).

In 2014, Steven Vanderputten and I agreed to edit a collection of sixteen essays offering a new history of the abbey of Cluny in the Middle Ages. No such collection had been published since 1971, when Noreen Hunt curated a decade's worth of European scholarship on Cluny and published it in English translation. Our goal was to produce a resource for the next generation of scholars interested in Cluniac monasticism that would provide them not only with a general history of the abbey from its foundation in 910 to the end of the Middle Ages, but also with specific studies written by specialists in monastic law, liturgy, hagiography, diplomatics, manuscripts, visual culture, and archaeology. The volume appeared in 2022 as *A Companion to the Abbey of Cluny in the Middle Ages*.

I contributed two state-of-the-question chapters to this collection. "The Relics of Cluny" surveyed the evidence for the cult of relics at Cluny from the trickle of saintly remains acquired primarily by purchase in the tenth century to the imperial gifts accumulated by Abbot Odilo in the eleventh century. It charted the rise of reverence for Cluny's abbots, which the brethren were slow to foster, and showed how the monks benefited from the donations of sacred remains made by warriors and pilgrims returning from the East in the era of the crusades (§ 9). "Cluny and the Crusades" picked up on the theme of Cluny's connections to Outremer. Although older generations of scholars had implicated Cluny in the rise of crusader ideologies, in no small part because Pope Urban II had been a monk there, this chapter argued that the brethren of Cluny were not active participants in the crusade movement. In fact, the sole crusading initiative aggressively encouraged by an abbot of Cluny, the so-called 1150 expedition in response to the failed Second Crusade, never materialized. Nonetheless, the brethren benefited financially by offering loans to Christian knights who took the cross and by receiving valuable donations, especially relics from the East, from returning crusaders. Individual monks made pilgrimages to Outremer in this period, most notably the exiled Abbot Pontius of Melgueil, and some new monastic foundations in the Crusader kingdoms claimed affiliation with the great Burgundian abbey, but the involvement of the Cluniacs in this movement was primarily opportunistic and restricted to the home front of Western Europe (§ 10).

When *A Companion to the Abbey of Cluny* appeared in print in 2022, I was already well underway with a new research project only loosely related to the great Burgundian abbey, but I return to Cluniac sources again and again as a way to teach monastic history.[9] In the summer of 2020, I collaborated with my doctoral student Mr. W. Tanner Smoot, who had received a Summer Research Fellowship from Fordham University to study an anonymous collection of miracles compiled in Souvigny at the tomb of Abbot Maiolus. This early eleventh-century text comprised fifty-four chapters detailing dozens of miracles attributed to the saint's healing power. Like many sources from Cluny, it had received no attention in modern scholarship. We set out to reconstruct a social history of the shrine based on the incidental information found in the miracle accounts. We started by tabulating the kinds of people who came to Souvigny to find relief from their maladies and calculated how far they had traveled. Many of these travelers suffered from motor disabilities and blindness, which drew our attention to the networks of family and friends who facilitated their journey to the saint's tomb. We also discovered pilgrims taking steps to increase their own agency by making use of personal mobility aids, including a rare reference to what may have been a wheelchair. The result of our inquiry was a vivid portrait of the thaumaturgical and social activities that took place at a bustling shrine at the dawn of the second millennium. It was published in 2023 under the title "The Social Life of an Eleventh-Century Shrine in the *Miraculorum sancti Maioli libri duo* (BHL 5186)" (§ 6).

The abbey of Cluny has not given up all her mysteries. The fourteen chapters collected here are gleanings from the "treasure of secrets" preserved in Latin texts written by medieval monks over a millennium ago, the echoes of a "centuries-old murmuring" preserved in manuscripts and on parchment fragments that attest to the cultural richness of a distant age, but they are not the end of the story. As renowned as it was in the Middle Ages, Cluny was one of hundreds of cloistered communities, where the industry of monks produced books

---

9. For an introduction to this new project, see S. G. Bruce, "The Lost Patriarchs Project: Recovering the Greek Fathers in the Medieval Latin Tradition," *Religion Compass* 14 (2020): 1–8.

for corporate worship, personal study, and private devotion. Countless texts from medieval Europe remain untouched and unread in libraries and archives, awaiting discovery from intrepid historians with the patience, endurance, and empathy to decipher their secrets. This book not only illustrates the value of pursuing historical research for the insight that it offers into the lived experiences and devotional practices of early medieval monks but also invites readers to pursue their own questions about the premodern past. The practice of historical inquiry is its own reward.

Acknowledgments

The epilogue of the book records many of the intellectual debts that I owe to my teachers at York University and Princeton University, including Richard C. Hoffmann, Michael W. Herren, Peter Brown, William Chester Jordan, and Giles Constable. Colleagues and students at the University of Colorado at Boulder and Fordham University have also been supportive in important ways, especially Paul Sutter, Nick Paul, and W. Tanner Smoot. My thanks to Mahinder Kingra for shepherding this project from proposal to print, to the staff of Cornell University Press for their care with the manuscript, and to the external reviewers for their criticism and encouragement. I am very grateful to Marc Edouard Gautier for his hospitality during my visits to Angers and for his permission to reproduce the cover image from Angers, Bibliothèque municipal 820, fol. 1v. W. Tanner Smoot, Benjamin A. Bertrand, and Curtis Rager kindly checked the page proofs. I prepared the manuscript for publication while I was the Edwin C. and Elizabeth A. Whitehead Member (2024-25) in the School of Historical Studies at the Institute for Advanced Study in Princeton, New Jersey, with funding provided by the Andrew W. Mellon Foundation.

Two people deserve special mention. Drew Jones has been a generous interlocutor and collaborator for almost two decades. The book's dedication is a small token of my admiration for his towering erudition and my gratitude for his friendship. None of this would have been possible, however, without Anne E. Lester, who has made innumerable sacrifices, small and large, over the years to forward my scholarship, while also pursuing her own research, managing her administrative and editorial responsibilities, and parenting our two children, Mira and Vivienne, with wisdom and grace.

Institute for Advanced Study
Princeton, New Jersey
9 April 2025

Bibliography

Manuscripts

Admont, Benediktinerstift, Codex 17
Admont, Benediktinerstift, Codex 567
Angers, BM 803
Angers, BM 820
Bamberg, Staatsbibliothek, Msc. Bibl. 126
Cluny, Bibliothèque du Musée d'art et d'archéologie de Cluny, MS 79
Einsiedeln, Stiftsbibliothek 199
Einsiedeln, Stiftsbibliothek 281
Florence, Laurentianus 70.3
Geneva, Bibliothèque Publique et Universitaire, Latin 169
Laon, BM 265
London, British Library, Additional 22820
London, British Library, Additional ms. 47678
London, British Library, Cotton Tiberius B V/1
London, British Library, Royal I.E.VII–VIII
Oxford, Bodleian Library, Laud Gr. 35
Oxford, Bodleian Library, Laud Misc. 636
Paris, BnF, Grec 437
Paris, BnF, Latin 2328
Paris, BnF, Latin 5365
Paris, BnF, Latin 5611
Paris, BnF, Latin 9665
Paris, BnF, Latin 17716
Paris, BnF, Latin 18304
Paris, BnF, Nouvelles acquisitions françaises 4336
Paris, BnF, Nouvelle acquisition latine 1438
Paris, BnF, Nouvelle acquisition latine 1490
Paris, BnF, Nouvelle acquisition latine 2246
Paris, BnF, Nouvelle acquisition latine 2483
Parma, Biblioteca Palatina, Ms. Parm. 1650
Saint Gallen, Stiftsbibliothek, Codex Sangallensis 1092
Troyes, Médiathèque de l'Agglomération troyenne 918
Valenciennes, BM 411
Vatican City, Biblioteca Apostolica Vaticana, Barberini Latini 671
Vatican City, Biblioteca Apostolica Vaticana, Reg. Lat. 134
Vatican City, Biblioteca Apostolica Vaticana, Reg. Lat. 1709

Primary Sources

Abelard, *Institutio seu Regula Sanctimonialium*, ed. D. Luscombe, in *The Letter Collection of Peter Abelard and Heloise* (Oxford, 2013), pp. 358–517.
Adalbero, *Carmen ad Robertum regem*, ed. and trans. C. Carozzi, in *Adalberon de Laon, Poème au roi Robert* (Paris, 1979).
Agobard of Lyons, *De iudaicis superstitionibus et erroribus (ad Ludouicum)*, ed. L. Van Acker, in *Agobardi Lugdunensis Opera Omnia*, CCCM 52 (Turnhout, 1981), pp. 199–221.
Alia miraculorum quorundam S. Hugonis relatione MS. collectore monacho quodam, ut videtur Cluniacensi, in *BC*, cols. 447–62.
Ambrose, *Expositio evangelii secundum Lucam*, ed. M. Adriaen, CCSL 14 (Turnhout, 1957).
"Ancienne traduction française des *Ecclesiastica officia, Instituta generalis Capituli, Usus conversorum* et *Regula sancti Benedicti*, publié d'après le manuscript 352 de la bibliothèque publique de Dijon," ed. P. Guignard, in *Les monuments primitifs de la règle Cistercienne* (Dijon, 1878), pp. 407–42 (Appendix I).
Anglo-Saxon Chronicle, ed. S. Irvine, in *The Anglo-Saxon Chronicle: A Collaborative Edition*, Vol. 7, *MS. E, A Semi-Diplomatic Edition with Introduction and Indices* (Cambridge, 2004).
The Anglo-Saxon Chronicle According to the Several Original Authorities, 2 vols. (London, 1861).
Annales de Wintonia, ed. H. R. Luard, in *Annales Monastici*, Vol. 2, *Annales Monasterii de Wintonia (A.D. 519–1277) and Annales Monasterii de Waverleia (A.D. 1–1291)* (London, 1865).
Annales Magdeburgensis, ed. G. Pertz, MGH Scriptores 16 (Hanover, 1859), pp. 105–96.
Anselm, *Liber de humanis moribus per similitudines*, ed. R. W. Southern and F. S. Schmitt, in *Memorials of St. Anselm*, Auctores Britannici Medii Aevi 1 (London, 1969), pp. 39–104.
Apuleius Madaurensis Metamorphoses Book IX: Text, Introduction, and Commentary, ed. B. L. Hijmans Jr. et al. (Groningen, 1995).
Augustine, *Confessiones*, ed. J. J. O'Donnell, in *Augustine: Confessions*, 3 vols. (Oxford, 1992).
Ausonius, *Epistolae*, ed. R. Green, in *The Works of Ausonius* (Oxford, 1991).
Baudric of Bourgueil, *Historia Ierosolimitana*, ed. S. Biddlecombe (Woodbridge, 2014).
Bede, *Historia abbatum*, ed. and trans. C. Grocock and I. N. Wood, in *Abbots of Wearmouth and Jarrow* (Oxford, 2013), pp. 22–75.
Bede, *In Samuelem prophetam allegorica expositio*, PL 91, cols. 499–714.
Benedict of Aniane, *Concordia Regularum*, PL 103, cols. 701–1380.
Bernard of Clairvaux, *Apologia ad Guillelmum abbatem*, in *SBO*, vol. 3, pp. 61–108.
Bernard of Clairvaux, *De gradibus superbiae et humilitatis*, in *SBO*, vol. 3, pp. 13–59.
Bernard of Cluny, *Ordo Cluniacensis sive Consuetudines*, in *Vetus Disciplina Monastica*, ed. M. Herrgott (Paris, 1726), pp. 136–364.
Bernard of Cluny, *De contemptu mundi*, ed. H. C. Hoskier, in *De Contemptu Mundi, A Bitter Satirical Poem of 3000 Lines Upon the Morals of the Twelfth Century by Bernard of Morval, Monk of Cluny (fl. 1150): Re-edited with Introduction and Copious Variants*

from *All the Known Manuscripts* (London, 1929); English translation: *Scorn for the World: Bernard of Cluny's De Contemptu Mundi: The Latin Text with English Translation and an Introduction*, trans. R. E. Pepin (East Lansing, MI, 1991).
Bernard of Cluny, *De octo vitiis*, ed. K. Halvarson, in *Bernardi Cluniacensis carmina de trinitate et de fide catholica, De castitate servanda, In libros regum, De octo vitiis* (Stockholm, 1963), pp. 97-138; English translation: R. E. Pepin, "De octo vitiis: A Satire by Bernard of Cluny," *Allegorica* 18 (1997): 31-99.
Bullarium sacri ordinis Cluniacensis, ed. P. Symon (Lyons, 1680).
Byrhtferth, *Vita Oswaldi*, ed. M. Lapidge, in *Byrhtferth of Ramsey: The Lives of St. Oswald and St. Ecgwine* (Oxford, 2009), pp. 1-203.
Calendar of Documents Preserved in France, Illustrative of the History of Great Britain and Ireland, Vol. 1, AD 918-1206, ed. J. H. Round (London, 1889).
The Cartulary of Flavigny, 717-1113, ed. C. Bouchard (Cambridge, MA, 1991).
The Cartulary of Montier-en-Der, 666-1129, ed. C. Bouchard (Toronto, 2004).
Cassiodorus, *Institutiones*, ed. R. A. B. Mynors (Oxford, 1937); English translation: Cassiodorus, *Institutes of Divine and Secular Learning and On the Soul*, trans. J. W. Halporn (Leeds, 2004), pp. 103-233.
Cicero, *De legibus*, ed. K. Ziegler (Freiburg, 1979).
Cicero, *Epistulae ad Atticum*, ed. D. R. Shackleton Bailey, in *M. Tullius Cicero: Epistulae ad Atticum*, 2 vols. (Stuttgart, 1987).
La Chanson de Roland, ed. L. Cortés, in *La Chanson de Roland* (Paris, 1994).
Chronicon novaliciense, ed. G. Pertz, MGH Scriptores 7 (Hanover, 1846), pp. 83-133.
Chronicon sancti Huberti Andaginensis, ed. G. Pertz, MGH Scriptores 8 (Hanover, 1848), pp. 565-630.
Conrad of Eberbach, *Exordium magnum cisterciense*, ed. B. Griesser, CCCM 138 (Turnhout, 1994).
Consuetudines Affligenienses, ed. R. J. Sullivan, in *Consuetudines Benedictinae variae (saec. XI-saec. XIV)*, ed. G. Constable, CCM 6 (Siegburg, 1975), pp. 123-99.
Consuetudines canonicorum regularium Springiersbacenses-Rodenses, ed. S. Weinfurter, CCCM 48 (Turnhout, 1978).
Consuetudines Cluniacensium antiquiores, in *Consuetudines Cluniacensium antiquiores cum redactionibus derivatis*, ed. Hallinger, pp. 9-150.
Consuetudines Cluniacensium antiquiores cum redactionibus derivatis, ed. Kassius Hallinger, CCM 7.2 (Siegburg, 1983).
Consuetudines Corbeienses, ed. J. Semmler, in *Initia consuetudinis benedictinae: Consuetudines saeculi octavi et noni*, ed. K. Hallinger, CCM 1 (Siegburg, 1963), pp. 355-422.
Consuetudines Floriacenses Antiquiores, ed. A. Davril and L. Donnat, in *Consuetudinum saeculi X/XI/XII monumenta non-Cluniacensia*, ed. K. Hallinger, CCM 7.3 (Siegburg, 1984), pp. 7-60.
De rebus in oriente mirabilibus, ed. A. Orchard, in *Pride and Prodigies: Studies in the Monsters of the Beowulf-Manuscript* (Toronto, 1995), pp. 175-81.
Defensor, *Liber scintillarum*, ed. D. H. M. Rochais, CCSL 117 (Turnhout, 1957).
Eadmer, *Vita sancti Anselmi*, ed. and trans. R. W. Southern, in *The Life of Anselm, Archbishop of Canterbury by Eadmer* (London, 1962).
Epistola Alexandri ad Aristotelem, ed. A. Orchard, in *Pride and Prodigies: Studies in the Monsters of the Beowulf-Manuscript* (Toronto, 1995), pp. 204-23.

Epistola cuiusdam ad domnum [Pontium] Cluniacensem abbatem, ed. H. E. J. Cowdrey, in "Two Studies in Cluniac History, 1049–1126," *Studi Gregoriani* 11 (1978): 9–395, at pp. 113–17.

Epistolae Senecae ad Paulum et Pauli ad Senecam, ed. L. B. Palagi, in *Epistolario apocrifo di Seneca e san Paolo* (Florence, 1985).

Expositio regulae sancti Benedicti, ed. R. Mittermüller, in *Vita et Regula SS. P. Benedicti una cum Expositio Regulae a Hildemaro tradita* (Regensburg, 1880).

Flodoard, *Annales*, ed. P. Lauer, in *Les Annales de Flodoard* (Paris, 1905); English translation: *The Annals of Flodoard of Reims, 919–966*, trans. S. Fanning and B. S. Bachrach (Peterborough, 2004).

Francisco de Rivo, *Chronicon Cluniacense*, in *BC*, cols. 589–602.

Galterius, *Vita Anastasii*, *PL* 149, cols. 427–32; English translation: "The Life of Anastasius of Cluny, Monk and Hermit," trans. S. G. Bruce, in *The Renaissance of the Twelfth Century: A Reader*, ed. A. J. Novikoff (Toronto, 2017), pp. 32–40.

Galand of Reigny, *Parabolarium*, ed. and trans. C. Friedlander, J. Leclercq, and G. Aciti, in *Galand of Reigny: Parabolarium*, SC 378 (Paris, 1992).

Gerbert of Aurillac, *Correspondance: Lettres 1 à 220*, ed. and trans. P. Riché and J.-P. Callu (Paris, 2008).

Gesta abbatum Lobbiensium 18, ed. W. Arndt, MGH Scriptores 21 (Hanover, 1869), pp. 307–33.

Gilo, *Historia Vie Hierosolimitane*, ed. and trans. C. W. Grocock and J. E. Siberry, in *The Historia Vie Hierosolimitane of Gilo of Paris* (Oxford, 1997).

Gilo, *Vita sancti Hugonis*, ed. H. E. J. Cowdrey, in "Two Studies in Cluniac History, 1049–1126," *Studi Gregoriani* 11 (1978): 9–395, at pp. 45–109.

Greek and Latin Narratives About the Ancient Martyrs, ed. and trans. E. Rebillard (Oxford, 2017).

Gregory the Great, *Homiliae in Euangelia*, ed. R. Étaix, CCSL 141 (Turnhout, 1999).

Haimo, *Expositio in epistolam II ad Corinthios*, *PL* 117, cols. 605–68.

Haimo, *Homilia 22 (Dominica in sexagesima)*, *PL* 118, cols. 163–72.

Hariulfus, *Chronicon*, ed. F. Lot, in *Hariulf, Chronique de l'Abbaye de Saint-Riquier (Vᵉ siecle-1104)* (Paris, 1894).

Helgaud of Fleury, *Epitoma vitae regis Rotberti Pii*, ed. R.-H. Bautier (Paris, 1965).

Herodotus, *Historiae*, ed. C. Hude, in *Herodoti Historiae*, 3rd ed., 2 vols. (Oxford, 1927).

Hildebert of Le Mans, *Vita sancti Hugonis*, in *BC*, col. 413–38.

Hilduin of Saint-Denis: The Passio S. Dionysii in Prose and Verse, ed. and trans. M. Lapidge (Leiden, 2017).

Hincmar, *De cavendis vitiis et virtutibus exercendis*, *PL* 125, cols. 857–930.

Hrosvit, *Opera Omnia*, ed. W. Berschin (Munich, 2001).

Hugo Candidus, *Chronicon*, ed. W. T. Mellows, in *The Chronicle of Hugh Candidus, A Monk of Peterborough* (London, 1949).

Idung, *Dialogus duorum monachorum*, ed. R. B. C. Huygens, in *Le moine Idung et ses deux ouvrages: "Argumentum super quatuor questionibus" et "Dialogus duorum monachorum"* (Spoleto, 1980), pp. 89–186.

Initia consuetudinis benedictinae: Consuetudines saeculi octavi et noni, ed. K. Hallinger, CCM 1 (Siegburg, 1963).

Instituta regalia et ministeria camerae regum Longobardorum et honorantiae civitatis Papiae, ed. A. Hofmeister, MGH Scriptores 30.1 (Hanover, 1934), pp. 1444-60.
Irimbert, *De incendio monasterii sui ac vita et moribus virginum sanctimonialium Parthenonis Admontensis narratio*, ed. B. Pez, in *Bibliotheca ascetica antiquonova*, 12 vols. (Regensburg, 1723-25), vol. 8, pp. 455-64.
Isidore de Séville, Étymologies, Livre I: La grammaire, ed. O. Spevak (Paris, 2020).
Isidore de Séville, Étymologies, Livre XII: Des animaux, ed. J. André (Paris, 1986).
Isidore of Seville, *Synonymorum liber*, PL 83, cols. 825-68.
Jacques de Vitry, *Sermones vulgares*, ed. T. F. Crane, in *The Exempla or Illustrative Stories from the "Sermones Vulgares" of Jacques de Vitry* (London, 1890).
Jerome, *Epistulae*, ed. I. Hilberg, CSEL 54-55 (Leipzig, 1910-12).
Jerome, *In Adbiam prophetam*, PL 25, cols. 1097-1118.
Jerome, *Vita Malchi*, ed. and trans. C. Gray, in *Jerome, Vita Malchi: Text, Translation, and Commentary* (Oxford, 2015).
John of Saint Arnulf, *Vita Iohannis abbatis Gorziensis*, ed. and trans. P. C. Jacobsen, in *Die Geschichte vom Leben des Johannes, Abt des Klosters Gorze*, MGH Scriptores rerum Germanicarum 81 (Wiesbaden, 2016).
John of Salerno, *Vita Odonis*, PL 133, cols. 43-86; trans. G. Sitwell, in *St. Odo of Cluny, Being the Life of St. Odo of Cluny by John of Salerno and the Life of St. Gerald of Aurillac by St. Odo* (London, 1958), pp. 3-87.
Jordanes, *Getica*, ed. T. Mommsen, MGH Auctores antiquissimi 5.1 (Berlin, 1882); English translation: *Jordanes: The Origins and Deeds of the Goths in English Version*, trans. C. C. Mierow (Princeton, 1908).
Jotsaldus, *Vita Odilonis*, ed. J. Staub, in *Iotsald von Saint-Claude, Vita des Abtes Odilo von Cluny*, MGH Scriptores rerum Germanicarum 68 (Hanover, 1999).
Julius Pollux, *Onomasticon*, ed. E. Bethe, in *Pollucis Onomasticon*, 3 vols. (Leipzig 1900-37).
Justin, *Epitoma historiarum Philippicarum Pompei Trogi*, ed. O. Seel (Stuttgart, 1972).
Lactantius, *De ira Dei liber*, ed. C. Ingremeau, in *Lactance, La colère de Dieu*, SC 289 (Paris, 1982).
Lanfranc, *Decreta*, ed. and trans. D. Knowles, in *The Monastic Constitutions of Lanfranc* (London, 1951).
Les plus anciens documents originaux de l'abbaye de Cluny, ed. H. Atsma and J. Vezin, 3 vols. (Paris, 1997-2002).
The Letter Collection of Peter Abelard and Heloise, ed. and trans. D. Luscombe (Oxford, 2013).
Libanii Opera, ed. R. Foerster, 12 vols. (Leipzig, 1903-63).
Liber monstrorum de diversis generibus, ed. A. Orchard, in *Pride and Prodigies: Studies in the Monsters of the Beowulf-Manuscript* (Toronto, 1995), pp. 254-317.
Liber Ordinis Sancti Victoris Parisiensis, ed. L. Jocqué and L. Milis, CCCM 59 (Turnhout, 1984).
Liber tramitis aevi Odilonis abbatis, ed. P. Dinter, CCM 10 (Siegburg, 1980).
Liudprand of Cremona, *Antapodosis*, ed. P. Chiesa, in *Liudprandi Cremonensis Opera Omnia*, CCCM 156 (Turnhout, 1998); English translation: *The Complete Works of Liudprand of Cremona*, trans. P. Squatriti (Washington, DC, 2007), pp. 41-202.

Miracula sancti Gorgonii, ed. P. C. Jacobsen, in *Miracula s. Gorgonii: Studien und Texte zur Gorgonius-Verehrung im 10. Jahrhundert*, MGH Studien und Texte 46 (Hanover, 2009).

Pope Martin I, *Epistolae, PL* 87, cols. 119-204.

Martin of Braga, *De ira*, ed. and trans. C. Torre, in *Martini Bracarensis de ira: Introduzione, testo, traduzione e commento* (Rome, 2008).

Miracula sancti Benedicti, ed. and trans. A. Davril, A. Dufour, and G. Labory, in *Les miracles de Saint Benoît: Miracula sancti Benedicti* (Paris, 2019).

Miraculorum sancti Maioli abbatis libri duo, in *BC*, cols. 1787-1814; repr. in *AASS* Maii 2, cols. 690-700.

Nalgod, *Vita sancti Maioli, AASS* Maii 2, pp. 657-67.

Nalgod, *Vita sancti Odonis*, in *Acta sanctorum ordinis sancti Benedicti in saeculorum classes distributa*, ed. J. Mabillon, 9 vols. (Paris, 1668-1701), vol. 5, pp. 186-99; repr. in *PL* 133, cols. 85-104.

Necrologium ecclesiae beatae Mariae Carnotensis, ed. R. Merlet and A. Clerval, in *Un manuscript chartrain du XIe siècle: Fulbert, évêque de Chartres* (Chartres, 1893).

Odilo of Cluny, *Epitaphium domine Adelheide Auguste*, ed. H. Paulhart, in *Die Lebensbeschreibung der Kaiserin Adelheid von Abt Odilo von Cluny* (Graz, 1962).

Odilo of Cluny, *Vita sancti Maioli*, in *BC*, cols. 279-90.

Odo of Cluny, *Collationes tres libri, PL* 133, cols. 517-638.

Odo of Cluny, *Occupatio*, ed. A. Swoboda, in *Odonis Abbatis Cluniacensis Occupatio* (Leipzig, 1900); and *The Occupatio of Odo of Cluny: Edition, Translation, and Commentary*, ed. and trans. C. A. Jones, 2 vols. (Turnhout, 2025).

Odo of Cluny, *Vita sancti Geraldi Auriliacensis*, ed. A.-M. Bultot-Verleysen, in *Odon de Cluny, Vita sancti Geraldi Auriliacensis: Édition critique, traduction française, introduction et commentaires* (Brussels, 2009); English translation: Odo of Cluny, *The Life of Saint Gerald of Aurillac*, trans. G. Sitwell, in *Soldiers of Christ*, ed. Noble and Head, pp. 293-362.

The Old English History of the World: An Anglo-Saxon Rewriting of Orosius, ed. and trans. M. R. Godden (Cambridge, MA, 2016).

Orderic Vitalis, *Historia Ecclesiastica*, ed. and trans. M. Chibnall, in *The Ecclesiastical History of Orderic Vitalis*, 6 vols. (Oxford, 1969-80).

Ordo Casinensis I, ed. D. T. Leccisotti, in *Initia consuetudinis benedictinae: Consuetudines saeculi octavi et noni*, ed. K. Hallinger, CCM 1 (Siegburg, 1963), pp. 94-104.

Orosius, *Historiarum adversum paganos libri septem*, ed. M.-P. Arnaud-Lindet, in *Orose, Histories (contre les païens)*, 3 vols. (Paris, 1990-91); English translation: *Orosius, Seven Books of History Against the Pagans*, trans. A. T. Fear (Liverpool, 2010).

Ovid, *Metamorphoses*, ed. G. Lafaye, 2 vols. (Paris, 2007-2008).

Paschasius Radbertus, *Cogitis me*, ed. E. A. Matter and A. Ripberger, in *Pascasius Radbertus, De partu Virginis/De assumptione sanctae Mariae Virginis*, CCCM 56C (Turnhout, 1985), pp. 97-162.

The Penguin Book of the Undead: Fifteen Hundred Years of Supernatural Encounters, ed. S. G. Bruce (New York, 2016).

Peter Damian, *Epistolae*, ed. K. Reindel, in *Die Briefe des Petrus Damiani*, MGH Die Briefe der deutschen Kaiserzeit 4.1-4, 4 vols. (Munich, 1983-93).
Peter of Poitiers, *Epistola 4*, ed. R. Glei, in *Petrus Venerabilis, Schriften zum Islam* (Altenberge, 1985), pp. 228-39; English translation: *Peter the Venerable, Writings Against Islam*, trans. I. M. Resnick (Washington, DC, 2016), pp. 163-71.
Peter the Venerable, *Adversus Iudeorum inveteratem duritiem*, ed. Y. Friedman, CCCM 58 (Turnhout, 1985); English translation: *Peter the Venerable, Against the Inveterate Obduracy of the Jews*, trans. I. M. Resnick (Washington, DC, 2013).
Peter the Venerable, *Contra Petrobrusianos*, ed. J. Fearns, CCCM 10 (Turnhout, 1968).
Peter the Venerable, *De miraculis*, ed. D. Bouthillier, CCCM 83 (Turnhout, 1988).
Peter the Venerable, *Sermo cuius supra in honore sancti illius cuius reliquiae sunt in presenti*, ed. G. Constable, in "Petri Venerabilis Sermones Tres," *Revue bénédictine* 64 (1954): 224-72, at pp. 265-72.
Peter the Venerable, *Sermo de sancto Marcello papa et martyre*, ed. G. Constable, in "Petri Venerabilis Sermones Tres," *Revue bénédictine* 64 (1954): 224-72, at 255-65.
Peter the Venerable, *Statuta*, ed. G. Constable, in *Consuetudines Benedictinae Variae (saec. XI-saec. XIV)*, CCM 6 (Siegburg, 1975), pp. 19-106.
Peter the Venerable, *Summa totius haeresis Sarracenorum*, ed. R. Glei, in *Petrus Venerabilis, Schriften zum Islam* (Altenberge, 1985), pp. 2-22; English translation: *Peter the Venerable, Writings Against the Saracens*, trans. I. M. Resnick (Washington, DC, 2016), pp. 34-50.
Pliny, *Naturalis historia*, ed. K. Mayhoff, in *C. Plinius Secundus: Naturalis Historiae Libri XXXVII*, 6 vols. (Berlin, 1967-70).
Plutarch, *De Herodoti malignitate*, ed. P. A. Hansen (Amsterdam, 1979).
Qualiter tabula sancti Basilii continens in se magnam dominici ligni portionem Cluniaceum delata fuerit tempore Pontii abbatis, in BC, cols. 561-64; and *Recueil des historiens des croisades: Historiens occidentaux*, 5 vols. (Paris, 1844-1895), vol. 5, pp. 295-98.
Quomodo reliquiae beati Stephani protomartyris Cluniacum delatae fuerunt tempore eiusdem Pontii abbatis, in BC, cols. 565-68; and *Recueil des historiens des croisades: Historiens occidentaux*, 5 vols. (Paris, 1844-1895), vol. 5, pp. 317-20.
Recueil des historiens des Gaules et de la France, 24 vols. (Paris, 1738-1904).
Redactio Wirzeburgensis, ed. R. Grünewald, in *Consuetudines Cluniacensium antiquiores cum redactionibus derivatis*, ed. K. Hallinger, CCM 7.2 (Siegburg, 1983), pp. 271-308.
Regesta pontificum Romanorum, ed. P. Jaffé, 2 vols. (Leipzig, 1885-88).
Regesta Regum Anglo-Normannorum 1066-1154, ed. H. W. C. Davis, C. Johnson, and H. A. Cronne, 3 vols. (Oxford, 1913-68).
Reginald of Canterbury, *Vita Malchi*, ed. L. Lind, in *The Vita Sancti Malchi of Reginald of Canterbury: A Critical Edition* (Urbana, IL, 1942).
Regula Benedicti, ed. and trans. A. de Vogüé and J. Neufville, *La Règle de saint Benoît*, SC 181-86, 7 vols. (the last of which is not included in the SC series) (Paris, 1971-72); English translations: *The Rule of Benedict*, trans. C. White (New York, 2008); and *The Rule of Saint Benedict*, trans. B. Venarde (Cambridge, MA, 2011).
Regula cuiusdam ad virgines, ed. and trans. A. Diem, in *The Pursuit of Salvation: Community, Space, and Discipline in Early Medieval Monasticism*, Disciplina Monastica 13 (Turnhout, 2021), pp. 60-151.

Regula Donati, ed. V. Zimmerl-Panagl and M. Zelzer, in *Monastica 1: Donati Regula, Pseudo-Columbani Regula monialium (frg.)*, CSEL 98 (Berlin, 2015), pp. 139–88.

Regula magistri, ed. A. de Vogüé, in *La règle de Maître*, 3 vols. SC 105–107 (Paris, 1964–1965).

Regularis Concordia Anglicae Nationis, ed. and trans. T. Symons, in *The Monastic Agreement of the Monks and Nuns of the English Nation* (London, 1953).

Regula Sancti Benedicti Anianensis, ed. J. Semmler, in *Initia consuetudinis benedictinae: Consuetudines saeculi octavi et noni*, ed. K. Hallinger, CCM 1 (Siegburg, 1963), pp. 515–36.

The Relatio metrica de duobus ducibus: A Twelfth-Century Cluniac Poem on Prayer for the Dead, ed. and trans. C. A. Jones and S. G. Bruce (Turnhout, 2016).

Renaud of Vézelay, *Vita domni Hugonis*, ed. R. B. C. Huygens, in *Vizeliacensia II: Textes relatifs à l'histoire de l'abbaye de Vézelay*, CCCM 42 Suppl. (Turnhout, 1980).

Robert of Torigni, *Chronica*, ed. and trans. T. Bisson, in *The Chronography of Robert of Torigni*, 2 vols. (Oxford, 2020).

Robert of Torigni, *Gesta Normannorum Ducum*, ed. and trans. E. Van Houts, in *The Gesta Normannorum Ducum of William of Jumièges, Orderic Vitalis, and Robert of Torigni*, 2 vols. (Oxford, 1995).

Rodulphus de Sully, *Vita Petri Venerabilis abbatis Cluniacensis*, ed. E. Martène and U. Durand, in *Veterum Scriptorum et Monumentorum Historicorum, Dogmaticorum, Moralium, Amplissima Collectio*, 9 vols. (Paris 1724–33), vol. 6, cols. 1187–1202; repr. in *PL* 189, cols. 15–28.

Rostang, *Narratio exceptionis apud Cluniacum capitis beati Clementis, ex ore Dalmacii de Serciaco, militis, excepta*, in *BC*, cols. 1481–90; repr. in *Exuviae sacrae Constantinopolitanae*, ed. P. Riant, 2 vols. (Paris, 1877–78), vol. 1, pp. 127–40.

Rudolphus Glaber, *Historiarum libri quinque*, ed. and trans. J. France, in *Rudolfus Glaber: The Five Books of Histories and the Life of St. William* (Oxford, 1989), pp. 1–253.

Rupert of Deutz, *In regulam sancti Benedicti*, PL 170, cols. 477–538.

Sacrorum Conciliorum Nova et Amplissima Collectio, ed. G. D. Mansi, 31 vols. (Florence, 1759–1798).

Sainted Women of the Dark Ages, ed. J. A. McNamara and J. Halborg (Durham, NC, 1992).

Seneca, *Apocolocyntosis*, ed. P. T. Eden (Cambridge, 1984).

Seneca, *De ira*, ed. L. D. Reynolds, in *Dialogorum Libri Duodecim* (Oxford, 1977), pp. 39–128.

Smaragdus, *Expositio in regulam sancti Benedicti*, ed. A. Spannagel and P. Engelbert, in *Smaragdi abbatis expositio in regulam s. Benedicti*, CCM 8 (Siegburg, 1974); English translation: *Smaragdus of Saint-Mihiel, Commentary on the Rule of Benedict*, trans. D. Berry (Kalamazoo, 2007).

Soldiers of Christ: Saints and Saints' Lives from Late Antiquity and the Early Middle Ages, ed. T. F. X. Noble and T. Head (University Park, PA, 1995).

Syrus, *Vita sancti Maioli*, ed. Iogna-Prat, in *Agni lmmaculati*, pp. 163–285.

Tertullian, *Apologeticum*, ed. and trans. J. E. B. Mayor (Cambridge, MA, 1917).

Thesaurus novus anecdotorum, ed. E. Martène and U. Durand, 5 vols. (Paris, 1717).

Thietmar, *Chronicon*, ed. R. Holzmann, MGH Scriptores Rerum Germanicarum n.s. 9 (Berlin, 1935).
Three Treatises from Bec on the Nature of Monastic Life, ed. G. Constable (Toronto, 2008).
Thucydides, *The Peloponnesian War*, trans. R. Warner (Baltimore, 1954).
Ulrich of Zell, *Consuetudines Cluniacensis*, PL 149, cols 643–779.
Vergil, *Georgics*, ed. R. A. B. Mynors, in *P. Vergili Maronis Opera* (Oxford, 1969).
Vita breuior sancti Maioli, in *BC*, cols. 1763–82.
Vita sancti Fulcrani, ed. F. Dolbeau, in "Vie inédite de Saint Fulcran, évêque de Lodève," *Analecta Bollandiana* 100 (1982): 515–44.
Vita sancti Petri Abbatis Cavensis, ed. L. A. Muratori, in *Rerum Italicarum Scriptores, Tomus Sextus* (Milan, 1725), cols. 217–28.
Wala of Bobbio, *Breve memorationis*, ed. J. Semmler, in *Initia consuetudinis benedictinae: Consuetudines saeculi octavi et noni*, ed. K. Hallinger, CCM 1 (Siegburg, 1963), pp. 420–22.
Walcher of Malvern, *Walcher of Malvern, "De Lunationibus" and "De Dracone": Study, Edition, Translation, and Commentary*, ed. and trans. C. P. E. Nothaft (Turnhout, 2017).
Walter Map, *De nugis curialium*, ed. and trans. M. R. James, in *Walter Map, De nugis curialium: Courtiers' Trifles*, rev. ed. (Oxford, 1983).
Widukind, *Res Gestae Saxonicae*, ed. P. Hirsch, in *Die Sachsengeschichte des Widukind von Korvei*, MGH Scriptores rerum Germanicarum 60 (Hanover, 1935).
William of Hirsau, *Constitutiones Hirsaugienses*, ed. C. Elvert and P. Engelbert, CCM 15.1–2, 2 vols. (Siegburg, 2010).
William of Tyre, *Chronicon*, ed. R. B. C. Huygens, in *Guillaume de Tyr, Cronique*, CCCM 63 (Turnhout, 1986).
Willibald, *Vita Bonifatii*, ed. W. Levison, in *Vitae sancti Bonifatii archiepiscopi Moguntini*, MGH Scriptores rerum Germanicarum 57 (Hanover, 1905), 1–58.
Wonders of the East (Old English Text), ed. and trans. A. Orchard, in *Pride and Prodigies: Studies in the Monsters of the Beowulf-Manuscript* (Toronto, 1995), pp. 184–203.

Secondary Scholarship

Aaij, M. "Boniface's Booklife: How the Ragyndrudis Codex Came to be a *Vita Bonifatii*," *The Heroic Age* 10 (May 2007).
L'abbaye de Gorze au Xe siècle, ed. M. Parisse and O. Oexle (Nancy, 1993).
Ackley, J. S. "Re-Approaching the Western Medieval Church Treasury Inventory, c. 800–1250," *Journal of Art Historiography* 11 (2014): 1–37.
Adil, S. F. "Memorializing al-Maqqarī: The Life, Work, and Worlds of a Muslim Scholar" (PhD diss., University of Chicago, 2015).
Aigrain, R. *L'hagiographie: Ses sources, ses methods, son histoire*, 2nd ed. (Brussels, 2000).
Airlie, S. "The Anxiety of Sanctity: St. Gerald and His Maker," *Journal of Ecclesiastical History* 43 (1992): 372–95.
Albert, B.-S. "*Adversus Iudaeos* in the Carolingian Empire," in *Contra Iudaeos: Ancient and Medieval Polemics Between Christians and Jews*, ed. O. Limor and G. Stroumsa (Tubingen, 1996), pp. 119–42.

Alciati, R. "The Invention of Western Monastic Literature: Texts and Communities," in *CHMM*, vol. 1, pp. 144–61.
Althoff, G. *Family, Friends, and Followers: Political and Social Bonds in Early Medieval Europe*, trans. C. Carroll (Cambridge, 2004).
d'Alverny, M. T. "La connaissance de l'Islam en Occident du IXe au milieu du XIIe siecle," in *L'Occidente e l'Islam nell'alto medioevo, Spoleto 2–8 aprile 1964*, 2 vols. (Spoleto, 1965), vol. 1, pp. 577–602, repr. in M. T. d'Alverny, *La connaissance de l'Islam dans l'Occident médiéval* (Aldershot, 1994), no. V.
Amargier, P.-A. "La capture de saint Maieul de Cluny et l'expulsion des Sarrasins de Provence," *Revue bénédictine* 73 (1963): 316–23.
The Amherst Papyri, ed. B. P. Grenfell and A. S. Hunt, 2 vols. (London, 1900–1901).
Angenendt, A. "Missa specialis: Zugleich ein Beitrag zur Entstehung der Privatmessen," *Frühmittelalterliche Studien* 17 (1983): 153–221.
Aniel, J.-P. "Le scriptorium de Cluny au Xe et XIe siècle," in *Le gouvernement d'Hugues de Semur*, pp. 265–81.
D'Arcier, L. F. *Histoire et géographie d'un mythe: La circulation des manuscrits du De excidio Troiae de Darès le Phrygien* (Paris, 2006).
Arnold, J. H. and C. Goodson, "Resounding Community: The History and Meaning of Medieval Church Bells," *Viator* 43 (2012): 99–130.
Atti del 4° congresso internazionale di studi sull'alto medioevo, Pavia-Scaldasole-Monza-Bobbio, 10–14 settembre 1967 (Spoleto, 1969).
Atwood, M. *The Blind Assassin* (New York, 2000).
Audoin-Rouzeau, F. *Ossements animaux de moyen âge au monastère de La Charité-sur-Loire* (Paris, 1986).
Augustine Through the Ages: An Encyclopedia, ed. A. D. Fitzgerald (Grand Rapids, MI, 1999).
Bailey, A. E. "Wives, Mothers, and Widows on Pilgrimage: Categories of 'Woman' Recorded at English Healing Shrines in the High Middle Ages," *Journal of Medieval History* 39 (2013): 197–219.
Bailey, A. E. "Miracle Children: Medieval Hagiography and Childhood Imperfection," *Journal of Interdisciplinary History* 47 (2016): 267–85.
Barlow, F. "The Canonization and Early Lives of Hugh I, Abbot of Cluny," *Analecta Bollandiana* 98 (1980): 297–334, repr. in F. Barlow, *The Norman Conquest and Beyond* (London, 1983), pp. 257–95.
Barlow, F. "William I's Relations with Cluny," *Journal of Ecclesiastical History* 32 (1981): 131–41, repr. in F. Barlow, *The Norman Conquest and Beyond* (London, 1983), pp. 245–56.
Barlow, F. *The Norman Conquest and Beyond* (London, 1983).
Barlow, F. *William Rufus* (London, 1983).
Barret, S. *La mémoire et l'écrit: L'abbaye de Cluny et ses archives (Xe-XVIIIe siècle)* (Munster, 2004).
Barret, S. "Cluny et les Ottoniens," in *Ottone III e Romualdo di Ravenna: Impero, monasteri e santi asceti, Atti del XXIV convegno del Centro Studi Avellaniti, Fonte Avellana, 2002* (Verona, 2003), pp. 179–213.
Barret, S. "Cluny et son scriptorium (Xe-XIe siècles)," in *Cluny ou la puissance des moines: Histoire de l'abbaye et de son ordre, 910–1790* (Dijon, 2001), pp. 48–53.

Bartlett, R. *Why Can the Dead Do Such Great Things? Saints and Worshippers from the Martyrs to the Reformation* (Princeton, 2013).
Bately, J. M. and D. J. A. Ross, "A Check List of Manuscripts of Orosius' *Historiarum Adversum Paganos Libri Septem*," *Scriptorium* 15 (1961): 329-34.
Baud, A. "Archaeology and the Abbey of Cluny," in *A Companion to the Abbey of Cluny in the Middle Ages*, ed. S. G. Bruce and S. Vanderputten (Leiden, 2022), pp. 146-72.
Beach, A. "Claustration and Collaboration Between the Sexes in the Twelfth-Century Scriptorium," in *Monks and Nuns, Saints and Outcasts: Religion in Medieval Society*, ed. S. Farmer and B. Rosenwein (Ithaca, 2000), pp. 57-75.
Beach, A. *Women as Scribes: Book Production and Monastic Reform in Twelfth-Century Bavaria* (Cambridge, 2004).
Beach, A. *The Trauma of Monastic Reform: Community and Conflict in Twelfth-Century Germany* (Cambridge, 2017).
Beales, D. *Prosperity and Plunder: European Catholic Monasteries in the Age of Revolution, 1650–1815* (Cambridge, 2003).
Becker, A. *Papst Urban II (1088–1099)*, MGH Schriften 10.1-3, 3 vols. (Stuttgart, 1964-2012).
Becker, C. L. "Every Man His Own Historian," *American Historical Review* 37 (1932): 221-36.
Beckett, K. S. *Anglo-Saxon Perceptions of the Islamic World* (Cambridge, 2003).
Benedict's Disciples, ed. D. H. Farmer (Leominster, 1980).
Bénet, A. "Le trésor de l'abbaye de Cluny: Inventaire de 1382," *Revue de l'Art chrétien* 6 (1888): 195-205.
Berman, C. "Later Monastic Economies," in *CHMM*, vol. 2, pp. 831-47.
Berry, V. "Peter the Venerable and the Crusades," in *Petrus Venerabilis, 1156–1956: Studies and Texts Commemorating the Eighth Centenary of His Death*, ed. G. Constable and J. Kritzeck (Rome, 1956), pp. 141-62.
Berschin, W. *Greek Letters and the Latin Middle Ages: From Jerome to Nicholas of Cusa*, trans. J. C. Frakes (Washington, DC, 1988).
Bischoff, B. *Manuscripts and Libraries in the Age of Charlemagne*, trans. M. Gorman (Cambridge, 1994).
Bischoff, B. *Katalog der festländischen Handschriften des neunten Jahrhunderts (mit Ausnahme der wisigotischen)*, 4 vols. (Wiesbaden, 1998-2017).
Bjornlie, M. S. *Politics and Tradition Between Rome, Ravenna and Constantinople: A Study of Cassiodorus and the Variae* (Cambridge, 2013).
Blennemann, G. "Ascetic Prayer for the Dead in the Early Medieval West," in *CHMM*, vol. 1, pp. 278-96.
Bodarwé, K. "Eine Männerregel für Frauen: Die Adaption der Benediktsregel im 9. und 10. Jahrhundert," in *Female "Vita Religiosa" Between Late Antiquity and the High Middle Ages: Structures, Developments and Spatial Contexts*, ed. G. Melville and A. Müller (Munster, 2011), pp. 235-72.
Boesch Gajano, S. "Gregorio Magno agiografo," in *Hagiographies: Histoire internationale de la littérature hagiographique latine et vernaculaire en Occident des origines à 1550*, ed. G. Philippart, M. Goullet, and F. Peloux, 9 vols. to date (1992-2024), vol. 7, pp. 11-94.

Bonde, S. and C. Maines, "The Archaeology of Monasticism: A Summary of Recent Work in France, 1970-1987," *Speculum* 63 (1988): 794-825.

Bouchard, C. *Sword, Miter, and Cloister: Nobility and the Church in Burgundy, 980–1198* (Ithaca, 1987).

Bouchard, C. "Monastic Cartularies: Organizing Eternity," in *Charters, Cartularies, and Archives: The Preservation and Transmission of Documents in the Medieval West: Proceedings of a Colloquium of the Commission Internationale de Diplomatique (Princeton and New York, 16–18 September 1999)*, ed. A. Kosto and A. Winroth (Toronto, 2002), pp. 22-32.

Boulc'H, S. "Le repas quotidien des moines occidentaux du haut Moyen Age," *Revue belge de philologie et d'histoire* 75 (1997): 287-328.

Bourdon, L. "Les voyages de Saint Mayeul en Italie: Itineraires et chronologie," *Melanges d'archéologie et d'histoire* 43 (1926): 63-89.

Boynton, S. "The Liturgical Role of Children in Monastic Customaries from the Central Middle Ages," *Studia Liturgica* 28 (1998): 194-209.

Boynton, S. "The Customaries of Bernard and Ulrich as Liturgical Sources," in *From Dead of Night to End of Day: The Medieval Customs of Cluny / Du coeur de la nuit à la fin du jour: Les coutumes clunisiennes au moyen âge*, ed. S. Boynton and I. Cochelin, Disciplina Monastica 3 (Turnhout, 2005), pp. 109-30.

Boynton, S. *Shaping a Monastic Identity: Liturgy and History at the Imperial Abbey of Farfa, c. 1000–1125* (Ithaca, 2006).

Boynton, S. "Music and the Cluniac Vision of History in Paris, Bibliothèque nationale de France, lat. 17716," in *Chant, Liturgy, and the Inheritance of Rome: Essays in Honour of Joseph Dyer*, ed. D. J. DiCenso and R. Maloy (London, 2017), pp. 407-30.

Boynton, S. "Shaping Cluniac Devotion," in *A Companion to the Abbey of Cluny in the Middle Ages*, ed. S. G. Bruce and S. Vanderputten (Leiden, 2022), pp. 125-45.

Bozoky, E. "Les reliques de La Voûte," in *Odilon de Mercœuer, L'Auvergne et Cluny, La "Paix de Dieu" et l'Europe de l'an mil: Actes du colloque de Lavoûte-Chilhac des 10, 11, et 12 Mai 2000*, ed. J. Vigier (Nonette, 2002), pp. 175-91.

Bragg, L. "Visual-Kinetic Communication in Europe Before 1600: A Survey of Sign Lexicons and Finger Alphabets Prior to the Rise of Deaf Education," *Journal of Deaf Studies and Deaf Education* 2 (1997): 1-25.

Braun, J. W. "Irimbert von Admont," *Frühmittelalterliche Studien* 7 (1973): 226-323.

Brown, M. P. "Spreading the Word," in *In the Beginning: Bibles Before the Year 1000*, ed. M. P. Brown (Philadelphia, 2006), pp. 45-75.

Brown, P. *The Cult of the Saints: Its Rise and Function in Latin Christianity* (Chicago, 1981).

Brown, P. "Relics and Social Status in the Age of Gregory of Tours," in P. Brown, *Society and the Holy in Late Antiquity* (Berkeley, 1982), pp. 222-50.

Brown, P. *Power and Persuasion in Late Antiquity: Towards a Christian Empire* (Madison, WI, 1992).

Brown, P. *Augustine of Hippo: A Biography*, 2nd ed. (Berkeley, 2000).

Brown, V. "Latin Manuscripts of Caesar's *Gallic War*," in *Palaeographica diplomatica et archivistica: Studi in onore di Giulio Battelli*, 2 vols. (Rome, 1979), vol. 1, pp. 105-57.
Bruce, S. G. "The Origins of Cistercian Sign Language," *Cîteaux: Commentarii cistercienses* 52 (2001): 193-209.
Bruce, S. G. "Hagiography as Monstrous Ethnography: A Note on Ratramnus of Corbie's Letter Concerning the Conversion of the Cynocephali," in *Insignis Sophiae Arcator: Essays in Honour of Michael Herren on his 65th Birthday*, ed. Gernot Wieland, Carin Ruff, and Ross C. Arthur (Turnhout, 2006), pp. 45-56.
Bruce, S. G. *Silence and Sign Language in Medieval Monasticism: The Cluniac Tradition, c. 900-1200* (Cambridge, 2007).
Bruce, S. G. *Cluny and the Muslims of La Garde-Freinet: Hagiography and the Problem of Islam in Medieval Europe* (Ithaca, 2015).
Bruce, S. G. "The Lost Patriarchs Project: Recovering the Greek Fathers in the Medieval Latin Tradition," *Religion Compass* 14 (2020): 1-8.
Bruce, S. G. "Textual Triage and Pastoral Care in the Carolingian Age: The Example of the *Rule of Benedict*," *Traditio* 75 (2020): 127-41.
Budde, T. "The *Versio Dionysii* of John Scottus Eriugena: A Study of the Manuscript Tradition and Influence of Eriugena's Translation of the *Corpus Areopagiticum* from the Ninth Through the Twelfth Century" (PhD diss., University of Toronto, 2011).
Bugyis, K. *The Care of Nuns: The Ministries of Benedictine Women in England During the Central Middle Ages* (New York, 2019).
Bull, M. *Knightly Piety and the Lay Response to the First Crusade: The Limousin and Gascony, c. 970-c. 1130* (Oxford, 1993).
Bullough, D. A. "Urban Change in Early Medieval Italy: The Example of Pavia," *Papers of the British School at Rome* 34 (1966): 82-130.
Bullough, D. A. "Early Medieval Social Groupings: The Terminology of Kinship," *Past & Present* 45 (1969): 3-18.
Bully, S., E. Destefanis, and E. Marron, "The Archaeology of the Earliest Monasteries in Italy and France (Second Half of the Fourth Century to the Eighth Century)," in *CHMM*, vol. 1, pp. 232-57.
Bultot, R. "La doctrine du mépris du monde chez Bernard le Clunisien," *Le Moyen Âge* 70 (1964): 179-204 and 355-376.
Buringh, E. *Medieval Manuscript Production in the Latin West: Explorations with a Global Database* (Leiden, 2011).
Burke, P. "A Survey of the Popularity of Ancient Historians, 1450-1700," *History and Theory* 5 (1966): 135-52.
Burman, T. E. *Reading the Qur'an in Latin Christendom, 1140-1560* (Philadelphia, 2007).
Burton, J. and J. Kerr, *The Cistercians in the Middle Ages* (Woodbridge, 2011).
Buyssens, E. "Le langage par gestes chez les moines," *Revue de l'Institut de Sociologie* 29 (1954): 537-45.
Bynum, C. W. *The Resurrection of the Body in Western Christianity, 200-1336* (New York, 1995).

du Cange, C. *Glossarium mediae et infimae latinitatis*, 10 vols. (Niort, 1883).
Carruthers, M. *The Craft of Thought: Meditation, Rhetoric, and the Making of Images, 400–1200* (Cambridge, 1998).
Casagrande, A. "Fondazione e suiluppo del monasterio cluniacense di San Maiolo di Pavia nei primi secoli," in *Atti del 4° congresso internazionale di studi sull'alto medioevo, Pavia-Scaldasole-Monza-Bobbio, 10–14 settembre 1967* (Spoleto, 1969), pp. 335–51.
Catalogue général des manuscrits des bibliothèques publiques des départments, 7 vols. (Paris, 1849–85).
Catalogue of Additions to the Manuscripts in the British Museum in the Years 1854–1860: Additional MSS. 19,720–24,026 (London, 1875).
Catalogue of Western Manuscripts in the Old Royal and King's Collections, ed. G. F. Warner and J. P. Gilson, 4 vols. (London, 1921).
Cavallo, G. "La circolazione dei testi greci nell'Europa dell'alto medioevo," in *Rencontres de cultures dans la philosophie médiévale: Traductions et traducteurs de l'antiquité tardive au XIVe siècle; Actes du Colloque international de Cassino 15–17 juin 1989*, ed. J. Hamesse and M. Fattori (Louvain and Cassino, 1990), pp. 47–64.
Ceillier, R. *Histoire générale des auteurs sacrés et ecclesiastiques*, 23 vols. (Paris, 1729–63).
Cesario, M. "Ant-Lore in Anglo-Saxon England," *Anglo-Saxon England* 40 (2011): 273–91.
Cesario, M. "The Shining of the Sun in the Twelve Nights of Christmas," in *Saints and Scholars: New Perspectives on Anglo-Saxon Literature and Culture in Honour of Hugh Magennis*, ed. S. McWilliams (Woodbridge, 2012), pp. 195–212.
Chardonnens, L. S. *Anglo-Saxon Prognostics, 900–1100: Study and Texts* (Leiden, 2007).
Chaume, M. "Les grands prieurs de Cluny: Compléments et rectifications à la liste de la *Gallia Christiana*," *Revue Mabillon* 28 (1938): 147–52.
Chevalier, P. "Le tombeau et les monuments funéraires médiévaux des saints abbés Mayeul et Odilon de Cluny," *Hortus Artium Mediaevalium* 10 (2004): 119–32.
Chibnall, M. "The Merovingian Monastery of St. Evroul in the Light of Conflicting Traditions," in *Popular Belief and Practice*, ed. G. J. Cumings and D. Baker, Studies in Church History 8 (Cambridge, 1972), pp. 31–40.
Christ, K. "In Caput Quadragesimae," *Zentralblatt für Bibliothekswesen* 60 (1943): 33–59.
Clark, C. "This Ecclesiastical Adventurer: Henry of Saint-Jean d'Angély," *English Historical Review* 84 (1969): 548–60.
Christ, M. R. "Theopompus and Herodotus: A Reassessment," *Classical Quarterly* 43 (1993): 47–52.
Clark, F. *The Pseudo-Gregorian Dialogues*, 2 vols. (Leiden, 1987).
Clark, F. *The "Gregorian" Dialogues and the Origins of Benedictine Monasticism* (Leiden, 2003).
Clark, F. "Authorship of the Commentary *In 1 Regum*: Implications of A. de Vogüé's Discovery," *Revue bénédictine* 108 (1998): 61–79.
Clark, F. *The First Pagan Historian: The Fortunes of a Fraud from Antiquity to the Enlightenment* (Oxford, 2020).

Clark, J. G. *A Monastic Renaissance at St. Albans: Thomas Walsingham and His Circle, c. 1350–1440* (Oxford, 2004).
Clark, J. G. *The Benedictines in the Middle Ages* (Woodbridge, 2011).
Clemens, R. and T. Graham, *Introduction to Manuscript Studies* (Ithaca, 2007).
Cochelin, I. "Peut-on parler de noviciat à Cluny pour les Xe-XIIe siècles," *Revue Mabillon*, n.s. 9 (1998): 17–52.
Cochelin, I. "Customaries as Inspirational Sources," in *Consuetudines et Regulae: Sources for Monastic Life in the Middle Ages and the Early Modern Period*, ed. C. M. Malone and C. Maines, Disciplina Monastica 10 (Turnhout, 2014), pp. 27–72.
Cochelin, I. "Monastic Daily Life (c. 750–1100): A Tight Community Shielded by an Outer Court," in *CHMM*, vol. 1, pp. 542–60.
Cochelin, I. "Discipline and the Problem of Cluny's Customaries," in *A Companion to the Abbey of Cluny in the Middle Ages*, ed. S. G. Bruce and S. Vanderputten (Leiden, 2022), pp. 204–22.
Cohen, A. "Monastic Art and Architecture, c. 700–1000: Material and Immaterial Worlds," in *CHMM*, vol. 1, pp. 519–41.
Colish, M. L. *The Stoic Tradition from Antiquity to the Early Middle Ages*, 2 vols. (Leiden, 1985).
Colombo, A. "I diplomati ottoniani e adelaidini e la fondazione del monastero di S. Salvatore di Pavia," *Biblioteca della Societa storica subalpine* 130 (1932): 1–39.
Comfort, W. W. "The Literary Role of the Saracens in the French Epic," *Proceedings of the Modern Language Association* 55 (1940): 628–59.
A Companion to the Abbey of Cluny in the Middle Ages, ed. S. G. Bruce and S. Vanderputten (Leiden, 2022).
A Companion to Medieval Miracle Collections, ed. S. Katajala-Peltomaa, J. Kuuliala, and I. McCleery (Leiden, 2021).
Conant, J. *Staying Roman: Conquest and Identity in North Africa and the Mediterranean, 439–700* (Cambridge, 2012).
Conant, K. J. *Cluny: Les églises et la maison du chef d'ordre* (Mâcon, 1968).
Conant, K. J. *Carolingian and Romanesque Architecture 800–1200* (Harmondsworth, 1979).
Constable, G. "Petri Venerabilis Sermones Tres," *Revue bénédictine* 64 (1954): 224–72.
Constable, G. "Opposition to Pilgrimage in the Middle Ages," *Studia Gratiana* 19 (1976): 123–46; repr. in G. Constable, *Religious Life and Thought (11th-12th Centuries)* (London, 1979), no. IV.
Constable, G. "Monachisme et pèlerinage au Moyen Âge," *Revue historique* 258 (1977): 3–27; repr. in G. Constable, *Religious Life and Thought (11th-12th Centuries)* (London, 1979), no. III.
Constable, G. *Religious Life and Thought (11th-12th Centuries)* (London, 1979).
Constable, G. "The Ceremonies and Symbolism of Entering Religious Life and Taking the Monastic Habit, from the Fourth to the Twelfth Centuries," in *Segni e riti nella chiesa altomedievale occidentale, Spoleto, 11–17 aprile 1985* (Spoleto, 1987), pp. 808–16; repr. in G. Constable, *Culture and Spirituality in Medieval Europe* (Aldershot, 1996), no. VII.

Constable, G. "Entrance to Cluny in the Eleventh and Twelfth Centuries According to the Cluniac Customaries and Statutes," in *Mediaevalia Christiana, XIe–XIIIe siècles: Hommage à Raymonde Foreville de ses amis, ses collègues et ses amciens élèves*, ed. C. É. Viola (Paris, 1989), pp. 335-54; repr. in G. Constable, *The Abbey of Cluny: A Collection of Essays to Mark the Eleven-Hundredth Anniversary of Its Foundation* (Berlin, 2010), pp. 143-62.

Constable, G. "Cluny in the Monastic World of the Tenth Century," in *Il secolo di ferro: Mito e realtà del secolo X (Spoleto, 19–25 aprile 1990)* (Spoleto, 1991), pp. 391-437; repr. in G. Constable, *The Abbey of Cluny: A Collection of Essays to Mark the Eleven-Hundredth Anniversary of Its Foundation* (Berlin, 2010), pp. 43-79.

Constable, G. *Culture and Spirituality in Medieval Europe* (Aldershot, 1996).

Constable, G. *The Reformation of the Twelfth Century* (Cambridge, 1996).

Constable, G. "The Commemoration of the Dead in the Early Middle Ages," in *Early Medieval Rome and the Christian West: Essays in Honour of Donald A. Bullough*, ed. J. M. H. Smith (Leiden, 2000), pp. 169-95.

Constable, G. *Crusaders and Crusading in the Twelfth Century* (Farnham, 2008).

Constable, G. "Cluny and the First Crusade," in G. Constable, *Crusaders and Crusading in the Twelfth Century* (Farnham, 2008), pp. 183-96.

Constable, G. "The Crusading Project of 1150," in G. Constable, *Crusades and Crusading in the Twelfth Century* (Farnham, 2008), pp. 311-20.

Constable, G. "The Three Lives of Odo Arpinus: Viscount of Bourges, Crusader, Monk of Cluny," in G. Constable, *Crusaders and Crusading in the Twelfth Century* (Farnham, 2008), pp. 215-28.

Constable, G. "Carolingian Monasticism as Seen in the Plan of St. Gall," in *Le monde carolingien: Bilan, perspectives, champs de recherches*, ed. W. Fałkowski and Y. Sassier (Turnhout, 2010), pp. 199-217.

Constable, G. "Souvigny and Cluny," in G. Constable, *The Abbey of Cluny: A Collection of Essays to Mark the Eleven-Hundredth Anniversary of Its Foundation* (Berlin, 2010), pp. 213-34.

Constable, G. *The Abbey of Cluny: A Collection of Essays to Mark the Eleven-Hundredth Anniversary of Its Foundation* (Berlin, 2010).

Constable, O. R. *Housing the Stranger in the Mediterranean World: Lodging, Travel and Trade in Late Antiquity and the Middle Ages* (New York, 2003).

Consuetudines et Regulae: Sources for Monastic Life in the Middle Ages and the Early Modern Period, ed. C. M. Malone and C. Maines, Disciplina Monastica 10 (Turnhout, 2014).

Courcelle, P. *Late Latin Authors and Their Greek Sources*, trans. H. E. Wedeck (Cambridge, MA, 1969).

Cowdrey, H. E. J. *The Cluniacs and the Gregorian Reform* (Oxford, 1970).

Cowdrey, H. E. J. "Cluny and the First Crusade," *Revue bénédictine* 83 (1973): 285-311; repr. in H. E. J. Cowdrey, *Popes, Monks, and Crusaders* (London, 1984), no. XV.

Cowdrey, H. E. J. "Two Studies in Cluniac History, 1049-1126," *Studi Gregoriani* 11 (1978): 9-395.

Cownie, E. *Religious Patronage in Anglo-Norman England, 1066–1135* (Woodbridge, 1998).

Craig, K. M. "Bringing Out the Saints: Journeys of Relics in Tenth- to Twelfth-Century Northern France and Flanders" (PhD diss., University of California at Los Angeles, 2015).

Craig, K. M. *Mobile Saints: Relic Circulation, Devotion, and Conflict in the Central Middle Ages* (London, 2021).

Craig, L. A. *Wandering Women and Holy Matrons: Women as Pilgrims in the Later Middle Ages* (Leiden, 2009).

Cribiore, R. *Gymnastics of the Mind: Greek Education in Hellenistic and Roman Egypt* (Princeton, 2001).

Cristiani, R. "Integration and Marginalization: Dealing with the Sick in Eleventh-Century Cluny," in *From Dead of Night to End of Day: The Medieval Customs of Cluny /Du coeur de la nuit à la fin du jour: Les coutumes clunisiennes au moyen âge*, ed. S. Boynton and I. Cochelin, Disciplina Monastica 3 (Turnhout, 2005), pp. 287-95.

Crivello, F. "Les débuts de l'activité artistique dans le *scriptorium* de Cluny: Fondements et œuvres," in *Cluny: Les moines et la société au premier âge féodal*, ed. D. Iogna-Prat et al. (Rennes, 2013), pp. 197-208.

Cucarella, S. "Corresponding Across Religious Borders: Al-Bājī's Response to a Missionary Letter from France," *Medieval Encounters* 18 (2012): 1-35.

Daniel, N. *Islam and the West: The Making of an Image*, rev. ed. (Oxford, 1993).

Davis, A. J. *The Holy Bureaucrat: Eudes Rigaud and Religious Reform in Thirteenth-Century Normandy* (Ithaca, 2006).

Davril, A. "Coutumiers directifs et coutumiers descriptifs: D'Ulrich à Bernard de Cluny," in *From Dead of Night to End of Day: The Medieval Customs of Cluny / Du coeur de la nuit à la fin du jour: Les coutumes clunisiennes au moyen âge*, ed. S. Boynton and I. Cochelin, Disciplina Monastica 3 (Turnhout, 2005), pp. 23-28.

de Hamel, C. *The Book: A History of the Bible* (New York, 2001).

D'Evelyn, C. "A Lost Manuscript of the *De contemptu mundi*," *Speculum* 6 (1931): 132-33.

Declercq, G. "Originals and Cartularies: The Organization of Archival Memory (Ninth-Eleventh Centuries)," in *Charters and the Use of the Written Word in Medieval Society*, ed. K. Heidecker (Turnhout, 2000), pp. 147-70.

DeFilippo, J. "*Curiositas* and the Platonism of Apuleius' *Golden Ass*," in *Oxford Readings of the Roman Novel*, ed. S. J. Harrison (Oxford, 1999), pp. 269-89.

Deissmann, A. *Licht vom Osten: Das Neue Testament und die neuentdeckten Texte der hellenistisch-römischen Welt*, 4th ed. (Tübingen, 1923).

Delisle, L. *Inventaire des manuscrits de la bibliothèque nationale: Fonds du Cluni* (Paris, 1884).

Delmulle, J. "Notes on the Text of the Twelfth-Century Cluniac *Relatio metrica de duobus ducibus*," *Journal of Medieval Latin* 34 (2024): 71-100.

Dictionary of Deities and Demons in the Bible, ed. K. van der Toorn et al. (Leiden, 1995)

Dictionnaire d'archéologie chrétienne et de liturgie, ed. H. Leclercq, 15 vols. (Paris, 1907-53).

Dictionnaire d'histoire et de géographie ecclésiastiques, 31 vols. to date (Paris, 1912-).

Diehl, J. and S. Vanderputten, "Cluniac Customs Beyond Cluny: Patterns of Use in the Southern Low Countries," *Journal of Religious History* 41 (2017): 22-41.

Diem, A. "Rewriting Benedict: The *Regula cuiusdam ad virgines* and Intertextuality as a Tool to Construct a Monastic Identity," *Journal of Medieval Latin* 17 (2007): 313–28.

Diem, A. "New Ideas Expressed in Old Words: The *Regula Donati* on Female Monastic Life and Monastic Spirituality," *Viator* 43 (2012): 1–38.

Diem, A. and P. Rousseau, "Monastic Rules (Fourth to Ninth Century)," in *CHMM*, pp. 162–94.

Dionisotti, A. C. "On Bede, Grammars, and Greek," *Revue bénédictine* 92 (1982): 111–41.

Documentary Culture and the Laity in the Early Middle Ages, ed. W. Brown et al. (Cambridge, 2013).

Dolbeau, F. "Un domaine négligé de la littérature médiolatine: Les textes hagiographiques en vers," *Cahiers de Civilisation Médiévale* 45 (2002): 129–39.

Doniol, H. "Cartulaire de Sauxillanges," *Mémoire de l'Académie des sciences, belles-lettres et arts de Clermont-Ferrand*, n.s. 3 (1861): 465–1199.

Donnat, L. "Les coutumiers du Moyen Âge et la règle de saint Benoît," *Regulae Benedicti Studia* 16 (1989): 37–54.

Donnat, L. "Les coutumiers monastiques: Une nouvelle entreprise et un territoire nouveau," *Revue Mabillon*, n.s. 3 (1992): 5–21.

Dreves, G. M. "Bernhardus Morlanensis, Monachus Cluniacensis, um 1140," *Analecta Hymnica* 50 (1907): 423–83.

Dubois, J. "Au temps des premiers Capétiens les moines en pleine expansion affirment leurs libertés," in *Pouvoirs et libertés au temps premiers Capétiens*, ed. É. Magnou-Nortier (Maulevrier, 1992), pp. 197–214.

Dubois, J. and J.-L. Lemaitre, *Sources et methods de l'hagiographie médiévale* (Paris, 1993).

Duby, G. "Le budget de l'abbaye de Cluny entre 1080 et 1155: Economie domaniale et économie monétaire," *Annales: Économies, Sociétés, Civilisations* 7 (1952): 155–71; repr. in G. Duby, *Hommes et structures du moyen âge: Recueil d'articles* (Paris, 1973), pp. 61–82.

Duby, G. *La société aux XIe et XIIe siècles dans la région mâconnaise* (Paris, 1953).

Duchet-Suchaux, M. and Y. Lefèvre, "Les noms de la Bible," in *Bible de Tous les Temps 4: Le Moyen Age et la Bible* (Paris, 1984), pp. 13–23.

Dunn, F. *The Emergence of Monasticism: From the Desert Fathers to the Early Middle Ages* (Oxford, 2000).

Early Medieval Rome and the Christian West: Essays in Honour of Donald A. Bullough, ed. J. M. H. Smith (Leiden, 2000).

Eco, U. *The Name of the Rose*, trans. Richard Dixon (New York, 2014).

Engelhardt, G. J. "The *De contemptu mundi* of Bernardus Morvalensis, Part One: A Study in Commonplace," *Mediaeval Studies* 22 (1960): 108–35.

Engelhardt, G. J. "The *De contemptu mundi* of Bernardus Morvalensis, Part Two: A Study in Commonplace," *Mediaeval Studies* 26 (1964): 109–42.

Engelhardt, G. J. "The *De contemptu mundi* of Bernardus Morvalensis, Part Three: A Study in Commonplace," *Mediaeval Studies* 29 (1967): 243–72.

Epp, V. *Amicitia: Zur Geschichte personaler, sozialer, politischer und geistlicher Beziehungen im frühen Mittelalter* (Stuttgart, 1999).

Erdmann, C. *The Origin of the Idea of Crusade*, trans. M. W. Baldwin and W. Goffart (Princeton, 1977).

The European Book in the Twelfth Century, ed. E. Kwakkel and R. Thomson (Cambridge, 2018).
Eyton, R. W. *Court, Household, and Itinerary of King Henry II* (London, 1878).
Evans, J. A. S. "Father of History or Father of Lies: The Reputation of Herodotus," *Classical Journal* 64 (1968): 11–17.
Falk, S. *The Light Ages: The Surprising Story of Medieval Science* (New York, 2020).
Farrer, W. *An Outline Itinerary of King Henry the First* (Oxford, 1920).
Fassler, M. "The Office of the Cantor in Early Western Monastic Rules and Customaries: A Preliminary Investigation," *Early Music History* 5 (1985): 29–51.
Feiss, H. "*Circatores*: From Benedict of Nursia to Humbert of Romans," *American Benedictine Review* 40 (1989): 346–79.
Février, P.-A. et al., *La Provence des origines à l'an mil: Histoire et archéologie* (Paris, 1989).
Fichtenau, H. "Reisen und Reisende," in H. Fichtenau, *Beiträge zur Mediävistik: Ausgewählte Aufsätze*, 3 vols. (Stuttgart, 1975–86), vol. 3, pp. 1–79.
Finucane, R. C. *Miracles and Pilgrims: Popular Beliefs in Medieval England*, 2nd ed. (New York, 1995).
Finucane, R. *The Rescue of Innocents: Endangered Children in Medieval Miracles* (London, 1997).
Flexner, A. *The Usefulness of Useless Knowledge* (Princeton, 2017).
Folz, R. "Pierre le Vénérable et la liturgie," in *Pierre Abélard—Pierre la Vénérable: Les courants philosophiques, littéraires et artistiques en Occident au milieu du XIIe siècle (Abbaye de Cluny, 2 au 9 juillet 1972)* (Paris, 1975), pp. 143–61.
Ford, A. J. *Marvel and Artefact: The "Wonders of the East" in Its Manuscript Context* (Leiden, 2015).
Foucault, M. *Discipline and Punish: The Birth of the Prison*, trans. A. Sheridan (New York, 1977).
Fouracre, P. "Merovingian History and Merovingian Hagiography," *Past & Present* 127 (1990): 3–38, repr. in P. Fouracre, *Frankish History: Studies in the Construction of Power* (Burlington, 2013), no. II.
Fouracre, P. *Frankish History: Studies in the Construction of Power* (Burlington, 2013).
Fournier, P.-F. "Histoire anonyme de la foundation du prieuré de Lavoûte-Chilhac par Odilon, abbé de Cluny," *Bulletin philologique et historique (jusqu'à 1715) du Comité des travaux historiques et scientifiques* 46 (1958): 103–15.
Frakes, J. C. "The Knowledge of Greek in the Early Middle Ages: The Commentaries on Boethius' *Consolatio*," *Studi Medievali*, 3rd ser., 27 (1986): 23–43.
France, J. "Rodulfus Glaber and the Cluniacs," *Journal of Ecclesiastical History* 39 (1988): 497–508.
Franklin, C. V. *Material Restoration: A Fragment from Eleventh-Century Echernach in a Nineteenth-Century Parisian Codex* (Turnhout, 2010).
Franz, A. *Die kirchlichen Benediktionen im Mittelalter*, 2 vols. (Graz, 1960).
Frazer, J. G. *The Golden Bough: A Study in Magic and Religion*, 3rd ed., 12 vols. (London, 1906–15).
Friedman, Y. "An Anatomy of Anti-Semitism: Peter the Venerable's Letter to Louis VII, King of France (1146)," *Bar-Ilan Studies in History* 1 (1978): 87–102.

From Dead of Night to End of Day: The Medieval Customs of Cluny / Du coeur de la nuit à la fin du jour: Les coutumes clunisiennes au moyen âge, ed. S. Boynton and I. Cochelin, Disciplina Monastica 3 (Turnhout, 2005).

Fryde, E. B. "Some Fifteenth-Century Latin Translations of Ancient Greek Historians," in E. B. Fryde, *Humanism and Renaissance Historiography* (London, 1983), pp. 87-99.

Garand, M.-C. "Copistes de Cluny au temps de saint Maieul (948-994)," *Bibliothèque de l'Ecole des Chartes* 136 (1978): 5-36.

Gautier, M.-É. "Les aménagements liturgiques de la prieurale de Souvigny et les tombeaux des saints abbés de Cluny, Mayeul et Odilon," *Bulletin Monumental* 162 (2004): 67-85.

Gautier, M.-É. "Les sépultures des saints abbés de Cluny, Mayeul et Odilon, à Souvigny: État de la question et réflexions nouvelles (XIe-XIVe siècle)," *Hortus Artium Mediaevalium* 10 (2004): 133-42.

Gazeau, V. *Normannia monastica*, 2 vols. (Caen, 2007).

Geary, P. "The Ninth-Century Relic Trade – A Response to Popular Piety?," in *Religion and the People, 800–1700*, ed. J. Obelkevich (Chapel Hill, NC, 1979), pp. 8-19; repr. in P. Geary, *Living with the Dead in the Middle Ages* (Ithaca, 1994), pp. 175-93.

Geary, P. "L'humiliation des saints," *Annales: Économies, Sociétés, Civilisations* 34 (1979): 27-42; English translation: P. Geary, "Humiliation of Saints," in P. Geary, *Living with the Dead in the Middle Ages* (Ithaca, 1994), pp. 95-115.

Geary, P. *Furta Sacra: Thefts of Relics in the Central Middle Ages*, 2nd ed. (Princeton, 1990).

Geary, P. "Saints, Scholars, and Society: The Elusive Goal," in *Saints: Studies in Hagiography*, ed. S. Sticca (Binghamton, 1996), pp. 13-20, repr. in P. Geary, *Living with the Dead in the Middle Ages* (Ithaca, 1994), pp. 9-29.

Geary, P. *Phantoms of Remembrance: Memory and Oblivion at the End of the First Millenium* (Princeton, 1996)

Genestout, A. "La Règle du Maître et la Règle de S. Benoît," *Revue d'Ascétique et de Mystique* 21 (1940): 51-112.

Genette, G. *La littérature au second degré* (Paris, 1982); English translation: G. Genette, *Palimpsests: Literature in the Second Degree*, trans. C. Newman and C. Doubinsky (Lincoln, 1997).

Ghosh, S. *Writing the Barbarian Past: Studies in Early Medieval Historical Narrative* (Leiden, 2016).

Gilsdorf, S. *The Favor of Friends: Intercession and Aristocratic Politics in Carolingian and Ottonian Europe* (Leiden, 2014).

Giocarinis, K. "Bernard of Cluny and the Antique," *Classica et Mediaevalia* 27 (1966): 310-48.

Gneuss, H. and M. Lapidge, *Anglo-Saxon Manuscripts: A Bibliographical Handlist of Manuscripts and Manuscript Fragments Written or Owned in England up to 1100* (Toronto, 2014).

Godlove, S. "The First *Life* of Boniface: Willibald's *Vita Bonifatii*," in *A Companion to Boniface*, ed. M. Aaij and S. Godlove (Leiden, 2020), pp. 152-73.

Goffart, W. *The Le Mans Forgeries: A Chapter in the History of Church Property in the Ninth Century* (Cambridge, 1966).

Goffart, W. *The Narrators of Barbarian History (A.D. 550–800): Jordanes, Gregory of Tours, Bede, and Paul the Deacon* (Princeton, 1988).
Golding, B. "The Coming of the Cluniacs," *Anglo-Norman Studies* 3 (1980): 65-77.
Gonthier, D. and C. le Bas, "Analyse socio-économique de quelques recueils de miracles dans la Normandie du XIe au XIIIe siècle," *Annales de Normandie* 24 (1974): 3-36.
Gougaud, L. "Le langage des silencieux," *Revue Mabillon* 19 (1929): 93-100.
Goullet, M. *Ecriture et réécriture hagiographiques: Essai sur les réécriture de Vies de saints dans l'Occident latin medieval (VIIIe-XIIIe s.)* (Turnhout, 2005).
Grafton, A. "The Republic of Letters in the American Colonies: Francis Daniel Pastorius Makes a Notebook," *American Historical Review* 117 (2012): 1-39.
Greek Papyri in the British Museum, 7 vols. (London, 1893-1974).
Green, J. A. *Henry I, King of England and Duke of Normandy* (Cambridge, 2006).
Griffiths, F. *Nuns' Priests' Tales: Men and Salvation in Medieval Women's Monastic Life* (Philadelphia, 2018).
Green, R. "Greek in Late Roman Gaul: The Evidence of Ausonius," in *"Owls to Athens": Essays on Classical Subjects Presented to Sir Kenneth Dover*, ed. E. M. Craik (Oxford, 1990), pp. 311-19.
Greenblatt, S. *The Swerve: How the World Became Modern* (New York, 2011).
Gross, F. "Reprise et réinterprétation de la tradition carolingienne dans la charte de fondation de Cluny," *Revue Mabillon*, n.s. 25 (2014): 45-78.
Guerreau, A. "Espace social, espace symbolique: À Cluny au XIe siècle," in *L'ogre historien: Autour de Jacques Le Goff*, ed. J. Revel and J.-C. Schmitt (Paris, 1998), pp. 167-91.
Guerreau-Jalabert, A. "Sur les structures de parenté dans l'Europe médiévale," *Annales: Economies, Sociétés, Civilisations* 36 (1981): 1028-49.
Guerreau-Jalabert, A. "La désignation des relations et des groups de parenté en latin medieval," *Archivum Latinitatis Medii Aevi* 46/47 (1988): 65-108.
Gyug, R. "Early Medieval Bibles, Biblical Books, and the Monastic Liturgy in the Beneventan Region," in *The Practice of the Bible in the Middle Ages: Production, Reception, and Performance in Western Christianity*, ed. S. Boynton and D. J. Reilly (New York, 2011), pp. 34-60.
Hafner, P. W. *Der Basiliuskommentar zur Regula S. Benedicti: Ein Beitrag zur Autorenfrage karolingischer Regelkommentare* (Munster, 1959).
Hagendahl, H. *Latin Fathers and the Classics: A Study on the Apologists, Jerome, and Other Christian Writers* (Stockholm, 1958).
L'hagiographie mérovingienne à travers ses réécritures, ed. M. Goullet, M. Heinzelmann and C. Veyrard-Cosme (Ostfildern, 2010).
Hahn, C. *Strange Beauty: Issues in the Making and Meaning of Reliquaries, 400–circa 1204* (College Park, PA, 2012).
Hallinger, K. "Klunys Bräuche zur Zeit Hugos des Grossen (1049-1109): Prolegomena zur Neuherausgabe des Bernhard und Udalrich von Kluny," *Zeitschrift der Savigny-Stiftung für Rechtsgeschichte: Kanonistische Abteilung* 45 (1959): 99-140.
Hallinger, K. "Das Phänomen der liturgischen Steigerungen Klunys (10./11. Jh.)," in *Studia historicoecclesiastica: Festgabe für Prof. Luchesius G. Spätling O. F. M.*, ed. I. Vázquez (Rome, 1977), pp. 183-236.

Hallinger, K. "Überlieferung und Steigerung im Mönchtum des 8. bis 12. Jahrhunderts," in *Eulogia: Miscellanea Liturgica in onore di P. Burckhard Neunheuser O.S.B.* (Rome, 1979), pp. 125-87.

Hallinger, K. "*Consuetudo*: Begriff, Formen, Forschungsgeschichte, Inhalt," in *Untersuchungen zu Kloster und Stift* (Göttingen, 1980), pp. 140-66.

Hamilton, B. and A. Jotischky, *Latin and Greek Monasticism in the Crusader States* (Cambridge, 2020).

Harlow, M. and W. Smith, "Between Fasting and Feasting: The Literary and Archaeobiological Evidence for Monastic Diet in Late Antique Egypt," *Antiquity* 75 (2001): 758-68.

Häussling, A. *Mönchskonvent und Eucharistiefeier: Eine Studie über die Messe in der abendländischen Klosterliturgie des frühen Mittelalters und zur Geschichte der Messhäufigkeit* (Munster, 1973).

Harvey, S. A. "Martyr Passions and Hagiography," in *The Oxford Handbook of Early Christian Studies*, ed. S. A. Harvey and D. G. Hunter (Oxford, 2008), pp. 603-27

Heale, M. *Monasticism in Late Medieval England, c. 1300–1535* (Manchester, 2009).

Heil, J. "Agobard, Amolo, das Kirchengut und die Juden von Lyon," *Francia* 25 (1998): 39-76.

Heinzelmann, M. *Translationsberichte und andere Quellen des Reliquienkultes* (Turnhout, 1979)

Heisig, K. "Die Geschichtsmetaphysik des Rolandsliedes und ihre Vorgeschichte," *Zeitschrift für romanische Philologie* 60 (1935): 1-87.

Helvétius, A.-M. "Re-Reading Monastic Traditions: Monks and Nuns, East and West, from the Origins to c. 750," in *CHMM*, vol. 1, pp. 40-72.

Hemmerdinger, B. *Les manuscrits d'Hérodote et la critique verbale* (Genoa, 1981).

Herren, M. W. "The Humanism of John Scottus," in *Gli Umanesimi Medievali: Atti di II Congresso dell' "Internationales Mittellateinerkomitee" (Firenze, Cretosa del Galluzzo, 11–15 settembre 1993)*, ed Claudio Leonardi (Florence, 1998), pp. 191-200.

Herren, M. W. "Pelasgian Fountains: Learning Greek in the Early Middle Ages," in *Learning Latin and Greek from Antiquity to the Present*, ed. E. P. Archibald, W. Brockliss, and J. Gnoza (Cambridge, 2015), pp. 65-82.

Hershbell, J. P. "Plutarch and Herodotus: The Beetle in the Rose," *Rheinisches Museum für Philologie* 136 (1993): 143-63.

Hiley, D. *Western Plainchant: A Handbook* (Oxford, 1993).

Hillgarth, J. N. "The *Historiae* of Orosius in the Early Middle Ages," in *De Tertullien aux Mozarabes, Tome II: Antiquité tardive et Christianisme ancient (VIe–XIe siècles): Mélanges offerts à Jacques Fontaine*, ed. L. Holtz and J.-C. Fredouille (Paris, 1992), pp. 157-70.

Histoire Litteraire de la France, 47 vols. (Paris, 1733-2021).

Hoffmann, H. *Gottesfriede und Treuga Dei* (Stuttgart, 1964).

Hoffmann, R. C. "Economic Development and Aquatic Ecosystems in Medieval Europe," *American Historical Review* 101 (1996): 631-69.

Hollister, C. W. *Henry I* (New Haven, 2001).

Horden, P. "Sickness and Healing," in *The Cambridge History of Christianity*, Vol. 3, *Early Medieval Christianities, c. 600–c. 1100*, ed. T. F. X. Noble and J. M. H. Smith (Cambridge, 2008), pp. 416-32.

Horn, W. and E. Born, *The Plan of St. Gall*, 3 vols. (Berkeley, 1979).
Hornblower, S. "Herodotus' Influence in Antiquity," in *The Cambridge Companion to Herodotus*, ed. C. Dewald and J. Marincola (Cambridge, 2006), pp. 306-18.
Hosler, J. D. *Henry II: A Medieval Soldier at War, 1147-1189* (Leiden, 2007).
Hourlier, J. "Cluny et la notion d'ordre religieux," in *A Cluny: Congrès scientifique, fêtes et cérémonies liturgiques en l'honneur des saints abbés Odon et Odilon, 9-11 juillet 1949* (Dijon, 1950), pp. 219-26.
Hourlier, J. "Saint Odilon bâtisseur," *Revue Mabillon* 51 (1961): 303-24.
Hourlier, J. *Saint Odilon, abbé de Cluny* (Louvain, 1964).
Houston, G. W. *Inside Roman Libraries: Book Collections and Their Management in Antiquity* (Chapel Hill, 2014).
Howe, J. *Church Reform and Social Change in Eleventh-Century Italy: Dominic of Sora and His Patrons* (Philadelphia, 1997).
Hunt, N. *Cluny Under Saint Hugh, 1049-1109* (Notre Dame, IN, 1967).
Huppenbauer, H. W. "Belial in den Qumrantexten," *Theologische Zeitschrift* 15 (1959): 81-89.
Hurel, D.-O. "La place de l'érudition dans le *Voyage littéraire* de dom Edmond Martène et dom Ursin Durand (1717 et 1724)," *Revue Mabillon* n.s. 3 (1992): 213-28.
Huyghebaert, D. N. "Un légat de Gregoire VII en France: Warmond de Vienne," *Revue d'Histoire Ecclésiastique* 40 (1944-45): 187-200.
Inglebert, H. *Les romains chrétiens face à l'histoire de Rome: Histoire, christianisme et romanités en occident dans l'antiquité tardive (IIIe-Ve siècles)* (Paris, 1996).
Innes, M. "Archives, Documents and Landowners in Carolingian Francia," in *Documentary Culture and the Laity in the Early Middle Ages*, ed. W. Brown et al. (Cambridge, 2013), pp. 152-88.
Innes, M. "On the Material Culture of Legal Documents: Charters and Their Preservation in the Cluny Archive, Ninth to Eleventh Centuries," in *Documentary Culture and the Laity in the Early Middle Ages*, ed. W. Brown et al. (Cambridge, 2013), pp. 283-320.
Iogna-Prat, D. *Agni Immaculati: Recherches sur les sources hagiographiques relatives à saint Maieul de Cluny (954-994)* (Paris, 1988).
Iogna-Prat, D. "La croix, le moine et l'empereur: Dévotion à la croix et théologie politique à Cluny autour de l'an mil," in *Haut Moyen-Age: Culture, Éducation et Société: Études offertes à Pierre Riché*, ed. C. Lepelley et al. (La Garenne-Colombes, 1990), pp. 449-75; repr. in D. Iogna-Prat, *Études clunisiennes* (Paris, 2002), pp. 75-92.
Iogna-Prat, D. "La geste des origines dans l'historiographie clunisienne des XIe et XIIe siècles," *Revue bénédictine* 102 (1992): 135-91; repr. in D. Iogna-Prat, *Études clunisiennes* (Paris, 2002), pp. 161-200.
Iogna-Prat, D. "Panorama de l'hagiographie abbatiale clunisienne (v. 940-v. 1140)," in *Manuscrits hagiographiques et travail des hagiographes*, ed. M. Heinzelmann (Sigmaringen, 1992), pp. 77-118; repr. in D. Iogna-Prat, *Études clunisiennes* (Paris, 2002), pp. 35-73.
Iogna-Prat, D. "La saint Maïeul à Cluny d'après le *Liber Tramitis Aevi Odilonis*," in *Saint Mayeul et son temps: Actes du congrès international de Valensole, 12-14 Mai 1994* (Dignes-les-Bains, 1997), pp. 219-32.

Iogna-Prat, D. "The Dead in the Celestial Bookkeeping of the Cluniac Monks Around the Year 1000," in *Debating the Middle Ages: Issues and Readings*, ed. L. Little and B. H. Rosenwein (Oxford, 1998), pp. 340–62.

Iogna-Prat, D. *Études clunisiennes* (Paris, 2002).

Iogna-Prat, D. "La place idéale du laïc à Cluny: D'une morale statutaire à une éthique absolue," in *Guerriers et moines: Conversion et sainteté aristocratiques dans l'Occident medieval (IXe–XIIe siècle)*, ed. M. Lauwers (Nice, 2002), pp. 291–316, repr. in D. Iogna-Prat, *Études clunisiennes* (Paris, 2002), pp. 93–124.

Iogna-Prat, D. *Order and Exclusion: Cluny and Christendom Face Heresy, Judaism, and Islam (1000–1150)*, trans. G. R. Edwards (Ithaca, 2003).

Jacobs, M. *Islamische Geschichte in jüdischen Chroniken: Hebräische Historiographie des 16. und 17. Jahrhunderts* (Tübingen, 2004).

Jacoby, F. *Griechische Historiker* (Stuttgart, 1956).

James, M. R. *The Wanderings and Homes of Manuscripts* (London, 1919).

Jamroziak, E. "Miracles in Monastic Culture," in *A Companion to Medieval Miracle Collections*, ed. S. Katajala-Peltomaa, J. Kuuliala, and I. McCleery (Leiden, 2021), pp. 36–53.

Jardine, L. and A. Grafton, "'Studied for Action': How Gabriel Harvey Read His Livy," *Past & Present* 129 (1990): 30–78.

Jarecki, W. *Signa Loquendi: Die cluniacensischen Signa-Listen eingeleitet und herausgegeben* (Baden-Baden, 1981).

Jaspert, B. *Die Regula Benedicti-Regula Magistri Kontroverse*, 2nd ed. (Hildesheim, 1977).

Jefferson's Literary Commonplace Book, ed. D. L. Wilson (Princeton, 1989).

Jensen, L. B. "Royal Purple of Tyre," *Journal of Near Eastern Studies* 22 (1963): 104–18.

Johnson, P. D. *Equal in Monastic Profession: Religious Women in Medieval France* (Chicago, 1991).

Johnson, W. A. *Readers and Reading Culture in the High Roman Empire: A Study of Elite Communities* (Oxford, 2010).

Jones, C. A. "Monastic Identity and Sodomitic Danger in the *Occupatio* by Odo of Cluny," *Speculum* 82 (2007): 1–53.

Jones, C. A. "Relatio prosaica de duobus ducibus / Relatio metrica de duobus ducibus," in *La Trasmissione dei testi latini del medioevo / Medieval Latin Texts and Their Transmission* 8, ed. L. Castaldi (Florence, 2023), pp. 145–64.

Jones, C. M. "The Conventional Saracen of the Songs of Geste," *Speculum* 17 (1942): 201–25.

Jones, L. W. "The Influence of Cassiodorus on Medieval Culture," *Speculum* 20 (1945): 433–42.

de Jong, M. "Carolingian Monasticism: The Power of Prayer," in *The New Cambridge Medieval History*, Vol. 2, *c. 700–c. 900*, ed. R. McKitterick (Cambridge, 1995), pp. 622–53.

de Jong, M. *In Samuel's Image: Child Oblation in the Early Medieval West* (Leiden, 1996).

de Jong, M. "The Empire as *Ecclesia*: Hrabanus Maurus and Biblical *Historia* for Rulers," in *The Uses of the Past in the Early Middle Ages*, ed. Y. Hen and M. Innes (Cambridge, 2000), pp. 191–226.

Jordan, W. C. *A Tale of Two Monasteries: Westminster and Saint-Denis in the Thirteenth Century* (Princeton, 2009).
Jotischky, A. *The Perfection of Solitude: Hermits and Monks in the Crusader States* (University Park, PA, 1995).
Judge, E. A. "The Earliest Use of *Monachos* for 'Monk': (P. Coll. Youtie 77) and the Origins of Monasticism," *Jahrbuch für Antike und Christentum* 20 (1977): 72–89.
Judic, B. "Lire Grégoire le Grand à Saint-Martial de Limoges," *Studia Patristica* 36 (2001): 126–33.
Kaczynski, B. M. *Greek in the Carolingian Age: The St. Gall Manuscripts* (Cambridge, 1988).
Kaldellis, A. *Procopius of Caesarea: Tyranny, History, and Philosophy at the End of Antiquity* (Philadelphia, 2004).
Kaldellis, A. *A New Herodotos: Laonikos Chalkokondyles on the Ottoman Empire, the Fall of Byzantium, and the Emergence of the West* (Washington, DC, 2014).
Kedar, B. Z. "Palmarée: Abbaye clunisienne du XIIe siècle en Galilée," *Revue bénédictine* 93 (1983): 260–69.
Kedar, B. Z. *Crusade and Mission: European Approaches Toward the Muslims* (Princeton, 1984).
Ker, N. R. *Catalogue of Manuscripts Containing Anglo-Saxon* (Oxford, 1957).
Keskiaho, J. *Dreams and Visions in the Early Middle Ages: The Reception and Use of Patristic Ideas, 400–900* (Cambridge, 2015).
Keynes, S. "Anglo-Saxon Charters: Lost and Found," in *Myth, Rulership, Church, and Charters: Essays in Honour of Nicholas Brooks*, ed. J. Barrow and A. Vareham (Aldershot, 2008), pp. 45–66.
King, E. "Henry of Winchester: The Bishop, the City and the Wider World," *Anglo-Norman Studies* 37 (2014): 1–24.
Klaniczay, G. "The Myth of Scythian Origin and the Cult of Attila in the Nineteenth Century," in *Multiple Antiquities, Multiple Modernities: Ancient Histories in Nineteenth-Century European Cultures*, ed. G. Klaniczay, M. Werner, and O. Gecser (Frankfurt, 2011), pp. 185–212.
Klingshirn, W. "Charity and Power: Caesarius of Arles and the Ransoming of Captives in Sub-Roman Gaul," *Journal of Roman Studies* 75 (1985): 183–203.
Knowles, D. "Peter the Venerable," *Bulletin of the John Rylands Library* 39 (1956): 132–45.
Knowles, D. *Great Historical Enterprises: Problems in Monastic History* (London, 1963).
Knowles, D. *The Monastic Order in England: A History of Its Development from the Times of St. Dunstan to the Fourth Lateran Council, 940–1216*, 2nd ed. (Cambridge, 1963).
Knowles, D., C. N. L. Brooke, and V. C. M. London, *The Heads of Religious Houses: England and Wales, 940–1216* (Cambridge, 1972).
Knowles, D. "Henry of Blois, Bishop of Winchester 1129-71," *Winchester Cathedral Record* 41 (1972): 28–36.
Kohnle, A. *Abt Hugo von Cluny (1049–1109)* (Sigmaringen, 1993).
Kolmer, L. *Odo, der erste Cluniacenser Magister* (Deggendorf, 1913)
Kolve, V. A. "Ganymede/*Son of Getron*: Medieval Monasticism and the Drama of Same-Sex Desire," *Speculum* 73 (1998): 1014–67.

Koopmans, R. *Wonderful to Relate: Miracle Stories and Miracle Collecting in High Medieval England* (Philadelphia, 2011).

Kottje, R. *Verzeichnis der Handschriften mit den Werken des Hrabanus Maurus* (Hanover, 2012).

Kreiner, J. *The Social Life of Hagiography in the Merovingian Kingdom* (Cambridge, 2014).

Kritzeck, J. *Peter the Venerable and Islam* (Princeton, 1964).

Krönert, K. "Le role de l'hagiographie dans la mise en place d'une identité locale aux Xe-XIe siècles: L'exemple de Trèves," in *Constructions de l'espace au Moyen Âge: Practique et representations* (Paris, 2007), pp. 379-89.

Krüger, K. "Monastic Customs and Liturgy in the Light of the Architectural Evidence: A Case Study on Processions (Eleventh-Twelfth Centuries)," in *From Dead of Night to End of Day: The Medieval Customs of Cluny / Du coeur de la nuit à la fin du jour: Les coutumes clunisiennes au moyen âge*, ed. S. Boynton and I. Cochelin, Disciplina Monastica 3 (Turnhout, 2005), pp. 191-220.

Kramer, R. "Monasticism, Reform, and Authority in the Carolingian Era," in *CHMM*, pp. 432-49.

Kuefler, M. *The Making and Unmaking of a Saint: Hagiography and Memory in the Cult of Gerald of Aurillac* (Philadelphia, 2013).

Labhardt, A. "*Curiositas*: Note sur l'histoire d'un mot et d'une notion," *Museum Helveticum* 17 (1960): 206-24.

Landes, R. "Popular Participation in the Limousin Peace of God," in *The Peace of God: Social Violence and Religious Response in France around the Year 1000*, ed. T. Head and R. Landes (Ithaca, 1992), pp. 184-218.

The Landmark Herodotus: The Histories, ed. R. B. Strassler (New York, 2009).

Lapidge, M. *The Roman Martyrs: Introduction, Translations, and Commentary* (Oxford, 2018).

Lauer, P. "Nouvelles acquisitions latines et françaises du Départment des Manuscrits de la Bibliothèque Nationale pendent les années 1932-1935," *Bibliothèque de l'école des chartes* 96 (1935): 205-45.

Lauwers, M. "Constructing Monastic Space in the Early and Central Medieval West (Fifth to Twelfth Century)," in *CHMM*, vol. 1, pp. 317-39

le Neve, J. *Fasti Ecclesiae Anglicanae 1066-1300: II. Monastic Cathedrals*, ed. D. Greenway (London, 1971).

Leclercq, J. *Aux sources de la spiritualité occientale* (Paris, 1964).

Leclercq, J. "S. Maiolo fondatore e reformatore di monasteri a Pavia," in *Atti del 4° congresso internazionale di studi sull'alto medioevo, Pavia-Scaldasole-Monza-Bobbio, 10-14 settembre 1967* (Spoleto, 1969), pp. 155-73.

Leclercq, J. *The Love of Learning and the Desire for God: A Study of Monastic Culture*, trans. C. Misrahi (New York, 1982).

Leclercq, J. "Prayer at Cluny," *Journal of the American Academy of Religion* 51 (1983): 651-66.

Leclercq, J. "*Curiositas* and the Return to God in St Bernard of Clairvaux," *Cistercian Studies* 25 (1990): 92-100.

Lehner, U. *Enlightened Monks: The German Benedictines, 1740-1803* (Oxford, 2011).

Lerner, R. E. *Ernst Kantorowicz: A Life* (Princeton, 2017).

Lester, A. E. *Creating Cistercian Nuns: The Women's Religious Movement and Its Reform in Thirteenth-Century Champagne* (Ithaca, 2011).
Lester, A. E. "What Remains: Women, Relics, and Remembrance in the Aftermath of the Fourth Crusade," *Journal of Medieval History* 40 (2014): 311-28.
Lester, A. E. "The Cistercians," in *The Oxford Handbook of Christian Monasticism*, ed. B. Kaczynski (New York, 2020), pp. 232-47.
Lexikon des Mittelalters, ed. Robert Auty et al., 9 vols. (Munich, 1977-99).
Lexikon für Theologie und Kirche, ed. M. Buchberger et al., 10 vols., 2nd ed. (Freiburg, 1957-65).
Lett, D. *L'Enfant des miracles: Enfances et familles au Moyen Âge (XIIe–XIIIe siècles)* (Paris, 1997).
Lewis, A. R. *Naval Power and Trade in the Mediterranean, A.D. 500–1100* (Princeton, 1951).
The Libraries of the Augustinian Canons, ed. A. G. Webber and A. G. Watson, Corpus of British Medieval Library Catalogues 6 (London, 1998).
Lifshitz, F. "Beyond Positivism and Genre: 'Hagiographical' Texts as Historical Narrative," *Viator* 25 (1994): 95-114.
Lifshitz, F. *Religious Women in Early Carolingian Francia: A Study of Manuscript Transmission and Monastic Culture* (New York, 2014).
Little, L. *Benedictine Maledictions: Liturgical Cursing in Romanesque France* (Ithaca, 1993).
Lohrmann, D. "Pierre le Vénérable et Henri Ier, roi d'Angleterre," in *Pierre Abélard—Pierre la Vénérable: Les courants philosophiques, littéraires et artistiques en Occident au milieu du XIIe siècle (Abbaye de Cluny, 2 au 9 juillet 1972)* (Paris, 1975), pp. 191-203.
Longo, U. "Riti e agiografia: L'istituzione della *commemoratio omnium fidelium defunctorum* nelle *Vitae* di Odilone di Cluny," *Bullettino dell'Istituto storico italiano per il Medio Evo e Archivio Muratoriano* 103 (2002): 163-200.
LoPrete, K. A. *Adela of Blois: Countess and Lord (c. 1067–1137)* (Dublin, 2007).
Lorain, M. P. *Histoire de l'abbaye de Cluny depuis sa fondation jusqu'à sa destruction à l'époque de la Révolution française* (Paris, 1845).
Lotter, F. "Methodisches zur Gewinnung historischer Erkenntnisse aus hagiographischen Quellen," *Historische Zeitschrift* 229 (1979): 298-356.
Lotter, F. "Das Idealbild adliger Laienfrömmigkeit in den Anfängen Clunys: Odos Vita des Grafen Gerald von Aurillac," in *Benedictine Culture, 750–1050*, ed. W. Lourdaux and D. Verhelst (Leuven, 1983), pp. 76-95.
Lovecraft, H. P. *The Call of Cthulhu and Other Weird Stories*, ed. S. T. Joshi (New York, 1999).
Lowden, J. "The Luxury Book as Diplomatic Gift," in *Byzantine Diplomacy*, ed. J. Shepard and S. Franklin (Aldershot, 1992), pp. 249-60.
Luppi, B. *I saraceni in Provenza, in Liguria e nelle Alpi occidentali* (Bordighera, 1952).
Lynch, K. M. "The Venerable Bede's Knowledge of Greek," *Traditio* 39 (1983): 432-39.
Mabillon, J. *Itinerarium Burgundicum*, in *Ouvrages posthumes de Jean Mabillon et de Thierri Ruinart*, ed. V. Thuillier, 2 vols. (Paris, 1724), vol. 2, pp. 1-33.
MacCormack, S. *The Shadows of Poetry: Vergil in the Mind of Augustine* (Berkeley, 1998).

Maenchen-Helfen, J. O. *The World of the Huns: Studies in Their History and Culture* (Berkeley, 1973).

Mairold, M. *Die datierten Handschriften in der Steiermark außerhalb der Universitätsbibliothek Graz bis 1600*, 2 vols. (Vienna, 1988).

Malone, C. M. "Interprétation des pratiques liturgiques à Saint-Bénigne de Dijon d'après ses coutumiers d'inspiration clunisienne," in *From Dead of Night to End of Day: The Medieval Customs of Cluny / Du coeur de la nuit à la fin du jour: Les coutumes clunisiennes au moyen âge*, ed. S. Boynton and I. Cochelin, Disciplina Monastica 3 (Turnhout, 2005), pp. 221–50.

Manitius, M. "Zu Petrus' von Cluni patristischen Kenntnissen," *Speculum* 3 (1928): 582–87.

Les manuscrits classiques latins de la bibliothèque Vaticane II.1: Fonds Patetta et fonds de la Reine, ed. E. Pellegrin et al. (Paris, 1978).

Marcon, F. *The Knowledge of Nature and the Nature of Knowledge in Early Modern Japan* (Chicago, 2015).

Marincola, J. M. "Plutarch's Refutation of Herodotus," *Ancient World* 25 (1994): 191–203.

Marquardt, J. T. *From Martyr to Monument: The Abbey of Cluny as Cultural Patrimony* (Newcastle, 2007).

Marrou, H. I. *A History of Education in Antiquity*, trans. G. Lamb (New York, 1956).

Martène, E. and U. Durand, *Voyage littéraire de deux religieux bénédictins de la Congregation de St. Maur*, 2 vols. (Paris, 1717–24).

Mason, E. "The Purposeful Patronage of Henry of Blois," *Medieval History* 3 (1993): 30–50.

Matthews, J. *The Roman Empire of Ammianus* (London, 1989).

Meyvaert, P. "The Medieval Monastic Claustrum," *Gesta* 12 (1973): 53–59; repr. in P. Meyvaert, *Benedict, Gregory, Bede and Others* (London, 1977), no. XVI.

Manaresi, C. "La fondazione del monasterio di S. Maiolo di Pavia," in *Spiritualità Cluniacense, 12–15 ottobre 1958* (Todi, 1960), pp. 274–85.

Matter, E. A. *The Voice of My Beloved: The Song of Songs in Western Medieval Christianity* (Philadelphia, 1990).

Mayer, H. E. *Bistümer, Klöster und Stifte im Königreich Jerusalem*, MGH Schriften 26 (Stuttgart, 1977).

Mayerson, P. "Saracens and Romans: Micro-Macro Relationships," *Bulletin of the American Schools of Oriental Research* 274 (1989): 71–79.

Mayr-Harting, H. "Functions of a Twelfth-Century Shrine: The Miracles of St. Frideswide," in *Studies in Medieval History Presented to R. H. C. Davis*, ed. H. Mayr-Harting and R. I. Moore (London, 1985), pp. 193–206.

McCleery, I. "Christ More Powerful Than Galen? The Relationship Between Medicine and Miracles," in *Contextualising Miracles in the Christian West, 1100–1500: New Historical Approaches*, ed. M. M. Mesley and L. E. Wilson (Oxford, 2014), pp. 127–54.

McCormick, M. "The Imperial Edge: Italo-Byzantine Identity, Movement, and Integration, A.D. 650–950," in *Studies on the Internal Diaspora of the Byzantine Empire*, ed. H. Ahrweiler and A. E. Laiou (Washington, DC, 1998), pp. 17–52.

McCormick, M. *Origins of the European Economy: Communications and Commerce* (Cambridge, 2001).
McKitterick, R. *The Carolingians and the Written Word* (Cambridge, 1989)
McNamara, J. A. *Sisters in Arms: Catholic Nuns Through Two Millennia* (Cambridge, MA, 1996).
Melville, G. "Action, Text, and Validity: On Re-Examining Cluny's *Consuetudines* and Statutes," in *From Dead of Night to End of Day: The Medieval Customs of Cluny / Du coeur de la nuit à la fin du jour: Les coutumes clunisiennes au moyen âge*, ed. S. Boynton and I. Cochelin, Disciplina Monastica 3 (Turnhout, 2005), pp. 67-83
Melville, G. *The World of Medieval Monasticism: Its History and Forms of Life*, trans. J. D. Mixton (Collegeville, MN, 2016).
Meeder, S. *The Irish Scholarly Presence at St. Gall: Networks of Knowledge in the Early Middle Ages* (London, 2018).
Meens, R. "The Frequency and Nature of Early Medieval Penance," in *Handling Sin: Confession in the Middle Ages*, ed. P. Biller and A. J. Minnis (Woodbridge, 1998), pp. 35-63.
Merrills, A. H. *History and Geography in Late Antiquity* (Cambridge, 2005).
Metzler, I. *Disability in Medieval Europe: Thinking About Physical Impairment During the High Middle Ages, c. 1100-1400* (London, 2006).
Metzler, I. "Have Crutch, Will Travel: Disabled People on the Move in Medieval Europe," in *Travels and Mobilities in the Middle Ages: From the Atlantic to the Black Sea*, ed. M. O'Doherty and F. Schmieder (Turnhout, 2015), pp. 91-117.
Miracles, vies et réécriture dans l'Occident médiéval: Actes de l'Atelier "La réécriture des Miracles" (IHAP, juin 2004) et SHG X-XII: Dossiers des saints de Metz et Laon et de saint Saturnin de Toulouse, ed. M. Goullet, M. Heinzelmann and C. Veyrard-Cosme (Ostfildern, 2006).
de Miramon, C. "Embrasser l'état monastique à l'âge adulte (1050-1200): Étude sur la conversion tardive," *Annales: Economies, Sociétés, Civilisations* 54 (1999): 825-49.
Mohr, R. "Der Gedankenaustausch zwischen Heloisa und Abaelard über eine Modifizierung der Regula Benedicti für Frauen," *Regulae Benedicti Studia* 5 (1976/77): 307-33.
Momigliano, A. "Note sulla leggenda del cristianesimo di Seneca," *Rivista storica italiana* 62 (1950): 324-44.
Momigliano, A. "The Place of Herodotus in the History of Historiography," *History* 43 (1958): 1-13, repr. in A. Momigliano, *Studies in Historiography* (London, 1966), pp. 127-42.
Momigliano, A. *The Classical Foundations of Modern Historiography* (Berkeley, 1990).
Monastic Archaeology, ed. G. Keevill, M. Aston, and T. Hall (Oxford, 2001).
Moran, P. "Greek in Early Medieval Ireland," in *Multilingualism in the Graeco-Roman Worlds*, ed. A. Mullen and P. James (Cambridge, 2012), pp. 172-92.
Mortensen, L. B. "The Diffusion of Roman Histories in the Middle Ages: A List of Orosius, Eutropius, Paulus Diaconus and Landulfus Sagax Manuscripts," *Filologia mediolatina* 6-7 (1999-2000): 101-200.

Munson, R. V. "Persians in Thucydides," in *Thucydides and Herodotus*, ed. E. Foster and D. Lateiner (Oxford, 2012), pp. 241–77.

Murray, A. "Confession Before 1215," *Transactions of the Royal Historical Society*, 6th ser., 3 (1993): 51–81.

Murray, O. "Herodotus and Hellenistic Culture," *Classical Quarterly* 22 (1972): 200–13.

Muthesius, A. *Studies in Byzantine and Islamic Silk Weaving* (London, 1995).

Muthesius, A. *Studies in Silk in Byzantium* (London, 2004).

Muthesius, A. *Studies in Byzantine, Islamic and Near Eastern Silk Weaving* (London, 2008).

Newhauser, R. "Towards a History of Human Curiosity: A Prolegomenon to Its Medieval Phase," *Deutsche Vierteljahrsschrift für Literaturwissenschaft und Geistesgeschichte* 56 (1982): 559–75.

Newhauser, R. "The Sin of Curiosity and the Cistercians," in *Erudition at God's Service: Studies in Medieval Cistercian History*, ed. J. R. Sommerfeldt (Kalamazoo, MI, 1987), pp. 71–95.

Newman, J. H. "The Mission of St. Benedict," in J. H. Newman, *Historical Sketches*, 3 vols. (London, 1906), vol. 2, pp. 365–87.

Nightingale, J. *Monasteries and Patrons in the Gorze Reform: Lotharingia, c. 850–1000* (Oxford, 2001).

Norberg, D. *Introduction to Latin Versification*, trans. G. C. Roti and J. de la Chapelle Skubly (Washington, DC, 2004).

Norman, A. F. "The Library of Libanius," *Rheinisches Museum für Philologie* 107 (1964): 158–75.

Nothaft, C. P. E. *Scandalous Error: Calendar Reform and Calendrial Astronomy in Medieval Europe* (Oxford, 2018).

Nussbaum, M. C. *The Therapy of Desire: Theory and Practice in Hellenistic Ethics* (Princeton, 1994).

Nussbaum, O. *Kloster, Priestermönch und Privatmesse: Ihr Verhältnis im Westen von den Anfängen bis zum hohen Mittelalter* (Bonn, 1961).

O'Donnell, J. J. *Cassiodorus* (Berkeley, 1979).

O'Hara, A. *Jonas of Bobbio and the Legacy of Columbanus* (Oxford, 2018).

O'Sullivan, S. "Glossing Vergil and Pagan Learning in the Carolingian Age," *Speculum* 93 (2018): 132–65.

Oberman, H. A. *Contra vanam curiositatem: Ein Kapital der Theologie zwischen Seelenwinkel und Weltall* (Zurich, 1974).

Olsen, B. M. *L'étude des auteurs classiques latins aux XIe et XIIe siècles*, 5 vols. (Paris, 1982–2020).

Orchard, A. *Pride and Prodigies: Studies in the Monsters of the Beowulf-Manuscript* (Toronto, 1995).

Ortenberg, V. "Archbishop Sigeric's Journey to Rome in 990," *Anglo-Saxon England* 19 (1990): 197–246.

The Oxford Handbook of Medieval Latin Literature, ed. R. J. Hexter and D. Townsend (Oxford, 2012).

The Oxford Handbook of Women and Gender in Medieval Europe, ed. J. M. Bennett and R. M. Karras (Oxford, 2013).

The Oxyrhynchus Papyri, 87 vols. to date (London, 1898–2023).

Page, S. *Magic in the Cloister: Pious Motives, Illicit Interests, and Occult Approaches to the Medieval Universe* (University Park, PA, 2013).
Palmer, J. *Early Medieval Hagiography* (Kalamazoo, MI, 2018).
Parsons, S. and D. Townsend, "Gender," in *The Oxford Handbook of Medieval Latin Literature*, ed. R. J. Hexter and D. Townsend (Oxford, 2012), pp. 423-46.
Paxton, F. *The Death Ritual at Cluny in the Central Middle Ages / Le rituel de la mort à Cluny au Moyen Âge central*, Disciplina Monastica 9 (Turnhout, 2013).
Pearson, K. L. "Nutrition and the Early-Medieval Diet," *Speculum* 72 (1997): 1-32.
Pepin, R. E. "Heaven in Bernard of Cluny's *De contemptu mundi*," in *Imagining Heaven in the Middle Ages: A Book of Essays*, ed. J. S. Emerson and H. Feiss (New York, 2000), pp. 101-17.
Perry, D. M. *Sacred Plunder: Venice and the Aftermath of the Fourth Crusade* (University Park, PA, 2015).
Petry, R. C. "Medieval Eschatology and Social Responsibility in Bernard of Morval's *De contemptu mundi*," *Speculum* 24 (1949): 207-17.
Philippart, G. "Hagiographes et hagiographie, hagiologes et hagiologie: Des mots et des concepts," *Hagiographica* 1 (1994): 1-16.
Phillips, J. *The Second Crusade: Extending the Frontiers of Christendom* (New Haven, 2007).
Pick, L. K. "Rethinking Cluny in Spain," *Journal of Medieval Iberian Studies* 5 (2013): 1-17.
Pierre Abélard—Pierre la Vénérable: Les courants philosophiques, littéraires et artistiques en Occident au milieu du XIIe siècle (Abbaye de Cluny, 2 au 9 juillet 1972) (Paris, 1975).
Poeck, D. "Laienbegräbnisse in Cluny," *Frühmittelalterliche Studien* 15 (1981): 68-179
Poly, J.-P. *La Provence et la société féodale (879-1166): Contribution à l'étude des structures dites féodales dans le Midi* (Paris, 1976).
Ponesse, M. "Smaragdus of St. Mihiel and the Carolingian Monastic Reform," *Revue bénédictine* 116 (2006): 367-92.
Priestley, J. *Herodotus and Hellenistic Culture: Literary Studies in the Reception of the Histories* (Oxford, 2014).
Pringle, D. *The Churches of the Crusader Kingdom of Jerusalem: A Corpus*, Vol. 3, *The City of Jerusalem* (Cambridge, 2007).
Prinz, F. *Frühes Mönchtum im Frankenreich: Kultur und Gesellschaft in Gallien, den Rheinlanden und Bayern am Beispiel der monastischen Entwicklung (4. bis 8. Jahrhundert)*, 2nd ed. (Munich, 1988).
Problems and Possibilities of Early Medieval Charters, ed. J. Jarrett and A. McKinley (Turnhout, 2013).
Purkis, W. J. *Crusading Spirituality in the Holy Land and Iberia, c. 1095–c. 1187* (Woodbridge, 2008).
Quirk, K. "Men, Women and Miracles in Normandy, 1050-1150," in *Medieval Memories: Men, Women and the Past, 700–1300*, ed. E. Van Houts (London, 2013), pp. 54-62.
Raaijmakers, J. *The Making of the Monastic Community of Fulda, c. 744–c. 900* (Cambridge, 2012).

Raby, F. J. E. *A History of Christian-Latin Poetry from the Beginnings to the Close of the Middle Ages* (Oxford, 1927).

Racine, F. "Herodotus' Reputation in Latin Literature from Cicero to the Twelfth Century," in *Brill's Companion to the Reception of Herodotus in Antiquity and Beyond*, ed. J. Priestly and V. Zali (Leiden, 2016), pp. 192-212.

La réécriture hagiographique dans l'Occident médiéval: Transformations formelles et idéologiques, ed. M. Goullet, M. Heinzelmann and C. Veyrard-Cosme (Ostfildern, 2003)

Rees, D. "The Benedictine Revival in the Nineteenth Century," in *Benedict's Disciples*, ed. D. H. Farmer (Leominster, 1980), pp. 282-307.

Regula–Consuetudines–Statuta: Studi sulle fonti normative degli ordini religiosi nei secoli centrali del Medioevo, ed. C. Andenna and G. Melville (Munster, 2005).

Reinaud, J.-T. *Muslim Colonies in France, Northern Italy and Switzerland*, trans. H. Kahn Sherwani (Lahore, 1955).

Remensnyder, A. G. *Remembering Kings Past: Monastic Foundation Legends in Medieval Southern France* (Ithaca, 1991).

Reynolds, L. D. "The Medieval Tradition of Seneca's Dialogues," *Classical Quarterly* 18 (1968): 355-72.

Reynolds, L. D. and N. G. Wilson, *Scribes and Scholars: A Guide to the Transmission of Greek and Latin Literature*, 4th ed. (Oxford, 2014).

Riche, D. "Un témoin de l'historiographie clunisienne a la fin du Moyen Âge: Le *Chronicon* de François de Rivo," *Revue Mabillon*, n.s. 11 (2000): 89-114.

Riché, P. "Gerbert d'Aurillac et Saint Mayeul," in *Saint Mayeul et son temps*, pp. 191-97.

Riemann, K.-A. *Das herodoteische Geschichtswerk in der Antike* (Munich, 1967).

Riley-Smith, J. *The First Crusade and the Idea of Crusading* (Philadelphia, 1986).

Riley-Smith, J. *The First Crusaders, 1095–1131* (Cambridge, 1997).

Ritchey, S. "Health, Healing, and Salvation: Hagiography as a Source for Medieval Healthcare," in *Hagiography and the History of Latin Christendom, 500-1500*, ed. S. K. Herrick (Leiden, 2020), pp. 417-36.

Röckelein, H. "Monastic Landscapes," in *CHMM*, vol. 2, pp. 816-30.

Rodriguez, J. "Financing a Captive's Ransom in Lace Medieval Aragon," *Medieval Encounters* 9 (2003): 164-81.

Rollason, D. "The Miracles of St. Benedict: A Window on Early Medieval France," in *Studies in Medieval History Presented to R. H. C. Davis*, ed. H. Mayr-Harting and R. I. Moore (London, 1985), pp. 73-90.

Rosé, I. *Construire une société seigneuriale: Itinéraire et ecclésiologie de l'abbé Odon de Cluny (fin du IXe-milieu du Xe siècle)* (Turnhout, 2008).

Rosenwein, B. H. "Feudal War and Monastic Peace: Cluniac Liturgy as Ritual Aggression," *Viator* 2 (1971): 129-57.

Rosenwein, B. H. "St. Odo's St. Martin: The Uses of a Model," *Journal of Medieval History* 4 (1978): 317-31.

Rosenwein, B. H. *Rhinoceros Bound: Cluny in the Tenth Century* (Philadelphia, 1982).

Rosenwein, B. H. *To Be the Neighbor of Saint Peter: The Social Meaning of Cluny's Property, 909–1049* (Ithaca, 1989).

Rosenwein, B. H., T. Head, and S. Farmer, "Monks and Their Enemies: A Comparative Approach," *Speculum* 66 (1991): 764-96.

Rosenwein, B. H. "Circles of Affection in Cluniac Charters," in *Écritures de l'espace social: Mélanges d'histoire médiévale offerts à Monique Bourin par ses élèves et ses amis*, ed. D. Boisseuil et al. (Paris, 2010), pp. 397-415.
Ross, D. *Alexander Historiatus: A Guide to Medieval Illustrated Alexander Literature* (Frankfurt am Main, 1988).
Rotter, E. *Abendland und Sarazenen: Das okzidentale Araberbild und seine Entstehung im Frühmittelalter* (Berlin, 1983).
Rudolph, C. *"The Things of Greater Importance": Bernard of Clairvaux's "Apologia" and the Medieval Attitude Toward Art* (Philadelphia, 1990).
Russell, J. B. *The Devil: Perceptions of Evil from Antiquity to Primitive Christianity* (Ithaca, 1977).
Saint Maïeul, Cluny et la Provence: Expansion d'une abbaye à l'aube du moyen âge, ed. D. Iogna-Prat and B. H. Rosenwein (Mane, 1994).
Saint Mayeul et son temps: Actes du congrès international de Valensole, 12-14 Mai 1994 (Dignes-les-Bains, 1997).
Sahner, C. C. "From Augustine to Islam: Translation and History in the Arabic Orosius," *Speculum* 88 (2013): 905-31.
Salter, R. J. *Saints, Cure-Seekers and Miraculous Healing in Twelfth-Century England* (York, 2021).
Samotta, I. "Herodotus and Thucydides in Roman Republican Historiography," in *Thucydides and Herodotus*, ed. E. Foster and D. Lateiner (Oxford, 2012), pp. 345-73.
San Maiolo e le Influenze Cluniacensi nell'Italia del Nord: Atti del Convegno Internationale nel Millenario di San Maiolo (994-1994) Pavia-Novara, 23-24 settembre 1994, ed. E. Cau and A. Settia (Como, 1998).
Schlotheuber, E. and J. McQuillen, "Books and Libraries Within Monasteries," in *CHMM*, vol. 2, pp. 975-97.
Schmidt, P. G. "Ars loquendi et ars tacendi: Zur monastischen Zeichensprache des Mittelalters," *Berichte zur Wissenschaftsgeschichte* 4 (1981): 13-19.
Schmitt, J.-C. *Ghosts in the Middle Ages: The Living and the Dead in Medieval Society*, trans. T. L. Fagan (Chicago, 1998).
Schroll, M. A. *Benedictine Monasticism as Reflected in the Warnefrid-Hildemar Commentaries on the Rule* (London, 1941).
Schulte, A. *Geschichte des mittelalterlichen Handels und Verkehrs zwischen Westdeutschland und Italien mit Ausschluss von Venedig*, 2 vols. (Leipzig, 1900).
de Seilhac, L. "L'utilisation de le Règle de saint Benoît dans les monastères féminins," in *San Benedetto nel suo tempo: Atti del 7. Congresso internazionale di studi sull'alto Medioevo (Norcia, Subiaco, Cassino, Montecassino, 29 Settembre-Ottobre 1980)*, 2 vols. (Spoleto, 1982), vol. 2, pp. 527-49.
Semmler, J. "Benedictus II: Una regula, una consuetudo," in *Benedictine Culture, 750-1050*, ed. W. Lourdaux and D. Verhelst (Louvain, 1983), pp. 1-49.
Sénac, P. *Musulmans et sarrasins dans le sud de la Gaule: VIIIe au XIe siècle* (Paris, 1980).
Sénac, P. *Provence et piraterie sarrasine* (Paris, 1982).
Settia, A. "Economia e società nella Pavia ottoniana," *Archivio storico Lombardo* 122 (1996): 11-28.
Shapiro, M. *The Parma Ildefonsus: A Romanesque Illuminated Manuscript from Cluny and Related Works* (New York, 1964).

Shepard, J. "The 'Muddy Road' of Odo Arpin from Bourges to La Charité-sur-Loire," in *The Experience of Crusading II: Defining the Crusader Kingdom*, ed. P. Edbury and J. Phillips (Cambridge, 2003), pp. 11-28.

Siegmund, A. *Die Überlieferung der griechischen christlichen Literatur in der lateinischen Kirche bis zum 12. Jahrhundert* (Munich, 1948), pp. 67-71.

Sigal, P.-A. "Comment on concevait et on traitait la paralysie en Occident dans le Haut Moyen Age (V^e-XIIe siècles)," *Revue d'histoire des sciences* 24 (1971): 193-211.

Sigal, P.-A. *L'homme et le miracle dans la France médiévale: XIe-XIIe siècle* (Paris, 1985).

Sillem, A. "St. Benedict (c. 480-c. 550)," in *Benedict's Disciples*, ed. D. H. Farmer (Leominster, 1980), pp. 21-40.

Sivan, H. *Ausonius of Bordeaux: Genesis of a Gallic Aristocracy* (London, 1993).

Smith, J. M. H. "The Problem of Female Sanctity in Carolingian Europe, c. 780-920," *Past & Present* 146 (1995): 3-37.

Smith, J. M. H. "Old Saints, New Cults: Roman Relics in Carolingian Francia," in *Early Medieval Rome and the Christian West: Essays in Honour of Donald A. Bullough*, ed. J. M. H. Smith (Leiden, 2000), pp. 317-39.

Smith, J. M. H. "Portable Christianity: Relics in the Medieval West (c. 700-1200)," *Proceedings of the British Academy* 181 (2012): 143-67.

Smith, K. A. *War and the Making of Medieval Monastic Culture* (Woodbridge, 2011).

Smith, L. M. *The Early History of the Monastery of Cluny* (Oxford, 1920).

Snijders, T. "Celebrating with Dignity: The Purpose of Benedictine Matins Readings," in *Understanding Monastic Practices of Oral Communication (Western Europe, Tenth-Thirteenth Centuries)*, ed. S. Vanderputten (Turnhout, 2011), pp. 115-36.

Snoek, G. *Medieval Piety from Relics to the Eucharist: A Process of Mutual Interaction* (Leiden, 1995).

Southern, R. W. *Western Views of Islam in the Middle Ages* (Cambridge, MA, 1962).

Southern, R. W. *Saint Anselm: A Portrait in a Landscape* (Cambridge, 1990)

Stacy, N. E. "Henry of Blois and the Lordship of Glasonbury," *English Historical Review* 114 (1999): 1-33.

Stadter, P. A. "Thucydides as 'Reader' of Herodotus," in *Thucydides and Herodotus*, ed. E. Foster and D. Lateiner (Oxford, 2012), pp. 39-66.

Stratford, N. "The Documentary Evidence for the Building of Cluny III," in N. Stratford, *Studies in Burgundian Romanesque Sculpture*, 2 vols. (London, 1998), vol. 1, pp. 41-59.

Stratford, N. "Un grand clunisien, Henri de Blois," in *Cluny 910-2010: Onze siècles de rayonnement*, ed. N. Stratford (Paris, 2010), pp. 238-44.

Stroll, M. *The Jewish Pope: Ideology and Politics in the Papal Schism of 1130* (Leiden, 1987).

Studies in Medieval History Presented to R. H. C. Davis, ed. H. Mayr-Harting and R. I. Moore (London, 1985).

Sullivan, R. "What Was Carolingian Monasticism? The Plan of St. Gall and the History of Monasticism," in *After Rome's Fall: Narrators and Sources of Early Medieval History*, ed. A. C. Murray (Toronto, 1998), pp. 251-87.

Sullivan, T. *Benedictine Monks at the University of Paris, A.D. 1229-1500: A Biographical Register* (Leiden, 1995).

Tanner, H. J. "In His Brother's Shadow: The Crusading Career and Reputation of Eustace III of Boulogne," in *The Crusades: Other Experiences, Alternative Perspectives*, ed. K. I. Semaan (Binghamton, NY, 2003), pp. 83-99.

Taylor, A. "Books, Bodies, and Bones: Hilduin of St-Denis and the Relics of St. Dionysius," in *The Ends of the Body: Identity and Community in Medieval Culture*, ed. S. C. Akbari and J. Ross (Toronto, 2013), pp. 25-60.

Taylor, A. *Epic Lives and Monasticism in the Middle Ages, 800-1050* (Cambridge, MA, 2013).

Taylor, A. "Hagiography and Early Medieval History," *Religion Compass* 7 (2013): 1-14.

Texts and Transmission: A Survey of the Latin Classics, ed. L. D. Reynolds (Oxford, 1983).

Theilmann, J. M. "English Peasants and Medieval Miracle Lists," *Historian* 52 (1990): 286-303.

Thompson, M. W. "Recent Excavations in the Keep of Farnham Castle, Surrey," *Medieval Archaeology* 4 (1960): 81-94.

Thucydides and Herodotus, ed. E. Foster and D. Lateiner (Oxford, 2012).

Tilliette, J.-Y. "Les modèles de sainteté du IXe au XIe siècle d'après le témoignage des récits hagiographiques en vers métriques," in *Santi e demoni nell'alto medioevo occidentale (secoli V-XI)* (Spoleto, 1988), pp. 381-406.

Tolan, J. V. *Saracens: Islam in the Medieval European Imagination* (New York, 2002).

Torrell, J.-P. and D. Bouthillier, *Pierre le Vénérable et sa vision du monde: Sa vie, son oeuvre, l'homme et le demon* (Leuven, 1986).

Travel, Pilgrimage and Social Interaction from Antiquity to the Middle Ages, ed. J. Kuuliala and J. Rantala (Abingdon, 2020).

Trenery, C. *Madness, Medicine and Miracle in Twelfth-Century England* (Abingdon, 2019).

Troncarelli, F. *Vivarium: I Libri, Il Destino* (Turnhout, 1998).

Tyler, J. E. *The Alpine Passes: The Middle Ages (962-1250)* (Oxford, 1930).

de Valous, G. *Le monachisme clunisien des origins au XVe siècle: Vie intérieure des monastères et organization de l'ordre*, 2 vols. (Paris, 1970).

Van Dam, R. *Leadership and Community in Late Antique Gaul* (Berkeley, 1985).

van den Eydne, D. "Les principaux voyages de Pierre le Vénérable," *Benedictina* 15 (1968): 58-110.

Van Engen, J. "The 'Crisis of Cenobitism' Reconsidered: Benedictine Monasticism in the Years 1050-1150," *Speculum* 61 (1986): 269-304.

Van Houts, E. *Married Life in the Middle Ages, 900-1300* (Oxford, 2019).

Van Nuffelen, P. *Orosius and the Rhetoric of History* (Oxford, 2012).

van Rijnberk, G. *Le langage par signes chez les moines* (Amsterdam, 1953).

Vanderputten, S. "A Time of Great Confusion: Second-Generation Cluniac Reformers and Resistance to Monastic Centralization in the County of Flanders (c. 1125-1145)," *Revue d'histoire ecclésiastique* 102 (2007): 47-75.

Vanderputten, S. "The First 'General Chapter' of Benedictine Abbots (1131) Reconsidered," *Journal of Ecclesiastical History* 66 (2015): 715-34.

Vanderputten, S. *Imagining Religious Leadership in the Middle Ages: Richard of Saint-Vanne and the Politics of Reform* (Ithaca, 2015), pp. 86-87.

Vanderputten, S. *Dark Age Nunneries: The Ambiguous Identity of Female Monasticism, 800–1050* (Ithaca, 2018).

Vanderputten, S. "'I Would Be Rather Pleased if the World Were to be Rid of Monks': Resistence to Cluniac Integration in Late Eleventh- and Early Twelfth-Century France," *Journal of Medieval History* 47 (2021): 22–41.

Vanderputten, S. "Imagining Early Cluny in Abbatial Biographies," in *A Companion to the Abbey of Cluny in the Middle Ages*, ed. S. G. Bruce and S. Vanderputten (Leiden, 2022), pp. 105–24.

Vanderputten, S. "Adalbero of Laon's Poem to King Robert (1023–25/7): A Discourse Against Cluniac Reform or a Commentary on Monastic Hypocrisy?," *Early Medieval Europe* 32 (2024): 159–83.

Vauchez, A. *Sainthood in the Later Middle Ages*, trans. J. Birrell (Cambridge, 1997).

Vocino, G. "Hagiography as an Instrument for Political Claims in Carolingian Northern Italy: The Saint Syrus Dossier (*BHL* 7976 and 7978)," in *An Age of Saints? Power, Conflict, and Dissent in Early Medieval Christianity*, ed. P. Sarris, M. Dal Santo, and P. Booth (Leiden, 2011), pp. 169–86.

de Vogüé, A. *Community and Abbot in the Rule of Benedict* (Kalamazoo, MI, 1979).

de Vogüé, A. *The Community and Abbot in the Rule of St. Benedict*, trans. C. Philippi and E. R. Perkins, 2 vols. (Kalamazoo, 1988).

de Vogüé, A. "L'auteur du *Commentaire des Rois* attribué à Saint Grégoire: Un moine de Cava?," *Revue bénédictine* 106 (1996): 319–31.

von Büren, V. "Le grand catalogue de la Bibliothèque de Cluny," in *Le gouvernement d'Hugues de Semur à Cluny: Actes du Colloque scientifique international (Cluny, septembre 1988)* (Mâcon, 1990), pp. 245–63.

von Büren, V. "Le catalogue de la bibliothèque de Cluny du XIe siècle reconstitué," *Scriptorium* 46 (1992): 256–67.

von Padberg, L. E. "Bonifatius und die Bücher," in *Der Ragyndrudis-Codex des Hl. Bonifatius*, ed. L. E. von Padberg and H.-W. Stork (Paderborn, 1994), pp. 7–75.

Voss, L. *Heinrich von Blois, Bischof von Winchester (1129–1171)* (Berlin, 1932).

Vulliez, C. "Le miracle et son approche dans les recueils de *miracula* Orléanais du IXe au XIIe siècle," in *Miracles, Prodiges et Merveilles au Moyen Age* (Sorbonne, 1995), pp. 89–113.

Walsh, P. G. "The Rights and Wrongs of Curiosity (Plutarch to Augustine)," *Greece and Rome* 35 (1988): 73–85.

Walther, H. *Initia Carminum ac Versuum Media Aevi Posterioris Latinorum: Alphabetisches Verzeichnis der Versanfänge mittellateinischer Dichtungen* (Gottingen, 1959).

Ward, B. *Miracles and the Medieval Mind* (Philadelphia, 1982).

Wathen, A. G. *Silence: The Meaning of Silence in the Rule of Saint Benedict* (Washington, DC, 1973).

Weinberger, S. "Paiens et mauvais chrétiens: L'explication du mal dans la Provence des Xe et XIe siècles," *Annales du Midi* 98 (1986): 317–26.

Welles, C. B. "Fragments of Herodotus and Appian from Dura," *Transactions and Proceedings of the American Philological Association* 70 (1939): 203–12.

West, S. R. "The Papyri of Herodotus," in *Culture in Pieces: The Proceedings of a Conference in Honour of Professor Peter Parsons*, ed. D. Obbink and R. Rutherford (Oxford, 2011), pp. 69–83.

Wichner, J. *Catalogus codicum manu scriptorum Admontensis* (Admont, 1889).
Wilmart, A. "Le couvent et la bibliothèque de Cluny vers le milieu du XIe siècle," *Revue Mabillon* 11 (1921): 89–124.
Wilmart, A. "Grands poèmes inédits de Bernard le Clunisien," *Revue bénédictine* 45 (1933): 249–54.
Wischermann, E. M. *Grundlagen einer cluniacensischen Bibliotheksgeschichte* (Munich, 1988).
Wolf, K. B. "The Earliest Spanish Christian Views of Islam," *Church History* 55 (1986): 281–93.
Wolf, K. B. "Christian Views of Islam in Early Medieval Spain" in *Medieval Christian Perceptions of Islam: A Book of Essays*, ed. J. V. Tolan (New York, 1996), pp. 85–108.
Wollasch, J. *Cluny, Licht der Welt: Aufstieg und Niedergang der klösterlichen Gemeinschaft* (Düsseldorf and Zürich, 1996).
Wollasch, J. "Das Schisma des Abtes Pontius von Cluny," *Francia* 23 (1996): 31–52.
Wood, I. N. "The Use and Abuse of Latin Hagiography in the Early Medieval West," in *East and West, Modes of Communication: Proceedings of the First Plenary Conference at Merida*, ed. E. Chrysos and I. Wood (Leiden, 1999), pp. 93–109.
Yarrow, S. *Saints and Their Communities: Miracle Stories in Twelfth–Century England* (Oxford, 2006).
Young, A. M. *Echoes of Two Cultures* (Pittsburgh, 1964).
Zerner, M. "La capture de Maïeul et la guerre de libération de Provence: Le départ des sarrasins à travers les cartulaires provençaux," in *Saint Mayeul et son temps: Actes du congrès international de Valensole, 12–14 Mai 1994* (Dignes-les-Bains, 1997), pp. 199–210.
Zimmermann, G. *Ordensleben und Lebensstandard: Die Cura corporis in den Ordensvorschriften des abendländischen Hochmittelalters* (Munster, 1973).

INDEX

Aachen, 41
Aachen assemblies (816–817), 15, 32
Abelard, 7, 23, 122
Abu al-Wadil Sulayman al-Bājī, 168
Adela of Blois, countess, 207, 210, 216
Adelaide, empress, 72, 76–77, 96
Admont, abbey, 232–35
Aethicus Ister, 6
Agobard of Lyons, archbishop, 56
Agricola, saint, 148
Alcuin, 5, 6, 41, 56
All Souls, Feast of (November 2), 75, 86, 89
Alfonso VI of León-Castile, king, 202
Ambrose of Milan, bishop, 5, 6, 8, 62, 224
Ammianus Marcellinus, 241
Anacletus II, antipope, 203
Anastasius, hermit, 168, 178, 200
Anglo-Saxon Chronicle. See *Peterborough Chronicle*.
Anne, saint, 157
Anselm of Bec, 7, 201, 208, 224–25, 235
Antioch, 172
Antony, saint, 37
Apuleius, 222
Arator, 4
archaeology, monastic, 42
Arimaspians (one-eyed men), 242
Aristarchus of Samothrace, 242
astrolabe, 225
Athanasius of Alexandria, archbishop, 36. See also *Life of Anthony*.
Athens, 240
Augustine of Hippo, bishop, 4, 5, 6, 8, 222, 224–26, 234, 238
Ausonius of Bordeau, 243–44
Ava, abbess, 144
Avitus of Vienne, 4
Aymard, abbot of Cluny (942–954), 75, 88

Baldric of Bourgueil, 176–77
Baldwin II of Jerusalem, king, 154, 171

Basil of Caesarea, 6, 14, 154
Bede, 4, 6, 8, 55, 66, 111, 225, 245
Belial, 50–52, 54–58
Benedict of Aniane, abbot, 15, 32, 113
Benedict of Nursia, abbot, 12–21, 32–34, 112, 158, 166
Benedict Biscop, abbot, 111
Benedictine, definition of, 11–13, 16–21
Benedictine Confederation of the Order of Saint Benedict, 20
Bernard of Clairvaux, abbot, 173–74, 203, 213–14, 221, 225–32, 234–35
Bernard of Cluny, 34, 125–41, 152
Bernard of Cluny, poet, 180–95
Berno, abbot of Cluny (910–927), 3, 75
Boethius, 244, 246
Boniface, archbishop and missionary, 59–60
Bouchard of Vendôme, count, 94

Caesarea, 155
Caesarius of Arles, 15
Cambyses, king, 241
canonization, 78
canons, regular, 121. See also Order of Saint Victor.
cartularies, 30, 142
Cassiodorus, 5–6, 244, 247–49, 252
Cato, 191
Cava (Santissima Trinità di Cava die Tirreni), abbey, 121
Cecilia, saint, 148
Charlemagne, 5, 17, 33, 41
charters, 28–32, 75, 81, 85, 88–89, 144–45, 152–53, 169–70, 232. See also cartularies.
Chartres, 95, 98, 161
Chrodogang of Metz, bishop, 145
Cicero, 4, 222, 240
Cistercians, 19, 20, 89, 225–32
Clement, pope and saint, 156–57, 178

317

INDEX

Clairvaux, abbey, 225
Cluniac General Chapter (1132), 206-7, 229
Cluny, abbey of, 1-10, 18-20, 25, 34, 37, 42, 46-47, 50-51, 60-61, 63-64, 66-67, 69-70, 74-76, 84-89, 95, 114-15, 118, 124-41, 242-61, 162-79, 180-95
Collationum tres libri, 180, 187
Columbanus, saint, 159
confession, 140
Constantinople, 144, 155-57, 177-78, 244
Consuetudines antiquiores, 152
Corbie, abbey, 113
Cornelius, pope, 147
Council of Anse (1025), 167
Council of Clermont (1095), 74, 163, 170, 176
crusades. *See* Council of Clermont (1095); First Crusade; Second Crusade; Third Crusade; Fourth Crusade.
cult of the dead, 33
Cunegonde, empress, 151
curiosity, 217-35
customaries, 17, 19, 34-36, 75, 112-41, 151-52. *See also* Bernard of Cluny; *Consuetudines antiquiores*; *Liber tramitis*; Ulrich of Zell; William of Hirsau.
Cuthbert Butler, 19
cynocephali (dog-headed men), 38-39
Cyprian of Carthage, 8
Cyrus the Great, king, 237, 239, 241

Dares, king, 241
Defensor of Ligugé, 224-25
Denis, saint, 22
Devil, 54-57, 226-27
Dido, 238
Didymus the Blind, 5
Dionysius the Areopagite, 40, 148
Donatus of Besançon, bishop, 23
Drauscius, bishop, 111
Dura-Europos, 242
Durand, Ursin, 142-43, 161
dye, 80

Eadmer, 201
Edessa, 154, 174
Eliot, T. S., 241
Elizabeth, saint, 157
England, 196-97, 200-216
environmental history, 42-43
Ephrem the Syrian, 6

Eugenius III, pope, 173-74, 182
Euripides, 246
Eusebius of Caesarea, bishop, 6
Eustace, saint, 159
Eustace III, count, 171
Evagrius, 36
Evroul, abbot, 111

Fabius Pictor, 241
Ferrara, 81
First Crusade, 45, 74, 155, 162-64, 167, 171-72, 176-79
fishponds, 42
Fleury-sur-Loire, abbey, 64, 118, 166
Flexner, Abraham, 220
Flodoard of Reims, 81
Folcuin of Saint-Bertin, 16
forgeries, 30
Fourth Crusade, 156-57, 178
Fraxinetum. *See* La Garde-Freinet.
friendship, 104-5
Fulbert of Chartres, bishop, 95
Fulcran of Lodève, bishop, 97
Fulda, abbey, 29

Galand of Reigny, 221, 225-28
Garnier (Warnerius), prior of Cluny, 153
Gebhard of Salzburg, archbishop, 232
Gennadius of Marseilles, 5
Geoffrey of Chartres, bishop, 203
Geoffrey of Roche-Vanneau, abbot and bishop, 225
George, saint, 148
Georgics, 26
Gerald of Aurillac, 81, 146, 165-66
Gerwin of Saint-Vanne, 66
Gilduin of Le Puiset, abbot, 171-72
Gilo of Cluny, 153
Godfrey of Bouillon, duke, 171
Gorgonius, saint, 145
Gorze, abbey, 31, 145
Great Saint Bernard Pass, 45, 47, 49, 58, 60, 76, 166, 169
Greek learning, 40, 243-48
Gregory I the Great, pope, 4-6, 8, 12, 14-15, 37, 148, 222-25, 234
Gregory VII, pope, 162, 201
Gregory Nazianzen, 8

hagiography, 36-40, 50, 60-61, 65, 69-70, 73, 78-89, 146, 166-67, 232. *See also Life of Anthony*; *Life of Christopher*; *Life*

INDEX 319

of Gerald of Aurillac; Life of Hugh; Life of Malchus; Life of Maiolus; Life of Martin of Tours; Life of Mary of Egypt; Life of Odo; Life of Peter of Cava; Life of Peter the Venerable.
hagiography, verse, 25–26, 39–40
Haimo of Auxerre, 6
Haimo of Fulda, 56–57
Hariulf, 66
Harvey, Gabriel, 238
Hector, 191
Helen of Troy, 191
Helmeradus of Riez, bishop, 153
Heloise, abbess, 23–24, 122
Henry I, king of England, 197–98, 202–4, 207–9, 211, 215–16
Henry II, king of England, 198, 212, 214–15
Henry II, emperor, 5, 151
Henry IV, emperor, 201
Henry of Angély, abbot, 205–6
Henry of Blois, abbot and bishop, 205, 207–12, 214–16
Herodotus of Helicarnassus, 236–61
Hilary of Poitiers, 5, 145
Hildebrand, master of the mint, 83–84, 86–87
Hilduin of Le Puiset, 154
Hildemar of Corbie, 33
Hincmar of Reims, 224
Hirsau, abbey, 115, 117
history, providential, 239
Holy Lance, relic, 172
Holy Land, 144, 154, 172, 177. *See also* crusades; Jerusalem.
Homer, 246
Honorantiae Civitatis Papiae, 81
Horace, 4, 182
Hrabanus Maurus, 5, 6, 8, 63
Hrotswitha of Gandersheim, 39
Hugh III, abbot of Cluny (1158–1161), 7
Hugh of Arles, count, 49
Hugh of Bourges, archbishop, 147
Hugh of Edessa, archbishop, 154
Hugh of Rouen, archbishop, 203
Hugh of St. Victor, 7
Hugh the Great, abbot of Cluny (1049–1109), 74, 115–16, 126, 143, 155, 158, 160, 162–63, 165, 168, 170, 178, 198–202, 207, 209
Hugh Capet, king, 94–95, 101
humiliation of saints, 153

Idung of Prüfening, 19, 229
Ildefonsus of Toledo, 9
Imad ad-Din Zengi, emir, 174
Innocent, saint, 148
Innocent II, pope, 203, 210, 233
Irimbert, abbot, 232–33
Isidore of Seville, 6, 8, 223–24, 246
Islam. *See* Muslims; Qur'an; Saracens.

Jacob, apostle, 148
Jacques de Vitry, 231
Jerome, 5, 6, 8, 25, 53, 70, 143, 158, 224, 243–44, 246. See also *Life of Malchus*.
Jerusalem, 44, 157, 163, 170–72, 177–78
Jews, 30–31, 55–57, 174, 211
John XV, pope, 77
John Cassian, 6, 14, 222–23, 225
John Chrysostom, 6, 8
John Henry Newman, cardinal, 19
John of Salerno, 65, 149. See *Life of Odo*.
John of Salisbury, 7
John Scotus, 4
John the Baptist, 153, 158
Josephus, Flavius, 4, 6
Julian of Toledo, 6
Juvenal, 4, 184

La Charité-sur-Loire, abbey, 42
La Garde-Freinet, 45, 48–50, 57, 60, 71, 76, 89, 169, 178
Lactantius, 246
Laonikos Chalkokondyles, 243
Lazarus, 148
Leo XIII, pope, 20
Leotadus, saint, 146
Lewes priory (East Sussex), 197, 201
Libanius of Antioch, 243, 246
Liber tramitis, 6, 115–16, 147–50, 153, 155, 158
Life of Anthony, 36
Life of Christopher, 38–39
Life of Gerald of Aurillac, 146, 165–66, 178
Life of Hugh, 153
Life of Malchus, 25
Life of Maiolus (*BHL* 5180), 73–74, 82–87, 100, 149, 164
Life of Maiolus (*BHL* 5177/79), 50, 86–87. *See also* Syrus of Cluny.
Life of Maiolus (*BHL* 5181), 65, 69–71. *See also* Nalgod of Cluny.
Life of Maiolus (*BHL* 5182/84), 64, 149. *See also* Odilo, abbot of Cluny.

INDEX

Life of Maiolus (BHL 5185), 150
Life of Martin of Tours, 36
Life of Mary of Egypt, 6
Life of Odo, 65–66, 84–85, 127, 149.
    See John of Salerno.
Life of Peter of Cava, 121
Life of Peter the Venerable, 197–98, 210–11
Liudprand of Cremona, 49
Livy, 6, 238, 241
Lothar III, emperor, 203
Louis VIII, king, 174, 177, 215
Louis IX, king, 22
Louis the Pious, 15, 17, 32, 40, 56, 113
Lourdes, 161
Lovecraft, H. P., 241
Luxeuil, 159

Mabillon, Jean, 62
Macrobius, 246
Maiolus, abbot of Cluny (954–994), 5, 29, 45–46, 49–52, 57–58, 60–67, 70–80, 82–108, 147–51, 160, 166–67, 169, 175–78, 213
Marcellus, pope, 148, 155
Marcellus of Chalon-sur-Saône, saint, 148
Marcigny, Cluniac nunnery, 208, 216
Martène, Edmond, 142–43, 161
Martial, saint, 146
Martin of Tours, saint, 4, 8, 37, 146, 166
Martin I, pope, 55
Mary. See Virgin Mary.
Mathilda of Flanders, queen, 199, 214
material culture, 40–42
Mathieu of Vendôme, abbot, 22
Maurice of Braga, archbishop, 155
Maurists, 197. See also Edmond Martène; Ursin Durand
Maurus, saint, 158
Mehmed II, sultan, 44
Mesopotamus, archdeacon, 154–55
Michael II, emperor, 40
Milo, bishop, 145
Minden, abbey, 145
mint, 82–84
miracles, 78–80, 82–84, 86–87, 90–108
Miraculorum sancti Maioli libri duo (BHL 5186), 90–108
Mohammad, 173, 175, 179, 213
Monte Cassino, abbey, 112
Moses, 148
Mount Garigliano, 49

Mount Saint Michel, 200
Mount Tabor, abbey, 172
al-Muktadir ibn Hud, 168
Murex brandaris (marine snail), 80
Muslims, 27–28, 44–46, 48–50, 52, 54, 57, 60, 65–68, 70–71, 76, 78–79, 89, 163–64, 166, 169, 173–75, 177–79, 213–14. See also Mohammad, Qur'an; Saracens.

Nalgod of Cluny, 62, 64–65, 69–71, 85, 149
Nicholas V, pope, 237
Novalesa, abbey, 27
novices, 109, 125, 127–41

oblates, 17, 35
Occupatio, 25
Odilo, abbot of Cluny (994–1049), 5, 29, 51, 64–65, 74–75, 85–88, 90–91, 95–96, 108, 115, 143, 147, 149–51, 153, 158, 160, 167, 178
Odo, abbot of Cluny (927–942), 3, 4, 9, 25, 64, 66, 69–70, 75, 85, 119, 146–47, 158, 164, 178, 180, 187. See also *Collationum tres libri*; *Life of Odo*; *Occupatio*.
Ordo Arpinus, viscount, 171
Order of Saint Victor, 121
Orderic Vitalis, 200, 206, 229
Origen of Alexandria, 6, 8
Orosius, Paul, 6, 8, 9
Oswald of Worcester, 68
Otto I, emperor, 76–77
Otto II, emperor, 61, 72, 77
Otto III, emperor, 41, 61
Ovid, 63
Oxyrhynchus, 242

pagans, 53–54
Paris, 61, 90
Parlement of Paris, 22
Paschasius Radbertus, 4, 70
Paul, apostle, 54–56, 80, 144, 147, 154
Paul the Deacon, 33, 66
Pavia, 47, 61, 64, 72–74, 76–88
Peace of God, 167, 178
Persius, 4
Peter, apostle, 143–44, 147–48, 154
Peter of Cava-Venosa, abbot, 15
Peter of Poitiers, 7, 213–14
Peter the Venerable, abbot of Cluny (1122–1156), 7, 9, 37, 44, 62, 65, 69, 88–89, 115, 149, 155–56, 164, 172–75,

INDEX 321

177–80, 182, 196–98, 203–16, 221, 229–31, 237–39, 248–53, 255–56
Peter Damian, 126
Peterborough Chronicle, 204–6
Petrobrusians (heretical group), 9, 237, 239
Philippe de Lozier, grand prior of Cluny, 158
pilgrims, 88–108, 154, 172, 179
Plan of St. Gall, 18, 42
Pliny the Elder, 241
Plutarch, 241
poetry, Benedictine, 24–26, 180–95
Pontius, abbot of Cluny (1109–1122), 147, 154, 172, 178–79, 207, 209, 229
prayer, intercessory, 75, 85–86, 89, 145, 175–77, 196–98
Priscian, 63, 246
Provence, 48–50, 60, 76, 88, 169
Prudentius, 227
Pseudo-Hegesippus, 4
Pseudo-Isidore, 5
purgatory, 29, 33

Qur'an, 44, 169, 173, 179, 213

Rainald of Paris, bishop, 94
Ramsey Abbey, 68
Ratramnus of Corbie, 38–39
Ravenna, 244
Raymond IV of Saint Gilles, 172
reconquista, 168
Reginald of Canterbury, 25–26. See also *Life of Malchus*.
Regula cuiusdam ad virgines, 23
Regularis Concordia, 119
Relatio metrica de duobus ducibus, 69, 89, 175–77
relics, 41–42, 142–61, 172, 178. See also Clement; relic inventories; reliquary of Saint Peter; True Cross; Virgin Mary.
relic inventories, 157–60
reliquary of Saint Peter, 152–53, 158
Remigius of Auxerre, 5–6
Rhine river, 83
Robert II, king, 96
Robert of Torigni, 202, 214
Rodulphus Glaber, 50–51, 62, 65–68, 71, 102, 108, 197–98
Rodulphus de Sully, abbot of Cluny (1173–1176), 197, 210–11
Romainmôtier, abbey, 64, 149

Rome, 45–47, 60–61, 77, 81, 85, 88, 145–47, 162, 166, 184
Rostang of Cluny, 156–57
roundsman (*circator*), 109–23
Rudolf, king, 146
Rule of Benedict (*Regula Benedicti*), 5, 10, 11–26, 32–36, 77, 110–13, 130, 138, 145, 217–21, 225, 230, 233–34
Rule of Columbanus (*Regula Columbani*), 15, 111
Rule of the Master (*Regula Magistri*), 14, 110
rules, monastic, 32–36. See also *Regula cuiusdam ad virgines*; *Rule of Benedict* (*Regula Benedicti*); *Rule of Columbanus* (*Regula Columbani*); *Rule of the Master* (*Regula Magistri*).
Rupert of Deutz, 21

Saint-Amand-les-Eaux, abbey, 246
Saint Apollinare in Classe, abbey, 76
Saint Calais, abbey, 30
Saint-Denis, abbey, 40, 90, 151
Saint Gall, abbey, 29–30, 245
Saint Maiolo, church, 78–79
Saint Maria, abbey, 72
Saint Martial of Limoges, abbey, 10
Saint Mary, cathedral, 95
Saint Mary of the Valley of Jehoshaphat, abbey, 171
Saint Maximin, abbey, 31
Saint Pietro in Ciel d'Oro, abbey, 72, 77
Saint-Riquier, abbey, 66
Saint Salvatore, abbey, 72, 77
Saint Syrus, church, 83, 86
saints' lives. See hagiography.
San Paolo fuori le Mure, abbey, 147
San Zoilo de Cordoba, abbey, 155
Santa Croce di Camese, abbey, 172
Saracens, 53
Sardinia, 175
satire, 167–68, 183–84, 246
Sebastian, saint, 148
Second Crusade, 164, 173, 179, 213
Sedulius, 4, 63
Seneca the Younger, 241, 246
Sicily, 177
Sidon, 73, 79–80, 82, 84, 86–87
Sigibert of Gembloux, 214
sign language, monastic, 18, 35, 117, 120–21, 124–41
silk, 47, 81

INDEX

Silvestrus, saint, 148
Simon of Clermont, lord, 22
silence, monastic, 33, 35, 120–21, 126–41
slaves, 81, 96
Smaragdus of Saint Mihiel, 34
Socrates, 191
Song of Roland, 53
Souvigny, abbey, 69, 90–108, 149–50
Spain, 49, 155, 168, 173, 178–79, 213
Sparta, 240
spices, 47
Stephen, king of England, 208, 211
Stephen, protomartyr and saint, 154, 178
Stephen of Blois, count, 208
Stephen of Bourbon, 231
Suger of Saint-Denis, abbot, 203
Sulpicius Severus, 36
Syrus of Cluny, 50–51, 64, 86, 149

Tatian, 60
Taurinus, saint, 146, 148
Tours, scriptorium, 3
Theophanu, empress, 77
Theopompus, 240–41
Theotokos Peribleptos, abbey, 156, 178
Thibaud of Vermandois, prior, 177
Third Crusade, 178
Thomas Becket, 177
Thucydides, 237, 240, 243
Truce of God, 167
True Cross, relic, 41, 148, 151, 154, 157, 178
Tyre, 73, 79–80, 82, 84, 86–87

Ulrich of Zell, 115, 117, 120, 125–41
University of Paris, 22
Urban II, pope, 74, 162–63, 170, 177, 176–78

Venantius Fortunatus, 63
Virgil, 4, 238. See also *Georgics*.
Virgin Mary, 41, 69–71, 89, 144, 148, 157, 159
Venice, 81
Vivarium, 244
Vivianus, prior of Cluny, 95

Wala, abbot, 113
Walcher of Malvern, monastic scientist, 225
Waldebertus, saint, 159
Walter of Doyde, 168, 200
Walter Map, 202
Warmund of Vienne, archbishop, 199
William II, abbot of Cluny (1207–1215), 9
William I of Aquitaine, duke, 18, 144–45
William I de Warenne, earl, 201
William of Arles, count, 50, 76
William of Hirsau, abbot, 115
William of Tyre, 171
William Rufus (William II), king of England, 201–2
William the Conqueror, 198–201, 207–208
Wolfhold, abbot, 232
wolves, 47
women, Benedictine, 22–24, 122, 217, 232–35
women, lay, 29, 184

Usuard, 233

Valla, Lorenzo, 237

Xenocrates, 191